Personation Plots

SUNY series, Studies in the Long Nineteenth Century
———————
Pamela K. Gilbert

Personation Plots

Identity Fraud in Victorian Sensation Fiction

CLAYTON CARLYLE TARR

Cover: "The Fearneaux Frauds." *Illustrated Police News* 952 (13 May 1882): 1–2.

Published by State University of New York Press, Albany

© 2022 State University of New York

All rights reserved

Printed in the United States of America

No part of this book may be used or reproduced in any manner without written permission. No part of this book may be stored in a retrieval system or transmitted in any form or by any means including electronic, electrostatic, magnetic tape, mechanical, photocopying, recording, or otherwise without the prior permission in writing of the publisher.

For information, contact State University of New York Press, Albany, NY
www.sunypress.edu

Library of Congress Cataloging-in-Publication Data

Name: Tarr, Clayton Carlyle, author.
Title: Personation plots : identity fraud in Victorian sensation fiction / Clayton Carlyle Tarr.
Description: Albany : State University of New York Press, [2022] | Series: SUNY series, Studies in the Long Nineteenth Century | Includes bibliographical references and index.
Identifiers: ISBN 9781438490830 (hardcover : alk. paper) | ISBN 9781438490854 (ebook) | ISBN 9781438490847 (pbk. : alk. paper)
Further information is available at the Library of Congress.

10 9 8 7 6 5 4 3 2 1

Who steals my purse steals trash; 'tis something, nothing;
'Twas mine, 'tis his, and has been slave to thousands:
But he that filches from me my good name
Robs me of that which not enriches him
And makes me poor indeed.

—Shakespeare, *Othello* (1603)

Contents

List of Illustrations	ix
Acknowledgments	xi
Introduction	1

Part I. Body

Chapter 1	
Skins to Jump Into	15
Clothes in *A Woman in Spite of Herself*	18
Cosmetics in *No Name*	23
Chapter 2	
Altered beyond Chance of Recognition	31
Surgery in *Checkmate*	33
Blood Transfusion in *Blood*	39
First Interlude: Alice Grey	49

Part II. Mind

Chapter 3	
That Lost Personality	61
Madness in *Lady Audley's Secret*	65
Epilepsy in *Thou Art the Man*	75

Chapter 4
This Unclean Spirit of Imitation   85
    Mesmerism in *The Notting Hill Mystery*   88
    Opium in *The Mystery of Edwin Drood*   99

Second Interlude: Mary Jane Furneaux   103

Part III. Matter

Chapter 5
A Daring Imposture   117
    Registers in *The Woman in White*   120
    Wills in *Verner's Pride*   127

Chapter 6
That Mysterious Paper Currency   135
    Refuse in *Our Mutual Friend*   138
    Photographs in *Unconventional*   146

Afterword: Reverse Personation   153

Notes   161

Works Cited   219

Index   245

Illustrations

I.1	Alice Grey	49
I.2	Grey's victims	50
II.1	Mary Jane Furneaux	103
II.2	Days with Celebrities. With Fearneaux	104
II.3	Furneaux, 3/4 face, with moustache	108
II.4	Furneaux, 3/4 face and wearing tall hat	108
II.5	Furneaux, in Stuart plaid shawl with hat and buckle at one side, nearly profile face	109
II.6	Furneaux in costume	110
II.7	Furneaux as Arthur Pelham Clinton	110
II.8	Furneaux's 1882 trial	113

Acknowledgments

Reckoning with the debts incurred by a book project can be daunting, especially when accounting for learning curves—twisting and retracing, often backtracking and rarely straight. Many people selflessly constructed guardrails along the way, sacrificing their own time and patience to keep the project moving forward. I appreciate the generous work of several anonymous readers. I am also grateful to Pamela Gilbert, who remained encouraging and inspiring throughout the revision process. But I am most deeply indebted to Rebecca Colesworthy, whose surname only partially suggests her extraordinary patience and boundless knowledge.

My mentors, colleagues, and friends have provided guidance, promoted collaboration, and promised honesty. But my family, who support the weight of my ambitions and anxieties with underappreciated strength, deserve the most recognition. Their affirmations and advocacy have empowered me to work through my own personation plots, academic and otherwise. To Bibi, Ellis, and my parents, I dedicate this book.

Introduction

In the summer of 1848, a twenty-four-year-old man from Troy, Maine, was approached by strangers, who recognized him as Rowland Hause, the missing son of James Hause, of nearby Corinna. Rowland, some three years earlier, had boarded the *Copia*, a whaling vessel bound for the Pacific Ocean. The young man, dressed in ragged work clothes, accompanied the strangers back to Corinna, where he met Rowland's parents. Although Mrs. Hause remembered her son as fairer and stockier than the young man, who had a "swarthy complexion," she eventually accepted him as her son, based primarily on some peculiar corporeal marks—scars on his knee, chest, and neck, and a toe that "lapped over the other."[1] Rowland's sister, a schoolteacher named Rebecca, was similarly incredulous, but ultimately identified her brother through another scar. The young man, now dressed like a gentleman, borrowed money, sold an heirloom watch, and later caused a disturbance in Bangor, where he signed "protection papers" and "stamped" Rowland's name "upon various articles of clothing."[2] Eventually, the young man was recognized by several acquaintances, and "the bubble of imposture burst."[3] During the January 1849 trial, Seth Hause (evidently no relation to the family in Corinna) identified the defendant as his son, Luther Hause. Although the packed courtroom heavily favored Luther, the jury quickly returned a guilty verdict.

Contemporary accounts marveled at the "absolute and entire deception of a whole family" and wondered how James Hause, "an intelligent man, and Justice of the Peace, and a man of property," fell for Luther's imposture.[4] Rebecca Hause, similarly, was a "fine looking intelligent girl, and it is astonishing that she could have been so deceived."[5] Although Luther and Rowland were generally dissimilar, the physical peculiarities they shared were an "infallible guide" to convince even the most intimate relations.[6] An 1874 account of the case observed that "the evidences of identity based on mere *personal appearance* [are] entirely deceptive."[7] The case proved extraordinary because Luther neither had foreknowledge of Rowland's scars nor "sufficient time . . . to produce on his own person an imitation of them."[8] The coincidence of the scars (and, perhaps less so, the overlapping toe) "weaken[ed] the evidence respecting identity that is based solely on the recollection of mere bodily resemblances."[9] Rather than providing unique forensic evidence, the body proved untrustworthy, a text that could be misremembered, duplicated, and counterfeited, what another reappraisal called "the frequent correspondence of marks of violence upon different men."[10]

The Hause imposture marks an important early development in debates over personal identity on both sides of the Atlantic. Although the case played out in Maine, it was retrospectively recognized for its "many features in common with the notorious . . . [Tichborne] imposture," which captivated the Victorian consciousness for nearly a decade.[11] Both Luther Hause and the Tichborne Claimant beguiled witnesses by exploiting the ambiguities and coincidences of corporeality.[12] As Pamela K. Gilbert observes, the Victorian era's "philosophical and anatomical knowledge . . . insists on a material self, located on the surface of the body."[13] This notion of material selfhood advanced in the decades between the Hause and Tichborne cases, particularly through the rise of forensics.[14] Under the influence of science and industry, early forensics granted sovereignty to the body as the exclusive seat of subjectivity, the sole signifier of the self. Yet this same period also saw the rise of the sensation novel, whose plots represented—and inspired— diverse forms of imposture that emphasized the body's incapacity to signify identity. The ubiquity of these plots not only demonstrates how identity fraud "loomed large in Victorian culture, . . . entering into many facets of daily life," but also highlights the paradox at the heart of this study: In the Victorian period, the body both formed and frustrated identity.[15] By resisting the confines of material identity, impostors reveal and exploit the inherent mutability of body, mind, and matter. Sensation fiction provided a reflection of and an incitement for this resistance.[16]

Sensation novels stage what I term *personation plots*—narratives of lost, mistaken, or stolen identities—to reflect a particular Victorian anxiety about the transformation of immaterial subjectivity into material identity.[17] The nineteenth century witnessed the development of increasingly intricate and accurate biometric techniques meant to identify individuals through particular bodily signifiers.[18] These techniques, which culminated in the rise of fingerprinting records at the end of the Victorian period, threatened subjectivity by marginalizing the soul and reducing human experience to the confines of embodiment.[19] This book argues that Victorian impostors, both actual and fictional, undermine the authority of material identity through methods that, while varied, persistently center on the inherent mutability of corporeality. I assert, in other words, that personation plots invariably focus on the body and its fundamental incapacity to signify subjectivity. More than expressing anxieties about shifting class dynamics in the wake of reform or the increasing influence of textual information—the contexts most critics of sensation fiction distinguish as the backdrop for identity fraud—Victorian imposture resists the scientific, medical, and legal promotion of corporeal identity as the sole indicator of human existence.[20] *Personation Plots* examines sensational narratives of mistaken, counterfeited, or otherwise stolen identities, in which impostors transform the body both inside and out; emphasize the instability of the mind; and explore the growing authority of external matter. The limitations and inconsistencies of corporeal identity, more so than strict socioeconomic factors, provide the conditions for each mode of imposture.

It is necessary, at the outset, to dispense with some terminology. This book distinguishes between *identity* and *the self*, the former being extrinsic, legible, and material, and the latter intrinsic, illegible, and immaterial. To understand and to control its populace, the state placed emphasis on identity, submerging the authority of the self beneath a host of material signifiers.[21] The materialization of personal identity began in the decades before biometric advances in photography, anthropometry, and fingerprinting, when medico-legal writers, following in the wake of pseudo-scientific proponents of physiognomy and phrenology, affixed identity to corporeal indicators.[22] Victorian science moved increasingly toward the materialization of identity, understanding even cognitive processes through physiological models.[23] As Peter Garratt observes, nineteenth-century epistemology "troubled the neat ontologies of self and world."[24] Industrial mechanization similarly constructed the individual subject as a laboring body suited for material production.[25] William A. Cohen notes that "[m]ass industrialism and urbanization provided new locations . . . in which conflicts over the relation between the body and its interior arose; mechanized labor produced [a] new kind of body."[26] Under the influence of science and industry, legal institutions began to recognize corporeal identity as the singular means to read, to classify, and to manipulate the populace, displacing the immaterial self from constructions of subjectivity.[27]

Personation Plots: Identity Fraud in Victorian Sensation Fiction argues that sensation fiction consistently highlighted the discrepancies in this narrow narrative of material identity. I equate *personal identity* with *subjectivity* throughout, following John Locke, whose chapter "Of Identity and Diversity" (1694) "revolutionize[d] the very conception of subjectivity."[28] Whereas Locke preferred the terms "human" (body) and "person" (mind/consciousness), the Victorians divided subjectivity between *identity* and *the self* (alternately "personality" or "ego"), the former being granted full legal authority as the sole signifier of subjectivity.[29] Ronald R. Thomas points to a "paradigmatic shift in the realm of subjectivity," signaled by "the process of 'materializing' personal identity."[30] This process resulted from the materialist pressures of science and industry, and sociojuridical disciplines followed suit. By the last decades of the nineteenth century, with the introduction of biometrics, identity became fully, but perhaps not irreversibly, tied to the body.[31] Here the cognates *identity* and *identify* become most treacherous. The elevation of identity over the self was the result of an institutional drive to identify, so that identity was always subjugative, promoted as a means to read, to locate, to control. Nevertheless, the self, displaced but never fully removed by materialist systems, regained some agency at the beginning of the twentieth century, primarily through Freudian psychoanalysis. I argue that sensation novelists untethered corporeality from subjectivity by emphasizing the mutability of body, mind, and matter, thus forging a path to modernist/postmodernist notions of the fragmented, fluctuating, dispersive self.

The central aims of this book are not only to highlight sensation fiction's representations of subjectivity but also to examine its interventions in Victorian understandings of the self. "To be a 'Victorian subject,'" J. Hillis Miller notes, "meant to be subjected to specific social, historical, and material conditions."[32] Subjectivity no longer meant only a Lockean notion of memorial consciousness but instead was constructed by cultural contexts. Miller imparts the threat that the word "subject" implies, meaning both being "thrown under" and "the way the self is always subject to something other than itself, something beneath it or beyond it that may be experienced more as an abyss than as a ground."[33] Being a subject means being forced under and into, pressed downward and inward, subjected and subjugated. In the Victorian period, for the first time, it also meant being publicized and fragmented among statistical and identificatory matter. The body was scrutinized, read as a text for the marks of meaning, and also rendered into text, documented, duplicated, and deployed. Subjectivity, as Miller explains, "is not a perdurable monad."[34] Victorians were forced to understand its transformation into identity, the material signifiers divorced from the signified self. Such a phenomenon resembles Derridean freeplay, wherein a "structure lacking any center represents the unthinkable itself."[35] It is in the mid–nineteenth century that the self becomes unthinkable. Kelly Hurley's convincing argument that the *fin de siècle* Gothic represented "the ruination of the human subject" could easily include the sensation novel as a less macabre, but no less dynamic, antecedent.[36] The body horror of the Gothic abhuman finds its forebear in sensation's spectrum of unstable matter.

Sensation fiction tests the limits of subjectivity, often modeling personation plots after actual events, but also imagining new impostures to predict the future of identity fraud. Rebecca Stern writes that sensation novels are "rife with contradictions between signifiers and signifieds, operating on symbolic systems in which appearances rarely correspond with actualities, in which it is nearly impossible to construe 'truth' or 'nature' from exterior signs."[37] Sensation impostors understand corporeal identity as a collection of signifiers that can be disguised, erased, and counterfeited. Henry Mansel warned of such an issue in his 1863 attack on the genre: "how exciting to think that under these pleasing outsides may be concealed some demon in human shape, a Count Fosco or a Lady Audley!"[38] Mansel's choice of characters, though not surprising, given their almost monarchial authority over the genre, is nonetheless significant. Both Wilkie Collins's Fosco and Mary Elizabeth Braddon's Lucy Audley are preternaturally malleable impostors, if not examples of Darwinian natural selection in real time.[39] Nicholas Daly notes that "it is . . . possible to see that these novels often dwell on the failure of the stable, centered subject."[40] Impostors suggest a further step: it is not just that the "centered subject" fails but that there is no center, no signified. The removal of the self from subjectivity meant "the disappearance of the Author," the chaos of autotelic life, where personal identity became impersonal.[41] Sensation novels signal when things fall apart.

Criticism on identity fraud in sensation fiction falls generally into two camps. The first recognizes imposture as the result of shifting class dynamics during the age of reform. As Andrew Radford observes, sensation fiction "can be perceived in . . . terms of class conflict."[42] The second camp understands imposture through the increasing authority that text commanded throughout the Victorian period. Sean Grass, for example, reads identity as a "textual and commodified thing," opposed to subjectivity, which had to be "cultivated" in response.[43] But the body—the subject of rich interpretations in other areas of sensation criticism—has not been fully articulated in such pursuits.[44] Pamela K. Gilbert identifies sensation fiction as "[t]he most physiological of genres, . . . with its careful attention to the body of both character and reader."[45] When "the surface of the body becomes the site of self," Gilbert argues, "realism becomes a dominant aesthetic mode of narrating that self."[46] I argue, conversely, that the fundamental fluidity of the body—its transformations and transformability—evidences the immateriality of the self, opposing any sense of a stable physiological identity. Sensation fiction, more so than any other genre, understood and emphasized the paradoxical position of the body, the slippage between signifiers of identity and the signified self. The explosion of identity fraud in the Victorian period signals a last-ditch effort to resist the materialization of subjectivity before late-nineteenth-century biometrics rendered such efforts largely impossible. In 1866, the *Saturday Review* accused sensation novelists of producing a "wave of materialism," but sensation writers actually swam against such a wave, resisting materialism through the formal and thematic elements of personation plots.[47]

Sensation fiction is preoccupied with identity fraud, to the point that some form of imposture seemingly figures into every text in the genre.[48] Yet scholarship on the device is relatively scarce.[49] In fact, Jonathan Loesberg's 1986 article "The Ideology of Narrative Form in Sensation Fiction" remains the most influential assessment of the genre's "question of identity."[50] According to Loesberg, debates over parliamentary reform in the 1850s and 1860s, which culminated in the Second Reform Bill (1867), shaped not only sensation fiction's conceptions of identity but also the genre's form. Reform threatened "to realign the balance of power in unpredictable and possibly threatening ways."[51] Sensation novels, Loesberg continues, "evoke their most typical moments of sensation response from images of a loss of class identity. And this common image links up with a fear of a general loss of social identity as a result of the merging of the classes."[52] But class anxiety, while a prominent theme in many sensation novels, does not adequately encompass the genre's diverse representations of identity fraud.[53] In Ellen Wood's *Verner's Pride* (1862–63), for example, John Massingbird personates his brother Frederick largely on a lark. In fact, class does not even fully account for the several impostures in Wilkie Collins's *The Woman in White* (1859–60), the focus of Loesberg's study.[54]

Although critics have subtly expanded on Loesberg's claims, the linkage between imposture and class identity has gone mostly unchallenged.[55] Jenny Bourne Taylor, for example, notes that Collins "breaks down stable boundaries," and explores "the shaping of social identity."[56] Taylor supplements Kathleen Tillotson's 1969 claim that "[t]he purest type of sensation novel is the novel-with-a-secret" to define the genre's "central narrative features—*secrecy* and *disguise*."[57] Identity, Taylor continues, "emerges as a set of elements that are actively constructed within a dominant framework of social interests, perceptions, and values."[58] Nicholas Daly has similarly studied the genre's "disruption of culture consumption stratified by class," which "encoded fears" over political reform that "the sphere of culture was not functioning to secure class distinctions."[59] Daly also focuses on *The Woman in White*, arguing that the novel's "most brilliantly realized moments dramatize the annihilation of all subjectivity in the revolutionary crowd."[60] Reform, in other words, meant some measure of societal leveling, an erasure of socioeconomic boundaries that threatened class hierarchy.

Critics have made similar connections between identity and textuality in sensation fiction. Ronald R. Thomas studies "devices of truth . . . aimed at making the body write or speak for itself."[61] Although he focuses on detective fiction, Thomas does not neglect the sensation novel, noting that the genre's search for truth is "achieved in a bitter struggle that pits one textual representation of the body against another."[62] In fact, sensation fiction often denies subjects an "autonomous moral self" in favor of understanding them through a "plot of identification that attends most closely to documenting the material facts of physical embodiment."[63] In *The Woman in White*, for example, both Laura Fairlie and Anne Catherick lose their subjectivity in favor of an identity that fixates on their bodies and documentation (registers, clothing, headstones). "While a person's character may be a deceptive act of impersonation shifting over time," Thomas observes, "her identity can be ascertained with finality because it is grounded in the verifiable and material truth of the body."[64] I argue, conversely, that bodies in sensation novels prove deceptive, continually transformed or nullified by other forces. Such a discrepancy might emphasize one disjunction between detective fiction and sensation novels: the former obsessively follows clues to concluding truths, while the latter often rejects resolution. Robert Audley's monomaniacal detective work in *Lady Audley's Secret* (1862), for example, ultimately translates Lucy Audley into Madam Taylor, "as a safe and simple substitute," further suggesting the limitations of corporeal identity.[65]

The Victorian conflation of identity and textuality has encouraged rich scholarship.[66] According to Sean Grass, the burgeoning genre of autobiography "ma[de] 'life' into a textual commodity," which "reshaped not only the legal, economic, and discursive practices associated with identity but also the narrative representation and ontological status of subjectivity."[67] Identity, Grass argues, became an "object of capitalist exchange."[68] Similar to my own distinction between "identity" and "the self," Grass reads identity as a "thing constituted in and through texts," in contrast to the "essential insubstantial interiority" of subjectivity.[69] Sensation fiction, which dwells on "proliferating texts," reflects "the anxieties engendered by autobiography's rise."[70] The displacement of identity from the individual, Grass argues, meant that identity was "subject to 'outright theft,'" especially in "the bold new age of its textual and mechanical reproduction."[71] Sensation novels, in particular, "began to treat subjectivity routinely as a thing alienated from its subject."[72] For example, Lucy Audley exists as a "profusion of texts," and John Harmon, the eponymous protagonist of *Our Mutual Friend* (1864–65), is "made up . . . of copies without an original."[73] Similar to Loesberg's claims about class, however, Grass's reading of textual identity cannot fully capture the greater picture of the body's role in displacing immaterial subjectivity. The authority that texts increasingly imposed on subjectivity is a symptom of corporeality's incapacity to signify identity. When bodies pose as legible texts—when their peculiar markings or measurable constructions come to signify unique individuals—they become canvases for forgery and counterfeiting.[74] Textual identity materializes from the failure of corporeal identity.[75]

Sensation fiction emerged during a tenuous period for identification practices, when the body continued to signify identity, despite complications.[76] In 1877, James Appleton Morgan championed the work of legal physicians, who are "not only indispensable, but absolutely omnipotent."[77] Given "the fallibility of human testimony in cases of personal identity," the physician is tasked with examining a "thousand . . . details which will more readily occur to a doctor than a lawyer."[78] For the physician "may be also a valuable detective."[79] According to Francis Wharton, writing in 1880, identity forms through "[p]ermanence of individuality," a condition defined solely by the body's "certain features . . . distinguishable from all others."[80] In spite of the promise that early forensics held, however, some criminologists remained skeptical, especially in cases of mistaken identity or intentional personation. In 1871, Robert Travers remarked: "[I]t is rarely, if ever, found that the matter [of mistaken identity] cannot be decided by other evidences than would be deducible from a laborious examination of physical signs, more or less obvious."[81] Travers's concluding remarks question the authority of corporeal evidence by asserting that there is "no physical sign from which alone the identity of a person may be proved."[82] Only an "approximation," based on "the number and value of the physical signs co-existing," can be ascertained.[83] Sensation novels often center on such corporeal ambiguities, promoting what Edward Higgs has called "the indeterminacy of the body as a means of identification."[84]

The explosion of personation cases in the 1850s signal an effort by criminals (or those otherwise desperate for change) to negotiate materialist structures of identity. While subjectivity was increasingly defined by and confined to the body, some subjects resisted, demonstrating that the signifiers thought to constitute identity never fully form into a signified subject. Just like names, physical peculiarities were arbitrary symbols that could be disguised or counterfeited. Sensation writers recognized not only that the body could be transformed through clothes, cosmetics, and even surgical procedures but also that the mind did not always present a continuum of stable consciousness; from madness and epilepsy to mesmerism and somnambulism, the mind was volatile and capable of being manipulated by outside forces. Is Helen Talboys, for example, the same person as Lucy Audley?[85] But challenges to corporeal definitions of identity did not end with examples of the flexible body and the fluctuating mind. Documentary evidence (registers, certificates, and wills) could alter a subject's past, present, and future, "fashioning individuals according to the terms of artificial codes, and turning life and death into figures of speech."[86] Official paperwork often meant as much to personal identity as persons themselves, a fact that sensation writers frequently exploited. As Sara Malton observes, sensation novels "dwell insistently on the unreliability of texts that apparently confirm identity."[87] Even technology could be manipulated. Simultaneously sensitive to current issues and prescient of future exigencies, sensation novels feature the first instances of photographic fraud.[88]

Imposture was always an essential ingredient of sensation fiction, and contemporary critics observed the genre's ubiquitous representations of the crime.[89] An 1864 review referred to "impersonation—an idea upon which there has been a somewhat inordinate run of late on the part of our novelists," while a later article noted that "[p]ersonation seems to be taking the place of bigamy."[90] In April 1866, *The Times* observed that a "sensation romance might be written with only two actual people [in] it, one of whom (the villain or villainess) shall, by skillful disguise, personate everybody else who is ever mentioned in the book."[91] This intentional hyperbole is not far off the mark. George Messenger, the protagonist of *The Old Roman Well* (1861), appears under a number of names and disguises, until he is hanged and resurrected as a respected and repentant doctor. A June 1864 article in *The Spectator*, aptly titled "Personation," makes the most of the device, noting that "[n]ovelists, weary of love and bigamy, are making a run just now upon personation."[92] The essay is most remarkable for how it separates the modern crime of personation from the fraud of old:

> There is no crime which it is so difficult to manage artistically, so hard to deprive of its excessive *primâ facie* improbability. It must be remembered that the offence is not that of assuming a rank to which the offender does not belong,—that has been done a thousand times, and will be done to the end of time, it is that of assuming the personality, the individual shape, character, and relations of another human being.[93]

At stake here is the ability for impostors to live entirely as someone else, to steal every facet of another person's identity, rather than briefly prospering off fraudulent legal claims. The article also provides a distinction between the two types of identity fraud that captured the Victorian consciousness—assumed names and personation. Braddon's Lady Audley exemplifies the first type, while Collins's Mercy Merrick, the criminal protagonist of *The New Magdalen* (1872–73), typifies the second. In contrast to *The Spectator* writer, however, I assert that both types of imposture fall under the wider category of identity fraud, and represent specifically Victorian concerns. Lady Audley and Mercy Merrick resist rigid physiological definitions of identity, each employing an arsenal of signifiers to assume a new life.

Until the nineteenth century, theories of personal identity hinged on concepts of either the metaphysical soul or mental consciousness. Under the influence of empirical science and industrial capitalism, however, medico-legal definitions of identity shifted attention to the body. Victorian impostors resisted strict corporeal definitions of personal identity, exploiting the mutability of body, mind, and matter. Sensation novelists reimagined these crimes, typically, and often hypocritically, punishing characters for identity fraud, depending on class, gender, and intent.[94] The general decline in media attention to imposture is the result of two factors: first, late-Victorian scientists became increasingly wary of corporeal definitions of identity attendant to the rise of psychology in the years before psychoanalysis emerged; second, the institution of increasingly intricate biometric technologies, including photography, anthropometry, and fingerprinting, made personation plots more difficult to imagine.[95] That sensation fiction not only developed during the explosion of diverse types of identity fraud but also declined simultaneous to new identificatory technologies demonstrates the genre's constitutional relationship with imposture.

Personation Plots unfolds in three parts—body, mind, and matter—that feature topic-specific chapters examining the ways that impostors in sensation fiction challenge rigid corporeal definitions of identity. The chronological range of the study is limited to the mid-Victorian period, roughly between the rise of criminology that focused on the body and the institution of precise biometric technologies. The earliest novel I examine is Collins's *The Woman in White*, though I am aware of, and responsive to, the work of critics who have traced sensation's beginnings to the 1850s, what Anne-Marie Beller has called "the genre's 'infancy.'"[96] On the other end of the spectrum, the sensation novel burned bright well into the 1890s, as Braddon's *Thou Art the Man* (1894) demonstrates. I offer readings of neglected sensation novelists, such as John Cordy Jeaffreson and Thomas Sutton, and occasionally refer to American authors who wrote sensation fiction, including Louisa May Alcott.[97] I have also featured two Dickens novels that were published at the height of the sensation craze, with the understanding that the inimitable could sometimes imitate.[98] Although I have included readings of the foundational novels of the genre, *The Woman in White* and *Lady Audley's Secret*, there are many popular novels featuring prominent personation plots that I have relegated to passing references or endnotes. My reasoning here is not limited to a desire to promote lesser-known novels; rather, the novels I have chosen are often exemplary of the chapter's individual theme.

Part I begins with the body, exploring how impostors transformed identity from both the corporeal exterior and interior. Chapter 1 studies imposture through the surface signifiers of clothes and cosmetics and offers readings of John Cordy Jeaffreson's *A Woman in Spite of Herself* (1872) and Wilkie Collins's *No Name* (1862–63). Chapter 2 probes interiors, scrutinizing surgical procedures and theories of blood transfusion in Sheridan Le Fanu's *Checkmate* (1871) and William Delisle Hay's *Blood: A Tragic Tale* (1888). Part II moves to the mind's role in representations of the unstable self. Chapter 3 charts the ways in which madness and epilepsy call to question notions of personal identity in Mary Elizabeth Braddon's *Lady Audley's Secret* (1862) and *Thou Art the Man* (1894). Chapter 4 reads the Victorian fascinations with mesmerism and opium through Charles Warren Adams's *The Notting Hill Mystery* (1862–63) and Charles Dickens's *The Mystery of Edwin Drood* (1870). Part III deals with material signifiers that exist beyond the subjective body and mind. Chapter 5 studies the impact of registration documents and wills in Collins's *The Woman in White* (1859–60) and Ellen Wood's *Verner's Pride* (1862–63). Chapter 6 investigates the mutable matter of refuse and photography in Dickens's *Our Mutual Friend* (1864–65) and Thomas Sutton's *Unconventional* (1866). The afterword describes the way that the Gothic, reappropriating the theme of identity theft from the sensation novel, converted imposture into monstrosity. The interludes that divide the parts tell the stories of two remarkable Victorian impostors who transformed their personal identities through a host of signifiers. These short criminal biographies are meant not only to typify the upsurge of identity fraud in the Victorian period but also to show how imposture worked outside of the sensation novel in ways that make truth stranger than fiction.

Part I

Body

The present is an age of sensation.

—*Argosy*, August 1, 1874

Chapter 1

Skins to Jump Into

Clothes and Cosmetics

In 1836, A. T. Thomson remarked, "If personal identity, where no fraud is intended, be rendered so difficult, how much greater must be the obstacles in the way of identifying criminals, whose object it is to disguise themselves?"[1] Thomson describes a mode of imposture that became a prominent concern in the Victorian period. Applying a disguise to evade the law was not a new phenomenon, of course, but the nineteenth-century growth of both the textile and the cosmetics industries gave particularly innovative criminals new ways to practice imposture, either to assume a new or alternate identity or to personate someone else. François Crouzet notes that the textile industry was "the first to be transformed and indeed turned upside down by the Industrial Revolution," witnessing a shift from domestic practice to mechanized process.[2] By 1851, textile production accounted for nearly 30 percent of the industrial labor force and dominated British exports. At the same time, a wealth of new cosmetic products, ranging from homeopathic to lethal, promised transformative effects for the consumer. The influx of new clothes and cosmetics, during what Thomas Richards terms "the era of spectacle," meant that Britons could alter their identities on the surface.[3] "As a booming consumer society," Laurence Talairach observes, "Britain was revamped into a *theatrum mundi* inhabited by performing actors and actresses concealed behind masks and costumes."[4] Some impostors took advantage of this growing subsection of consumer culture, using fashion products to commit diverse forms of identity fraud. "It is impossible," Mary Eliza Haweis remarked in 1878, "to separate people from their looks."[5]

Victorian commodity culture went hand in hand with imposture. Rebecca Stern notes that "the suspicion of characterological falseness was one among many offshoots of industrial culture, an effect of the growing alienation within interpersonal relationships."⁶ Both Marxian reification (the transmogrification of objects into subjects) and alienation (the related mechanization and objectification of the laborer) produced the culture of imposture that permeated and fascinated Victorian society. Personal identity became material, a product that could be bought, sold, and counterfeited. In 1845, Karl Marx railed against Ludwig Feuerbach's failure to ground human experience in industrial capitalism. For Marx, Feuerbach "resolves the essence of religion into the essence of man. . . . But the essence of man is no abstraction inherent in each single individual. In reality, it is the ensemble of the social relations."⁷ These "social relations" are constructed through capitalist labor production, meaning that material structures precede and produce individual consciousness. In *The German Ideology* (1846), Marx emphasizes how capitalism cheapens products and promotes fraud through "fabricated and fictitious production, deterioration in quality, adulteration of the raw materials, falsification of labels, fictitious purchases, bill-jobbing, and a credit system devoid of any real basis."⁸ He argues that "[t]he social structure of the state" understands individuals "as they *really* are; i.e. as they operate, produce materially."⁹ Intriguing connections emerge between Marx's materialism and Victorian realism, a genre arguably predicated on representing "things as they are," especially in regard to the way sensation fiction challenged both modes through the device of imposture.

The rise of material culture encouraged Victorian subjects to resist material models of personal identity. Mary Poovey draws attention to "material innovations," which "brought groups that had rarely mixed into physical proximity with each other and represented them as belonging to the same, increasingly undifferentiated whole."¹⁰ Mass industrial reproduction of wearable commodities encouraged the stratification of British subjectivity according to class. By exploiting the social codes and contemporary fashions of clothes and cosmetics, impostors could enter higher economic stations. In Mary Elizabeth Braddon's *Henry Dunbar* (1863–64), for example, the impostor Joseph Wilmot acquires a "complete rig-out" by patronizing a tailor and having his "ragged moustache trimmed into the most aristocratic shape."¹¹ Katherine Montwieler points to Braddon's "canny recognition of her culture's materialism."¹² Never mind that Wilmot is a lower-class convict; he becomes Henry Dunbar because consumer culture materialized class status. Kimberly Harrison observes that sensation novels "suggest that it might be clothes, cosmetics, and a cultivated bearing that make the lady and gentleman, not birth."¹³ But clothes and cosmetics could also be occupational accessories or even lower one's status. In Florence Marryat's *Her Father's Name* (1876), for example, Leona Lacoste disguises herself as part of her detective work.[14] Indeed, sensation fiction demonstrates that personal identity was a matter of appearances rather than the appearances of matter.

An interesting late-Romantic case of criminal disguise sets the stage for a flurry of Victorian occurrences, both actual and fictional. In 1825, a beggar woman was spotted "dressed in rags" with a "face [that] bore all the marks of the most inveterate cancer."[15] After a man accosted her, she "slowly and reluctantly removed the mask" to reveal "not a skeleton reduced to skin and bone, whose juices, forsaking their natural channels, oozed out in blotches and putrid sores; but a plump, comely, buxom queen, little more than thirty years of age."[16] The woman's disturbing appearance was "the effect of fraud and stratagem," which included "linen rags, ingeniously folded and intertwisted," and a "painted or stained" face that she habitually squirted with water "to make it appear that the sores were running."[17] She was brought before a magistrate, who sentenced her to being "publicly exhibited on a temporary pillory" in her disguise, and affixed with the label "Behold an infamous impostor."[18] At the end of her sentence, she was forced to remove her disguise "to exhibit[] a transformation, the effect of which was quite electrical upon the risible muscles and faculties of the mob."[19] The conclusion of the case is most significant. When the woman removed her disguise, "[e]very one thought it a pity to deform so fair a face."[20] The description of the scene resembles the way that sensation novels would vacillate between condemnation over and fascination with impostors, especially in regard to women. Wilkie Collins's Magdalen Vanstone, for example, is simultaneously "the heroine and pervading spirit" of *No Name* (1862–63), while also a "determined, dangerous woman."[21]

Such a dichotomy, however, was not always the case. In *Behind a Mask, or A Woman's Power* (1866), Louisa May Alcott (writing under the pseudonym A. M. Barnard) constructed a sensation plot clearly influenced by *Lady Audley's Secret* and *No Name*. The novella centers on Jean Muir, who becomes governess to the Coventry family. Although she claims to be nineteen, Jean is actually thirty, "small, thin, and colorless."[22] She achieves the transformation through cosmetic tricks: "she unbound and removed the long abundant braids from her head, wiped the pink from her face, [and] took out several pearly teeth."[23] Gerald Coventry, who initially distrusts Jean, eventually falls for the "contagious fever" of her preternatural charms: "I rather like romances in real life," he boasts.[24] Simultaneous to her flirtations with Gerald, Jean draws the attention of John Coventry, Gerald's uncle, and heir to the family fortune. As with Magdalen Vanstone, Jean displays her stage acumen, depicting a character in "barbaric splendor" through clothes and cosmetics: "She had darkened her skin, painted her eyebrows, [and] disposed some wild black locks over her fair hair."[25] Eventually, Gerald discovers the treachery of the "Scotch witch," but not before Jean and John Coventry are married under special license.[26] One of the principal themes of Alcott's novella is that, under the "metamorphosis" of clothes and cosmetics, Jean adopts an entirely new identity, not just to others, but also to herself. During the costume dinner, she admits that the "absurd dress . . . makes me feel so unlike myself," and later, gazing into a mirror, "she hardly knew herself."[27] With the transformation endorsed by the added matter of a marriage certificate, Jean fully becomes Lady Coventry.

Sensation novelists were intrigued by the potential that clothes and cosmetics provided to challenge rigid corporeal definitions of identity. Tara MacDonald observes that sensation fiction "frequently details how women's familiarity with elaborate clothing and cosmetics make them naturally gifted in the act of imposture."[28] Although this chapter examines two novels in which women use clothes and cosmetics to transform their identities, sensation writers regularly represent male impostors who resort to similar techniques. Braddon's *Henry Dunbar* is the best example of such sartorial imposture, but several sensation novels also feature storylines in which male characters practice cosmetic alterations. Imposture performed on the surface of the body, then, was a culturally pervasive issue not confined to women.[29] Consumer culture provided any Victorian subject with the opportunity to transform personal identity, to disguise the prior or alternate self under commodities that could be purchased readily and legally. As the body increasingly became the sole evidence for identity, especially in medico-legal definitions, clothes and cosmetics offered a way not just to disguise physical peculiarities but also to create new ones. Through clothes and cosmetics, personal identity could be conceived as a cultural construct, the self never more than skin deep.

Clothes in *A Woman in Spite of Herself*

In 1829, a writer for the *Pocket Magazine* asserted, "No one is so merry at the expense of a tailor as a dandy, and yet to that meritorious artist he owes all he has 'that may become a man'; his make and shape, his 'form and pressure'; his very personal identity: he is the tailor's handywork, who sets his mark upon him, and knows him for his own."[30] The parallels here to Thomas Carlyle's *Sartor Resartus* (1833–34) are many, including the focus on tailors and dandies. But the suggestion that "clothes make the man"—that dress constitutes personal identity—is the most significant link. Carlyle's magnum opus, simultaneously sprawling and labyrinthine, introduces Diogenes Teufelsdröckh's "Philosophy of Clothes," which the fictional editor attempts to stitch together. Teufelsdröckh looks "at all Matter and Material things as Spirit," thus affording him the ability to see the "Body and Cloth [as] the site and materials whereon and whereby his beautified edifice, of a Person, is to be built."[31] Carlyle confronts the onslaught of materialism, brought on by advancements in the natural sciences, by locating divinity in the physical world.[32] Personal identity, even when fixed in and on the body, remains spiritual.

Carlyle's philosophical treatise, which uses clothes as a metaphor to probe ontological mysteries, was surprisingly influential for mid-Victorian books on fashion. In 1849, for example, the anonymous author of *Secrets in the Art of Dress*, argued that "[t]here is a moral, a philosophy in dress."[33] Mary Eliza Haweis, one of the most prominent voices for Victorian fashion, even quoted from *Sartor Resartus* in *The Art of Dress* (1879). But her words the year prior, in *The Art of Beauty*, are more important. "Dress is the second self," she writes, "a dumb self, yet a most eloquent expositor of the person."[34] For Haweis, clothes do not just reflect personal identity but help to construct it.[35] In 1891, the pioneering psychologist William James made Carlyle's claims part of his model of subjectivity. For James, one facet of personal identity is the "material self," which consists of the body foremost and clothes secondarily. "We so appropriate our clothes," he writes, "and identify ourselves with them that there are few of us who, if asked to choose between having a beautiful body clad in raiment perpetually shabby and unclean, and having an ugly and blemished form always spotlessly attired, would not hesitate for a moment before making a decisive reply."[36] Clothes can disguise deficiencies, transform corporeal structure, and determine personal identity. Rosy Aindow observes that "[c]lothing by its very nature is ambiguous. It can be taken off, removed, or used as a form of disguise. Ultimately it can be employed as a means of subverting identity."[37] It is no surprise, then, that many Victorians attempted to fashion new identities through new fashion.[38]

The most frequent sartorial fraud in sensation novels occurs when an impostor exchanges clothes with another person (living, dead, or missing) to assume that person's identity.[39] This device was used regularly in other genres during the nineteenth century, appearing in such novels as Charles Dickens's *A Tale of Two Cities* (1859) and Mark Twain's *The Prince and the*

Pauper (1881). But sensation fiction positively obsesses over the way that clothes could transfer personal identity between characters.[40] The most significant example occurs in Collins's *The Woman in White* (1859–60), when Laura Fairlie, having been drugged and ensconced in an asylum, is mistaken for Anne Catherick because she is wearing Anne's marked clothes. Rebecca Stern notes the way that clothes figure as evidence of identity and implicate Laura's madness: "Metonymically marking Laura's body as that of the woman who has died in her place, this ink translates Laura from a realm of credibility to one of madness where her stories are understood *as* stories rather than truth."[41] *The Woman in White* demonstrates that material definitions of personal identity rest not just on bodies but also on clothes. Indeed, clothes determine Laura's identity as her half-sister, which she retains well after her hospitalization. The testimony of recognition provided by Walter Hartright and Marian Halcombe has no bearing against textile evidence. Numerous novelists composed similar plots, but perhaps the most innovative example occurs in John Cordy Jeaffreson's *A Woman in Spite of Herself* (1872).[42]

Jeaffreson's novel centers on Felicia Avalon, who is forced to personate her dead brother Felix to escape the clutches of the villainous Major Tilbury. Although personation by twins was a well-worn trope in sensation novels by the 1870s—used prominently by Mary Elizabeth Braddon in *The Trail of the Serpent* (1860), *The Captain of the Vulture* (1861–62), and *Sir Jasper's Tenant* (1865)—the Avalon siblings, though similar physically, are not twins. Felicia's personation of her brother instead relies on a combination of her own masculinity and Felix's femininity. The success of the personation plot, in other words, requires both siblings to possess a certain level of androgyny. *The Athenaeum* commended the novel as a "powerfully-written and exciting tale," yet criticized the "improbability of the incident."[43] Significantly, the latter criticism points to the unconvincing success of Tilbury's revenge conspiracy, and has nothing to do with Felicia's plot, during which she "avail[s] herself of a strange whim for masquerading in [Felix's] clothes, to personate his manhood after his untimely death."[44] More so than perhaps any other sensation novel, clothes determine identity in *A Woman in Spite of Herself*. The bodies of the novel's sibling protagonists are indistinguishable, so dress remains the sole factor to maintain distinct individuality.

Jeaffreson begins *A Woman in Spite of Herself* by foreshadowing the personation plot that occupies the latter half of the novel. Felicia Avalon, a "colonial belle" in Quebec, and her brother Felix, a respected reverend, are a "startlingly similar pair."[45] The siblings are the same height, with Felicia unusually tall and Felix "almost . . . undersized" (1.43), and they possess the same profile, lips, eyes, eyebrows, hair, and complexion: "On a microscopic comparison of the two faces, it was seen that even in their most delicate lines and shadows, no less than in their general design, the one was a precise reproduction of the other" (1.42). Even their phrenological resemblance is exact: "the most precise comparison and measurement of their two heads would have found them almost identical in massiveness and weight, as well as in conformation" (1.43). The likeness remains striking because Felix cannot grow facial hair, meaning that "in his twenty-sixth year he was as downless and smooth-faced as any girls of eighteen summers" (1.43). Felicia's figure, which "has no more shape than a pump or a gate-post" (1.112), also plays into the resemblance. In short, the Avalon siblings are living copies because "the features and expression which appeared masculine in the young woman, seemed effeminate in the somewhat younger man" (1.43).

The villain of the novel, in an innovative twist, participates in his own personation plot. Major Joseph Curtain Tilbury, who has gained a reputation for his "sartorial art" (1.19), obsesses over Felicia. Whereas Felicia later uses clothes to personate her brother, Tilbury dresses lavishly to claim unearned authority. "Kerbstone's Patent Hair-Restorer" (1.113), among other products, evidences his artificiality. Felicia immediately distrusts Tilbury, identifying "the evil of his nature, which he hides under an affectation of kindly temper and boisterous affability. . . . He is a dangerous man, all the more so because he is not altogether deficient in cunning and tact" (1.54). Receiving no signs of reciprocation, Tilbury nonetheless continues his advances, being the first suitor to address her "with a view to business" (1.111). Tilbury eventually proposes marriage, which Felicia refuses, but she errs in her relish at cutting him down. Incensed by the disrespect, Tilbury vows revenge: "The time shall come when I will clothe her with shame, compared with which my disgrace shall appear honor" (1.147). Tilbury's words hint at one of the primary methods for his retaliation—the use of clothes to personate Felicia.

Tilbury engages several different methods to effect his imposture, the first of which is to practice documentary fraud. He writes to England to have a handwriting expert analyze the manuscript pages of Felicia's novel, which features portraits of prominent colonial figures. These papers portray a woman's hand disguised as a man's, and Tilbury works to mimic this style. Eventually, almost every person of rank in Quebec receives an anonymous letter threatening blackmail, "written in the handwriting of a woman feigning a masculine hand" (1.217). Here Tilbury begins the second part of his imposture, the sartorial personation of Felicia. Each letter was conveyed to the post office by a "tall lady, wearing a dark dress and a considerable quantity of sable fur, and having her face concealed by a thick veil" (1.255). At this point, the novel makes an implicit connection between Tilbury's lavish style and his willingness, if not dexterity, at dressing in women's clothes. Whereas desperation and circumstance force Felicia's personation of Felix, something more inherent motivates Tilbury's imposture.

Felicia's personation plot results from Tilbury's machinations, the circumstantial evidence that brings her to trial and ensures her conviction. Following her release, the Avalon siblings, ostracized and penniless, prepare to immigrate to England. Before they embark, however, Tilbury arrives. "You may unsex yourself," he seethes, "and disguise yourself in man's clothing, but I will hunt you out, strip you of your disguise, and proclaim you to be the woman who was once a convict in the gaol of Quebec" (2.28). Felicia realizes his divination. Aboard the ship, she dresses herself in Felix's clothes to stay warm: "The completeness of the masquerade was all the more astonishing. . . . No stranger would have suspected her sex, or questioned that she was a young and decidedly handsome Anglican clergyman" (2.48). When the ship hits bad weather and wrecks, Felix and Felicia manage to board an emergency boat, but only Felicia survives. Rescuers identify her as Felix, however, because she possesses his papers and his coat. Clothes complete Felicia's accidental imposture, and she assumes Felix's identity.

The "completeness of the masquerade" allows Felicia's personation to proceed uninhibited in Sunningwold, a remote English town. So convincing is her imposture that Ada Clissold, the squire's daughter, falls madly in love, forcing Felicia to reveal her original identity. Felicia's personation plot fully unravels after she establishes a friendship with Noel Truelock, an artist. "His manliness is perfect," Noel remarks, "and it is allied with such a puzzling womanliness" (2.146). As his surname suggests, Noel sees through Felix's masculine attire, locating personal identity in vaguely gendered mannerisms that would have also applied to Felix, whose femininity his father deemed "defective" (1.63). Noel subsequently works to restore Felicia's identity by forcing Tilbury, mortally ill, to repent. Following Tilbury's deathbed confession, Felicia and Noel marry, while Ada, recovered from the shock of Felicia's personation, marries Reuben Bloxham, unattractive and rudely mannered, but goodhearted. Jeaffreson concludes the novel with the revelation that the narrator has been Rueben, who refers to "*my* nursery" with Ada (294), suggesting that *A Woman in Spite of Herself* has been itself a sort of personation all along. As *The Examiner* opines, "It is a fairly good novel in spite of itself."[46]

Clothes in *A Woman in Spite of Herself* belie the claim Jeaffreson makes in the title. For Felicia's personation of Felix proves successful until she falls under Noel's penetrating gaze. "Felicia," a reviewer for *The Graphic* noted, "has become a new person."[47] *The Spectator* similarly observed that Felicia "goes through not only a change of scene and a change of garb, but a change of life."[48] While personal identity in *A Woman in Spite of Herself* relies on customs of dress, the novel seems just as interested in the fluidity of gender, seeming to anticipate the conventions of performativity that Judith Butler has notably emphasized. "That the gendered body is performative," Butler writes, "suggests that it has no ontological status apart from the various acts which constitute its reality."[49] Thus, gender is a "fantasy instituted and inscribed on the surface of bodies."[50] Not only do Felicia and Felix seem to resist binary gender categories, but so too does Tilbury, whose masculine military identity relies entirely on sartorial performativity. If clothes make the man, then clothes can also unmake the man. Tilbury's obsessive pursuit of Felicia affords him the opportunity to adopt a new identity, mimicking her voice and handwriting, and displaying her stolen handkerchief as the chief totem of his imposture. But Jeaffreson, in spite of the affordances he makes to Felicia "unsexing [her]self" (2.286), ultimately punishes Tilbury's similar performance. Tilbury's descent into alcoholic "torpor" (2.67) leads the "maniac" into a "straight waistcoat" (2.68), clothing that strips him of any identity besides madness.

Cosmetics in *No Name*

To transform personal identity, cosmetics could achieve something that clothes could not: physical alteration at the level of the skin, the closest possible point at which the bodily surface remains relatively unbreeched. In fact, Victorian cosmetics interacted with the body at such an intimate level that they often proved irritative rather than cleansing or, at worst, lethal rather than rejuvenating. As Laurence Talairach observes, "cosmetics map out the female body as a territory open to invasion and contamination," and thereby "subordinate[] woman to her physiology."[51] By the mid-nineteenth century, makeup was used sparingly by professedly respectable women. Victorian consumers, in contrast to occasionally garish eighteenth-century styles, preferred subtle, if not imperceptible, applications.[52] Beauty was increasingly perceived as natural, and artificial enhancements were the sign of an immoral or lascivious character. Cora Pearl, the courtesan known for experimental and heavy-handed applications of makeup and hair dye, drew attention for being an outlier. Contemporary beauty manuals consistently promoted natural applications. An 1825 writer claimed that cosmetics "can often perform wonders," serving "only [to] assist nature, and make amends for her defects."[53] By 1840, however, another writer advocated "cleanliness to cosmetics, and . . . natural complexion to artificial paints."[54] An 1862 article, published alongside the serial run of Wilkie Collins's *No Name*, referred to subtle applications of eyeliner "to whom no suspicion of enameling need attach."[55] By the end of the century, Baroness Staffe, the French "expert on manners," pleaded with her readers "to give up the deplorable and disfiguring habit of painting themselves."[56]

But these developments did not mean the cosmetics industry disappeared. As Carolyn A. Day observes, "[m]ake-up went underground."[57] The decline of makeup as a respected form of fashion meant that women often produced their own samples and that "charlatans and perfumers" flourished.[58] Sarah Rachel Leverson, aka Madame Rachel, swindled Londoners during the early 1860s with fraudulent concoctions that promised customers would be "beautiful for ever." Wilkie Collins based Maria Oldershaw, the swindling adviser to Lydia Gwilt in *Armadale* (1864–66), on Leverson. Makeup also became part of sensational criminal trials. In 1857, Madeleine Smith poisoned her secret lover with arsenic that she allegedly claimed to have purchased to improve her complexion. Collins, as even Victorian critics noted, was likely inspired by this case when plotting the mysterious death at the center of *The Law and the Lady* (1874–75): Sara Macallan keeps arsenic on hand to alter her complexion and later uses it to commit suicide.[59] What is more, the cosmetics industry was not directed only toward women. John Scoffern, a well-regarded medical writer and teacher, acknowledged that cosmetics refer to "the beautifying of the already beautiful sex," but admits that "the ugly sex has something to do with cosmetics too."[60] Men, Scoffern claims, dye their hair more than women. "Let it never be affirmed," he concludes, "that the use of cosmetics is so especially a feminine accomplishment."[61]

Actual cases of cosmetic imposture, similar to other forms of identity fraud, were perhaps inspired by personation plots in sensation fiction. In 1872, Marguerite Dixblanc, a Belgian cook, murdered her former employer in London, and fled to Paris. Upon her arrest, the *Daily News* reported, she was found to have "blackened her face in order to conceal her identity, and seemed . . . as though she had done nothing all her life but measure out coals and charcoal."[62] An even more notorious case occurred in 1882, this time *in* Belgium. Armand Peltzer convinced his brother Léon to murder

Wilhelm Bernays, a barrister, because Armand was having an affair with Bernays's wife. Lifelong criminal conmen, the Peltzer brothers lured Bernays to a business meeting, where Léon shot him in the neck. Before the murder, Léon had "ordered a wig and false beard of a Paris wigmaker, representing that he was going to a fancy ball."[63] Then, on the day of the murder, he also "bought a cosmetic for blackening his eyelashes and darkening his complexion."[64] Although both Dixblanc and Peltzer were quickly apprehended, their attempts to alter their skin signal a new, or at least advanced, species of imposture that tested the limits of corporeal definitions of personal identity. As Rebecca Kling notes, cosmetics "destabilized the physiognomic paradigm."[65] Cosmetics, especially when applied expertly, could transform the body, confusing recognition testimonies and troubling identification efforts.

Victorian sensation fiction overruns with cosmetic disguises, giving impostors a powerful weapon to add to their criminal arsenals. By making cosmetics an instrument of imposture, sensation novelists further solidified the connection between makeup and immorality. One Victorian fashion book decried the use of cosmetics and asserted that "[w]hiteness is the most essential quality of the skin."[66] In *The Woman in White* (1859–60), Anne Catherick's "colorless, youthful face," in addition to her all-white attire, marks her innocence and virtue.[67] Conversely, Count Fosco's face, which is "smoother and freer from all marks and wrinkles than [Marian Halcombe's], though . . . he is close on sixty years of age," suggests that the villain uses makeup to alter his complexion.[68] But Collins's *No Name* (1862–63) fixates on cosmetics even more energetically, demonstrating how makeup can be used to disguise unique corporeal marks.[69] Whereas cosmetics in *The Woman in White* signal immorality, they effect transformation in *No Name*, as Magdalen Vanstone's body becomes a blank canvas to be painted over with new identities.

No Name begins among the domestic bliss of the affluent Vanstone family. Unlike the Avalon siblings in *A Woman in Spite of Herself*, sisters Norah and Magdalen are a study in opposites, the former humble and introspective, the latter haughty and impetuous. Collins immediately draws attention to Magdalen's curious features: "The whole countenance—so remarkable in its strongly-opposed characteristics—was rendered additionally striking by its extraordinary mobility."[70] Kylee-Anne Hingston notes that "nearly all bodies" in *No Name* "reveal themselves to be uncontrollable and atypical, and managing one's identity preoccupies every character."[71] But Magdalen's "strangely-constituted organization" (9) especially resists constancy, functioning as a cipher that can account for any equation. Her hair is of "monotonous purity," her eyes of "colourless grey," and her complexion a "pure monotony of tint . . . , without a tinge of colour in the cheeks" (8). Similar to Anne Catherick in *The Woman in White*, Magdalen's colorlessness makes her the perfect vehicle for fraud. But even more so than Collins's previous novel, *No Name* fixates on the implications of corporeal identity, which is constructed, and sometimes counterfeited, by material signifiers.

The combination of Magdalen's "white changeless blank" (83) complexion with the erasure of her documentary inheritance creates a further crisis of subjectivity that renders her a ghostly specter.[72] Miss Garth first passes by Norah's bedroom and hears "[v]oices inside, the voices of the two sisters" (112), and then she hears Magdalen as a "voice, behind her" (113). Thereafter, Norah worries that "I couldn't speak to her; I couldn't look at her" (115). Magdalen's disembodied voice and Medusa-like repellence might be read through Jacques Lacan's *objet petit a*, the permanent lack formed by entrance into the symbolic order that the subject strives unsuccessfully to fill.[73] She becomes lack personified, and having "no name" affords her a precarious, spectral position in symbolic reality. Magdalen's face, once only colorless, is now "blank bloodless pallor" (121), and she later admits, "I have struggled against myself" (144), signaling her ruptured subjectivity that now consists only of material signifiers. But this rupture leaves behind traces of her former self: "[t]he traces of heavy tear-drops" (117) on her father's letter; the "trace" (145) of the acting teacher's card; the "trace" (435) of the Allonby postmark on her anonymous letter; the "fragment" (237) of her brown alpaca dress; and, most significantly, her "two little moles" (151). Jacques Derrida writes that "[t]he trace is the erasure of selfhood, of one's own presence, and is constituted by the threat or anguish of its irremediable disappearance, of the disappearance of its disappearance."[74] Cosmetics function as Magdalen's primary means to efface her trace, to remove the one corporeal signifier of identity. "I am nothing to myself" (273), she declares.

Magdalen possesses one trace, however, that she cannot remove on her own. Her most ambitious personation plot requires the aid of a professional impostor. Before the tragic deaths of Mr. and Mrs. Vanstone, Captain Horatio Wragge, a distant relation of Mrs. Vanstone, unexpectedly called at the house. Wragge, whose surname conjures anxieties over paper money as empty rags, is Magdalen's physical opposite. Whereas Magdalen's "flexible face" (190) affords her everywoman abilities, Wragge cuts a distinct figure, "deeply pitted with the small pox, and characterized, very remarkably, by eyes of two different colours" (17). Wragge's heterochromia cannot be concealed, and his conspicuous scars suggest that he, although an expert in cosmetology, does not use makeup. Under Wragge's counsel, Magdalen abandons her acting career, and decides to infiltrate Noel Vanstone's life with the goal of winning back her original inheritance. She plans to persuade Noel to reconsider the terms of the inheritance by personating Miss Garth, a performance that requires professional cosmetic acumen.[75] Magdalen wears false eyebrows, "stain[s] her face," and draws "[t]he lines and markings of age" (217). In addition to feigning a "slight limp" and disguising her voice, she "deliberately disfigured herself by artificially reddening the insides of her eyelids" (218). This "hideous transformation" (218) succeeds, Magdalen reasons, because "not even Norah" (219) could recognize her. Whatever part of her immaterial self that remains has been fully submerged beneath new material identities.

Magdalen eventually enters a full partnership with Wragge, who has proudly identified himself as a "[s]windler" and "moral agriculturist" (169), though he never reveals that he has been blackmailing Mrs. Vanstone. Wragge keeps a meticulously managed "Index," where he records his transactions. "Here is my commercial library," he boasts: "Day Book, Ledger, Book of Districts, Book of Letters, Book of Remarks, and so on. Kindly throw your eye over any one of them. I flatter myself there is no such thing as a blot or a careless entry in it from the first page to the last" (172). Indeed, Wragge's textual fastidiousness later emerges when he erases Magdalen's "blots," her identifying moles. The book also includes "Adopted Handwritings of public characters" (173), which Wragge uses to forge documents. Knowing that Magdalen is a "born actress" (184), Wragge hatches a plan to exploit her skills for his criminal plots: "I have discovered that she possesses extraordinary talent as a mimic. She has the flexible face, the manageable voice, and the dramatic knack which fit a woman for character-parts and disguises on the stage" (190). Wragge's interest in Magdalen rests on her "endlessly reconstructible self," the capability of her body to be perpetually transformed.[76]

Whereas Magdalen's first personation relied on heavy cosmetics, she reenters Noel's circle, now under Wragge's tutelage, with "[n]o paint" (291). After her performance as Miss Garth proved ineffective, she "tore off her cloak, bonnet and wig; and threw them down out of sight, in the blank space between the sofa-bedstead and the wall" (245). Collins obsesses over "blank spaces" in *No Name* (surpassing even the blank spaces of the marriage register, the gravestone, and even Anne Catherick herself in *The Woman in White*), but Magdalen's disposal of the disguise into a sort of purgatory realm signals her criminal development.[77] She has relinquished every element of her past self, "her mind empty of all impressions, and conscious of no thoughts" (290), finally becoming no one by becoming everyone. "Give me any name you like," she declares: "I have as much right to one as to another" (194). Wragge eagerly supplies her new identity:

> My books . . . contain, under the heading of *Skins To Jump Into*, a list of individuals retired from this mortal scene, with whose names, families, and circumstances, I am well acquainted. Into some of those Skins I have been compelled to Jump in the exercise of my profession, at former periods of my career. Others are still in the condition of new dresses, and remain to be tried on. The Skin which will exactly fit us, originally clothed the bodies of a family named Bygrave. I am in Mr. Bygrave's skin at this moment—and it fits without a wrinkle. (263)

Wragge's "skins" provide Magdalen a different level of imposture, one based more on immersion than mimicry. That Wragge describes the process, specifically in regard to Mrs. Wragge, as "hammer[ing] her new identity *into* her head" (288) suggests his species of imposture is cerebral rather than cosmetic.

Although Magdalen's "clever masquerade" (240) becomes a "transformation" (263) through Wragge's Bygrave skins, one remnant of her past self threatens exposure. "We must discover her," Miss Garth explains, "by personal description—we can trace her in no other way" (144). The authorities, led by Sergeant Bulmer, circulate a handbill, which identifies "two little moles, close together, on the side of her neck" (151). Virginie Lecount, Noel's perspicacious housekeeper, sees through Magdalen's initial performance, and later procures a letter from Miss Garth that "provided a means of establishing Magdalen's identity" through a "personal description minute enough to be used to advantage" (324).[78] As with the handbill, this description identifies Magdalen through a particular bodily signifier. Andrew Mangham observes that Lecount's detective work "reads like a surgical procedure."[79] Indeed, Lecount had previously cut out a portion of the brown alpaca dress that Magdalen had worn as Miss Garth, which becomes a textile puzzle piece to expose Magdalen's fraudulent identity. Tatiana Kontou observes that the piece of dress "assume[s] a double (perhaps multiple) function," representing Magdalen's identity while also demonstrating how her "false identity is only skin deep—she steps out of character as if out of a dress."[80] Reading Magdalen's shifting identities as shedding skins also renders her reptilian/amphibian, not only as a snake or even a chameleon, but also generally as a figure of degeneration, level with the grotesque toad that occupies the centerpiece of Lecount's aquarium.

Desperate to forestall Noel's suspicions, Wragge proposes the "Crucial Test" (336) to scrutinize Magdalen's neck for the identifying moles. With time running out, Wragge hastily orders Magdalen's "whole collection, brushes, palette and everything" (336), and he "carefully mix[es] his colour with liquid glue, and with a strong 'drier' added from a bottle in his own possession" (337). Magdalen warns that the moles "can't be painted out" (337), but Wragge proceeds, "passing a cambric handkerchief with some white powder on it," and then "plac[ing] two layers of colour on the moles, with the tip of the brush" (337). In spite of the success of his potentially hazardous composition, Wragge still relies on Noel maintaining a "distance of two or three feet," suggesting that "the closest inspection" (337) would be an improper transgression between the would-be lovers.[81] Yet, even after they are married—the prelude to which nearly drives Magdalen to suicide—Noel "can't say" whether his new bride possesses the moles, given her propensity "to wear [her hair] low" (445). Noel's unfamiliarity with Magdalen's body suggests their lack of intimacy, the terms of which further permit Magdalen's eventual reformation.

Following Noel's death, Magdalen wears another "skin" to access a secret trust, agreeing to fund her maid Louisa's passage to Australia in exchange for Louisa's identity. But Admiral Bartram's drunken old coxswain Mazey catches the "land-shark in petticoats" (555) reading the document. Banished from the house, Magdalen assumes the name Gray (perhaps a reference to the notorious impostor Alice Grey), and retires to a derelict lodging, ill and despondent. Wragge visits to announce that he has graduated from identity theft to consumer fraud, having "shifted from Moral Agriculture to Medical Agriculture" (585). Captain Robert Kirke, "bewitched" (284) by Magdalen since their first incidental encounter, also appears to precipitate her restoration. That Kirke's name corresponds to the Scottish word for the Church of Scotland (and roughly to the German *Kirche*) suggests Magdalen's transformation is implicitly religious, if not outwardly spiritual.

By means of some astoundingly complex legal maneuvers, even for Collins, Magdalen wins back a portion of the Vanstone inheritance. Since the terms of the secret trust were not enacted, half the Vanstone inheritance returns to Magdalen. Armed with this information, however, Magdalen "t[ears] the Trust to pieces" and "cast[s] the fragments into the street" (607). She destroys her newly restored identity to erase her past: "I have parted with it as I have parted with those torn morsels of paper" (607). The death of Magdalen's parents tied her personal identity directly to her body, but the legal reestablishment of her inheritance restores her documentary self. Yet Magdalen resists this latter identity, reforming herself spiritually under the absurdly Christian name Magdalen Kirke.[82] While this final transformation defines personal identity through the soul, rather than the body or the document, it also maintains the condition for imposture. Magdalen's spiritual identity, in other words, cannot be documented, proved, or discovered; it is, instead, entirely immaterial, intrinsic rather than cosmetic. "Somebody's Wife" (484) achieves a perfect imposture, shedding skins to reveal the incorporeal soul.

Chapter 2

Altered beyond Chance of Recognition

Surgery and Blood Transfusion

Impostors in sensation novels were the first to challenge corporeal definitions of personal identity by altering the form or composition of the body itself. Whereas clothes and cosmetics disguised identity from the skin outward, surgery and blood transfusion demonstrated that the body could be transformed from the skin inward. If personal identity was based on physical peculiarities, then subcutaneous/intravenous modifications could either create new identities or, especially in the case of blood transfusion, transfer identities between subjects. Unlike imposture through clothes and cosmetics, which was represented in sensation novels and recorded in actual cases, imposture through surgery and blood transfusion was limited to the fictional sphere. These personation plots, then, gesture toward the preternatural or the prophetic, perhaps more suited to the Gothic novel or science fiction than to sensation fiction. Yet the means that fictional impostors used to alter personal identity are grounded in nineteenth-century advancements in surgical procedures and hematology. Although the results remain farfetched, the origins are plausible, at least in the case of plastic surgery. Imposture through blood transfusion, in contrast, relies on a combination of science and myth, wherein the transfusion itself is medically sound, but the blood retains traces of vitalism. In either case, the body becomes a site for manipulation from within—at the very least subcutaneously—contesting definitions of personal identity that are tied to particular corporeal marks or measurements.

In 1880, Francis Wharton, an American criminologist, claimed that full-scale identity theft would require impostors "to obliterate their own peculiar features."[1] Wharton rests on the assumption that, no matter the disguise, "the nose, the mouth, the voice remain, each of which possesses traits which cannot be defaced by any means short of destruction."[2] Yet the "peculiar features" that proved identity in Victorian courts were often scars and tattoos. In 1874, Alfred Swaine Taylor noted that an impostor, "to prevent a discovery of his identity," might "remove[] the marks by cautery or other means."[3] Taylor subsequently recounts the 1843 story of a man named Aubert, who was arrested for robbery. Concocting an alibi, Aubert claimed to have been in prison at the time under the assumed name Solignon. Prison records noted Solignon's particular tattoos. None were conspicuously present on Aubert, who claimed he had "removed the marks by a chemical process," consisting of an "ointment of strong acetic acid, then a weak solution of potash, and afterwards hydrochloric acid."[4] In spite of Aubert's efforts, careful examination revealed vestiges of his former tattoos, which did not match Solignon's records. Although Victorian impostors did not resort to plastic surgery (or, for that matter, blood transfusion), they did practice forms of body modification, manipulating the skin and soft tissue either to conceal their own identities or to personate someone else.[5] "Criminals," one 1877 medical writer remarked, "are great adepts at personal disguisement."[6] As the body became the sole site of personal identity, impostors adapted, demonstrating the mutability of corporeal matter.

Sensation fiction frequently represented the body as a site for modification. Tattoos, scars, and brands, whether decorative, occupational, or punitive, regularly perform as identification signifiers, permanently altering the composition, topography, and pigmentation of the skin, from the epidermis layer inward. One of the most intriguing examples of body modification in sensation fiction occurs in Mary Elizabeth Braddon's *Sir Jasper's Tenant* (1865).[7] As in many sensation novels, twin personation structures the plot: Leonora personates her sister Caroline to access a pension, among other financial pursuits. To complete the imposture, Leonora burns herself with the "red-hot point" of a fireplace poker to counterfeit Caroline's scar.[8] George Pauncefort (aka Godfrey Pierrepoint), who was married to Caroline, initially trusts the authenticity of this fraudulent scar, and believes that Leonora is his estranged wife. *Sir Jasper's Tenant* approaches body modification in an innovative way. Since Leonora inflicts the burn upon her own body to personate her twin sister, a peculiar corporeal mark does not differentiate between subjects, but rather permits imposture. She modifies her body to alter her personal identity.

Whereas clothes and cosmetics have intrinsic limitations—that is, their functionality relies on application and removal—body modification hinges on permanency. In Wilkie Collins's *No Name* (1862–63), Magdalen Vanstone wears the "skins" of both Captain Wragge's "individuals retired from this mortal scene" and the associates she personates, but these disguises transform her body outwardly, and are readily exchanged, revised, and discarded.[9] The panic over Magdalen's dual moles, which serve as unique identification marks, never broaches surgery. Braddon's Leonora Fane, however, permanently alters her corporeal constitution. While she burns herself, her face becomes "horribly distorted," as if her personal identity transforms through the counterfeit mark.[10] The two novels I analyze below extend the imposture that Braddon promotes, if not introduces, in *Sir Jasper's Tenant*. In Sheridan Le Fanu's *Checkmate* (1871), extensive plastic surgery alters the antagonist's personal identity, making his former self unrecognizable and only traceable via a sort of makeshift death mask that the eccentric surgeon categorizes and stores. William Delisle Hay's *Blood: A Tragic Tale* (1888) similarly deals in body modification but focuses on blood rather than tissue. The aftermath of a blood transfusion transmogrifies the personal identity of the donor into the body of the patient.

Surgery in *Checkmate*

Nineteenth-century developments in surgery coalesce behind innovations in anesthesia applications and antiseptic techniques. Surgeons began to use nitrous oxide as an anesthetic in 1844 but moved to ether and chloroform in 1846 and 1847, respectively. By the end of the century, the medical profession finally accepted Joseph Lister's advocacy and techniques for the antiseptic treatment of wounds and surgical devices. Before these innovations, surgery was defined by pain, suffering, and the likelihood of infection and disease. Frances Burney's unnerving 1812 account of her mastectomy evidences the horror of early-nineteenth-century surgical experience. Most late-eighteenth- and early-nineteenth-century surgeons were either students or followers of John Hunter, the eminent Scottish doctor, who served as a war surgeon early in his career. As W. J. Bishop points out, "[w]ar continued to be the great school for the surgeon."[11] Indeed, the Napoleonic Wars proved to be a testing ground for surgical innovation. The severity and extent of battlefield injuries prompted the formal introduction of plastic surgery into the field of medicine.

Plastic surgery dates back several millennia, at least to ancient India, where surgeons first attempted rhinoplasty on subjects whose noses were punitively, ritually, or criminally removed.[12] The most important innovator in plastic surgery before the nineteenth century was Gaspare Tagliacozzi, whose *De Curtorum Chirurgia per Insitionem* (1597) is widely considered the field's pioneering text. Tagliacozzi is best known for adapting the Indian method of nose reconstruction by transplanting skin from the arm. Recovery required the patient's arm to remain connected to the nose until the graft was established. In 1814, Joseph Constantine Carpue successfully performed the first rhinoplasty in Britain, and two years later Karl Ferdinand von Graefe, a German surgeon, performed a similar procedure. In the late nineteenth century, Baroness Staffe, "[t]he great French authoress on the toilet," offered advice for at-home rhinoplasty in her wildly popular *The Lady's Dressing Room* (1893).[13] Under the section "The Science of Rhinoplasty," Staffe encouraged her readers, following the "millionaires" in New York City, to "[w]ear eye-glass frames during the night, and as much as possible during the day," in order to "change their noses into either Greek, Roman, or Hebrew, as they prefer."[14] Staffe also suggested that her readers blow their noses "exclusively on the defective side until [they] become[] perfectly straight."[15] Staffe's nonsurgical advice notwithstanding, early nineteenth-century developments in rhinoplasty paved the path for plastic surgery to become a respected subfield in the medical community.

Eduard Zeis, a German surgeon, coined the term plastic surgery in 1838, and encouraged the work of Johann Friedrich Dieffenbach, "the earliest true founder of the specialty."[16] Dieffenbach, as Sander L. Gilman notes, "draws the line between reading a procedure as having a 'real medical' as opposed to merely an 'aesthetic' function."[17] Under Dieffenbach's influence, plastic surgeons gained prominence as reconstructive specialists rather than cosmetic artists. In 1846, an English reviewer provided a translation of Dieffenbach's definition of plastic surgery: "the replacement of a lost, or the restoration of the form of a mutilated . . . part of the human body."[18] Although J. M. Chelius claimed in 1847 that "[p]lastic [s]urgery has found little sympathy" in England, the practice took off in the latter decades of the Victorian period, perhaps not coincidentally during the expansion of antiseptic methods.[19] In the 1860s and 1870s, simultaneous to the rise of sensation fiction, several surgeons, including Jacques Louis Reverdin, Karl Thiersch, and John Reissberg Wolfe, made important innovations in skin grafting.

For Chelius, "[t]he value of plastic operations" rested on "effectual improvements" that ranged from correcting congenital deformations to "the restoration of any important function, and the removal of any very serious inconvenience."[20] No medico-legal writers in the nineteenth century seem to have expressed concern over the potential for plastic surgery to affect personal identity. Sensation fiction, ever prescient, made such a connection. Indeed, Ellen Wood's *East Lynne* (1861), one of the genre's most noteworthy early novels, features a surgical procedure that transforms the protagonist's identity. Isabel Vane, having been abandoned by her duplicitous lover Captain Levison, is involved in a horrifying train accident that kills both her child and her maid. Isabel, initially thought dead, barely survives with severe injuries to her leg and "the lower part of her face."[21] The surgeons save her life, but she is permanently disfigured: "A scar extends from her chin above her mouth, completely changing the character of the lower part of her face."[22] This major surgical procedure, though perhaps not plastic surgery per se, nonetheless involves reconstructive efforts that "altered [her] beyond chance of recognition."[23] Thereafter, Isabel assumes the name Madame Vine, and surreptitiously reenters the house of the family she abandoned. As Audrey Jaffe observes, she is "both a victim of disguise . . . [and] the manipulator of her own image."[24]

One other surgical procedure in a sensation novel is worth mentioning because it involves the brain. In Vere Clavering's *Barcaldine* (1889), Stephen Callender is thought to have personated his double, Gerald Fairfax. The *Saturday Review* played spoiler, noting that the supposed personation causes a "vast deal of unnecessary trouble" because the "case of mistaken identity . . . turns out not to have been mistaken after all."[25] Clavering, clearly influenced by the familiar model of the personation plot, turns it on its head. Unlike many other sensation novels, true mystery defines *Barcaldine*. Readying readers for the expected revelation of personation, Clavering subverts the device. Stephen, who laid the groundwork to personate Gerald, actually dies, never having succeeded with his plan, while Gerald, thought to be an impostor, ultimately retains his rightful position as heir of Barcaldine. Surgery plays a significant role in this development. Gerald and Stephen independently decide to emigrate from Australia to England, but the ship they share wrecks in the Mediterranean Sea. Clavering encourages readers to believe that Gerald died in the wreck, giving Stephen the opportunity to personate his acquaintance. After much intrigue, a doctor examines Gerald and finds that a "small portion of bone *was* pressing unduly upon the brain, and was undoubtedly the primary cause of the loss of memory, the violent pains in the head, and general irritability of the patient."[26] As it turns out, this brain injury, sustained during the shipwreck, caused Gerald to forget his own identity and to assume, based on the suspicions of some unscrupulous characters, that he was actually Stephen. *Barcaldine* thus participates in late-Victorian advances in localization and neurology that underscored the materiality of the brain, which organizes memory, and can be modified through injury and surgery.

A far more pervasive, though perhaps not as permeating, surgery structures Sheridan Le Fanu's *Checkmate* (1871). Walter Longcluse, the novel's criminal protagonist, undergoes facial reconstruction, altering his nose, jaw, and eyebrows to assume a new identity that allows him to lead a more virtuous life. *The Examiner* noted Le Fanu's interest in plastic surgery, declaring that there is "some ingenuity, or rather novelty, in the notion . . . of a criminal who baffles the detective police by submitting to the Taliacotian operation."[27] But remarks in the *Saturday Review* are most significant to the novel's central theme: "in novel-writing, as well as in wax-work shows, a Chamber of Horrors is found to pay only too well. Madame Tussaud has at all events the decency to keep her horrors in a chamber to themselves."[28] The reference to waxworks emphasizes the novel's interest in the pliability of corporeal personal identity. Anna Maria Jones observes that Le Fanu's fiction "explores the persistent problem of individual agency, engaging in Victorian debates about the nature of subjectivity and the limits of individualism."[29] In *Checkmate*, "the Mephistophelian eyebrowed hero" literally molds himself new facial features to escape his criminal atrocities.[30] Ultimately, however, the novel's amateur detective locates the death mask of a previous identity, which acts as a sort of fossilized record of a past that no longer exists.

Checkmate begins among the domestic circle of the Arden family. Siblings Alice and Richard Arden are joined by Walter Longcluse, a "thin, tall man—the only sinister figure in the group. . . . Who is that pale, thin-lipped man, 'with cadaverous aspect and broken beak,' whose eyes never seem to light up, but maintain their dismal darkness while his pale lips smile?"[31] The narrator's vampiric portrait also includes Longcluse's "slightly underhung" jaw, which joins "the depression of his nose" (5). Longcluse plots to install himself in the Arden family as personal penance for murder, which he committed under his previous identity as Yelland Mace. His surgical disguise begins to fail, however, when the housekeeper, Martha Tansey, recoils in shock after meeting him. Martha can trace the voice to the scene of Henry Arden's murder, but the face is neither Mace nor his accomplice, who was caught after the crime. Notably, the surgical procedure deteriorates, rather than improves, Longcluse's image. He is described as possessing a "bad color. . . . A bad white . . . and pock-marked something; a broad face and flat, and a very little bit of a nose" (22). His skin is scarred, and his nose no longer aquiline. It is as if the promise of a new identity has made him syphilitic, complete with lesions and a saddle nose.

As in many sensation novels, unraveling the mystery of Longcluse's previous identity requires the work of an amateur detective. David Arden, Richard's virtuous uncle, travels to Paris to meet with the surgeon Vanboeren, whose "savage energy" and "brutal vulgarity" (164) embodies the malevolence of his dark arts. Peppered with questions about Longcluse and Mace, Vanboeren remains cryptic: "I can bring you face to face with both" (165). He leads David into his "catacombs" (165), which contain shelves of locked boxes. "[M]y mummies are cased in hieroglyphics," Vanboeren remarks: "Come! *Here* is the number, the date, and the man" (166). He opens one of the boxes labeled Yelland Mace and removes a plaster mask, in which David "saw a face with large eyes closed, a very high and thin nose, a good forehead, a delicately-chiseled mouth; the upper lip, though well formed after the Greek model, projected a little, and gave to the chin the effect of receding a little. This slight defect showed itself in profile; but the face, looked at full front, was on the whole handsome, and in some degree even interesting" (166). Vanboeren then removes a mask from a shelf of "*resurrections*" (167), which shows Longcluse "sharply defined in every line and feature, in intense white and black, against the vacant shadow behind. There was the flat nose, the projecting under-jaw, the oblique, sarcastic eyebrow, even the line of the slight but long scar that ran nearly from his eye to his nostril. The same, but younger" (167). Anna Maria Jones's remark that Le Fanu's novels have a "revenant quality to them" applies forcefully to this scene. The death mask resurrects the identity of a man who is not dead but reborn.[32]

Longcluse's imposture requires a method of surgical precision that makes Vanboeren a kind of Victor Frankenstein for the criminal underworld. Vanboeren reveals that Mace approached him under the assumed name Herr von Konigsmark, and he describes, in intricate detail, the surgical process, which resembles a sculptor describing his artistry:

> I opened the skin with a single straight cut from under the lachrymal gland to the nostril, and one underneath meeting it . . . along the base of the nose from the point. Then I drew back the skin over the bridge, and then I operated on the bone and cartilage, cutting them and the muscle at the extremity down to a level with the line of the face, and drew the flap of skin back, cutting it to meet the line of the skin of the cheek; *there*, you see, so much for the nose. Now see the curved eyebrow. Instead of that very well marked arch, I resolved it should slant

> from the radix of the nose in a straight line obliquely upward; to effect which I removed at the upper edge of each eyebrow, at the corner next the temple a portion of the skin and muscle, which being reunited and healed, produced the requisite contraction, and thus drew that end of each brow upward. And now, having disposed of the nose and brows, I came to the mouth. (169)

Although the masks provide evidence of the faces of Yelland Mace and Walter Longcluse, they do not prove any link beyond both being taken in 1844. Vanboeren knows that his account is the only connective tissue: "Without me you can never lift the veil; without me you can never unearth your skulking Yelland Mace, nor without me identify and hang him" (168). When David refuses to be extorted for a testimony, Vanboeren furiously "dashed the two masks to pieces on the hearth-stone at his feet, and stamped the fragments into dust with his clumsy shoes" (170). David departs with neither evidence nor testimony.

Vanboeren's insistence on taking masks of dead identities resembles a sort of biometric technology, for which he creates an intricate classification system that even relies on copies. Initially resistant to David's inquiry, Vanboeren reveals that he possesses the "original matrix of each mask" (172), meaning that the shattered mask is not the only surviving evidence of Longcluse's original identity. Before David can react, however, Vanboeren is found murdered. Meanwhile, Longcluse has abducted Alice with the intention of marrying her against her will. But officers arrest him under the charge of murder. The main deposition comes from Martha Tansey, who noticed that Longcluse had a scar, "a very peculiar mark indeed, on the back of his left hand" (180). Mace, she recalls, had the same scar. Although extensive plastic surgery successfully erases Mace's face, his personal identity remains tied to a corporeal particularity. In prison, Longcluse pays Richard's debts, leaves the remainder of his fortune to David and Alice, and commits suicide. During a raid of his house, investigators discover "proofs . . . of Longcluse's identity" (181) and also the elements of a disguise he used to confront his enemies with impunity. Plastic surgery gave Yelland Mace a permanent new identity, but clothes allow him to assume several other identities on a temporary, and far less intrusive, basis.

The *British Quarterly Review* identified Le Fanu as a "master of what it has become the fashion to call 'sensation,'" and observed that *Checkmate* "is a real puzzle, based upon an original contrivance."[33] To understand Longcluse's physical transformation under the knife of an incipient cosmetic surgeon as a "contrivance," however, reduces the novelty and the prescience of Le Fanu's project. *Checkmate* illustrates how impostors could exploit medico-legal definitions of personal identity that focused solely on the body. Longcluse's face is not a forgery because there is no original to copy; instead, Vanboeren, following in the footsteps of Victor Frankenstein, creates an entirely new subject. As in many sensation novels, however, Le Fanu ultimately champions corporeal identification, as a bodily peculiarity provides evidence of personal identity. But Martha Tansey's initial suspicion, which eventually leads her to notice Longcluse's scar, rests on the disembodied voice. For Francis Wharton, writing in 1880, "the face is not the only test. Voices are equally distinguishable, and their distinguishability has been made the basis of convictions in criminal courts."[34] Although an earlier legal manual asserted that "the voice should have very little weight in determining controverted questions of personal identity," both Le Fanu and Wharton gesture toward twenty-first-century biometric technologies, especially voice recognition.[35]

Blood Transfusion in *Blood: A Tragic Tale*

The modern history of blood transfusion traces to the seventeenth century, with William Harvey's anatomical research on the circulation of blood. The body increasingly became understood as a complex machine, especially in the case of blood, which the heart pumped outward through arteries and collected back through veins. The first transfusions that involved humans began with animal donors. Douglas Starr notes that early practitioners of transfusions considered blood to be a "therapeutic liquid," meaning that the procedure was performed "to treat not blood loss or anemia but insanity."[36] Sensation novels offer a curious blend of ideas about blood transfusion. On the one hand, they advocate realistic medical benefits for patients who have undergone severe trauma, and their scenes of blood transfusion always occur between human subjects, suggesting a rejection of xenotransfusion, the transfer of blood between different species. On the other hand, sensation novels perpetuate vitalist notions of blood's properties, imagining an exchange of some or all aspects of personal identity between donor and patient. Such a conflict not only allows sensation novelists to compose simultaneously realistic and fantastic plots but also reflects contemporary notions of blood transfusion, most often a mix of science and myth, before blood types were discovered at the turn of the century.

The most notorious and influential case occurred in 1667. Jean-Baptiste Denis, hoping to minimize Antoine Mauroy's violent outbursts that were thought to evidence insanity, transferred artery blood from a bovine calf into a vein in Mauroy's arm. Following a second transfusion, the patient vomited and went into shock, but then he recovered and was released. Unexpectedly (and incorrectly), Mauroy's insanity was said to be cured. Nevertheless, Mauroy returned for a third transfusion, but he died before the procedure began. As it turns out, he had been poisoned by his wife Perrine, whom he had abused for years. Denis' experiments with transfusion caused immediate controversy, and many officials petitioned to have the practice made illegal. In 1670, the French Parliament banned blood transfusion altogether, and the practice largely died out in the medical community, only to reemerge in the nineteenth century. As Holly Tucker observes, the 150-year hiatus was not the result of worry about patient health, but rather stemmed from anxiety over "the moral and religious implications of mixing the blood of different species."[37]

James Blundell, an early-nineteenth-century obstetrician, is widely credited with performing the first successful blood transfusion that involved a human donor and a human host. Rather than attempt to cure insanity, Blundell used transfusion as a last resort for patients who experienced postpartum hemorrhages, and he correctly ascertained: "[I]n performing the operation of transfusion on the human body, the human blood should alone be employed."[38] Notably, one patient reported that she "felt as if *life* were infused into her body."[39] In spite of the initial success, Harold A. Oberman notes, blood transfusion during the nineteenth century was, "at best, primitive."[40] Mid-nineteenth-century procedures that adapted Blundell's method appeared successful but were quickly followed by a spate of tragedies. "To-day," one writer asserted in 1885, "enthusiasm has utterly died out."[41] Sanctions from the professional medical community, however, did not mean that the practice died out; rather, it moved underground. During an 1877 "death by misadventure" trial in Liverpool, one doctor claimed to have "performed 15 cases of blood transfusion, using a special apparatus of his own."[42] Only after Karl Landsteiner identified blood groups in 1900–1901 did transfusion become safe and widely exercised. The demand for on-site blood during World War I subsequently led to advancements in preservation and storage.

At the time of the sensation novel's cultural dominance, blood transfusion was largely discouraged by medical professionals. In cases of traumatic injury where doctors resorted to transfusion, it may have been the transfusion itself, and not the injury, that hastened the patients' deaths.[43] George Henry Lewes warned in 1859 that transfusion, in the case of curing diseases, is "useless, or worse."[44] Jules Law points out that Lewes's cautionary remarks demonstrate an updated conception of blood as a "neutral medium devoid of all the occult qualities attributed to it. . . . Thus one should not expect the exchange or sharing of blood to change dramatically the character of the organism."[45] One 1874 case, of questionable authenticity, contrasted Lewes's claims. A doctor transfused the blood of a goat into his mortally ill patient, who revived, "jumped out of bed, and, twitching his head about after the fashion of a goat, made a savage attempt to butt the doctor."[46] Lewes, whose writing in the natural sciences contributed to an increasingly materialist characterization of personal identity, understood blood as purely material, absent of any mythic or immaterial force that would affect patients. Sensation novelists disagreed, composing personation plots that hinged on the capacity for blood transfusion to transfer some, if not all, aspects of personal identity between subjects.

In spite of Lewes's intervention, popular notions of blood continued to promote mythic properties, such as vitalism, the capacity for blood to act as the elemental substance of personal identity. Ann Louise Kibbie notes that an "increasingly mechanistic view of the function that blood serves in the body [did] not entirely displace a rhetoric regarding blood's special powers that continue[d] to verge, at times, on the mystical or supernatural."[47] Well before Bram Stoker interposed blood transfusion and monstrosity in *Dracula* (1897), sensation novelists imagined ways that the transfer of blood between subjects could transform personal identity, calling into question corporeal definitions of the self. For Kibbie, nineteenth-century writers represented a "bodily economy that extends beyond the boundaries of the individual person," so that "transfusion could . . . lead to imaginative speculations about how such incorporation might challenge our notion of a stable individual identity."[48] Sensation novelists led the charge for such concepts, imagining a way to transmit personal identity between subjects through material means. The first of these designs, not coincidentally, occurs in George Eliot's story "The Lifted Veil" (1859), published the same year that Eliot's partner, George Henry Lewes, downplayed the effects of blood transfusion.

Latimer, the doomed narrator of "The Lifted Veil," possesses what he calls a "double consciousness," which not only forces him to see images of the future but also grants him unwanted access to other peoples' minds.[49] Following the tragic death of his brother, Alfred, Latimer marries Bertha Grant, who was set to become his sister-in-law. Gradually, Bertha comes to understand Latimer's "abnormal power of penetration," and avoids his company.[50] Bertha then employs a new maid, Mrs. Archer, who becomes a trusted adviser, only to have a sudden falling out. Latimer's old friend Charles Meunier, a respected continental physician, visits, and Mrs. Archer experiences a "sudden severe illness."[51] Meunier diagnoses her with peritonitis and declares her case beyond the aid of customary procedures. He convinces Latimer to help him perform a blood transfusion to be initiated after her death. Having found success experimenting on animals, Meunier "want[s] to try it on a human subject," and volunteers himself as donor.[52] That the operation must be kept a secret—Meunier is worried that a "disagreeable foolish version of the thing might get abroad"—suggests the danger and recklessness of his enterprise.[53] The transfusion initially succeeds. Mrs. Archer revives, sees Bertha, who has just entered the room, and reveals that Bertha was planning to poison Latimer. Eliot stops short, in "The Lifted Veil," of asserting that blood transfusion affects personal identity in terms of hematological imposture. But she does suggest that transfusion, in some way, bridges donor and host. As Kate Flint observes, "the combined power of Meunier's body and profession . . . gives Mrs. Archer new power to speak."[54]

"The Lifted Veil" seems to have inspired a wave of sensational plots that involve blood transfusion.[55] Mary Elizabeth Braddon's "Good Lady Ducayne" (1896), for example, places the supernatural vampire tale in the real world, making blood transfusion a disturbing means of revivifying life. In the short story, Bella Rolleston takes a job as a companion to Lady Ducayne, an eccentric elderly woman. Bella travels to Italy with her mistress, where she meets Dr. Parravicini, who attends Lady Ducayne. Bella begins to waste away, having curious dreams, and hearing reports of previous companions who mysteriously died. When she finds a small wound on her arm, Parravicini blames mosquitos. It is only after Herbert Stafford, a young doctor, makes Bella's acquaintance that the truth comes out. Stafford confronts Parravicini with evidence that he has "been bleeding Miss Rolleston after putting her under chloroform. . . . A practice so nefarious, so murderous, must, if exposed, result in a sentence only less severe than the punishment of murder."[56] Lady Ducayne allows Bella to depart with substantial hush money, and Bella later marries Stafford. Whereas earlier novels represent blood transfusion as a practical and realistic medical treatment for traumatic injury, "Good Lady Ducayne" highlights the potential rejuvenating or life-sustaining effects of transfusions. In contrast, Charles Reade's *Griffith Gaunt* (1865–1866), which he considered his "masterpiece," demonstrates the potential effects that transfusion can have on personal identity.[57]

The first half of *Griffith Gaunt* progresses like a historical romance, but the remainder ramps up the sensational elements, focusing on a particularly innovative imposture, in which Griffith Gaunt personates his illegitimate half-brother Thomas Leicester because they share the "infallible mark" of a hereditary mole.[58] Following the intrigue of a lengthy trial, Griffith reunites with Kate, whom he had married, abandoned, and committed bigamy against. But in the novel's most outrageous scene, Kate falls ill after childbirth (perhaps indicating the Reade had Blundell's operations on postpartum hemorrhages in mind). The doctor declares that a blood transfusion is her only hope, and Griffith steps forward, ostensibly to restore his tarnished reputation. "Take every drop I have," he proclaims: "No man's blood shall enter her veins but mine."[59] The doctor works quickly and "sen[ds] some of Griffith Gaunt's bright red blood smoking hot into Kate Gaunt's veins."[60] Surely, Bram Stoker had this scene in mind when Van Helsing calls Lucy Westenra a "polyandrist" and himself a "bigamist" following the multiple transfusions in *Dracula*.[61] Similar to Lucy's experience, Kate reveals that she has been altered by the event: "[S]he had never been quite the same woman since she lived by Griffith's blood; she was turned jealous; and moreover it had given him a fascinating power over her, and she could tell blindfold when he was in the room."[62] Ann Louise Kibbie observes that "the transfusion . . . seems to have created a kind of telekinetic communication from husband to wife."[63] But in a novel so concerned with imposture, the scene seems even more forcefully to question definitions of corporeal identity, to rupture the bodily limits of the self. Whereas Griffith successfully personates Thomas, he infiltrates Kate. It is not that Kate partially assumes Griffith's identity, in other words, but rather that Griffith, through the fusion of their blood, has breached Kate's identity and thus made himself her vampiric master.

Although William Delisle Hay's *Blood: A Tragic Tale* (1887) focuses on blood transfusion and identity, the novel never broaches the topic of vampirism. Instead, Hay explores the implications of vitalism on personal identity, transgressing the boundaries of corporeality. The narrator, Cornelius Steggall, arranges an experimental blood transfusion between his sickly niece, Luris Lyonscourt, and an associate, Seth Seamore. The procedure, rather than merely rejuvenating Luris, kills Seamore and transfers his consciousness into Luris's body. In spite of the novelty of the narrative, critics were underwhelmed. The *Literary World* noted that *Blood* "belong[s] to the highly tragical order" and criticized the novel for relying on the hackneyed trope of the found manuscript.[64] The *Saturday Review* argued that *Blood* "might be described as *Dr. Jekyll* out of *Frankenstein*. . . . Dr. Steggall has created a monster, like Frankenstein; his creation has a double identity, like its ancestors Jekyll and Edward Hyde; and in the end he has to pay the piper."[65] The reviewer correctly detects the novel's clear allusions to *Frankenstein*, including the transfusion's stormy setting, but the comparison to *The Strange Case of Dr. Jekyll and Mr. Hyde* (1886) is most intriguing. For the identity of the "monster" is a true Cartesian duality—the mind of Seamore in the body of Luris. The *Westminster Review* was most critical of the novel, specifically taking issue with the identity transfer. "Happily," the reviewer asserts, "the phenomena described are utterly impossible. Blood-transfusion, on such a scale as is here supposed, as well as the psychological effects produced by the operation, belong to the domain of *la haute fantasie*."[66]

The scale of the blood transfusion, however, is the event that drives the novel. Dr. Steggall accidentally allows it to proceed unchecked for thirty minutes, thus transfusing some thirty ounces. Given Luris's small stature and emaciated frame, this volume could amount to almost one-third of her total blood supply. Hay's project is to imagine the implications that such a large transfusion could have on personal identity. Ann Louise Kibbie observes that Hay "uses the fiction of transfusion to present his readers with the kind of thought experiment that has animated discussions about personal identity since" Locke.[67] Hay seems to explore a new possibility for the fission theory first introduced in the early eighteenth century and then taken up by William Hazlitt at the beginning of the nineteenth.[68] In this case, however, identity does not split between subjects but, rather, transfers wholesale from one subject to another. And the vehicle for this transference is blood, suggesting that Hay understands blood as both a physiological and a mythic substance that contains empirically verified material elements *and* imaginatively conjectured immaterial powers. Regardless of this dual character, blood in *Blood* challenges inflexible definitions of personal identity that center on the peculiarities of the body. Whereas Longcluse in *Checkmate* is ultimately identified by a particular mark that was not removed by plastic surgery, Seamore successfully—and permanently—personates Luris, as he possesses her entire body, which provides the only evidence necessary to prove personal identity.

Blood begins with a series of questions from its first-person narrator, Cornelius Steggall: "Who am I, or you? What am I, or you? What laws controlled my entrance into conscious life, and what shall control the extinction or metamorphosis of that consciousness?"[69] Steggall plays coy, of course, because his narrative is retrospective, and he already understands that blood answers each of these questions. "What is it that is ME, apart from YOU?"

he continues: "What is Personality, Individuality, Identity—call it what you will—and how is its existence begun, separated from other existences, and ended?" (2). The only substance that separates existences, the novel suggests, is blood, which can be transferred between bodies. The capacity of blood to be transfused between donor and host was, in the nineteenth century, an exclusive property of the material body, as tissue transplantation had only just occurred in 1883, and organ transplantation did not follow until the twentieth century. Blood, in other words, was almost unique in its capacity to be shared. If it were passed and repassed, what were the limitations to the distribution of the self among others? *Dracula*, of course, extends this potential to a horrifying magnitude, as the vampire relocates to London "to be in the midst of the whirl and rush of humanity."[70]

Blood stops short of such vampiric threats, instead examining the implications of hematological identity on a smaller, but no less disturbing, scale. Luris comes under the care of Steggall, her uncle-in-law, early in the novel when her parents reluctantly send her away in hopes of finding a cure for her increasingly dire illness. Steggall admits to "monomania" in his "yearning desire to restore Luris" (10), and he finds a "suitable agent—perhaps I ought to write *victim*—by means of whom to accomplish my design" (11). Seth Seamore, an Australian who immigrated to London to study medicine, disgusts Steggall with his pleasure seeking. More crucial to the imposture, Seamore "possessed an organization of a type extremely rare, in the male sex, at least. It was one of those emotional, hypersensitive, extraordinarily sympathetic natures which are usually associated with hysterical females of a particular class" (13). Steggall explains that the experiment "consist[s] in a certain delicate manipulation and the employment of appliances not yet introduced into Europe. . . . By those means the *arterial* current of the blood giver—not the *venous*—can be made to pass into the circulation of the patient without an intermediary" (24). Following the protracted transfusion, Steggall observes a "wondrous, an awful alteration in [Luris's] face," which is accompanied by a full-body transformation: "Her eyes are open and distended, her sunken cheeks now appear full and round, her lips puffed and swollen, and above all—above all, a crimson flush overspreads her once pale face and neck and floods downwards over her heaving bosom" (38). Gorged with Seamore's blood, Luris awakens Steggall's sexual desire, which he struggles to suppress for the remainder of the novel.

Although *Blood* questions corporeal identity through the blood transfusion between Seamore and Luris, the novel nonetheless relies on procedural forensics to convict Steggall of Seamore's murder. Following the transfusion,

Steggall hastily disposes of Seamore's body in a large furnace, hoping that "[t]hose indistinguishable atoms in the ashes . . . can reveal nothing—nothing!" (45). The professionals hired to investigate the ashes, however, discover "the left side of the lower jaw-bone of a man or woman" (179), with intact teeth. One tooth is missing from the bone, and the prosecution confidently declares: "there is . . . a means of actually identifying the individual to whom this jaw, and, therefore, probably the other remains, belonged. For if it can be shown that a missing person possessed a false first lower molar on the left side, and other facts tend to the same conclusion, I suppose there would be little doubt about identity" (180). According to Francis Wharton, teeth represent "the chief mode of identification, when the features of the deceased have lost their shape."[71] Yet the surviving bones merely identify Seamore's body, not his immaterial self. Investigators subsequently consult Seamore's dentist, who corroborates the evidence, dooming Steggall. Shortly thereafter, Luris visits Steggall's prison cell and produces an untraceable poison from a location only Seamore would have known. As Steggall slowly dies, Luris reveals herself as Seamore, and boasts: "The creature has worsted her creator" (189). At the end of the novel, Luris, in her "new womanhood and its ambitions" (194), prepares to marry a duke.

The implications of this marriage are intriguing, but Hay stops short of any conspicuous commentary on the circumstances of a male consciousness inhabiting a female body. Ann Louise Kibbie notes that blood transfusion in the novel "effects its own complicated gender transformation," which "entertains the problem of how *sexual* identity is or is not constitutive of personal identity."[72] Seamore, in fact, seems perfectly content in his new body, perhaps more *complete* than he was before. Seamore, according to Steggall, seeks pleasure "without scruples or moral principles of any sort or kind" (12). But Steggall's principal unease with Seamore stems from his associate's "incomplete character" (14), as if Seamore's identity is not legible according to the standardized codes that construct Victorian sexual literacy. For Jolene Zigarovich, the sensation novel's "emphasis on the plasticity and fungibility of identity" means that it "often explores the shifting gender codes of the nineteenth century."[73] One might read Seamore as queer, if not trans, in that he appears to find some level of "completeness" by inhabiting Luris's body. Steggall recalls that "[t]here were moments when I caught myself wondering whether there was not something *feminine* about this young man" (13). The blood transfusion gives Seamore the body that corresponds with his mind; it is, in some sense, a sex-affirmation procedure. At the very least, Seamore challenges corporeal definitions of personal identity *even before* the transfusion relocates his consciousness. His personal identity, which encompasses his sexual identity, cannot be identified with his body. Investigators discover and analyze his calcified remains, but they are not, and never were, Seth Seamore.

First Interlude
Alice Grey

I.1. Alice Grey: "The Female Impostor, Alice Grey." *The Illustrated Usk Observer and Raglan Herald* 21 (November 24, 1855): 3.

Alice Grey, one 1856 writer remarked, was "the most notorious imposter that we had had in England for so many years."[1] Grey's criminal enterprise, the bulk of which occupied only one year, spread throughout the British Isles,

	Apprehended.	Discharged.	Convicted.
Birmingham	1	1	—
Bath	1	1	—
Bristol	1	1	—
Chester	3	1	2
Cork	2	2	—
Dublin	2	2	—
Galway	1	0	1
Glasgow and Greenock	3	3	—
Liverpool	3	1	2
London	5	5	—
Macroom	1	1	—
Waterford	2	0	2
Wolverhampton	4	2	2
	29	20	9

I.2. Grey's victims: "The Female Impostor at Wolverhampton." *Jackson's Oxford Journal* 5,350 (November 10, 1855): 6.

and her victims, several of whom served unjust prison sentences, numbered at least into the twenties. A table of her "episode in the annals of artifice" appeared in several publications.[2]

In 1855, *The Times* reported:

> The catalogue of ships in the *Iliad* is not a very amusing portion of the poem, for the simple reason that it is a catalogue—a dry recital of facts and names. The same remark must necessarily apply to any attempt at describing the various enormities which have been committed by a young woman who has been unfavorably known in various parts of the [U]nited [K]ingdom as Alice Grey, Alice Christie, Agnes Hemans, Anastasia Haggard, Jane Turean, Mary Anne O'Brien, and by a dozen *aliases* besides.[3]

The connection between Grey's performance as a "new heroine" who "had played many parts" and characters in sensation novels is promising, especially in the case of Mary Elizabeth Braddon's Lucy Audley and Wilkie Collins's Magdalen Vanstone.[4] In fact, W. S. Gilbert named his heroine Alice Grey in his satirical play *A Sensation Novel* (1871). So notorious were Grey's crimes that, at least into the 1860s, women impostors were referred to as "Alice Greys," with one reporter warning that the copycats would mean "Alice Grey without end."[5] But Grey was not without her supporters. In 1856, following her conviction, a pamphlet was published titled *The Ballad of Alice Grey and the Grand Jury: A Lay of Modern Staffordshire*, which highlighted the legal corruption imposed on "poor Alice."[6]

Alice Grey was an assumed name, which the impostor may have lifted from the titles of either William Mee's 1815 poem or John T. Haines's 1839 melodrama.[7] Grey's actual name was probably Annastasia Haggard, and she was born somewhere around Limerick, Ireland, in the early 1830s.[8] As a teenager, Grey may have started a relationship with a man named Keeffe, who published their banns, but the marriage never occurred. One dubious source claims that she escaped from a Liverpool reformatory at fifteen, and another writer describes how she sued a rich man in Limerick for "breach of promise of marriage."[9] Although her age matches an "Alice Grey" featured in *The Man of Pleasure's Pocket Book* (1850), her name is too common to substantiate the connection. In August 1853, Grey married Timothy Brazil, a soldier in the 68th Regiment, and later gave birth to a son, Henry.[10] It appears that she abandoned her family shortly thereafter and fled to England. But other reports claimed that her flight resulted from Brazil's conviction and transportation for bigamy. Allegedly he wrote her two letters while she was jailed in Scotland, claiming he had been pensioned and sent to Bermuda.

The first public mention of Grey's "long and successful . . . career of guilt" appears in late October 1855.[11] In a Wolverhampton court, she accused four boys of robbery; two held her down, she claimed, while the other two fled with her purse. Although no other witnesses came forward, two of the boys, Perry and Randall, were found guilty. Subsequent evidence proved that they were not in the vicinity at the time of the crime, and the boys were released, "deserv[ing] much sympathy."[12] At one of her trials, Grey, who claimed to be a governess, was "[d]ressed with a simple neatness that approached elegance, with a face whose freshness seemed to have lost nothing by a long journey."[13] Another article went into more detail, noting that Grey was "about 21 years of age, about 5 feet 7 inches high, fair complexion, high cheek bones, and dark hair," with "the appearance of a respectable servant girl."[14] Yet another witness noted her "good figure," and the *London Review* described her "pretty face, white skin, delicate colour, and . . . soft voice."[15] She was, for one writer, a "fallen angel."[16] Nearly every article that reported on Grey's crimes mentioned her "fair and frail" appearance, which "appealed to a man's most chivalrous instincts."[17] In fact, following another trial in Liverpool, "the barristers at the session actually made a collection to send the forlorn Anastasia back to Ireland."[18] She was, for the *Law Times*, "the interesting perjurer, whose innocent face and plaintive tones imposed upon judges, juries, counsel and clergymen."[19] As news spread of her multiple trials, Grey became a celebrity: "She has received presents of money; scraps of her handwriting are carefully treasured; and her portrait, taken a few days ago, is very eagerly sought after."[20] Devotees cheered her during the trials, bought strands of her hair and shreds of her dress, and clamored for autographs. So popular was the market for her hair that "two wigs failed to keep pace with the demand."[21] "Alice Grey is the rage," one writer noted: "She is . . . worth her weight in gold to a Barnum."[22]

Shortly after the Wolverhampton trial, Grey appeared in front of a Birmingham judge, further establishing "that wonderous and charming person's vogue in the courts."[23] This time, "jocose and eccentric as usual," she was the accused, having been recognized in a train station as Alice Christie, who had charged a worker with stealing her traveling box.[24] Information flooded the court describing Grey's myriad impostures. She had earlier complained of being left destitute after having fled the home of her abusive stepfather, a reverend in Leeds, and she also claimed in Kent to have been a Catholic escaping from her Baptist father. Elsewhere, she alternately claimed to be a "Protestant escaped from Catholic coercion, at others a Baptist, a Wesleyan, a nursery governess, [and] a young woman who had run away to be married, but could not find her intended."[25] Grey subsequently turned up in a Liverpool workhouse, where she produced a forged letter of introduction, asserted that her brother was a student at Oxford, and claimed to have worked in an artist's studio where she was abandoned by her husband. In addition to these declarations, Grey spread "tales of high ancestral descent," which included "queer notions" of a legacy from the East India Company.[26]

Grey thereafter maintained that she had left her purse at a railway station, asserted that her purse had fallen through a hole in her pocket, and announced that she had been attacked and robbed. She then claimed that her traveling box was stolen by Joseph Stanton, Owen Brogan, and a woman named Keighley. As usual, however, the evidence was scant, "rest[ing] upon a piece of gimp, some buttons, and some plush velvet found in the house where the prisoners lived."[27] Whereas Brogan was eventually acquitted, Stanton and Keighley were sentenced to nine and six months, respectively. Later, a man named Fenton testified that Grey worked as his nurse for three weeks under the name Anastasia Huggard. Evidence of more crimes arrived through telegraph. In Chester, she had accused three men, John Robinson, Robert Writer, and John White, of robbery. Although White had an alibi, Grey's claims won out, and the men were each sentenced to three months in prison. More accounts emerged accusing Grey of crimes in Coventry and Greenock, Scotland, where she went by Anastasia Carter and Anastasia Brazil, and charged Duncan Gillies, a porter, with stealing her property. Then, in Glasgow, she accused three people, Marion M'Gilvray, a widow, Neil M'Gilvray, her son, and John Paterson, a ham-curer, of theft. But the accused were acquitted. The *Morning Chronicle* warned that "a just *denouement* awaits her extraordinary and reckless career."[28]

At the Staffordshire Assizes, Grey was accompanied by an assistant, who supplied her with periodic refreshments. Nearly every reporter commented on the extraordinary crowds at the trial, which attracted even "persons of considerable county standing."[29] During her deposition, Grey used "disgusting language," which formed a "disgusting contrast to that gentle, modest, sweet, ingenuous manner" she had earlier displayed.[30] As another writer put it, Grey "transformed into a coarse blearing creature, who shocked the court with foul expressions."[31] "[H]er person was changed," the *Morning Post* declared: "there was more of the tigress than the dove in the unhappy woman's disposition."[32] Grey continued to display "animal excitement," when inquiry began, describing the clerk as a "nasty-looking thing," calling other members of the court "the filthiest names," and telling them that "they might all go to———."[33] Alternate reports spelled out the epithet, "go to hell," noting that she "conducted herself with the utmost affrontery."[34] At one point, Grey told a guest: "If you were that magistrate, I would pull your whiskers."[35] For her most notorious performance, after "showering this filth about her," Grey attempted to exit the crowded court, and "sprang from the chair . . . and skipped across the table."[36]

The prosecution's case was largely built on witness testimony, during which Grey "manifested a considerable acquaintance with the law of evidence."[37] Witnesses were brought to court to identify Grey based on photograph copies circulated at the locations of her various crimes. When Grey was arrested, officers discovered a daguerreotype of herself in her possession. Colonel Gilbert Hogg may have given the daguerreotype to Oscar Rejlander, the pioneering and controversial photographer, who made twenty calotype copies. Investigators then disseminated these copies to her known whereabouts, which "secured her identification, and will hereafter as effectually mark her as though scarred with a heated iron."[38] Nine other applications came forward requesting Grey's photograph, which subsequently produced information that she had spent at least one year in either a Dublin prison or an asylum. Another report arrived claiming that Grey was Ann Wills, a woman "discovered in a state of nudity . . . by three fishermen," claiming she had been robbed.[39]

The court's star witness was Reverend Joseph Morris, who claimed he gave Grey money and bought her coffee in Birmingham. Under scrutiny, he admitted to taking her to a "temperance hotel," but denied that they went to a pub where he drank three glasses of wine.[40] He also rejected the accusation that he "kiss[ed] her 9000 times."[41] When Morris was led into court, Grey allegedly began "rapidly thrusting out and withdrawing her tongue," and said, "Oh, you delicate little man—you bad man!"[42] Grey continued her diatribe against Morris: "You, a man of God! Sit down. Make a seat for the gentleman!"[43] She also handed out verses, titled "Pitching into the Parson," to members of the press:

> One evening, by the Railway Station,
> I met a Vicar spruce and gay,
> Who got with me in conversation,
> And then invited me to tea.
> As we were sitting at the table,
> We talk'd of things more pleasing still—
> He says, "To keep you I am able,
> Take my offer if you will."
> I told him I was quite a stranger,
> And felt unwilling to engage;
> He kindly bade me fear no danger,
> And wish'd to know my name and age.
> "This night," he said, "if you are ready,
> I will take you off for life,
> And ever keep you like a lady,
> As I kept my former wife."
> At this fair speech I seemed delighted,
> But would defer it for some time,
> Saying, "If you speak your mind in writing,
> I will speak the truth of mine."

Four pounds he gave me then with pleasure,
To buy a suit of muslin fine,
And bad me come and sit at leisure,
Where we could have a glass of wine.
A minute found us in the "Palace,"
Where there was a pleasant fire,
Sealing all we said with kisses,
Drinking all we could desire.
At length I ask'd him his profession,
Thinking he look'd somewhat odd;
By law, he said, he got his living;
But did not mean the law of God.
Thus we sat, quite cheerful-hearted,
Till the moon began to shine,
The clock cried out, "We should be parted,"
And then I lost my old divine.[44]

The *Staffordshire Sentinel*, which published the verses, eventually wrote Morris a letter of apology, after he threatened a lawsuit. Morris also threatened the *Morning Advertiser*, another paper that ran the verses, but he received no such reply. Morris failed to attend subsequent court dates, complaining of being "seriously ill of paralysis."[45] Delivered this news, Grey opined: "Perhaps he is in love."[46]

Another witness, John Smedley, wrote a letter to *The Times* meant to dispel rumors about his association with Grey. "The way," Smedley demurred, "in which my name has been mentioned in the local papers in connexion with the impostor Alice Grey is calculated to place my conduct in at least an equivocal light."[47] Smedley, a philanthropist, was the owner of hydropathic hospitals in Derbyshire named Lea Mills, which his father founded near Lea Hurst with a relation of Florence Nightingale, who lived there periodically. According to Smedley, a woman of "superior manners and education" arrived at Lea Mills and applied for lodging, claiming to have escaped from a convent.[48] "I was confirmed in my first impression," Smedley asserted, "that she was an impostor, and I considered it a duty to the public to put a stop to her practices."[49] In spite of his reservations, Smedley "determined to give her a trial" as a worker at the mill, "on condition she consented to be locked up at night until we had confidence in her reformation."[50] Grey remained in the position for a short time, but then absconded, leading Smedley to report her as a "rogue and vagabond."[51]

To the surprise of many, the accusation against Grey in Birmingham was dismissed. Shortly before her release, "more than one publican" offered her employment "in the hope that the notoriety she has gained might render her an attraction to customers."[52] After exiting the prison, however, Grey was apprehended at a train station, and brought to trial on alternate charges relating to perjury in Wolverhampton. Crowds increased as news of her "spicy manner spread," with spectators obsessing over the "romantic interest with which her life of crime has been invested."[53] Grey would appeal to these crowds, especially asking after the health of Reverend Morris, and claiming that she will "be well tried and crucified."[54] Grey's antics eventually lost their charm, and the media, which was formerly favorable, turned against her. *The Times* opined that Grey's "thoroughly vicious" career has led to the wish that "she may now be properly disposed of."[55] And another writer hoped that her sentence would be severe enough "to deter others from following her example."[56]

During portions of her trial, Grey "put on the appearance of insanity, and still continue[d] to simulate aberration of mind."[57] Prosecutors claimed that, at earlier trials, she "appeared to be in full possession of all her faculties."[58] Undaunted, she continued the routine, "tearing her clothes and performing other wild freaks."[59] But the doctors in attendance maintained the "opinion that her insanity is feigned."[60] The court order for Grey to be "attended by one or more female turnkeys" was one night overlooked, and nearby staff heard a noise, finding that Grey had "fallen against the door, apparently in a state of partial suffocation, produced from the smoke of straw which was burning in her cell."[61] Grey claimed she had attempted "to burn herself to death."[62] Grey's suicide attempt led one writer to criticize the "wonders in our gaols," which have led people to "commit[] acts of violence in order to obtain the[ir] comforts."[63] In years past, the writer argues, "that interesting impostor and pathetic perjurer" would have "looked in vain for a cell lighted with gas, or a mattress capable of ignition."[64] News of Grey's alleged madness and suicide attempt only added to her notoriety. Crowds of people visited the prison hoping she "would be exhibited to them."[65]

Further developments in the "epic" investigation prompted inquiries in Ireland, where several writers reported a series of impostures starting in 1849.[66] (One accuser alleged that Grey began her criminal career as early as 1840, when she would have been a child.) At that time, Grey allegedly went by the name Armstrong in Dublin, claiming to be the abused daughter of a constable to gain charity. Later information indicated that Grey might have made fraudulent claims about the paternity of a child in 1848. A

Newcastle man claimed knowledge that Grey's father was shot to death in Limerick when she was four years old and that Grey had "to escape from the slavery of a low stepfather's house," with plans to sail to America.[67] An official from Limerick also asserted that Grey's mother had married Thomas Walsh. When Grey was convicted of two felonies, which stemmed from false accusations of robbery and subsequent perjury, she "found Ireland 'too hot' to hold her, [so] she came to England."[68]

Grey's change of scenery was brief; it appears she returned to Ireland regularly throughout the early 1850s. Possessing an "elegant taste in names," she altered her identity at seemingly every stop.[69] Given her Irish origin, several articles referred to Grey as a "female Jesuit," linking her to Jemima Luke's 1851 anti-Catholic novel *The Female Jesuit; or, the Spy in the Family*. Grey was simultaneously a heroine in a sensational court drama and a villain spreading popery into Protestant households. In 1851, Grey charged four women with robbery in London, and the same year, under the name Anastasia Finlary, she accused a man of robbery in County Cork, Ireland. In 1852 she was in Bath, under the name Agnes Hemans, where she claimed Thomas Stone had robbed her. She was subsequently known in Scotland as Anastasia Carter and in London as Mary Ann O'Brien. In Regent's Park, she worked as a servant under the name Jane Turean, and was accused of robbing her upper-class employer. By March 1854, Grey was back home in Limerick, where she charged a man with seduction.

Each of these alleged crimes were presented during the Staffordshire Assizes, where S. R. Goodman, the chief clerk, boasted he "could identify her out of a thousand."[70] During the trial, *The Times* highlighted her unparalleled criminal career: "who can be quoted as at all a rival of the interesting personage," who has "made such good use of her time that a mere enumeration of her achievements must necessarily run to a considerable length."[71] So notorious was Grey that crimes she did not commit were pinned on her.[72] Mr. Bartlett, her attorney, argued that "[a]ll the offences which had been committed in the United Kingdom by women during the last nine years, had been attributed to that innocent woman."[73] Grey herself claimed she was "not guilty of one sixteenth or twentieth part of what I am charged with."[74] At least one writer, having acquired Grey's photograph, reported that accusers had "fallen into error" by suggesting that Grey committed a crime as Anna Maria Armstrong in 1851.[75] Conflicting evidence notwithstanding, Grey's trial for perjury proceeded. She was represented by Mr. Motteram and Mr. A. S. Hill, while the prosecution was led by Mr. Huddlestone and Mr. Scotland. The defense argued that it was "at the worst only a case of mistaken identity."[76] But the jury was not convinced. Under her false name, Grey was convicted of perjury in March 1856 and sentenced to four years' imprisonment. "A change," one writer opined, "had come over her dream."[77] As Grey left the court, she muttered that "the Learned Judge could not make her live so long."[78] That May, she was transferred to Millbank Prison in Westminster, London.

In 1862, Henry Mayhew and John Binny visited Millbank during their investigations of London prisons. "One woman was at work picking coir," they recalled, "with her back turned towards us. We looked at her register number above the door, and read on the back of the card the name of *Alice Grey*."[79] The same year, Frederick William Robinson, as part of his quasi-fictional prison narratives written under the anonym "A Prison Matron," also described a visit to Grey's cell. "It was always her desire to be famous," Robinson asserts: "her struggles in prison to assume a position to which she considered herself entitled by her past notoriety, were unremitting."[80] Robinson observes that Grey acted disrespectfully toward prison staff and refused to perform manual labor. *The Athenaeum* described Grey's experience in "durance vile," where she "paraded her resolution to make laws for herself."[81] Having been transferred to Brixton Prison, notorious for its overcrowding and squalor, Grey mimicked her earlier suicide attempt, setting fire to the coir and the sheets in her cell. She was quickly removed, however, and remanded to "the 'dark,'" where she was kept for twenty-eight days.[82] Grey's time was not without some happiness, however. She adopted a pet sparrow, which one 1863 writer connected to Wilkie Collins's "amiable villain Fosco . . . and his pet canaries."[83] In 1875, Arthur Griffiths also mentioned Grey in his *Memorials of Millbank*, noting that "the most notorious prisoners . . . were not always to be found on the 'male side.'"[84]

The conclusion to Grey's story remains unclear. Robinson, in a footnote, claims that she was "assisted to emigrate by the Prisoners' Aid Society on the 28th of March, 1860."[85] Robinson also asserts that Grey wrote a letter "stating that she was in an excellent situation and contented with her new life."[86] Another source indicates that Grey's adventures were not finished. In 1866, Charlotte Ward provided an anecdote about a friend who noticed an interesting-looking woman on an omnibus in south London. The woman was "every inch the lady," yet her clothes were "mean and rusty."[87] The stranger then complained of faintness, so Ward's friend purchased restorative drugs and offered her mother's house as a nearby resting place. The woman claimed to have fled from home because her father married a Catholic woman who wanted to place her in a convent. The friend's husband, armed with legal connections, began an investigation, hoping to "restore her to her rights."[88] At length, this inquiry revealed the stranger's true history, which the friend detailed in an angry letter: "[S]he is the greatest liar, hypocrite, and imposter, that I ever heard of in modern times," and she is best known "under the name of Alice Grey."[89] It was around this year, according to several sources, that she "drank herself to death."[90]

In the early twentieth century, Grey's story reemerged in a series of accounts that border on hagiography. These biographical sketches, similar to contemporaneous reports, base their positive appraisals on Grey's alleged beauty. "If pretty Alice Grey had not chosen to lead the life of a criminal adventuress," C. L. McCluer Stevens claims in 1924, "she might easily have achieved fame and fortune on the stage, for she was one of the most consummate, natural-born actresses, probably, that ever lived."[91] In Stevens's wildly inaccurate account, Grey is "timorous," "shrinking," "modest," and "timid" to the point that "[i]t savoured almost of blasphemy to imagine anything evil of so frail and beautiful a personality."[92] Somehow more inaccurate is another retrospective by Charles Kingston, who asserts that Grey "would have made a perfect model for either painter or sculptor who wished to depict Innocence."[93] Similar to Stevens's description, Kingston notes Grey's "fragile daintiness," "angelic mouth," and "Madonna-like features."[94] Four years in prison, however, distorted her "innocent and guileless expression."[95] Whereas Stevens admits that Grey was eventually "poisoned by drink," Kingston blames her downfall on her altered appearance: "with the loss of her Madonna-like beauty, Alice Grey was reduced to the ranks of the criminal underworld, and there she existed precariously until her death."[96] These sketches reform Grey into a heroine—and explicitly so in Kingston's case, where she was "the heroine of the hour" at her trial—idealizing her brazen criminality into a picture of exquisite desperation.[97] In many respects, Grey resembles Lucy Audley through depictions of her devious beauty. But she is perhaps better associated with Magdalen Vanstone, who similarly, and just as controversially, earned full reclamation after a flurry of impostures. In either case, twentieth-century interest in Grey's extraordinary identity fraud speaks to sensation's cultural durability, lasting well after the genre's allegedly precipitous decline. "I am the fascinating Alice Grey," the incarcerated impostor maintained: "You have heard of the celebrated Alice Grey."[98]

Part II

Mind

Personation is an unworked mine.
—*The Spectator*, May 13, 1882

Chapter 3

That Lost Personality

Madness and Epilepsy

Following her violent, warranted outburst at the beginning of Charlotte Brontë's *Jane Eyre* (1847), the eponymous narrator recalls feeling "beside myself; or rather *out* of myself," while being dragged "like a mad cat" into the ghostly red room.[1] She recollects that her "head still ached and bled with the blow and fall I had received" and notes that her "brain was in tumult."[2] Shortly thereafter, she "had a species of fit: unconsciousness closed the scene."[3] When Jane regains consciousness, Bessie will say only that she "fell sick," which is perhaps not euphemistic but directly descriptive of her fall.[4] Bessie then remarks that "it's such a strange thing she should have that fit: I wonder if she saw anything."[5] Indeed, Jane reports to have seen "[s]omething . . . all dressed in white," with a "great black dog behind him."[6] The narrator admits that the event "gave my nerves a shock of which I feel the reverberation to this day," which manifests as "fearful pangs of mental suffering."[7] Leonard Guthrie, a late-nineteenth-century pediatrician, referred to the "neurotic child" in *Jane Eyre*, who experiences a "fit of apparently hysteron-epilepsy, in which the child has visions."[8] Although Jane's narrative doubling with Bertha Mason potentially includes madness, the type of mental abnormality they possess differs along the lines of acquired versus hereditary. Rochester claims that Bertha "came of a mad family; idiots and maniacs through three generations!"[9] Jane, in contrast, experiences a traumatic head injury—immediately manifested in spasms and loss of consciousness—the effects of which she endures into adulthood.[10] But the women share in their alleged madness some form of mental disassociation, a loss of personal identity, whether temporary, recurrent, or permanent.

This chapter examines representations of madness and epilepsy in sensation fiction to demonstrate how novelists used imposture to test the limits of personal identity. Since epilepsy was often understood as a symptom of madness, the chapter begins broadly and makes a more specific intervention in the second section. Increased knowledge of brain chemistry in the latter half of the nineteenth century led medico-legal writers to investigate the criminal responsibility of insane subjects. To do so meant defining personal identity against cognitive abnormality. In 1862, James Crichton Browne, a prominent neurologist who specialized in brain injury, attempted to delineate the specific forms of madness that would constitute a loss of personal identity. He begins by underscoring the power that naming has on personal identity, imagining that a subject being stripped of a title would "produce a mental confusion bordering upon double consciousness."[11] Similar to his peers, such as Alexander Bain and Henry Maudsley, Browne correlates "corporeal and mental identity" through "the influence of the nervous system."[12] But ultimately he is interested in "errors of identity" that "exercise a powerful sway over the sane or insane who are subject to them."[13] Consciousness, for Browne, is an "experience of the vital actions and changes perpetually taking place within us," and "errors" in personal identity occur when "the corrigent sequence of teleorganic changes is interrupted."[14]

The cardinal issue, for Browne, is that many "false convictions" have been accepted in which modifications of "encephalic conditions" affect personal identity.[15] Browne argues that a patient who "believes himself transmuted into some brute or inanimate object[] does not lose the consciousness of continuous self-existence."[16] But he does note that cases exist in which "the insane notion is so prominent as to obliterate all recollection of the healthy period prior to its incursion," meaning that all sense of an original personal identity has been lost or replaced.[17] Browne concludes his essay with a lengthy examination of "double consciousness," when "the individual is separated into two distinct beings," a phenomenon proving that "mental identity is something more than consciousness."[18] This inquiry leads Browne to promote the term "double identity" over "double consciousness" because "[o]ne identity is laid aside, with all the remembrances connected with it, but another is put on."[19] Therefore, double identity is the "result of diseased action," which can manifest in a range of conditions, defined against one another by "the mental symptoms, and by the relations to each other of the lucid and insane or of the two insane 'oscillations.' "[20] One might read Brontë's Jane and Bertha as a sort of double identity that has also divided corporeally. Rochester attempts to establish the difference: "Compare these clear eyes with the red balls yonder—this face with that mask—this form with that bulk."[21] But we might note that the "fall" Jane experiences at

Gateshead Hall in some sense prefigures Bertha's dramatic plunge from Thornfield Hall, where "her brains and blood were scattered."[22]

Jane Eyre's thematic interest in madness and identity does not embrace imposture into its fold. (The novel's primary men—Brocklehurst, Rochester, and Rivers—are frauds, certainly, but never fully impostors.) Instead, Brontë attends to the way that madness disrupts personal identity, potentially linking the lives of Jane and Bertha. In 1855, Margaret Oliphant anticipated the wave of sensation in the coming decades, referring to Jane Eyre as "the impetuous little spirit which dashed into our well-ordered world, broke its boundaries, and defined its principles," inspiring "the most alarming revolution of modern times."[23] Indeed, *Jane Eyre* prefigures many sensational themes, especially through its focus on madness. Jenny Bourne Taylor notes that "the sensation novel was seen as a collective cultural nervous disorder, a morbid addiction within the middle class that worked directly on the body of the reader."[24] Victorian reviewers often claimed an association between the sensation market and madness, deploying the moniker "sensational mania." In an 1866 article, for example, the *Saturday Review* remarked that "[t]he writing of a sensation novel may, perhaps, henceforth be regarded as the last stage of mental disease."[25] This assessment would mean, if taken seriously, that the genre's novelists possess a form of "double identity," displacing previous or potential authorial identity with the less respectable self of sensation.[26] Reviewers regularly pleaded with sensation novelists, especially Mary Elizabeth Braddon and Wilkie Collins, to write what the *Saturday Review* called a "novel of character."[27] The *Ladies' Companion*, for example, remarked that Braddon is "in literature what a mercenary is in an army," satisfying the public's demand for criminality, while "rank[ing] . . . the foremost and most talented writer of her class in England."[28] In any case, issues of personal identity and mental illness are coded into the sensation agenda, especially intertwining within personation plots.

Madness in *Lady Audley's Secret*

An 1866 article titled "Madness in Novels" reacquaints readers with Mary Elizabeth Braddon's singular style. "For her purpose," the reviewer explains, "it was necessary to strengthen the old machinery of novel-writing, to introduce changes more frequent, acts more unaccountable, catastrophes more violent and appalling."[29] These changes, acts, and catastrophes often centered on madness, which "may intensify any quality, courage, or hate, or jealousy, or wickedness."[30] The decision to make Helen Talboys mad in *Lady Audley's Secret* (1862) allowed Braddon to be "released from the irksome *régime* of the probable."[31] Since the actions of mad characters cannot be predicted by readers, the reviewer claims, sensation novels are able to capitalize on improbability, without approaching the supernatural. As Jessica Cox notes, madness "is a theme which dominates the genre."[32] The *Saturday Review* put it best in 1866: "madness pure and simple, as an element in sensation novels, ha[s] become by this time rather stale."[33] Indeed, seemingly every sensation novel deals with madness in some form, often with the objective to interrogate personal identity. Madness not only challenges corporeal definitions of personal identity, demonstrating that the self can contain complex, conflicting, and changeable cognitive states, but also questions mental models that rely on a stable continuum of memory or consciousness. Thus, madness inherently resists identity, suggesting the diversity of the human experience, the postmodern concept of the fragmented self.

In 1830, John Conolly, the eminent psychiatrist and asylum reformer, observed that the cultural fascination concerning madness stemmed from the fact that "no man can confidently reckon on the continuance of his perfect reason."[34] Two decades later, a writer for *The Times* emphasized that "[n]othing can be more slightly defined than the line of demarcation between sanity and insanity."[35] The definition for madness is both too narrow and too broad, with the result that "we are all mad when we give way to passion, to prejudice, to voice, to vanity."[36] In *Lady Audley's Secret*, Braddon similarly reflects on "how many minds must tremble upon the narrow boundary between reason and unreason, mad to-day and sane to-morrow, mad yesterday and sane to-day."[37] Just one year before the initial serial part of Braddon's novel, Thomas Laycock noted "the increase of insanity" that is "exciting a spirit of inquiry as to the best means of treating and preventing that disease."[38] Two years later, Andrew Wynter similarly remarked that asylum statistics might "lead the public to believe that certain powerful emotions were sufficient to disorganize the material instrument of thought."[39] Such concerns occupied part of the "Lunacy Panic," which emerged as the result of an influx of private asylums accused of unjust incarcerations. Both Collins's *The Woman in White* and Braddon's *Lady Audley's Secret* were published in the wake of movements to reform the diagnosis and treatment of madness.[40] And both novels contain plots in which questionably mad characters are incarcerated against their will to maintain class distinctions. *Lady Audley's Secret*, especially, fixates on the fact that, to borrow from Lewis Carroll's Cheshire Cat, "we're all mad here."[41]

Victorian brain specialists frequently explored the ways that mental abnormality affected personal identity. An 1856 writer conflated madness and dreams, noting that in both "the thoughts wander in the same wild manner," often creating "the same confusion as to personal identity."[42] And in 1858, Joshua Burgess noted that patients who endure hallucinations and illusions may experience a "suspension of personal identity."[43] Less than a decade later, another medical writer qualified such pronouncements, arguing that "consciousness generally remains unimpaired in lunatics," though the patient "sometimes expresses himself as if his notion of personal identity were strangely confused."[44] The issue was also taken up by leading phrenologists. In *A System of Phrenology* (1848), George Combe emphasized "the existence of a plurality of mental functions, each connected with a particular part of the brain," and claimed that "one of them supplies the feeling of Personal Identity, or the *I* of consciousness."[45] For Combe, madness supports the phrenological model of the brain because "patients are sometimes insane in this feeling, and in no other faculty of the mind. Such individuals lose all consciousness of their past and proper personality, and imagine themselves different persons altogether."[46] Other researchers on mental abnormality opposed such models. In 1865, James F. Duncan referred to the "immaterial nature" of cognitive faculties, which means "[w]e cannot . . . determine whether the mind is divisible into parts or not."[47] If "the mind is indivisible," Duncan continues, "there can be no such thing as partial insanity."[48] In spite of these disagreements, physicians were responsible for "inquir[ing] into . . . the loss or obscuration of the sense of continuity of life, and therefore personal identity."[49]

The study of brain abnormality as a physiological phenomenon was a particularly Victorian concern that stemmed from advances in cerebral localization and neurological mapping.[50] At the end of the eighteenth century, "moral" theories transformed the way that patients were treated, focusing on "appeals to the sufferer's intellect and feeling," rather than linking madness to a "disorder of the body."[51] Initial efforts were led by William Tuke, who founded York Retreat in 1796. In the Victorian period, "the domestication of insanity" emerged from asylum reforms led by such advocates as John Conolly.[52] Jenny Bourne Taylor notes that moral management encouraged a "notion of a common subjectivity to which all have equal access," but in its promotion of a "stable, sane identity," the movement also "tacitly suggest[ed] the fragility of the identity that it aimed to sustain."[53] Developments in neuroscience meant that physiological approaches gradually vied for attention alongside moral models. L. S. Jacyna observes that a "more complete polarization" occurred at the end of the nineteenth century, when "British psychiatric orthodoxy adhered to both somaticist aetiology and treatment, to the rigid exclusion of other more psychological approaches."[54] In 1862, for example, Andrew Wynter sought to determine the "first beginnings" of madness, noting that the brain "always affords notable signs, easily capable of being read by an accomplished physician."[55] Remarkably, the very same year Wynter drew attention to "[t]he injurious effects of blows upon the head," Braddon associated Stephen "Softy" Hargraves's madness in *Aurora Floyd* to a "fall in the hunting-field," which left him a "little bit touched in the upper story."[56] At the same time that personal identity became increasingly tied to corporeal attributes, the diagnosis, study, and treatment of madness shifted progressively toward determining the distinct physiological processes of the mind, including research on brain hemispheres and lesions caused by trauma or disease.[57] In *The Pathology of Mind* (1879), Henry Maudsley asserted that the "moral commotions and mental overstrains" that cause madness "do it by straining or breaking the molecular ties of the nerve-structure and so injuring or destroying its vital elasticity."[58]

Sensation novelists regularly used madness to illustrate personal identity as an unstable and mutable construct. As Rebecca Stern notes, sensation fiction spoke to "popular interest in recorporealizing madness."[59] Whereas the dominant practice in the study and treatment of mental abnormality focused on the material mind, sensation novels frequently showed how such rigid models rely on arbitrary and changing definitions of normalcy. Lyn Pykett notes that Wilkie Collins's *The Woman in White* (1859–60) is significant for its "inversion of the dominant code," as madness in the novel is represented by "passive, controlled, domestic women."[60] Ostensibly sane characters, in contrast, including Percival Glyde and Count Fosco, are physically violent, mentally abusive, and manipulative, which demonstrates the ambiguous borders between sanity and insanity. As Andrew Mangham notes, "[w]hat appears to be a search for the hidden improprieties of female identity actually lays bare the latent horrors of the *male* psyche."[61] Through this inversion, Collins also establishes how madness could be used to interrogate corporeal structures of identity. Anne Catherick's madness is associated with her blankness, both mental and sartorial. When Hartright first meets Anne, she is "dressed from head to foot in white garments."[62] Her face is "colorless" and her hair a "pale, brownish-yellow hue" (24), as if either her manuscript pages are weathered with age or that Collins associates her with the populist sensations of yellow-back novels. John Kucich argues that Anne's "psychological emptiness . . . is a metaphor for the 'lie' of all understanding about identity, all possibilities for honesty about the self."⁶³ And Diane Elam similarly observes that Anne "stands before the narrative as an absence, a blank, denying the possibility of the universal, of the all, of visible presence."⁶⁴ Yet she is also a vault of information, possessing an "unusual tenacity in keeping [ideas]" (60). The woman in white is a palimpsest for personation, able to absorb Laura's identity.

The Woman in White suggests that madness can influence personal identity in two ways. First, Anne's madness effectively erases her identity, rendering her powerless to assert her own personhood as distinct from Laura. Second, Laura's drugging disturbs her sense of personal identity, making her appear mad to the asylum staff, and thus able to personate Anne. For Ann Cvetkovich, this substitution "suggest[s] that identity is contingent, that the body is not a guarantee of individuality."⁶⁵ Subsequent sensation novelists connected madness to personal identity in different ways. One frequent trope was for an impostor to become mad due to the pressure of the personation.⁶⁶ The most common depiction of madness in sensation novels, however, was initiated by Braddon in *Lady Audley's Secret*, in which hereditary madness eventually emerges from Lucy Audley's fraudulent identity.⁶⁷ This phenomenon is just what Henry Mansel described in 1863: "under these pleasing outsides may be concealed some demon in human shape."⁶⁸ Mansel, in part, was referring to Lady Audley, whose polished exterior conceals hereditary madness.

In *Lady Audley's Secret*, Helen Talboys's gift for imposture seems to be linked to her mental instability. But Braddon revises the relationship between identity and madness that Collins employed in *The Woman in White*. Whereas Anne Catherick's madness renders her a passive body to sustain personation, Helen's madness activates imposture, triggering her performance of a new personal identity as Lucy Graham. Victorian critics saw Lucy Audley's duplicitous criminality as a threat to polite society. For the *London Review*, the success of the novel evidences a "growing tendency to pry into the dark recesses of . . . feminine nature[]."⁶⁹ Other reviews emphasized similar issues that implicitly targeted anxieties over degeneration. "Have we," the *Critic* inquired, "by following the criminal course of a beautiful woman's life, gained one step in either our moral or intellectual progress? Far from it—we have retrograded."⁷⁰ *Lady Audley's Secret*, which the *Athenaeum* called "just the sort of book to be read by everybody," was doubly dangerous.⁷¹ It not only exhibited the potential degeneration of aristocratic lines through the crimes of a woman but also spread the intrigue of such crimes through an unprecedented readership, acting as a sort of genetic (or generic) mutation.

Critics also commented on the novel's depiction of madness. *The Reader* made the most intriguing observation, asserting that Lucy is "such a combination of conflicting qualities, that [Braddon] has to reconcile them by starting a new theory of madness."[72] These "conflicting qualities," however, could be understood as the symptoms of Lucy's madness, wherein she cannot present a stable, unitary personal identity. "Lady Audley is mad," the reviewer continues, "in what Greek grammarians call the paulo-post future sense. If something else was to happen, she knows that she would be mad, and this hypothetical insanity gives her the double privileges of a sane person and a lunatic."[73] This duality lies at the heart of Braddon's project. The novel's protagonist is simultaneously Helen and Lucy, sane and insane, "at once the heroine and the monstrosity."[74] Her personal identity, constructed by madness, is never undivided. In fact, the same year that the novel finished its complete serial run in *Sixpenny Magazine* (January–December 1862), James Crichton Browne published his theories on "double identity."

The first chapter of *Lady Audley's Secret* is titled "Lucy" and begins with the pronoun "It" (8). Subsequent sentences gradually reveal that the pronoun refers to Audley Court, but the withholding effect subtly objectifies Lucy Audley, while also de-signifying the home she has invaded. For although Audley Court is the ancestral home of Sir Michael Audley, it is reigned over by a false monarch. Sir Michael's estate, in other words, becomes empty of signification, similar to the foreboding "stagnant well" on the property. Audley Court boasts being "no thoroughfare" (7) and also a "stronghold" (8), yet it fails to protect against "one of those apparently advantageous matches" (10). Braddon early on demonstrates how identity consists of material signifiers that can be forged or counterfeited. Although Lucy's past remains mysterious, she readily produces a reference letter from Mrs. Vincent, her former employer. The letter guarantees her work as a governess under the surgeon Mr. Dawson, "without any more special knowledge of her antecedents" (189), much like the "It" that begins the novel. Mrs. Vincent's recommendation letter, together with the appearance of "Helen Talboys" in the "list of deaths" (36) in *The Times*, allows Lucy to erase her past and to create a new future: "every trace of the old life melted away—every clue to identity buried and forgotten" (16).[75] Lucy errs, however, by retaining evidence of her past, including a "ring wrapped in an oblong piece of paper" (17), and the "secret drawer" in her jewelry case that contains a "baby's little worsted shoe rolled up in a piece of paper, and a tiny lock of pale and silky yellow hair, evidently taken from a baby's head" (31–32). Lucy's forged recommendation letters and fraudulent death register compete against the material signifiers of her past, the "terrible chain of evidence" that Robert Audley "slowly forge[s]" (49).[76]

Robert gradually embraces "the office of spy, the collector of damning facts that led on to horrible deductions" (168), as his earlier listlessness transforms into monomania.[77] An early stop to find "every record of [Lucy's] life" (188) is to interview Dr. Dawson, her previous employer. When Lucy provided her reference letter, Dawson recalls, he checked its accuracy by locating the address of Mrs. Vincent, the referee, in a directory. The documentary signifiers of Helen's past form into a figurative paper body—or a personified novel—that Robert reconstructs: "I have still a blank of three years to fill up" (190). That Lucy's "one fault" is her "absence of color" (27) suggests, similar to Collins's Anne Catherick, she is a blank canvas, able to be painted into various identities. Similar to the cosmetic imposture employed by Collins's Magdalen Vanstone in *No Name* (1862–63), moreover, Lucy's "sweet smile is more false than Madame Levison's enamel, and far less enduring" (286). Jenny Bourne Taylor notes that *Lady Audley's Secret* promotes "the notion that identity itself is built on masquerade."[78] As a "wax-dollish young person" (33) who is "only ornamental" (202), Helen becomes Lucy, as she subtly admits to her maid Phoebe Marks, through a "bottle of hair dye" and a "pot of rouge" (54–55).[79]

Helen's outwardly artificial nature conceals the distinct turmoil of her interior existence, which only two characters are able to observe. The first is the anonymous pre-Raphaelite painter, who composes a portrait of Lucy that was "so like and yet so unlike" and "had something of the aspect of a beautiful fiend" (65). Robert is particularly struck by the portrait, taking a masturbatory pose "with the candlestick grasped in his strong right hand" (65). But George Talboys, understandably most affected by the image of his wife, loses his glove, and "ha[s] no candle" (68). Sean Grass observes that the portrait scene "has a breathtaking symbolic efficiency" because the characters "speculate on a matter at the heart of the novel: whether her identity has been made material and inaugurated into dynamics of ownership and exchange."[80] Indeed, Helen is reconstructed by the matter that Robert collects, and his completion of the case means that he takes control over her body, and thus any identity that she manifests. The final material that Robert retrieves is a letter from Dr. Alwyn Mosgrave, which certifies her "latent insanity" (323). Robert earlier explains that painters can see what is "not to be perceived by common eyes" (66), much like Dr. Mosgrave's failed attempt to find "the diagnoses of madness in [Robert's] face" (317), which he subsequently locates during his brief interview of Lucy.

In addition to "hidden relics," Lucy leaves behind documentary evidence of her past. "[T]he novel," Grass observes, "abounds with texts that materialize Lucy's identity and circulate through the novel."[81] During Robert's trip to interview Mrs. Vincent, who is hiding from debts, he secures the assistance of Miss Tonks, who provides him with Lucy's bonnet-box. "[S]craps of railway labels and addresses . . . were pasted here and there upon the box," and Robert notices that one address "had been pasted over another" (203). The palimpsest travel box, which materializes the impostor's double identity, features Helen Talboys overwritten by Lucy Graham. Robert retains the labels by placing them "between two blank leaves of his pocket-book" (203), again reconstructing Helen into a legible book. This paper trail leads Robert to Mrs. Barkamb, formerly the landlady of Lucy's father, who recorded "the whole business in black and white" (212). She leads Robert to an "old-fashioned mahogany desk lined with green baize, and suffering from a plethora of documents, which oozed out of it in every direction. Letters, receipts, bills, inventories, and tax-papers were mingled in hopeless confusion" (212). Among these papers is a letter from Helen Talboys. "I go out into the world," Helen boasts, "dissevered from every link which binds me to the hateful past, to seek another home and another fortune" (212). With "[t]he evidence of handwriting" (230), Robert only needs to account for the time that separates Helen Talboys from Lucy Graham, as if she needed time to emerge from a chrysalis. "The sole ground upon which my suspicions rest," Robert remarks, "is the identity of two individuals who have no apparent connection—the identity of a person who is supposed to be dead with one who is living" (221). The connection, of course, is madness, which empowers Helen and Lucy as a double identity housed in one body.

Braddon provides clues to Lucy's secret well before she confesses to Robert. The first clue stands at the center of Lucy's room, an "octagon ante-chamber" within Audley Court, which Robert, George, and Alicia Audley, Robert's cousin, enter without permission. Alicia, who leads the men through a "trap-door" (63) unknown to Lucy, asserts that the room is "very provoking" (62), blaming the victim for possessing secrets. This room is at once vaginal, or perhaps womb-like, making the transgression a rape or perhaps an insemination (especially given Robert's pose with the candlestick and George's missing glove). Or it is a more metaphorical "rape," akin to *The Rape of the Lock*, since Lucy, like Pope's Baron, possesses "fairy-like silver-mounted embroidery scissors" (71). But Braddon's description of the space best conjures an image of Lucy's brain. (Phoebe and Luke Marks are the first to enter the room, and Phoebe steals the baby hair and shoe, as if she has retrieved one of Lucy's memories.) The "ante-chamber" indicates its location within the house with no other egress, and the trap-door suggests psychosurgery or cranial trepanning. "There are some things," Robert ominously remarks, "which . . . cannot be hidden" (148). That *Lady Audley's Secret* was published during pioneering experiments on cerebral localization perhaps transforms the invaders into surgeons, ones who find Lady Audley's brain in "elegant disorder" (63). After all, the "physiologist" Dr. Mosgrave later "found his way to the octagon ante-chamber" (322) to interview Lucy. Lucy's room, in other words, resembles the "unnatural activity of her mind" (270) and the "wild chaos of her brain" (288), when she "run[s] riot in a species of intellectual tarantella" (94).

This image of Lucy's "dancing" brain resembles her explanations of the way that madness affects her personal identity. Lucy explains the phenomenon during both her confession and her attempt to prove Robert's madness. George's desertion was the initial triggering event, when her "mind first lost its balance" (301). She next experiences a fit of madness when the "idea flashed upon me" (304) of faking her own death. Subsequent fits emerge during the scene at the well and when she attempts to burn Robert to death in Luke Marks's public-house. "Sometimes a paroxysm seizes them," she projects to Sir Michael, "and in an evil hour they betray themselves" (244). During this "mental aberration," she continues, "[t]he mind becomes stationary; the brain stagnates; the even current of the mind is interrupted" (244). The narrator later describes the descent into madness as "the terrible process," which "was to transform her from a woman into a statue" (264). This stupor precedes full disassociation, in which "[s]he spoke with an unnatural clearness, and an unnatural rapidity" (266). Understanding personal identity through Lockean continuity marks these interruptions as breaks in subjectivity. "[M]y mind," Lucy further explains, "utterly lost its balance" (294). Significantly, George plummets down the well because Lucy noticed that a "rusty iron spindle rattled loosely whenever he shifted his position," and then "drew the loose iron spindle from the shrunken wood" (335). Before this act, she admits, "[i]t was then that I was mad" (335), meaning that, at the very same moment, both characters lose their balance.

Lucy's madness also manifests in physical signs, particularly the "four slender, purple marks, such as might have been made by the four fingers of a powerful hand" (80), the bruise resulting from her altercation with George at the well. But Lucy's madness also seems curiously contagious, as if both pathological and transmittable. As Phoebe remarks, "[s]he set every body mad about her wherever she went" (29). With the exception of Robert's already eccentric habits, which make him an "inoffensive species of maniac" (101), Lucy's presence spreads discontinuity. Robert himself questions whether he has "become a monomaniac" (127), wonders whether he experiences a "monition or a monomania" (217), and explains that a letter from Clara Talboys will "wrench me out of myself" (179). Harcourt Talboys, moreover, levels the accusation, "you are mad!" (165), and Sir Michael, under Lady's Audley's influence, remarks, "I think that boy is half mad" (240). Lucy's bewildering presence triggers madness elsewhere. Just before he absconds for Australia, George explains that Lucy's "tears and reproaches drove me almost mad; and I flew into a rage with her" (23). Yet since Lucy identifies George's abandonment as the trigger for her madness, George has just as much claim to being the novel's patient zero as Helen Graham's maternal ancestors.

Once Robert has found "those missing links" (229) in his chain of evidence—wording that suggests Lady Audley's degenerative qualities—he eventually confronts Lucy with a rhetorical question: "What do people generally do when they wish to begin a new existence. . . . *They change their names*" (231).[82] Although Lucy's assumed name temporarily allows her to "sink[] her identity" (231), George's arrival at Audley Court means that she must literally sink his. George's own use of an assumed name as Thomas Brown suggests that Lucy's plan, by and large, succeeds. He ostensibly agrees to start his own fraudulent life in New York. But Lucy is ultimately undone by Robert's maniacal collection of documentary evidence, leading her to reveal the "hereditary taint" (300) of madness, which is, as she herself explains, *the* secret of *Lady Audley's Secret*. Although Elaine Showalter has influentially argued that the "real secret is that she is *sane*," the more significant secret is the bigamy that the Audley family must themselves suppress.[83] Proving Lucy is mad means the Audleys can remove her from England and prevent "any exposures" (323). Dr. Mosgrave—a "physiologist" (324) who would denounce moral management—determines that Lucy suffers from "latent insanity" (323), ensuring her incarceration in a "*maison de santé*" (324) in Belgium, and effectively signing her death sentence.

But Lucy's "discontinuous personhood," to borrow Maia McAleavey's phrase, does not end with her removal.[84] That Robert rests on Madame Taylor as Lucy's new name (thereby also denying her a forename) is suggestive of Helen's "tailoring" of new identities through visual and documentary signifiers. Even more suggestive is Dr. Mosgrave's descriptor as a "mad doctor" (320), rather than a "doctor of madness." But one of the most important lessons that *Lady Audley's Secret* imparts is that prejudices over imposture depend on class. Helen is a "designing and infamous woman" (204), an "arch conspirator" (216), an "arch trickster" (219), an "all-accomplished deceiver" (219), and an "artful woman" (228), among other epithets. But George's use of an assumed name to disappear is understood as a reasonable reaction, and the Audleys' live burial of Lucy under the name Madame Taylor is treated as a practical recourse to preserve the honorific dignity of their family name. This discrepancy demonstrates that the homeostasis of Victorian society relies on the endurance of symbolic class distinctions. Pamela K. Gilbert argues that *Lady Audley's Secret* "provides a clear working example of how interests, issues, and themes gendered female are subordinated and sacrificed in order to maintain a classed and gendered hierarchy."[85] Whereas Lucy is punished for climbing the social ladder through a fraudulent identity, the Audleys are rewarded for deploying assumed names to maintain their respectability.

Helen's madness, Jill L. Matus argues, is a "cover-up" that "serves to displace the economic and class issues already raised in the novel and to deflect their uncomfortable implications."[86] What imperial exploits, one might ask, have stockpiled Lucy's "fairy boudoir" (322)? How close was Phoebe Marks, who worked with Lucy at Dr. Dawson's, to becoming Lady Audley? Why must Lucy become an afterthought in Robert's quest narrative?[87] In this sense, Helen acts as a vessel to contain not only the Audleys' prejudices and misdoings but also those of Victorian society at large. Thus, her madness is reflective rather than innate. "According to [Braddon]," Leila Silvana May argues, "the very essence of consciousness in its relation to the external world determines that madness is an inevitable natural condition: we are all mad. . . . [T]his is arguably the real secret of *Lady Audley's Secret*."[88] To put it another way, Helen's madness authorizes a double subjectivity that reveals identity as a construct formed from arbitrary signifiers. Braddon, who acted under the stage name Mary Seyton, who used the pseudonym Lady Caroline Lascelles, and who committed "literary crime of the first magnitude" under the pseudonym Babington White, demonstrates that the belief in unitary personal identity, whether spiritual or material, is madness.[89]

Epilepsy in *Thou Art the Man*

Victorian critics frequently noted sensation fiction's interest in epilepsy. In 1866, for example, Thomas Arnold, younger brother of Matthew Arnold, described the genre as "the convulsional school."[90] And three years earlier,

Henry Mansel claimed that "[t]he sensation novel is the counterpart of the spasmodic poem," the former of which "aims at convulsing the soul of the reader."[91] Most remarkable, however, is that Henry Maudsley, in the same book in which he scrutinized the effects of epilepsy on personal identity, notes that "the modern sensation novel, with its murders, bigamies, and other crimes, was an achievement of the epileptic imagination."[92] Maudsley's words resemble the *Saturday Review*'s 1866 claim that sensation novelists appear to suffer from a "mental disease." Both assessments imply that the genre's writers possess double identities, as if their sensational imaginations come from a diseased hemisphere of the brain. Regardless, it is remarkable that modern critics have also understood sensation fiction through the coded language of epilepsy. D. A. Miller, for example, argues that the sensation novel "renders our reading bodies . . . theatres of neurasthenia" by "address[ing] itself primarily to the sympathetic nervous system."[93] Sensation novels cause readers to experience involuntary physiological responses that could resemble symptoms of epilepsy, thus impacting personal identity beyond the parameters of the text.

Epilepsy was a particularly intriguing disorder for Victorian medical experts because it demonstrated the link between mind and body, wherein brain abnormalities triggered corporeal responses. Epilepsy, in other words, seemed to evidence the physiology of cognitive processes. John Hughlings Jackson's empirical research on epilepsy furthered brain localization endeavors in the latter half of the nineteenth century.[94] But one of the most controversial figures in Victorian epilepsy research was Henry Maudsley. As Lynn M. Voskuil has noted, Maudsley "insisted that the human mind is factually, physiologically, and visually accessible if only one knows what to look for."[95] Epilepsy made the brain legible through the movements (or sometimes immobility) of the body. Similar to madness (with which epilepsy was often associated), epilepsy was also studied for its potential effects on personal identity. German E. Berrios observes that, by the end of the nineteenth century, "it was the accepted view that there was a positive correlation between the number of seizures and the memory impairment."[96] Epilepsy's influence on cognition and memory meant that it could affect the subject's sense of self. Sensation novelists seized on this potential, connecting epilepsy and imposture by illustrating how abnormal brain functionality could produce conflicting states of personal identity.

Nineteenth-century terminology for different types of epileptic activity survives today.[97] Seizures termed *le petit mal*, also called absence seizures, are characterized by temporary loss of consciousness. *Grand mal* seizures, in contrast, cause convulsive episodes. The seizures that are symptomatic of epilepsy are classified as either focal or generalized. Focal seizures "result from epileptic activity occurring in a circumscribed region of the brain tissue" and manifest in a range of features, including "alterations of behavior, experience, cognition, or automatic function."[98] The bodily responses depend on the cerebral location of the neurological dysfunction. Motor cortex seizures cause spasms of the limbs on the opposite side of the affected brain hemisphere; occipital lobe seizures produce visual abnormalities, from color variations to hallucinations; parietal lobe seizures "give rise to paroxysmal disturbance of bodily sensation, including out-of-the-body experiences"; and temporal lobe seizures generate a "rising sensation" that can lead to "more complex alterations of experience and cognition, including *déjà vecu*, 'dreamy states,' intense emotions, and transient amnesia."[99] With the exception of motor cortex seizures, each of these epileptic events has the potential to disturb personal identity, to displace the subject's habitual self with what Joel Peter Egan calls an "alter presence that manifest[s] behavior and attitudes sharply discrepant from, and often in direct opposition to, the 'host.' "[100] In some sense, epilepsy causes a form of personation, the theft of personal identity by an alien impostor.

In his influential essay "A Study of Convulsions" (1862), John Hughlings Jackson observes that a convulsion is a "symptom of disease of the same region of the brain," meaning that epileptic events confined to half of the body were triggered by a dysfunction within the opposite side of the brain.[101] Elsewhere, he asserts that convulsions "result[] from excessive discharges of nerve cells, meaning . . . liberation of energy during rapid decomposition . . . of some matter in, or of part of, those cells."[102] The descriptor "decomposition" is telling of the way that epilepsy was often correlated with degeneration. Henry Maudsley claimed that epilepsy in children is "associated with idiocy and imbecility," while adults suffer from "maniacal paroxysms, monomania, dementia, or total fatuity."[103] In the mid–nineteenth century, Bénédict Morel was the leading researcher on hereditary mental illness, and proposed connections between epilepsy and degeneration, which he articulated in two influential texts in 1857 and 1860.[104] What is more, since epilepsy often resulted in twisting, writhing convulsive episodes, it "appeared to validate evolutionary theory."[105] As Gillian Beer notes, Charles Darwin "saw the source not only of creativity but of loss. Evolutionary theory emphasized extinction and annihilation equally with transformation."[106] In *Psychopathia Sexualis* (1886), Richard Von Krafft-Ebing tied degenerative sexual impulses to epilepsy, arguing that "cerebral changes which accompany the epileptic outbreak may induce an abnormal excitation of the sexual instinct."[107] And Cesare Lombroso, in the fourth edition of *Criminal Man* (1889), positions epilepsy as a "universal substructure of all criminal behavior."[108] Degeneration, for Lombroso, can be traced to epileptic episodes, whether convulsive or "hidden," because "congenital criminality and moral insanity are nothing but special forms of epilepsy."[109]

Physiological symptoms were not the only concern for medical professionals. Epilepsy also affects memory and cognition, meaning that it can alter personal identity, both for the subject's sense of self and for medico-legal definitions. Maudsley draws attention to "*aura epileptica*," which is a "striking example of the disturbance of general sensation and organic sensibility."[110] Of note here is "the remarkable unconsciousness of what [the subject] has done during the attack," meaning that Maudsley expresses concern over not just the cognitive ramifications of epilepsy but legal ones as well.[111] During an episode, an epileptic subject's "intimate physiological sympathy and synergy of the organs of the body . . . are suspended," which alters "the real foundation of the *ego*."[112] In *Responsibility in Mental Disease* (1874), Maudsley brings together the legal implications for epilepsy's potential effects on personal identity: "When a murder has been committed without apparent motive, and the reason of it seems inexplicable, it may chance that the perpetrator is found on inquiry to be afflicted with epilepsy."[113] The question for courts, then, is "how far the existence of this disease affects his responsibility."[114] Joel Peter Egan observes that *vertigé épileptique*, which referred to nonconvulsive epilepsy, "signified the first use of a medical term to address the likelihood of thoroughly unconscious behavior."[115]

Maudsley's analysis of the legal implications of epilepsy contrasts with the results of the 1843 M'Naughten case, which helped to codify the insanity defense in courts.[116] Maudsley sees in some epileptics "mental derangement of a furious kind," which results from "epileptic mania," and the subject remains "unconscious of what he is doing, his senses perhaps possessed with frightful hallucinations."[117] But this "excitement" eventually "subsides, and the person comes to himself."[118] These episodes displace personal identity temporarily, problematizing legal definitions. Maudsley particularly draws attention to what he calls "mental epilepsy," which displays no physiological symptoms such as convulsions but instead "fixes upon the mind-centers and issues in a paroxysm of mania."[119] As a result of this condition, the subject "may lose the consciousness of personal identity," which undermines the work of "metaphysicians who lay such great stress on the unity of the *ego*."[120] Remarkably, Maudsley disputes any unitary notion of personal identity, labeling these cases of mental epilepsy "the phenomena of disordered identity," which prove that the self is nothing but "the full and harmonious action of the different parts of the mental organization."¹²¹ The simple answer for "the physiologist" is that "the defacing action of decay" interferes with "the harmony of function and a disruption of the unity of consciousness."¹²² Such a declaration not only explodes rigidly corporeal definitions of personal identity but also challenges even a Lockean model that relies on a continuum of consciousness and memory. The sensation novel seized on such a potential for cerebral dysfunction to transform personal identity.¹²³

Wilkie Collins's *Poor Miss Finch* (1872) was the first sensation novel to connect, in a detailed manner, epilepsy and personal identity. In the novel, Oscar Dubourg is robbed and left "senseless, in a pool of his own blood," having experienced a "concussion of the brain . . . with a blunt instrument."¹²⁴ Oscar was set to marry Lucilla, the eponymous Miss Finch, but he unexpectedly suffers an "epileptic fit," in which "his whole body was wrenched round, as if giant hands had twisted it, toward the right."¹²⁵ Peter Wolf explains that Collins "virtually gives us a clinical case study . . . of a seizure."¹²⁶ As in Charles Reade's *Griffith Gaunt* (1865–66), epilepsy causes an initial rupture in Oscar's personal identity, triggering a personation plot involving his twin brother Nugent.¹²⁷ "That Nugent should personate Oscar," *The Athenaeum* remarked, "and that poor Miss Finch should be in love with both at once and yet with only one, was inevitable."¹²⁸ Collins stops short, however, of making epilepsy the cause of an internal imposture, wherein Oscar would unconsciously exhibit the traits of an alternate identity. Instead, Oscar ingests silver nitrate to treat his condition, which causes his skin to turn "blackish-*blue*," and the personation plot instead hinges on the machinations of his identical twin Nugent, together with Lucilla's "imaginary antipathy to dark people and to dark shades of color of all kinds."¹²⁹

In George Eliot's *Silas Marner* (1861), the eponymous weaver suffers from a form of catalepsy, which Eliot describes as "mysterious rigidity and suspension of consciousness."¹³⁰ Since these episodes can be "mistaken for death," Marner is susceptible to William Dane's scheme to frame him for robbery.¹³¹ Mary Elizabeth Braddon stages a similar plot in *Thou Art the Man* (1894). Brandon Mountford, who suffers from hereditary epilepsy, is framed for a brutal murder by the spurned aristocrat Hubert Urquhart. Although the novel features a complex narrative structure and vivid characterizations, critics were generally unimpressed, and suggested that the age of sensation had already passed.¹³² The *Saturday Review*, for example, criticized Braddon for her "old love of sensation," and asserted that Mountford's epilepsy "forms an excuse for the kind of crime without which the author would . . . be a changeling."[133] This last point is most significant because it draws attention to the way that epilepsy transforms Mountford's personal identity. In contrast to Silas Marner, whose trances leave him immobile, Mountford violently convulses, and allegedly performs acts directed by an alternate consciousness that represents degenerative brutality. But Braddon's inherent goal is to dispute pernicious notions of epilepsy that understood the disease as manifesting either weak moral character or evidential atavism. For Mountford, though he never knows it, did not commit the crime. Since the actual murderer, Urquhart, is an aristocrat, degeneracy, rather than accompanying disease, in fact lurks within upper-class bodies.

Thou Art the Man follows two periods in the life of Sibyl Higginson. In the outer frame narrative, Sibyl, the Countess of Penrith, receives an unsigned note from a mysterious stranger that displays a "madman's scrawl, no doubt, inspired by some half-cloudy purpose in the troubled brain of lunacy."[134] Coralie Urquhart, the daughter of Sibyl's brother-in-law Hubert Urquhart, willingly enters Sibyl's orbit, and her father demands letters detailing her everyday activities. A few of these letters intersect with the third-person frame narrative. Coralie, acting as a "spy" (15), functions as an audience surrogate, learning about Sibyl's history with both her father and a mysterious figure named Brandon Mountford.[135] The embedded narrative begins by explaining Mountford's entrance into the Higginson household over a decade earlier. Shortly after Mountford's birth, his mother "went out of her mind," and his father learned that "there had been madness in her family" (36). Sibyl's mother, Lucy, had been in love with Mountford's father, her cousin, but she instead married Sibyl's father, Sir Joseph Higginson. Although Mountford and Sibyl are distant cousins, "just one stage further apart on the family tree" (63), only Mountford contains hereditary madness, which he evinces through epilepsy. Ordered by his doctor "to live in the open air" (61), Mountford has spent most of his life traveling and hunting in Africa, which Braddon uses "to map out the civilized man's struggle against his own primitivism."[136] In search of smaller game, however, Mountford has recently traveled to the Scottish property of his distant relatives.

Braddon ingeniously stages Hubert Urquhart as a villainous double to the hero Mountford, suggesting that the rivals possess commonalities beyond their pursuit of Sibyl. Urquhart has designs to access Sir Joseph's considerable mining fortune and immediately considers Mountford a "dangerous interloper" (65), appearing to sense the visitor's tainted bloodline. Sir Joseph initially encourages Mountford to marry his illegitimate daughter, Marie Arnold, because he "believe[s] in heredity" (73). But Mountford explains that he cannot marry because he possesses a "strain of madness in his blood" (75). Foreshadowing his own imprisonment, Mountford relates that his mother was "no better off than a state prisoner" (76). As a child, she suffered from epilepsy, which gradually degraded into full-scale madness. At eighteen, Mountford suffered his first epileptic episode, which rendered him a "creature apart from his fellows, marked with the signs of revolting disease" (77). His "horrible convulsive seizures" worsened "until reason would be wrecked in the struggle, and madness would close the scene" (77–78). The cognitive effects of Mountford's epilepsy are most significant to the plot because he suffers "sudden lapse[s] of consciousness," recalling only "the knowledge that he had lost himself" (78). Traveling in open environments helped him to mitigate the episodes, but stress and confinement effect relapses. In a sense, Mountford's "loss" is not just consciousness but also personal identity. The part of himself that emerges during epileptic events is an impostor, taking control of his body.

Unlike Mountford, Sibyl appears to embody stability, as if she is impervious to imposture. Mountford refuses to make addresses to Marie, but he struggles to resist Sibyl's magnetic constancy. On one occasion, he calls himself a "modern Othello with a pair of Desdemonas" (90), suggesting not only his status as an "other" but also that he will be duped by Urquhart, who plays the role of Iago. Sibyl feels equally strongly about Mountford, but the "hideous specter" of epilepsy prevents their union. Mountford knows that the "face she loved would be convulsed and changed, and the lips she had kissed would be disfigured with foam and blood" (92). Yet again, however, the issue with Mountford's affliction is less physical than it is mental. The "transformation" (93) that he undergoes affects his identity, potentially displaying a "homicidal fury" (94) and putting Sibyl's life in danger. Urquhart takes advantage of not only the actual physiological effects of Mountford's epilepsy but also the potential cognitive outcomes. Envious of the attention that both Sibyl and Marie pay to Mountford, Urquhart brutally stabs Marie, and positions Mountford's recovering body next to the corpse. Mountford had just suffered his "longest lapse of consciousness" (111), during which he emitted a "strange half-savage sound" (108). This heightened episode is triggered by the dual stresses of leaving Sibyl and his "improper reading" of sensational epilepsy accounts, which he believes, as Courtney A. Floyd notes, might be "disabling him."[137] One of the men who stumbled upon the scene reports that Mountford was "like a lunatic" (119), and the murder, which "seemed motiveless, savage, the act of a maniac" (126), becomes tied to the epileptic man, coated in Marie's blood, recovering at the scene.

Since Mountford "know[s] nothing," with the exception of an "interval of darkness, a blank of my existence" (128), he cannot mount a defense. The impostor that emerges during his latest epileptic episode is a completely separate identity, unlike the shared memory of Robert Louis Stevenson's Jekyll and Hyde. Although Mountford asserts that "the impulse to slay was never upon me" (129), he does admit to an earlier suicide attempt. At this point, Mountford considers himself a murderer, remarking that "[t]here sometimes are two natures in the same man—the nature in calm and well-being—the nature in storm and madness" (129). Urquhart convinces him to flee and tells Sibyl that Mountford has boarded a boat. When word arrives that the ship has wrecked, Sibyl travels to the site to investigate, but Mountford's body never resurfaces. Years later, she receives an anonymous note, and convinces herself that Mountford is alive, having been "spirited away" (237) by Urquhart and Mr. Carpew, the pastor of St. Jude's parish. John Coverdale, a virtuous reverend, assists Sibyl in the search, and accuses Carpew of being "the keeper of a lunatic asylum" (238). Indeed, similar to his mother's experience, Mountford became a prisoner, and his confinement exacerbated epilepsy into madness. Coverdale locates Mountford and informs Sybil that he is "desperately ill—a changed man" (279), as if his alternate identity has completed an irrevocable personation.

In the end, Braddon offers neither reclamation nor rejuvenation. Mountford never learns that he was not Marie's murderer. And he never recovers his previous identity: "Nothing could bring back that lost personality" (317). Following Mountford's death, Urquhart begins to succumb to a vague cancer, and his medication leaves him "very often in a state of semi-delirium" (320). He calls Sibyl to his deathbed, "the victim of an inexorable scheme of Creation" (322), to confess to Marie's murder. But he does not admit to the earlier murder of his brother, Sibyl's husband, which remains recognized as a hunting accident. Fratricide, for whatever reason, is a bridge too far. Although Urquhart's reference to a "scheme of Creation" suggests that he suffers from a hereditary illness, there is some evidence that his disease is acquired rather than inherited. Yet Braddon suggests such a distinction only to refute it, leaning on the implicit notion that hereditary disease, however shuttered by the aristocracy, knows no class boundaries.

Sibyl, hoping to punish Urquhart, spurned him in a public scene, by agreeing to marry his brother, Archibald. During the resulting argument, Urquhart "behaved like a lunatic" (190), prompting Archibald to throw his younger brother through a glass door. The violence of the event caused Urquhart to "suffer[] from a slight concussion of the brain" (190), and later he "laugh[s] a spasmodic laugh" (321). The possibility exists, then, that Urquhart experienced his own "homicidal fury" (94) during an epileptic episode, and that he truly has no memory of murdering Archibald. That Urquhart's cerebral trauma occurs well after Marie's murder, however, suggests his savage brutality is just as innate as Mountford's epilepsy. Both men struggle to control their bodies, and both experience lapses of reason. Sibyl, in contrast, "goes through life like an animated statue" (18) with a "spotless" (20) character. Allen Bauman observes that Braddon "focuses on epilepsy in a male character . . . to demonstrate the vulnerability of gentlemanly masculinity to 'nervous' disease as one variant of male degeneration and weakness of will."[138] If this is the case, then Braddon simultaneously promotes the evolutionary stability of women, evidenced by Sibyl's relentlessly unitary personal identity.

Chapter 4

This Unclean Spirit of Imitation

Mesmerism and Opium

Wilkie Collins's *The Moonstone* (1868) demonstrates that stable, unitary personal identity, especially when under assault from outside sources, is impossible. Seemingly every character in the novel struggles to maintain cognitive consistency, further complicating the whodunit puzzle. Two primary forces produce this disunity—mesmerism and opium. The majority of *The Moonstone* fixates on mesmerism and especially the mesmeric hold of the titular diamond. The dénouement, however, refocuses on opium, and the role that the narcotic plays in the theft of the Moonstone. In either case, Collins emphasizes the power of external stimuli on notions of personal identity. Whether under the influence of mesmerism or opium, characters in *The Moonstone* persistently find themselves unable to sustain unitary consciousness, suggesting that the self can be manipulated, divided, and counterfeited by outside forces.[1] Such a reading can be applied contextually. Collins was fascinated by mesmerism, having contributed his "longest work of non-fiction" on the subject to *The Leader* in 1852.[2] And together with Charles Dickens, Collins called on mesmeric mediums and patients in 1853, and performed in a play titled *Animal Magnetism* in 1857. That this interest continued well after the public disavowal of mesmerism by the medical community typifies the pseudoscience's prolonged influence in the mid–nineteenth century.[3]

In the 1868 preface to *The Moonstone*, Collins asserts that the "physiological experiment" that closes the novel "actually does happen."[4] This experiment, constructed and supervised by Ezra Jennings, himself an opium addict, requires Franklin Blake to rehearse the exact conditions from the night the Moonstone was displaced, to prove that the laudanum he unknowingly ingested triggered an episode of somnambulism. Before this point, however, the novel had been more concerned with the influence of mesmerism, and specifically the pernicious power of the Moonstone over characters in its vicinity. The "curse" is both its attraction, which goes well beyond its material value, and its ability to destabilize identity. The novel opens with a narrative detailing Colonel John Herncastle's sanguinary, and perhaps opium-induced, colonial theft of the Moonstone, during which he acted "like a madman" (5), with a face that "looked possessed by the devil" (31). From there, the diamond spreads its insidious influence throughout the "scattered and disunited household" (182).[5] John Sutherland observes that *The Moonstone* is "primarily the story of a diamond," but its "other main subject matter is narcotics."[6] Collins, however, appears to conflate the two, suggesting the materiality of both mesmerism and opium.

Rosanna Spearman, the lovelorn servant, is doubly entranced, impelled by both the Moonstone and the Shivering Sand, which "has laid a spell on me" (25). In some sense, the Shivering Sand functions as a symbol for addiction, a swirling, hypnotic agency that drags subjects into a bottomless abyss. Blake embodies the Moonstone for Rosanna, triggering a mesmeric effect. Penelope, the steward Gabriel Betteredge's daughter, explains that Blake's rebuff "turn[s Rosanna] into stone" and causes her to be "like a woman in a dream" (144). Rosanna complains, moreover, that "[m]y past life still comes back to me sometimes" (24), a life of "frauds and deceptions" (323), which she reexperiences through the imposture of wearing Blake's soiled nightgown. In addition, Lady Verinder, who "suffer[s] under an insidious form of heart disease" (213), takes "drops"—likely laudanum—to "put me right" (208). And even Godfrey Ablewhite, whom the zealot Drucilla Clack considers "very complete" (201), turns out to be a "smooth-tongued impostor" (268), whose "life had two sides to it" (448). Ablewhite's particular danger is that his duplicity comes naturally; his imposture is intrinsic and not reliant on the outside forces of mesmerism or opium.

Most significant is the effect the Moonstone has on Blake, who is "nothing of his old self" (27). Betteredge observes Blake's "puzzling shifts and transformations" (42) that bring out the "many different sides to his character," causing him to live "in a state of perpetual contradiction with himself" (43). More so than any other character, Blake's personal identity remains constantly in flux, the result of his proximity to the Moonstone and, later, his unknowing ingestion of laudanum. Being in "twenty different minds about the Diamond" (59) suggests that Blake struggles to stabilize his identity, to contain "the foreign sides of his character" (171), under the assault of mesmeric forces, coupled with nicotine withdrawal. It is no wonder that the laudanum triggers the sleepwalking episode, during which Blake retrieves the Moonstone and gives it to Ablewhite. When Sergeant Cuff assertively declares that "*Nobody has stolen the Diamond*" (105), focus initially rests on "stolen," for Blake plays supplier rather than thief. Yet one should also linger over "nobody," which might suggest that the sleepwalker is not Blake, but merely his corporeal form, an automaton body without a personal identity. Indeed, *The Spectator* asserted that "[t]he hero has no qualities at all."[7] For Joel Peter Egan, "[t]he sleepwalker revealed not one soul asleep, but one physical body housing 'two souls.'"[8] When Blake assembles a series of narrators "to lend me the assistance of their memories" (360), he reconstructs the part of his identity lost to opium but never addresses the indelible effects of the Moonstone's mesmerism.

Collins regularly refers to the cognitive confusion that characters experience as an obscuring "cloud" (56), "darkness" (94), or "mist" (355) that clears when new information emerges. But it seems that every character, with the exception of Cuff and the "immovable" (72) Mr. Murthwaite, is a "sensitive subject," meaning they are highly susceptible to "mesmeric influence" (282).[9] *The Spectator*'s claim that Collins introduces an "array of dummies," and *The Nation*'s allusion to them as "mere puppets," both insinuate the way that the characters are never themselves, but rather props manipulated by mesmerism and narcotics.[10] The Indians' "boy" is a "Seer of things invisible to their eyes" (282) but is no more under thrall than the detectives' child-spy Gooseberry, so named for the "extraordinary prominence of his eyes" (429). It is here that Collins's connection with Ezra Jennings comes into play, for Jennings possesses "*unsought self-possession*" (365), even when wrenched by opium abuse.[11] Thus is Collins both the mesmeric "Seer," the one who knows the solution to the mystery, and also the opium addict who expertly solves the case, the doctor "whirling through empty space with the phantoms of the dead" (392). At the very least, Jennings behaves like a play director, a role with which Collins was himself familiar, restaging an anniversary performance with an unconscious leading actor.

In 1863, following the publication of *No Name* (March 1862–January 1863), Collins's gout, having moved into both feet, became debilitating. Since Frank Beard, who prescribed Collins's laudanum, was himself indisposed, Collins reached out to John Elliotson, the leading professional advocate of mesmerism since the late 1830s. Elliotson recommended mesmerism to ease the pain and to assist with sleep. Collins wrote to Beard that Elliotson wanted to "mesmerize me into sleeping so as to do without the opium!"[12]

The initial result was promising, but withdrawal symptoms persuaded Collins to return to his increasingly heavy doses of laudanum. This event demonstrates the way that mesmerism and opium were linked as palliative measures in the Victorian period. Yet both remedies remained controversial, the former labeled as a pseudoscience and eventually displaced by hypnotism, and the latter increasingly understood as dangerously addictive, becoming a principal motivator for the 1868 Pharmacy Act. Mesmerism and opium were further linked by the similar effect they had on personal identity. Both destabilize the self, calling into question unitary subjectivity, and challenging corporeal definitions of identity. Sensation novelists exploited this reality, composing personation plots involving mesmerism and opium that illustrate the vulnerability of the self, the way that identity could be manipulated by invisible energies and addictive intoxicants.

Mesmerism in *The Notting Hill Mystery*

Mesmerism, named after Franz Anton Mesmer (1734–1815), was initially a scornful, derisive label that became a recognized procedural term during its British heyday in the 1830s. Mesmer introduced the term "animal magnetism," which claimed that invisible, circulating fluids structured organic life. This sphere of fluids could be harnessed and manipulated, often with magnets or a metal rod, to relieve pain, to cure disease, and to correct mental abnormalities. Robert Darnton refers to Mesmer's "eighteenth-century cult of nature" that hinged on "fascinating performances."[13] These performances required an intimate connection between mesmerist and patient, which prompted accusations of immorality from Mesmer's time forward. By the dawn of the Victorian period, mesmerism had infiltrated British culture and fascinated its people, many of whom, Alison Winter notes, "saw in [it] the fulfillment of the mind's greatest potential."[14] The mesmeric séance entered domestic spaces in the mid-nineteenth century, fascinating people of all occupations and classes. Mesmerism became a spectacle, in which the mesmerist took control over the subject's body and mind, establishing a sort of telepathic connection that also presented as mimicking bodily movements. Thus, mesmerism became associated with questions over personal identity, since mesmerized subjects not only temporarily lost their own conscious selves but also personated the mesmerist's mind and body. As Winter argues, mesmerism "could display forms of interpersonal communication and influence that seemed to dissolve the boundaries between two people or to subsume one person's identity in another's."[15] Mesmerism, alongside related theories of spiritualism and hypnotism, challenged corporeal definitions of personal identity by demonstrating the fluid, permeable nature of the self.

Mesmerism's greatest advocate in the 1830s was John Elliotson, a respected writer on physiology who introduced the stethoscope to widespread medical practice. Influenced by phrenology, Elliotson reported his "conviction of the possibility of mesmerizing distinct cerebral organs."[16] Referring to one of his female patients—with the sort of euphemistic rhetoric that drummed up accusations of sexual impropriety—Elliotson claimed he could "play upon her head as upon a piano."[17] One of the cardinal virtues of mesmerism was that it allegedly cured ailments and diseases without physical contact, let alone breaking the skin, meaning it could displace surgery, which remained precarious in the decades before sterilization was widely practiced. Elliotson also parried attacks against mesmerism, chief among them the claim that the patient merely mimicked the emotions or state of mind of the mesmerist through sympathetic connection. "I never could discover," he writes, "any sympathy between the mental state of my youthful patients and myself."[18] Critics also claimed that mesmerism relied on materialism, which carried charges of atheism and immorality. Elliotson refused to placate such worries, arguing that "[t]he brain and its functions are subject to precisely the same laws as the other portions of the body and their functions," and any concept of the "spirit, or something distinct from matter, is . . . childish."[19] Elliotson's chief acolyte, Chauncy Hare Townshend, noted not only that "mesmerized persons speak with freedom" but also that the "mesmeric sleepwalker" exhibits an "improvement both of thought and motion."[20] Townshend goes even further, arguing that mesmerism can produce "the perfection of motion and superior coherence of thought."[21] The mesmeric subject, for Townshend, is liberated from the constraints of waking life, and perhaps freed from the limits of unitary personal identity.

Elliotson's fall from grace was precipitous. Following a series of controversial experiments on the O'Key sisters, who were accused of being frauds, he was forced to resign from University College Hospital in December 1838. In spite of the professional dismantling, however, mesmerism regained footing among amateur practitioners in the 1840s, and remained in the cultural milieu during the rise of sensation fiction. In fact, Elliotson founded *The Zoist*, a periodical devoted to the practice and promotion of mesmerism, in April 1843, years after he was discredited. As evidence of mesmerism's enduring hold, Dickens attended one of Elliotson's exhibitions in 1838, and then himself practiced mesmerism on his beleaguered wife

Catherine in 1842. In 1844, this time alongside Collins, Dickens treated Madame de la Rue in Genoa. Martin Willis and Catherine Wynne note that this experiment "demonstrated the mutual need in the operator-patient relationship—a need that helped to destabilize Dickens's marriage and tapped into one of the central debates surrounding mesmeric controversy in the nineteenth century—sexual morality."[22] No matter the setting, Susan Poznar states, "the Victorian mesmerist was usually male and his subject female."[23] Sensation novelists represented the discomforting impropriety that mesmeric séances could introduce. In Charles Warren Adams's *The Notting Hill Mystery* (1862–63), for example, Baron R** yields mesmeric control to his female associate Rosalie rather than himself practice on Gertie Anderton.

Elliotson was also aware of the effect mesmerism could have notions of the self. In an 1852 letter in *The Zoist*, Joseph Aylieff noted that he was able to "affect [his patient's] sense of personal identity, causing them to ride chairs as imaginary horses, to suffer excruciating pains, perspiration to start on their face."[24] Writers who carried the torch for mesmerism similarly argued that a "person is seen to be, at one and the same time, in two distinct states, and to possess, at once two consciousnesses."[25] For William Gregory, writing in 1851, this double consciousness was the result of the two hemispheres of the brain, one in "ordinary waking state," and the other "passed into the mesmeric state."[26] Perhaps the second most important figure in mesmerism, next to Elliotson, was the American spiritualist John Bovee Dods, who claimed to have "located . . . the organ of Individuality," which "constitutes our individualism, or personal identity."[27] To combat accusations of materialism, Dods not only claimed that a "*spiritual* organ of Individuality correspond[s] to the *physical* one of the brain" but also noted that "*sympathy*" connected different parts of the human body" and "one individual and another."[28] In fact, the "phrenological organs of the human brain are but a daguerreotype manifestation" of the "spiritual organs of the living mind."[29] Thus, Dods argued that patients could be "*electrically* and *psychologically* controlled" by pinpointing the "family of nerves" that "constitutes, phrenologically, our individualism or personal identity."[30] Although doing so permits "electro-psychological communication," involving magnetic circles of electric energy, this phenomenon works only with "those persons . . . who are very sensitive."[31]

Without ignoring substantial support from Dickens and Collins, mesmerism's greatest advocate in the literary world was Harriet Martineau. In a series of letters to *The Athenaeum*, contributed in late 1844, Martineau extolled the virtues of mesmerism after having recovered from a prolonged illness. Beth Torgerson notes, however, that Martineau did not accept the practice wholesale, but rather "emphasized that mesmerism was an unknown phenomenon in need of research and that this research would develop its full significance."[32] Martineau's letters focus on not only the mesmeric treatment of Jane Arrowsmith, referred to as "J" throughout, but also the other potential effects, including clairvoyance. In the introduction to the compiled edition of the letters, Martineau criticizes "[t]he systematic disingenuousness of some Medical Journals," who "assail every case or cure or relief by Mesmerism."[33] Martineau herself engaged this "great curative agency," which released her from being a "prisoner from illness."[34] During one session, Jane fell into a "mesmeric sleep," which was an "absolute blank," and she reported witnessing "spiritual things. I can see diseases; and I like to see visions."[35] These visions were not like "dreams in common sleep" but instead "things out of other worlds;—not the things themselves, but impressions of them."[36] For Rachel Ablow, mesmerism allowed Martineau to understand the physical "transmi[ssion] of energies or intensities that oftentimes bypass cognition entirely," a phenomenon that revealed "the illusory nature of the distinction between selves."[37] Such a concept provokes profound implications on personal identity and imposture. The individual self becomes a construct, constantly dissolving and merging with other subjects, never the unitary entity that the state, let alone our own psyches, require it to be.

Mesmerism faced its fair share of hostility, none more fervent than attacks from John Hughes Bennett, who wrote of the "mesmeric mania" of 1851. Hughes considered mesmerism a "delusion" and a "disorder" that has infected polite society, carried on by charlatans who "depend[] on collusion and imposture."[38] Taking an empirical approach, Hughes made his own tests and observations on "Animal Magnetism," and came to the conclusion that "no such principle exists."[39] Ultimately, Hughes asserted that the performances of patients were "suggested by the words and actions of others," meaning he fell squarely in the camp of detractors who believed that the patient merely mirrored the state of mind and movements of the mesmerist. Hughes's public condemnation in many respects echoes the private misgivings expressed by Jane Welsh Carlyle in 1844. Bedridden with an illness, Welsh Carlyle explains that she has just read Martineau's "outpourings in the Athenaeum" but had already determined that mesmerism was tantamount to "witch craft" and "demonical possession" that produced a "damnable sort of tempting of Providence."[40] Welsh Carlyle had witnessed a mesmeric exercise performed by a "distinguished Magnetiser," who rendered his patient "the image of death—no *marble* was ever colder, paler, or more motionless."[41] She then offered herself as subject, recalling that he was superior to her only by "animal strength" and could never broach her "moral and intellectual superiority."[42] By 1877, William Benjamin Carpenter, whose work is championed by Ezra Jennings in *The Moonstone*, would call mesmerism an "Epidemic Delusion," arguing it had "been disproved by scientific investigation: all that is genuine in [its] phenomena having been accounted for by well-ascertained Physiological principles."[43] At least for the scientific community, this was a death knell.

Sensation novelists were more receptive to mesmerism's charms.[44] Charles Warren Adams's *The Notting Hill Mystery*, initially serialized in *Once a Week* and then published in a single volume in 1863, might go further than any other sensation novel to express the dangers of mesmerism. The plot is relatively straightforward: Baron R** uses mesmerism to kill off three people in line to a substantial inheritance. The presentation, however, is convoluted, featuring the testimonies of an assortment of characters framed by the investigatory conclusions of a life insurance agent. The *St. James Magazine* called the novel "[o]ne of the cleverest and most cleverly written books of the kind we have ever met with."[45] The *London Review* was more discerning, calling it a "carefully-prepared chaos" but ultimately mocking its focus on mesmerism by claiming that "the magnetic influence of life-like character and a well-considered sequence of events are alike wanting."[46] *The Athenaeum* was even less complimentary, pointing out the "mass of ill-arranged and incongruous papers," and similarly criticizing the lack of "human interest."[47] This last reviewer also asserted that Adams sought "to reproduce some of the mannerisms of 'The Woman in White,'" a charge echoed by modern critics.[48] Yet Adams ultimately departs from Collins's example. The personation plot in *The Notting Hill Mystery* promotes the truth of even the most spectacular powers of mesmerism, while Fosco's identity swap in *The Woman in White* remains grounded in material matters. Thus, Adams works to question notions of stable personal identity by representing an imposture that takes place via invisible forces spanning significant distances. The personation plot, in other words, does not involve the replacement of one body *for* another body but instead the infiltration of a body *through* another body.

The Notting Hill Mystery begins with prefatory statements from Ralph Henderson, a life insurance agent commissioned to investigate the dubious payment of £25,000 to Baron R**.[49] As part of his inquiry, Henderson is also interested in Baron R**'s access to another £25,000, paid through the inheritance of the Boleton family. The first piece of evidence that Henderson presents is the curious death of Madame R** by poisoning in March 1857. Witnesses testify that Madame R** was sleepwalking when she ingested the "powerful acid," but Henderson indicates "there is no admission of any propensity to somnambulism."[50] Working backward, Henderson also exposes the deaths of Gertie and William Anderton, the first by suspected poisoning and the second by suicide. Yet an autopsy of Mrs. Anderton revealed no traces of poison, leading Henderson to entertain the possibility of "Mesmeric Agency" (8). Even when the details definitively prove that Baron R** used mesmerism, however, Henderson remains incredulous, allowing his addressee at the insurance agency to construct his own conclusions. *The Notting Hill Mystery*, then, refuses completion; its frame narrative remains open-ended. This structural fragmentation also works at the level of character. As Baron R**'s unrevealed name suggests, identity in the novel is never complete but open to interpretation and invasion.

Henderson closes the frame by bringing in some final pieces of documentary evidence, including a letter from a "leading Mesmerist" that details "the power claimed by mesmeric operators over those subjected to their influence" (238). But the more significant evidence arrives from an actual extract from John Elliotson's periodical *The Zoist*. This extract describes the mesmerist himself ingesting food to relieve the complaint of his patient. Henderson speculates that Baron R** was inspired by this article and used Rosalie, who is actually Katie Boleton, as a medium to convey "mesmeric fluid" (250), meaning that the biological sympathy between the twin sisters allowed the Baron to manipulate Gertie's body *through* Rosalie. But knowing that Gertie, William, and Katie must die in succession for him to win the inheritance meant the Baron was forced to play an intricate game. He had to poison Gertie, with meticulous care, through Katie, all the while keeping Katie alive, then subtly encourage William's suicide, and finally establish Katie as a sleepwalker who rummaged through his laboratory chemicals. The curious circumstances of Katie's eventual death brought Henderson into the case because the Baron stands to win both the Boleton inheritance and an equal life insurance policy he had taken out on his wife.

Henderson concludes with a decidedly inconclusive question: "are crimes thus committed susceptible of proof, or even if proved, are they of a kind for which the criminal can be brought to punishment?" (284). Unlike Collins's Count Fosco, who is eventually murdered by the Brotherhood he betrayed, the Baron escapes with impunity. No material evidence implicates the Baron in their deaths: Gertie died with no trace of poison, William appeared to commit suicide, and Katie took poison herself during a sleepwalking episode. Lara Karpenko reads *The Notting Hill Mystery* through the concept of sympathy, which was a "physiological phenomenon—one that could erase physical boundaries, destroy bodily integrity, and infect populations. Sympathy . . . is a physical experience of connection and community."[51] This reading of mesmerism's physiological powers calls to mind its implications concerning personal identity. For mesmerism, embodied through Gertie's and Katie's sympathetic physiology, challenges corporeal notions of the self. Under the Baron's influence, the twins occupy one identity. Thus, Henderson's question stands. How could the Baron be convicted of a crime without material evidence? Even if it were proved that he was poisoning Katie, he never directly administered poison to Gertie. Baron R** commits the perfect crime.

That the Baron escapes with impunity runs counter to the conclusions of early sensation novels. Collins's Sir Percival Glyde and Count Fosco in *The Woman in White* both meet their demise as punishment for their crimes. And in *Lady Audley's Secret*, Braddon's Lucy Audley dies shortly after her incarceration in a Belgian madhouse. The Baron's escape and financial windfall are part of the *The Notting Hill Mystery*'s complicated relationship with sensation fiction. According to Karpenko, the novel "showcases a surprising moment in the Victorian history of reading," in which Adams "conceives of the sympathetic experience as dangerously grounded in the body, and as frighteningly communal."[52] This attention to the threat of sympathetic identification corresponds with the dangers of sensation fiction's "embodied pleasure and sympathetically engaged reading style."[53] The fragmented form of *The Notting Hill Mystery* "resists this sort of deep absorption," critiquing sensation fiction's mesmeric properties, while also capitalizing on the genre's popularity.[54] Adams's novel thus becomes a sort of impostor, masquerading with sensational trappings that disguise its true nature.

In 1844, *Punch* ran an article that satirically wondered whether mesmerized subjects should be held accountable for their crimes. "[P]rofessors of mesmerism," the writer remarks, "are suffered to sap the very foundations of civil society . . . by making the innocent unintentional felons."[55] To solve this civil issue, parliament should "appoint a committee to inquire into the philosophy of 'mesmeric coma'" so that innocent subjects who acted in a "state of mesmeric oblivion" are not convicted.[56] This "newest Black Art," the writer concludes, "turn[s] the moral self of man inside out," and renders subjects "monstrous libels upon themselves."[57] The suggestion here, regardless of the article's venue, is significant. Mesmerized patients, in some sense, personate themselves, acting through the same body, but with an alternate consciousness. *The Notting Hill Mystery* takes this phenomenon a step further, performing the imposture through another body, without altering consciousness. Katie/Rosalie personates her sister Gertie through a mesmeric connection that does not require corporeal counterfeiting or cerebral manipulation. Through mesmerism, personal identity becomes immersive, rather than contained, suggesting that subjectivity might be defined as personal *diversity*, the erratic, fleeting, assimilating, cooperative nature of the human experience.

Opium in *The Mystery of Edwin Drood*

Samuel Taylor Coleridge's "Kubla Khan," composed in 1797 and circulated privately until its 1816 publication, can be read as a failed or interrupted imposture. The exotic and erotic visions that occupy the first two-thirds of the fragment give way to the speaker's desire to personate the "Abyssinian maid," whose "symphony and song" gives him "deep delight."[58] Yet this desire remains conditional—"Could I revive within me . . . // I would . . ."— suggesting that the speaker fails to counterfeit her visionary song.[59] That Coleridge's opium dream was interrupted by a "person on business from Porlock" potentially provides an excuse for this failure.[60] But the linkage between opium and imposture remains significant. Coleridge, at the outset of his decades-long addiction to laudanum, very nearly occupied a new identity, one he could have exercised (or exorcised) to finish the fragment. Especially late in life, Coleridge rued his "craving for the Poison," which seems diametrically opposed to "the milk of Paradise" in "Kubla Khan."[61] Arthur Symons noted that Coleridge's "imagination required no wings, but rather fetters; and it is evident that opium was more often a sedative than a spur to his senses."[62] One might speculate, then, whether Coleridge's drugless life became an imposture, for "[t]he effect of opium on the normal man is to bring him into something like the state in which Coleridge habitually lived."[63]

In a note to his *Confessions of an English Opium-Eater* (1821), Thomas De Quiney writes that Coleridge "has greatly exceeded me in quantity."[64] De Quincey had a complex relationship with both opium *and* Coleridge, wavering between feelings of pleasure and pain for the poetic drug and the drugged poet. Grevel Lindop notes that "the most intense accounts of De Quincey's opium-induced nightmares in the *Confessions* seem to emulate the visionary Orientalism of *Kubla Khan* but render it horrible by organizing it around the self-tormenting psychic divisions of [Coleridge's 1803 poem] *The Pains of Sleep*."[65] These "psychic divisions" demonstrate the opium user's potential for self-imposture. Similar to what Coleridge expresses in "Kubla Khan," De Quincey experienced what John Barrell has called a "*hybrid* identity," grown from a "symbiotic interdependence . . . between a self and an other."[66] Perhaps most significant, in *Confessions* De Quincey focuses on the way that opium disinters buried memories: "there is no such thing as *forgetting* possible to the mind. . . . [T]he inscription remains for ever."[67] In Lockean terms, opium, rather than introducing alternate selves, in fact confirms personal identity, conjuring memories to be restored along life's continuum. De Quincey adds that opium "introduces amongst [the mental faculties] the most exquisite order, legislation, and harmony."[68] Sobriety from opium, one might say, summons an impostor that disguises its inherent deconstruction.

Mid-nineteenth-century medical writers were more attentive to opium's effect on consciousness than the alleged enhancements of memory. In 1855, Thomas Laycock, the noted physiologist and pioneering psychologist, asserted that the "first result of the action of opium" is to "exalt the feeling of corporeal well-being," and that opium also "act[s] upon the organs of self-consciousness and thought."[69] John Elliotson, the leading British promoter of mesmerism, was also interested in opium. As with many of his phrenology-influenced peers, Elliotson believed that the two hemispheres of the brain meant that subjects could possess "the consciousness of two persons."[70] Elliotson quotes Franz Joseph Gall on the effects of various modes of "intoxication," including opium, wherein patients are "transformed into perfectly different beings."[71] This observation potentially pinpoints the difference, increasingly widened by advancements in neurology, between Romantic and Victorian judgments on opium. For De Quincey (and less so Coleridge), opium manifested the true self, unearthed the treasures of the memory, and fired creative impulses. Victorian writers, conversely, saw this second self through a glass darkly, an anchor that submerged the moral virtues of sobriety, a narcotic that tranquillized the duties of industrial society—in short, a criminal impostor.

Professional and amateur researchers who specialized in the study of opium came to more specific conclusions about the narcotic's influence on personal identity. Alonzo Calkins, for example, remarked that, "[a]mid the ever-shifting spectacular scene[,] the *sense of personal identity* is never perhaps entirely lost," yet the potential exists for a "duality of existence," which embraces "the idea of one and the same soul in duplication and bipartition . . . and present in two bodies."[72] An 1867 article on the effects and treatment of opium addiction notes that "habituation invariably tends to reduce the man to the *automatic* plane," and that this "disorganization" results in a "personality defrauded of its completion."[73] A similarly themed 1892 article focuses on "morphinomaniacs," whose "will is paralyzed and personality destroyed."[74] In Dickens's *The Mystery of Edwin Drood* (1870), John Jasper becomes a "mere automaton" under the influence of opium, his former personal identity as Cloisterham choirmaster almost fully erased.[75] In 1878, Charles Richet, a French immunologist, noted that opium causes a "pleasurable feeling of *abandon*," wherein "the thoughts are like the ever-shifting sense of a phantasmagoria."[76] Most significant, Richet observes that "[t]he active, conscious *Me* exists no more, and another personality seems to have taken its place."[77] Paraphrasing Richet's work, an 1884 writer asserted that, under the influence of opium, "the *ego* of consciousness has disappeared."[78] Such a phenomenon also applies to Jasper in *Edwin Drood*, whose primary ego, assaulted by opium abuse, has seemingly been submerged, like his nephew's corpse, in quicklime.

In January 1862, Dickens advised Collins not to be "satisfied with Frank Beard's patching you."[79] This warning about Collins's opium use was neither unfounded nor uninformed. In *Bleak House* (1852–53), Dickens had staged a particularly meaningful death by opium overdose. When the lawyer Tulkinghorn enters Nemo's squalid lodgings, he views the corpse as a "banshee of the man," with a "yellow look," directly the result of "the spectral darkness of a candle," but indirectly evoking a racial slur for East Asian peoples, and specifically the Chinese, who were most often the operators of Victorian opium dens.[80] The effect of opium on personal identity also comes into play: Nemo is Captain Hawdon, Lady Dedlock's former lover, and Esther Summerson's father. Opium has transformed Hawdon from respected army captain into a decrepit law-copier, whose assumed name is the Latin for "nobody," while also serving as a backward "omen" both for Lady Dedlock's secret past and for the addictive, debilitating nature of the drug.[81] Six years later, Dickens posed another warning to Collins, this time veiled. Although he was initially excited about *The Moonstone*, Dickens ultimately soured on the novel, writing in a July 26, 1868, letter: "The construction is wearisome beyond endurance, and there is a vein of obstinate conceit in it that makes enemies of readers."[82] The timing of the letter is notable. Dickens would have recently read the fourth "narrative" of *The Moonstone*, which was running in his periodical *All the Year Round*, meaning the opium-episode restaging directed by Ezra Jennings had lately wrapped. What was, for Dickens, a "very curious story—wild yet domestic," degenerated into a narrative of "obstinate conceit."[83] One might speculate that the novel's shift from mesmerism to opium triggered Dickens's reaction, especially because Collins uses the narcotic as a *deus ex machina*, a key to solving the mystery rather than a means further to obscure it.

For Dickens, both *The Moonstone* and its author possessed dual identities fueled, in some sense, by opium. It is hardly surprising, then, that Dickens's most overt foray into the sensation genre, *Edwin Drood*, would focus on opium and identity. As Thomas Dormandy argues, "Dickens gave vent to his dislike of opium" by creating John Jasper, "one of his most rivetingly repulsive creations."[84] Indeed, since Jasper "dominates the manifest content of the novel," as Ronald R. Thomas notes, he seems to stand as a particularly forceful commentary.[85] Similar to Henry Jekyll's progressively dire inability to prevent Edward Hyde's emergence, Jasper appears incapable of inhibiting the visibly transportive effects of opium. Lillian Nayder argues that Dickens "rework[s] Collins's vision of empire and race relations to a more conservative end," by crediting Jasper's "violence to his corruption by opium and the East."[86] One way of doing so is to contrast *The Moonstone*'s engagement with laudanum, a domesticated, liquified form of the drug prescribed by doctors and available in stores, by illustrating the sordid details of opium, consumed illicitly in squalid dens and prepared primarily by immigrants. Another important element of opium's Oriental contagion is, for Barry Milligan, its "general tendency toward the dilution of all kinds of identity."[87] In some sense, opium acts like vampire blood, infecting subjects and transforming them into identical, and perhaps inhuman, creatures.

For Miriam O'Kane Mara, *Edwin Drood* "suggests that colonial infection begins, not in the colonies, but with the British themselves and their attempts to ingest other cultures."[88] Indeed, opium becomes a contagion in the novel, evidencing a form of what Stephen Arata has called "reverse colonization," by seeming to pass between characters through a range of interactions.[89] And Jasper does his part to spread it, like some kind of Typhoid Mary, dosing the drinks of his nephew Drood and Neville Landless, while also offering an adulterated draught to the stonemason Durdles. Rosa Bud also "shrinks" (169) from Jasper's touch and correctly warns her fiancé Drood not to let "Mr. Jasper . . . come between us" (70). The most significant contamination in the novel, however, occurs during the disturbing courtyard meeting between Rosa and Jasper, held months after Drood's disappearance. Jasper, "leaning on a sun-dial" (168), draws his shadow over time, "setting . . . his black mark upon the very face of day" (170). With mesmeric hold, "he draws her feet towards him. She cannot resist" (169).[90] Jasper finally admits his obsessive love, causing Rosa to enter a kind of cataleptic shock: "A film comes over the eyes she raises for an instant, as though he had turned her faint" (171). This physiological reaction mirrors the novel's calling card for an opium-induced event. Drood had earlier noted of his uncle, for instance, that "[t]here's a strange film come over your eyes" (9), and later "a curious film passes over" (126) Princess Puffer. The effect of this infection is that the East, through both East Asian production and consumption and the opium dens of East London, slowly infiltrates the West, a dissolving-view effect that Dickens orchestrates in the first paragraph of the novel.

Readers come to consciousness alongside Jasper during the initial lines of *Edwin Drood*. As he awakens, or rather emerges, from an opium haze, he gradually comes to understand his distorted surroundings. The image of an "ancient English Cathedral town" mixes with the scene of an Eastern "Sultan's . . . palace" (1). Jasper's "scattered consciousness . . . fantastically piece[s] itself together" to show the actual view of a broken bed, collapsing under the weight of its four inhabitants. Contemporary reports on opium dens surprisingly coalesced around beds. The den that Dickens visited in 1869 with Inspector Field, for example, featured a "tattered bed."[91] In addition, an 1866 article noted "half a dozen of 'em in one bed . . . a-smoking and sleeping away like so many dormice," and another reporter noticed a "large bedstead, with a bed made the wrong way on it."[92] On the one hand, the shared and collapsing beds signal the distorted domesticity that opium introduces. That Princess Puffer measures out her potion by the "thimbleful" demonstrates what Barry Milligan calls the "commercialized distortion of the maternal ideal."[93] But on the other hand, Dickens suggests a likeness between Princess Puffer's bed and Jasper himself. As Jasper regains consciousness, on the "large, unseemly bed," he "supports his trembling frame upon his arms" (1). Not only are both "frames" unstable, they also contain mixing and disforming identities. Princess Puffer, both creator and consumer, reminds Jasper about her particular skill in forming the concoction, a feat not even equaled by her neighbor "Jack Chinaman." Yet again, Dickens demonstrates the duality inherent in the novel, as "Jack" and "John" Chinaman, a pejorative label given to East Asian immigrants, parallels Jasper, who goes by "Jack" and "John" alternately throughout the novel.

Having regained consciousness, Jasper "looks with repugnance at his three companions," and observes that Princess Puffer has "opium-smoked herself into a strange likeness of the Chinaman. His form of cheek, eye, and temple, and his color, are repeated in her" (2). As Jeremy Tambling observes, "[o]pium addiction makes identity pass into identity, all identity being imitation."⁹⁴ But Jasper cannot grasp that the homogenizing effects of opium also apply to himself. The alliteration of Princess Puffer pertains not only to "Sally the Opium Smoker," the real proprietor of an opium den that Dickens visited, but also to John Jasper.⁹⁵ Victorian accounts of opium dens routinely noted how customers "meet on perfect equality," as if these spaces dissolve class, race, and gender boundaries.⁹⁶ And several writers noted the atavistic effects of opium smoke on the skin, describing actual addicts as a "hideous and long-forgotten mummy," and "present[ing] the appearance of an Egyptian mummy."⁹⁷ Drood's arrangement to "go engineering into the East" (11), and specifically "to wake up Egypt a little" (54), takes on new meaning. For the mummy that he should fear has already awakened in a London opium den. To avoid this "unclean spirit of imitation" (2), Jasper departs by "pass[ing] out" of the house, after which he "falls into procession" (3) during a church service. These terms render unclear whether Jasper has truly regained his actual identity, or whether his Cloisterham life has become an imposture. When Drood remarks that Jasper is "very unlike [his] usual self" (11), we might question which identity has become "usual."

In one of the novel's most provocative passages, Dickens refers to "cases of drunkenness" and "animal magnetism," wherein "there are two states of consciousness which never clash, but each of which pursues its separate course as though it were continuous instead of broken" (14). Intentionally misleading readers, Dickens claims that such a dual consciousness presents in Miss Twinkleton, the proprietor of the girls' seminary in Cloisterham. At best, however, Twinkleton offers a binary to Princess Puffer (both entrepreneurs who specialize in molding minds), analogous to the fundamental opposition between Miss Pross and Madame Defarge in *A Tale of Two Cities*. The more fitting "two states of consciousness," of course, is Jasper, who is both a "conscientious master" (51) at the cathedral and a "[m]onster" (51) stalker, bent relentlessly on pursuing Rosa. Jasper maintains that he takes opium "for a pain—an agony—that sometimes overcomes me. The effects of the medicine steal over me like a blight or a cloud and pass" (9). But Jasper later admits he has "been taking in now and then in my own way" (207), suggesting that, in Cloisterham, he imbibes laudanum, which he would be able to purchase legally and without scrutiny. To go on his "journey," however, he must travel to London to sample Princess Puffer's "real receipt" (206). The laudanum in Cloisterham acts as a palliative for his withdrawal symptoms, embodied by his "filmy" (208) eyes that signal a "stage of transition between the two extreme states" (11). During this "kind of fit," Jasper's "memory grew DAZED" (4), as he alternates between selves.⁹⁸

Jasper's apparent inability to control these states of consciousness introduces legal implications regarding his probable murder of Drood. In 1880, Francis Wharton noted that "forms of unconsciousness may be noticed as constituting a defense to a criminal charge."[99] When the accused was "under the influence of opium," Wharton asks, "[w]as the defendant at the time of the act a free agent?"[100] Stephanie Peña-Sy takes another step to argue that Dickens sought, through Jasper's opium use, to make a "distinction between simple intoxication and the syndrome of 'fixed and continued' delusion resulting from habitual intoxication."[101] A good barrister, in other words, might have been able to exploit "[t]he discontinuity of Jasper's selfhood and the disconnection of that discontinuous selfhood from personal identity."[102] That Jasper experiences "perfect self-command" (129) following the murder initially indicates cognitive stability. But after he hears from Grewgious the postdated news of Drood and Rosa's broken engagement, his alternate identity appears to reemerge with a "terrible shriek" (138). Thereafter, he promises to "pursue [Rosa] to the death" (175), engaging in "ghostly following of her" (177). Just as he "lean[s] on a sun-dial" (168), shadowing the "face of day" (170), Jasper "sets his face toward London" (205), shadowing Rosa with the sort of premeditation that discredits claims of unconsciousness.

Once in London, however, Jasper travels "[e]astward and still eastward," arriving at the opium den to begin a new "journey" that this time threatens Rosa. "Now," Princess Puffer observes, "you begin to look like yourself" (206). Her new concoction functions doubly as a narcotic and as a truth serum, suggesting that she knows the details of the murder. Although Jasper's punishment or exoneration must remain hypothetical, given the hearsay evidence of Dickens's plan, we might take seriously the choirmaster's promise to "begin the next volume with a clearer vision" (130). Rather than pledge a new life of sobriety, this statement suggests clarity of purpose, one that requires preplanning the performance countless times amid the fumes of the opium den. The "stout gate of iron bars" (183) that encircle Rosa offer no more protection than the "hill or highest wall" that Satan contemptuously "overleap[s]" in *Paradise Lost*.[103] For Jasper is both split between selves and divided between worlds, a fallen angel of Cloisterham constructing a pandemonium in London. "I loved you madly," he confesses to Rosa, "wandering through Paradises and Hells . . . , carrying your image in my arms" (170). Indeed, Dickens constructs Cloisterham as Eden, penetrated by the "devil himself" (109). And in this Victorian version of Genesis, Eve has fled from Satan's assault, while Adam is dead.

Second Interlude
Mary Jane Furneaux

II.1. Mary Jane Furneaux: "The Fearneaux Frauds." *London Journal* 75.1,937 (March 25, 1882): 188.

In April 1882, an Australian newspaper remarked that Mary Jane Furneaux's career of imposture "bids fair to eclipse the once celebrated Alice Grey case."[1] Two primary elements distinguish the criminal careers of Grey and Furneaux (alternately Fearneaux and Ferneaux). First, Grey's crimes preceded the rise of sensation fiction, whereas Furneaux's largely occurred after the genre was fully established. For this reason, Grey likely influenced sensation plots, while Furneaux was probably influenced by them. Second, Grey's impostures relied primarily on assumed names, whereas Furneaux employed both assumed names and personation. Indeed, Furneaux's personation of Arthur Pelham Clinton—who was deceased—might be the nineteenth century's greatest imposture, even more brazen and calculated than the notorious personation by the Tichborne Claimant. Furneaux practiced forgery and personation to unprecedented lengths, twice returning to her life of crime after prison sentences.

II.2. Days with Celebrities. With Fearneaux: "Days with Celebrities." *Moonshine* (March 18, 1882): 121.

Furneaux's second trial created a sensation from February to May 1882. In a retrospective on the case, *The Spectator* declared that a "large section of the lower middle-class are capable of believing that any vulgar impostor is a millionaire Duke in hiding, and in want of a few hundreds, because his grandmother is trying to take his life."[2] Indeed, Furneaux preyed upon credulous subjects who believed her various claims of being either an aristocratic descendant in line for a substantial inheritance or a disgraced nobleman about to be restored by a pardon from Queen Victoria.

At the beginning of Furneaux's 1882 trial, the *Saturday Review* described her crimes as "the simple and old-fashioned fraudulent device known as 'the confidence trick'" perpetrated by a "Master Thief."[3] But the methods of Furneaux's crimes are strictly a product of her time. Just as Arthur Orton may have been inspired by Mary Elizabeth Braddon's *Aurora Floyd* (1863), Furneaux seems, almost unquestionably, to have been influenced by sensation novels. One writer blamed her criminality on reading "yellow-backed novels."[4] Her most astounding crime, the personation of Clinton, resembles several sensation plots.[5] The *Birmingham Daily Post* fittingly referred to Furneaux's "sensational case" at the start of her trial.[6] Other writers argued that her career exceeded any plots by either a "sentimental novelist" or a "sensation novelist."[7] And the *New York Times* noted that, "like Count Fosco, she had pets, and was fond of them."[8] Indeed, it is intriguing that both Grey and Furneaux were likened to Wilkie Collins's corpulent criminal mastermind, for Fosco is himself not much of an impostor, but mostly stands to benefit from impostures that he either directs or encourages.

Mary Jane Furneaux was born on October 21, 1839, in Liverpool to Frederick and Sarah Furneaux. Her father, whose name might have inspired her alias "Frederica," worked as a Liverpool police officer, and died in 1846. Before her life of crime began, it appears that Furneaux attempted to open a school near Wolverhampton, worked as a governess and a barmaid in Oxford, and was employed as an attendant at Prestwich Lunatic Asylum in Manchester. The asylum job is intriguing because Furneaux would later be blamed, on several occasions, for driving women to insanity. One such accusation came early on. Furneaux had begun dressing in men's clothes, and had assumed the name Arthur Rudd, through which "she courted a girl named Wood," who "became insane, and had to be removed to a Bromsgrove Asylum."[9] It is likely that the women in Furneaux's life were her lovers, who were subsequently institutionalized by family members. Contemporary reports often approached the truth of these relationships, though never described them directly. One American newspaper noted, for example, that Furneaux "amused herself, if not by marrying women, at least in making love to them."[10]

The Times began following the Furneaux case on February 10, 1882, relying heavily on correspondents from Birmingham and Liverpool. Initial estimates of Furneaux's criminal profits during her decade of fraud ranged from £6,000 to over £15,000. Details of her life gradually came to light, revealing that her criminal career began in Wolverhampton. As with Alice Grey, nearly every account of the trial's day-to-day development described Furneaux's appearance and dress. She claimed to be forty-two but "looked considerably younger," and was "attired in a Newmarket coat, which gave her a somewhat masculine appearance."[11] Testimonies from other witnesses trickled in. One of her victims described her voice as "like neither a male's nor a female's," and a witness claimed: "That person you suppose to be a lady is a man by the way she handles the reins."[12] The *London Journal* thought it worth mentioning that she "does not possess the least pretensions of good looks."[13] And another writer mentioned "something of the feline in the expression of her face."[14] Although Furneaux practiced several simultaneous criminal plots—including the claim that she was set to inherit property through a distant connection to Lord Lanesborough—only one imposture set her apart from similar frauds, ensuring her national notoriety.[15]

Living up to her former charge of being "a lady of 'great expectations,'" Furneaux personated Arthur Pelham Clinton, who, by the time of the 1882 trial, had been dead for nearly twelve years.[16] Clinton had gained his own notoriety just before his suspicious death, having been arrested on April 28, 1870, together with several other men, "for conspiracy to commit, or to incite to the commission of felonious and unnatural crime."[17] The primary actors, Ernest Boulton (aka Stella) and Frederick William Park, were "taken into custody in women's dresses coming from a theater."[18] During an official search, officers discovered letters from Clinton and ascertained that Boulton and Clinton lived together. This evidence led to the charge of a "*general* conspiracy to debauch the public, and several *separate* conspiracies to debauch each other."[19] At Clinton's lodgings, Boulton "always dressed as a woman, wearing a wedding ring, called by a female name, 'Stella,' sleeping with him constantly, and described by him as his wife."[20] Before the trial commenced, Clinton allegedly died from "exhaustion following an attack of scarlet fever," having denied any serious crime besides "the foolish continuance of the impersonation of theatrical characters, which arose from a simple frolic, in which he permitted himself to become an actor."[21] One writer acknowledged that "his lordship died quite suddenly, and somewhat mysteriously," suggesting the media's misgivings with the medical report.²²

Furneaux began personating Clinton in 1871. Although the imposture was less intricate than what she would practice later in the decade, the primary ingredients were already present. Always associated with voluminous paperwork, she transported thousands of letters that related to her fraud, including bills of sale that she abandoned. In Birmingham, she became acquainted with the Moorcroft family (alternately Morecroft), claiming to be a dressmaker. During the initial stage of her crime, she would apply to Mrs. Moorcroft's friends for money, which she would pocket. And she also borrowed money by claiming to be in line for a legacy from the Lanesborough family. At the same time, Furneaux defrauded local businessmen and clergymen, by claiming to be Clinton, describing herself as not a "member of the 'fair sex,'" and having been "compelled to don female attire."²³ She explained, in "graphic manner," how she was administered chloroform, placed in a coffin, and then "at an opportune moment burst the lid off" and escaped burial.²⁴ This performative breakout from Clinton's coffin does not appear in her later claims concerning the burial, perhaps because they proved too wild.

Furneaux was eventually arrested and brought to court in November 1871. The *Nottinghamshire Guardian* anticipated much of the rhetoric that would emerge a decade later by noting the "extraordinary and romantic case of female swindling."²⁵ And the *Hampshire Telegraph* called Furneaux a "heroine," suggesting her connection to popular novels.²⁶ As in the later trial, newspapers regularly highlighted Furneaux's appearance. The *Bristol Mercury*, for example, described her as "somewhat masculine in her appearance, although slenderly built."²⁷ And the *York Herald* described her clothes as a "mixture of a man's and a woman's."²⁸ During the trial, more information came to light concerning Furneaux's similar impostures around the West Midlands, and she was sentenced to one year in prison. Shortly after her release, Furneaux visited George Adam Green's photography studio in Birmingham, where she "put on a scarf and a moustaches, and in this masculine guise had a few cartes-de-visite struck off."²⁹ She later patronized Henry Proctor's studio in Liverpool.

Furneaux's claims about Clinton's faked death became less wild, though perhaps no more realistic, as the decade wore on. As part of the "unprecedented ingenuity of her crime," Furneaux claimed that Clinton had "feigned to die" and that his coffin was "filled with stones and buried, while the lawyers and doctors were bribed not to say too much."³⁰ By dressing

II.3. Furneaux, 3/4 face, with moustache: National Archives, UK: COPY 1/56/352

II.4. Furneaux, 3/4 face and wearing tall hat: National Archives, UK: COPY 1/56/353

II.5. Furneaux, in Stuart plaid shawl with hat and buckle at one Side, nearly profile face: National Archives, UK: COPY 1/56/475

in men's clothes, including the occasional army uniform, Furneaux's personation passed the eye test. But the primary evidence against her emerged through a collection of forged letters reported to number well over four thousand. Masquerading as Clinton, Furneaux claimed that she was set to be pardoned by Queen Victoria, with the result that she would regain both his title and property. Although few contemporary newspaper accounts bring up the context of this pardon, Furneaux evidently knew that Clinton had died under scandal. Abigail Joseph argues that, for Furneaux, the Boulton-Park affair "became a resource for the fashioning of a queer self."[31] On a practical level, however, Furneaux chose Clinton to personate not only because he was indicted in a scandal involving crossdressing but also because he was a suitable candidate to be restored by the Queen's forgiveness. The former point allowed Furneaux to dress "as a man in the height of fashion," under the auspices that she had "got in disgrace owing to the 'Boulton and Park' case, and was hiding."[32]

The latter maneuver was more difficult to establish and required Furneaux to forge letters from Sir John Coleridge, the Lord Chief Justice of England; Edward VII, the Prince of Wales; and Queen Victoria herself.[33]

II.6. Furneaux in costume: "Owl-La Podrida." *The Birmingham Owl* 7.3 (March 10, 1882): 4.

II.7. Furneaux as Arthur Pelham Clinton: "The Romantic Career of Miss Fearneaux." *Penny Illustrated Paper and Illustrated Times* 1,078 (March 4, 1882): 137.

In the late 1870s, Furneaux lived with James Gething, who either became her primary mark or partnered in her myriad schemes. The "[n]ew dupes . . . being daily brought to light in every part of the country" saw themselves as "highly favored in being permitted to advance money to 'his lordship' pending the settlement of his affairs."[34] Gething, who maintained to the end that he was ignorant of Furneaux's true identity, gave her lodging and money under the promise that she would reimburse him with substantial interest after Clinton's title and property were restored. That he fraudulently registered his newborn child as Arthur Pelham Clinton Gething might betray his claims of innocence. At one point, Furneaux produced a letter from Lord Coleridge that sought to arrange a meeting with the Queen.[35] Furneaux traveled to the meeting with Edward Beynon (alternately Benyon), an engineer who had previously employed Gething. Beynon later claimed that he sold all of his property to fund Furneaux, during the stress of which "his wife had become insane, and was at present in an asylum."[36] Furneaux took Gething and Beynon to meet the Queen at Balmoral Castle, but Beynon took ill beforehand and could not attend. Although Beynon testified that he was actually sick, it was alleged that Furneaux might have drugged him. Furneaux would also travel to London, claiming to have arranged meetings with dignitaries, where she was "described as most lavish in the expenditure of money, taking a cab even to go a few yards or across the street."[37] Furneaux also "lavishly furnished" a Liverpool home, complete with several musical instruments she could not play.[38]

Furneaux subsequently developed a relationship with Gething's niece, Jenny Ward, who was taken to a mental asylum following the revelation of Furneaux's identity. The *London Times* reported that Furneaux "made violent love to a young woman, who reciprocated the feigned attachment so strongly, that on the discovery of the deceit which had been practiced upon her she became insane, and is now the inmate of a lunatic asylum."[39] Allegedly, Ward was told that she was going on an innocent "drive in her carriage," but quickly "surmised where she was, and said they had brought her to gaol."[40] Another account claimed that Ward "went out of her mind" after Furneaux began a relationship with "Miss Horan," a Sunday school teacher.[41] Ward allegedly performed as Furneaux's runner to retrieve letters from the post office, which itself employed some "remarkably clever accomplices."[42] In letters to Ward, including one that detailed a suicide attempt with a concoction of "chloroform and laudanum and hydric acid," Furneaux referred to herself as "Fred."[43] At the end of Furneaux's trial, Ward, still an inmate at Rubery Hill Asylum, "relapsed into a state of semi unconsciousness" after hearing the details of the case.[44] Other newspaper accounts disputed Gething's claims that no one in the family saw through Furneaux's personation, and Furneaux herself later claimed that both Gething and Ward knew. Adding to the sensational aspects of Furneaux's plot, yet another woman, who had been scammed out of £3,000, was taken to an asylum.

Furneaux's criminal plot initially began to unravel through an 1875 connection she formed with Benjamin Fowell, a Liverpool gasfitter whom she scammed out of money using similar promises that she made to Gething. As with Beynon, Furneaux induced Fowell to sell property, and to entrust her with advances on a forthcoming inheritance. Before she moved in with Gething, Furneaux lived with Fowell, partially altering her name to Frederica Elliott de Furneaux. Her criminal plot, at this point, involved the claim that she was set to secure an inheritance from the Lanesborough estate, through her mother's distant connection.[45] Fowell testified that Furneaux was continually in "frightful moods" and that she spoke about "spies being after her."[46] When Fowell spotted two police officers outside his house, Furneaux allegedly fainted. The next day, she borrowed Mrs. Fowell's clothes and escaped.

Fowell lost track of Furneaux for years, though he hunted her throughout England and Scotland, publicly advertising a reward of five pounds for her whereabouts, and identifying her photograph at a police station. Fowell eventually reconnected with Furneaux in 1879. She gave him some money, and promised more, but again disappeared. Fowell was arrested in 1880 under the charge of having threatened Furneaux's life. Two letters were produced as evidence, the latter of which Fowell claimed not to have written. It is likely that Furneaux used the previous letter, which Fowell admitted was his, to forge the second letter. This species of threat reverses one of Furneaux's favorite methods, which was to forge letters from respected lawyers threatening people who sought repayment. Mr. Manton, an "ornamental writer" from Liverpool, was brought in as a handwriting expert, and determined that the two letters came from the same hand.[47] Fowell was convicted of the crime and served a one-year prison sentence. Following his release, Fowell started "making known the facts of the case with a view to obtaining some restitution," publicly calling Furneaux "the blackest she-devil upon earth."[48]

After Beynon came forward with accusations of fraud and conspiracy, Furneaux and Gething were eventually arrested. Similar to the trials of Alice Grey, the court was "crammed to excess with local nobilities."[49] The prosecution's evidence featured the testimonies of Mr. Screen, who sold his property for Furneaux, and Mr. Auerbach, a Liverpool moneylender, who

II.8. Furneaux's 1882 trial: "The Alleged Frauds by Miss Fearneaux—The Magisterial Examination at Birmingham." *Graphic* 25.640 (March 4, 1882): 16.

possessed a "large number of letters" and a collection of IOUs.[50] But the most influential testimony came from Lord Coleridge, who examined several of the letters seized during the investigation. "That is not my handwriting," he testified: "it is not the least like my handwriting."[51] Furneaux's forged letters from Queen Victoria also appeared as evidence, often eliciting "outbursts of hilarity" in the courtroom, mostly due to frequent misspellings, such as "Common Please" rather than "Common Pleas," "Great Brittain," and "collonel."[52] Visitors at the court were also tickled by Beynon reportedly referring to Furneaux as "My Lord." According to the thousands of letters at the prosecution's disposal, Furneaux had evidently combined the two strands of her "double personation," having the Queen both pardon Clinton and award him the title and lands of the Earl of Lanesborough.[53] One such letter described "[h]is lordship [as] in height 5ft. 3in.; brown hair, feminine appearance," and granted Clinton land in London, Leicestershire, and Ireland, along with £200,000.[54]

Following a court order, Ann Lovesey, "[t]he female searcher at the Birmingham Gaol[,] proved that the prisoner was a woman."[55] According to one writer, Lovesey was also the searcher during Furneaux's 1871 trial.

Other reports of this search claimed that Furneaux was "delivered some years ago of a female child."[56] Furneaux maintained that she "never thought of passing herself off as a man until Gething instigated her to do so" and claimed that Jenny Ward always knew she was a woman.[57] Mr. Cheston, Furneaux's lawyer, argued that his time for cross-examination was insufficient. Furneaux's case appears to have been transferred to Mr. Stubbins (alternately Stebbins). Under the prosecution of Mr. Pollard, the "Director of Public Prosecutions," and later Mr. Merewether, Furneaux was eventually found guilty of fraud, conspiracy to defraud, and forgery, and was sentenced to seven years in prison. Gething, charged only with conspiracy, was acquitted.

Similar to her 1871 conviction, Furneaux almost immediately resumed her crimes following her release from prison, "carr[ying] on the same life though in a less ambitious way."[58] In 1894, she was arrested in Leeds under the name of Frederica Furneaux—for "sweet alliteration's sake"—and charged with fraud.[59] Officials claimed that this new series of frauds had been occurring since at least 1891, but one writer asserted 1889, which would have been directly after her release from the seven-year 1882 sentence. Upon her arrest, Furneaux intimated that she was maintaining several simultaneous crimes, reportedly asking: "Which case is it?"[60] The primary fraud concerned an artist named Phillips, who entrusted her with two paintings based on her claim of being included in the substantial will of Katherine Dickinson, her cousin-in-law. Eventually, Phillips visited Somerset House in London to inquire about the will, and found that it did not exist. In fact, neither Dickinson nor her deceased husband Colonel Dickinson ever existed.

During the trial, Phillips was "not at all disinclined to tell the story of how he had been duped by a clever woman."[61] Beginning in 1891, Furneaux applied to Phillips for funds while traveling throughout England, after having been cornered in London by a victim named Ellen Miller (alternately Millar), who claimed she had "been reduced almost to poverty" by advancing money to Furneaux."[62] Phillips reportedly claimed that the story "would make a sensational *feuilleton*" and described Furneaux's reading habits and dress, which was "ahead even of the New Woman."[63] Through the testimony of Phillips and Miller, Furneaux was sentenced to prison, this time under the name Frederica Furneaux. In 1900, she was granted release from Aylesbury Prison, with the stipulation that she be removed to the Elizabeth Fry Refuge. It appears that she died in late summer 1901. As the *Evening News* claimed, "there is no doubt that she has had a most sensational career."[64]

Part III

Matter

Cases of mistaken identity constitute the romance of the law.
—*Criminal Law Magazine*, September 1885

Chapter 5

A Daring Imposture

Registers and Wills

In *The French Revolution* (1837), Thomas Carlyle refers to the decade from 1774 to 1784 as "The Paper Age." What was the "Age of Gold," Carlyle re-labels as paper, "which in many ways is the succedaneum of Gold."[1] Indeed, paper currency flooded the marketplace, acting as a symbol for the gold it promised to guarantee. The material properties of paper are displaced once paper assumes exchange value. In the sense that paper circulates, whether as currency, as a letter, or even as a book from a lending library, it achieves a dynamism that borders on subjectivity. "[T]here are endless excellences in Paper," Carlyle writes.[2] When paper fails adequately to represent its referent, however, it seemingly loses its value and becomes empty matter, "*rags* of things that did once exist."[3] Once paper is invested with value, it resists its material origins, defying Bill Brown's "thing," which occurs when "objects . . . stop working for us . . . , when their flow within the circuits of production and distribution, consumption and exhibition, has been arrested."[4] Sigmund Freud refers to his "Mystic Writing-Pad" as the "materialized portion of my mnemic apparatus," suggesting that paper, once endowed with writing, becomes a physical embodiment of psychic processes.[5] For Jacques Derrida, paper is a "limited 'subject,'" which can assume three states—priceless, supportive, and disposable.[6] Since documents—copied, delivered, stored, and sold—often support the subject's identity claims, they are also priceless. Without them, the subject is no one; with them, the subject can be anybody.

Carlyle's "Paper Age" more appropriately applies to the Victorian period, especially the decades that followed the repeal of "taxes on knowledge" in the 1850s. As late as 1885, one writer remarked: "We are in reality only just entering upon the borders . . . of the genuine paper age."[7] In 1850, Frederick Knight Hunt writes that the Registrar General produces "[p]ages enough to line the Waterloo Bride from end to end—tons weight of paper and of parchment."[8] The founding and growth of a range of state-endorsed statistical entities, together with London's bureaucratic and financial sectors, produced a staggering amount of paperwork. In a December 1857 article in *Household Words*, John Hollingshead provides a fascinating description of central London's paper industry:

> Within a certain circle, of which the Royal Exchange is the center, lie the ruins of a great paper city. Its rulers—solid and substantial as they appear to the eye—are made of paper. They ride in paper carriages; they marry paper wives, and unto them are born paper children; their food is paper, their thoughts are paper, and all they touch is transformed to paper. They buy paper and they sell paper; they borrow paper, and they lend paper,—a paper that shrinks and withers in the grasp like the leaves of the sensitive plant; and the stately-looking palaces in which they live and trade are built of paper,—small oblong pieces of paper, which, like the cardboard houses of our childhood, fall with a single breath. That breath has overtaken them, and they lie in the dust.[9]

Hollingshead's account is significant because it not only notes the sheer breadth of London's documentary industry but also suggests the fleeting, fragile nature of paper. As Lisa Gitelman notes, "paper is a figure both for all that is sturdy and stable . . . and for all that is unsubstantial and ephemeral."[10] London is a house of cards, the foundation of which is paper currency. Karl Marx describes money as an "almighty being" that determines the subject's individuality, with far more authority than innate qualities.[11] Coins, in the form of gold and other precious metals, possess value, but paper currency is merely symbolic: "Only in so far as paper money represents gold, which like all other commodities has value, is it a symbol of value."[12] When paper currency is no longer tied to gold reserves, as was the case in England from 1797 to 1821, it becomes a fictional construct, an empty symbol. England became "a society without substance," Kevin McLaughlin notes, "a paper society."[13]

In much the same way that mid-nineteenth-century England's financial foundation was constructed from paper, its populace was paper, as well. Peter

Brooks has observed that identity "seems to have become a problem with entry into the modern age in a way that it wasn't before."[14] Brooks further notes that identity became "the business of the state."[15] Such business, according to James C. Scott, involved making "society legible."[16] And any means of legibility was material in nature, whether in the form of registration documents or corporeal identification. Ian Hacking notes that the nineteenth century's "avalanche of printed numbers" led to "new technologies for classifying and enumerating, and new bureaucracies with the authority and continuity to deploy the technology."[17] The modern state became a "registering machine" that provided statistics for what Michel Foucault describes as "effective instruments for the formation and accumulation of knowledge."[18] Edward Higgs notes that registration of children's births "place[s] them on the road to formal recognition by the state as citizens."[19] Being citizens gives subjects a national identity and keeps them from becoming one of Dickens's "blank children, . . . those little gaps in the decorous world."[20] Subjects are registered at birth, documented at marriage, and posthumously immortalized through death registers and wills.[21] As John Guillory observes, "the dominion of the document is a feature of modernity."[22]

In 1861, George Graham, the second Registrar General, argued that "the art of writing secures by simpler means permanent evidence, which can be preserved, transcribed, and produced in any place on any occasion."[23] Birth certificates especially "afford[ed] sufficient legal proof" that a subject "was really born, and [was] not a mythical personage."[24] Higgs notes that civil registration indicates the state's concern with "the legal rather than the biological person."[25] Once birth, marriage, and death records became the duty of the state, a subject's identity was no longer innate; it was pledged to a government official, certified, copied, delivered, proofread, recopied, and stored, and then, without the consent of its referent, displayed and sold for the nominal fee of one shilling. For Henry Wyldbore Rumsey, the leading Victorian proponent of public medicine, civil registration's "physical" purpose is "to aid in disclosing *causes of disease*," whereas its "legal" aim is "to provide the means of tracing descent and proving personal identity."[26] This definition conflates the body with the document in determining identity through the eyes of the state. Claudine Dardy observes that documentation papers "provide us with identities" and "replace bodies and individuals."[27]

Sensation writers were fascinated by this new world of documentary identities. Sara Malton observes that sensation novels "insist on a connection between corrupt individuals who have refashioned their identities by means of falsified texts."[28] Registers, especially, could transform personal identity, allowing impostors to introduce themselves into an existing lineage or to create an entirely new life. Lost, stolen, and forged wills and codicils were ubiquitous in sensation novels. Seemingly every sensation plot, regardless of whether it featured a form of identity theft, hinges at some point on missing or fraudulent documents. The trope was not limited to the sensation genre, of course. Wills and codicils appear in countless narratives that fall under the amorphous category of realism.[29] But sensation novels, also interested in matters of inheritance, were just as concerned with the potential effects that wills had on personal identity. Registration documents and wills demonstrate that, in the new paper age, identity could consist of a collection of documentary signifiers that did not merely represent, but rather replaced, the individual subject.

Registers in *The Woman in White*

The first modern civil registration system was instituted in France in 1792, following the French Revolution.[30] Although England had experimented with registration for centuries, it did not follow France's example for over four decades.[31] The Births, Deaths, and Marriages Act went into effect on July 1, 1837—just days after Queen Victoria took the throne.[32] The previous fall, Thomas Henry Lister (1800–42) had been appointed the first Registrar General by William IV. Lister and his associates had the good sense to use the union infrastructure already established by the 1834 Poor Law. These unions served dual functions as districts manned by superintendent registrars, who then controlled the registrars that populated their districts. When registrars filled five hundred entries in any of their books, they delivered a copy to the superintendent registrar, who checked them for accuracy and forwarded them each quarter to the General Register Office in London. Superintendent registrars were also responsible for disseminating notices, which were pinned to relevant public buildings.

In the first year of the Registration Act, Lister boasted that the returns to the General Register Office featured nearly one million entries. Nathan K. Hensley has credited Lister with developing "the state's new human databank."[33] As information about registration requirements disseminated broadly in the subsequent years, numbers rose. Muriel Nissel asserts that by 1842, when Lister died, registration was "well established and accepted."[34] This is not to say, however, that the initial years were not without setbacks. To begin with, Lister was a controversial choice. Some questioned his qualifications for the post because he was best known as a novelist and had even written an early example of science fiction. Quieting his detractors, Lister acquitted himself admirably at the position, handling the undertaking with an eye to detail and efficiency. Some issues, however, were out of his control: books were lost in the mail or delayed by being overweight, copyists made spelling errors, and registrars incorrectly recorded names from illiterate subjects. As Frederick Knight Hunt explains, "when thousands of different persons have this simple duty divided amongst them, it is difficult, almost to impossibility, to get the thing done with accuracy."[35] But Lister's greatest challenge was resistant clergy members, who were understandably concerned not only with marriage becoming a civil ceremony but also with decreased attention to baptisms and burials.

Lister oversaw an efficient system of fact-checking in his "Error Department."[36] Workers were allocated to complete four tasks—examination, arrangement, indexing, and abstracting. Registration books sent from superintendent registrars were recopied at the central office and checked for accuracy.[37] Inquiries were then sent to the corresponding registrars, who were responsible for addressing the mistake. Lister's workers sent over ten thousand such letters in the first year alone. To defend against fraud, registrars were provided special forms "on paper of a durable kind, having a peculiar water-mark as a safeguard against the substitution of false entries."[38] Lister's note to the registrars also contained specific instructions concerning the state that the forms were to maintain: "every leaf should be delivered to the Superintendent-Registrar entire, and without any part of it having been torn or cut. It is also very desirable that the leaves should not be soiled, and that they should not be creased by folding more than can be helped."[39] Even the ink was regulated, for "[a]ny erasure is a deadly sin, and so is the cancelling of any entry."[40] Finally, the books were required to be kept in a fire-proof lockbox that the government supplied. The superintendent registrar and the registrar kept duplicate keys.

In 1842, Lister died of consumption and George Graham (1801–88) took over the post of Registrar General. Graham immediately began to make improvements, occupying the "center of a grand piece of official mechanism."[41] Admitting that unregistered births numbered in the "several thousands," he hoped that registrars would "be induced to employ more vigilance in discovering the births that occur in their districts."[42] Graham's greatest contributions, however, were to engage registration data even more fully and to ensure that registration remained secure and accurate.[43] In 1865, he recommended the move from handwritten to typeset books. In his initial act to stamp out corruption, he dismissed four registrars and hired four inspectors—"gentlemen of great keenness, who travel about all the year round, never telling when they are likely to visit any place."[44] Payment by entry meant that registrars were sometimes tempted to practice fraud. Nissel points out that, during a four-year period in the district of Marylebone, the rate of fictitious entries "led to recalculation of the district's birth rate and prosecution of the registrar for felony."[45] Hoping to deter these crimes, Graham included a note of warning in each register book that detailed the punishments.

Frequent revisions to the Registration Act, outlined in the yearly reports, were made to safeguard the system against fraud. Accurate returns proved vital to the accumulation of numbers, which were engaged to understand the health, wealth, and movement of the populace. As Pamela K. Gilbert observes, "[t]he management of the social body through public medicine and discourses of health became the principal discourse with which to negotiate . . . new questions of citizenship and the Condition of England."[46] Once the 1874 Registration Act made registration compulsory, the state could surveil with seemingly unlimited authority and punish those who refused to comply. "[O]bservers," Graham writes in 1876, "like watchmen on the walls, are ever on the look out, so that men see exactly what is going on."[47] Registration was one of the state's primary methods to make "society legible," to translate its populace into written records that could be deposited, studied, and manipulated.[48] What Ronald R. Thomas calls the "institutionalization of the textual construction of identity" paved the way for various forms of documentary identity fraud, as the self became paperwork to be destroyed, forged, or counterfeited.[49]

Sensation fiction exploited the particular power of registration documents to transform personal identity.[50] The genre's most complex registration forgery occurs in Wilkie Collins's *The Woman in White* (1859–60), suggesting the significant role that registration played in its genesis.[51] Sean Grass observes "identity's flimsy basis" in the novel, signified by "church registers, wills, letters, death certificates, and tombstone inscriptions."[52] Collins early on establishes the importance of paperwork in forming individual identity. Whereas Hartright is to be trusted because he can produce "[v]olumes of letters and portfolios of testimonials," Percival Glyde's fraudulent claim to his family baronetcy demonstrates that these paper identities can be counterfeited.[53] Vincent Gilmore, the novel's initial lawyer, determines that Glyde is "a gentleman, every inch of him" (144), based solely on appearance and deportment. Glyde does not need to perpetrate physical or intellectual fraud because he has always lived as a gentleman. His issues are tied to paperwork rather than to person and involve a secret that would "deprive him, at one blow, of the name, the rank, the estate, the whole social existence that he had usurped" (500). For Sara Malton, Glyde's fraud is a "violation of cultural memory, its temporary success suggestive of a kind of cultural hypnosis."[54] Although his parents lived as a married couple, they never lawfully wed. Glyde's mother had been married in Ireland to an abusive man who left her for another woman. Since Glyde is born out of wedlock, he has "no more claim to the baronetcy and to Blackwater Park than the poorest laborer" (500). Faced with crippling debt prior to the events of the novel, his first recourse was to borrow money against his family's property. To do so, he was required to produce both his birth certificate and his parents' marriage certificate. The latter, of course, does not exist, prompting Glyde to forge the entry into a parish register.

Jane Catherick, Anne's estranged mother, confirms the details of Hartright's investigation and fills in most of the remaining gaps. By blackmailing Mrs. Catherick with the threat to publicize their nonexistent affair, Glyde gained entry to the vestry at Old Welmingham church, where he located the register book from 1803. Mrs. Catherick claims that Glyde's initial plan was "to tear the leaf out (in the right year and month), to destroy it privately, to go back to London, and to tell the lawyers to get him the necessary certificate of his father's marriage, innocently referring them of course to the date on the leaf that was gone. Nobody could say his father and mother had *not* been married after that" (522). When he located the corresponding page, however, Glyde was surprised to see a "blank space left" (522).[55] By claiming that he was born prematurely, Glyde could account for any discrepancy between the marriage certificate and his birth certificate. The space where Glyde forged the entry confirms the evidence that Hartright had earlier gathered. Searching for clues concerning Glyde's mysterious lineage, Hartright travels to the Old Welmingham Church vestry, and enters a "dim, moldy, melancholy old room, with a low, raftered ceiling" (488). The registry documents are in disorder: "a litter of dusty papers; some large and rolled up, like architects' plans; some loosely strung together on files, like bills or letters" (488). Hartright accesses the correct book, which contains the entry for the Glydes' marriage. Although Glyde had taken pains to copy the ink color, and to "practic[e] the handwriting" (522), Hartright notices the "narrowness of the space" (491) in which the entry is recorded.

Hartright confirms his suspicions by comparing the original register at Old Welmingham with a copy located in Knowlesbury, the neighboring town. At Knowlesbury, Hartright speaks with Mr. Wansborough, a lawyer who acts as the vestry clerk. Wansborough's father, Robert, performed as a failsafe for the disordered registration system at Old Welmingham. In a sense, he was civil registration personified, singlehandedly demanding accurate records decades before government intervention. For Hartright is not the only person to be "struck by the insecurity of the place in which the register was kept" (490). Years earlier, the elder Wansborough had "kept a copy of this book, in his office at Knowlesbury, and had it posted up regular, from time to time, to correspond with the fresh entries here" (490). The 1837 Registration Act employed district registrars, entrusted with maintaining accurate records of births, deaths, and marriages. These registrars then sent copies of their register books to superintendent registrars, who sent their own copies to London. Wansborough acts as a proto-registrar, copying the original register in "smartly bound" books, which he then kept "securely locked" (499). Similar to the one-shilling charge levied by the General Register Office in London, moreover, Hartright even pays "the necessary fees" (498) to access the record. As he suspects, there is no entry to indicate the marriage of Glyde's parents. "That space," he reflects, "told the whole story!" (499).

Indeed, blank spaces serve as the central image in *The Woman in White*, and this blankness is always a symptom of the characters' textualities.[56] John Kucich has noted how both heroes and villains in the novel are "centrally concerned with the manipulation of texts," and the "mutual engagement in the play of textual deception points to a common contagion."[57] Anne Catherick is herself a blank space, both physically and mentally, that Hartright fills with narrative, and that Fosco fills with Laura Fairlie.[58] And Laura similarly becomes a blank space, not only drugged and installed in an asylum but also denied the narrative agency afforded to the darker, inkier Marian. Nicholas Daly has noted that "the novel's plot is not so much a woman in white as a piece of blank paper."[59] That Glyde's "identity is founded on a blank" connects him to other characters in the novel, "in which loss of identity, or suppression of identity, is more or less the norm."[60] Such an "all-pervasive concern with questions of the instability of identity" does not anticipate postmodern concepts of the fragmented self but rather "mark[s] it very much as a novel of its time."[61] Modernity, in other words, fosters the environment for identity loss, exchange, or otherwise confusion, and it consequently creates, to fill the blank spaces that emerge from fragmented identities, the impostor.

Another document features prominently in the novel's second personation plot. One of the reasons the "complete transformation of two separate identities" (591) succeeds in *The Woman in White* relates to the mismanagement of Laura's death certificate. Shortly before Anne's death, Alfred Goodricke, a professionally licensed local doctor, is summoned under the impression that he will care for Lady Glyde. When Anne dies, Goodricke takes the extraordinary measure to commence legal obligations: "Your master is a foreigner. . . . Does he understand about registering the death? . . . I don't usually do such things . . . but it may save the family trouble in this case, if I register the death myself. I shall pass the district office in half an hour's time; and I can easily look in" (396). Goodricke relies entirely on the word of Fosco and the recognition of the cook, Hester Pinhorn, to confirm identity, and he proceeds to the "REGISTRAR of the Sub-District" to document Laura's death: "I hereby certify that I attended Lady Glyde, aged Twenty-One last Birthday; that I last saw her, on Thursday, the 25th July 1850; that she died on the same day at No. 5, Forest-road, St. John's Wood; and that the cause of her death was, Aneurism. Duration of Disease, not known" (397). Goodricke's willingness to help the "foreigner" comply with civil registration law leads directly to Anne being buried under Laura's name. Since no next-of-kin is present, two subjects with no relation confirm identity. Jane Gould, brought in by Goodricke to make preparations for burial, can offer nothing but confirmation that the body was "laid in the coffin, in my presence, and I afterwards saw the coffin screwed down, previous to its removal" (398). The register and the "narrative" tombstone engraving certify Laura's death, becoming documentary signifiers of her personal identity.

Glyde's forgery, foiled by a neighboring lawyer's meticulous record keeping, demonstrates the vulnerability of parish registers. But the details of Fosco's scheme, which only succeeds by coincidence of an overzealous doctor, similarly shows the liability of civil registration. Human error, ranging from unintentional carelessness to deliberate dishonesty, undermines the Registration Act's complex system of safeguards. And these issues still do not account for errors in recognition. When Marian brings the recently liberated Laura to see her uncle, Frederick Fairlie refuses to identify her: "Mr. Fairlie declared . . . that he did not recognize the woman who had been brought into his room; that he saw nothing in her face and manner to make him doubt for a moment that his niece lay buried in Limmeridge churchyard" (421). This misrecognition, as much the result of Mr. Fairlie's apathy as it is Laura's "fatal resemblance" (426), calls to mind actual mistaken identity cases, including Lady Tichborne's resolute certainty that Arthur Orton was her long-lost son, Roger. Valerie Pedlar notes that Collins "reveals the anxieties of an age in which the certainties of a small-scale society based on face-to-face familial and working relationships have been lost."[62] Faced with the assurance that recognition testimonies are fruitless, Hartright turns to other "proofs" (435) to reestablish Laura's identity.

The lawyer Kyrle, though pessimistic about the prospect of success, informs Hartright that the only chance to reverse the results of the dual personation would be to present material evidence that shows a discrepancy between Anne's death and Laura's removal to London. Three documents become the novel's most significant paper trails. Hartright easily acquires the death certificate, and a trip to a carriage service secures him the testimony and the dated entry of Fosco's trip with Laura, which occurred after the official date of Anne's death. The third piece, acquired as part of Hartright's final arrangement with Fosco, is a letter from Glyde announcing Laura's trip, also dated postmortem. Whereas names are slippery, interchangeable symbols in *The Woman in White*, dates fix bodies in time. Hartright boasts of the "written evidence about me" (605), which he takes to Kyrle to begin restoring Laura's identity.

Possessed with sufficient evidence to undermine the "daring imposture" (406), Hartright nonetheless also requests a narrative from Fosco, as part of an agreement to allow the villain to escape with impunity. In a tense scene, Fosco "make[s] this a remarkable document" (583), writing with prodigious urgency: "Each slip as he finished it, was paged, and tossed over his shoulder, out of his way, on the floor. . . . Slip after slip, by dozens, by fifties, by hundreds, flew over his shoulders on either side of him, till he had snowed himself up in paper all round his chair" (584). When finished, Fosco gathers the "white chaos of paper" (584), binds it together, undertakes revisions, and finally recites the complete manuscript to Hartright. Fosco acts not only as novelist and editor but also as reader, echoing Dickens's first public readings in 1858–59 and anticipating Collins's own readings over a decade later.

Fosco's authorial and editorial performance also connects him to Hartright, who arranges and revises the novel's voluminous collection of first-person documents. The ultimate success of Hartright and Marian's investigation is not only that it restores Laura's original identity but also that it punishes imposters. Glyde's fiery death, set at the very site of his initial forgery, is presented as an appropriate penalty for his crime. And Fosco, the brains behind the identity exchange between Anne and Laura, is ceremoniously stabbed in Paris by a fellow member of the Brotherhood. Ronald R. Thomas notes that Fosco, "[d]espite all the aristocratic titles he bears, . . . is ultimately identified by that secret mark on his arm that brands him a member of a foreign organization."[63] A master at manipulating other bodies, Fosco is betrayed by his own. Rebecca Stern argues that *The Woman in White* "may be understood as a tirade against 'personation' and a paean to the unitary self."[64] Indeed, the novel sanctions assumed names, while it sentences personation to death. Fictional lives are acceptable elements of the modern world, but identity theft, and its assault on hereditary order, cannot be tolerated. Ann Gaylin observes that the conclusion "ultimately reaffirms the social and institutional status quo."[65] And Hartright occupies the best of both worlds. According to Mariaconcetta Costantini, Hartright "confounds traditional sets of values, since he appropriates the ideological tenets of the two classes between which he moves."[66] Yet Hartright finishes his narrative by identifying his child as "one of the landed gentry of England. . . . *the Heir of Limmeridge*" (617). Marriage to Laura elevates him from artist to aristocrat, demonstrating one final time the power of documents to transform personal identity.

Wills in *Verner's Pride*

Similar to the secularization of civil registration ratified by the 1837 Births, Deaths, and Marriages Act, legislation on wills transformed dramatically during the Victorian period, shifting the processes of certification and storage from the church to the state. The same year as the Registration Act, the Wills Act passed parliament, functioning as the first of several legislative maneuvers that simplified the process of writing and certifying wills in the nineteenth century. The next significant legislation occurred in 1857 with the installation of the Court of Probate, which resembled, in its bureaucratic centrality, the General Register Office. Before the Principal Probate Registry opened, wills were managed by the Church of England and ostensibly conducted by legally trained members of the clergy, who held "lucrative and much coveted" positions in various Diocesan Courts.[67] The establishment of the Court of Probate "swept away" these ecclesiastical lawyers, which was a controversial and expensive process, because "[l]arge compensations had to be paid to the superseded functionaries."[68]

The 1837 Wills Act was meant to condense and to clarify a discursive cacophony of existing laws on the composition, legality, and implementation of wills.[69] Cathrine O. Frank observes that the Wills Act "made the will a distinctly modern document."[70] Similar to registration documents, this new legislation on wills affected personal identity. The will not only outlined the material and symbolic possessions that helped to construct the subject but also certified that the subject continued to exist beyond death, making posthumous claims about the distribution of the self that could affect generations of descendants. And this is not to mention the way that a will could transform a subject's civil status, replacing symbolic signifiers, such as names and titles. But this subjectivity, Frank notes, became "inseparable from the legal structures that enable it."[71] The will's amalgamation of the testator's voice with legal jargon "complicated the idea of the intentional subject," meaning that personal identity was permeated by bureaucratic rhetoric.[72] The will became especially important to a society structured by industrial capitalism, "align[ing] . . . social identity with materialism."[73] As personal identity became associated with the abundance, value, and arrangement of assets, the will transferred a subject's possessions to other subjects, achieving a sort of material immorality by dispersing the self through a form of commodity genetics.

Victorians were fascinated by wills, reporting on their dynamic, often peculiar forms, and understanding their profound impact on civil life. "Most people are interested in wills," L. S. Lewis wrote in 1897, "directly or indirectly."[74] Several Victorian writers on wills commented on potential effects on identity. An 1860 writer noted the revelatory nature of wills: "In their wills few men can keep up an assumed character."[75] Although Wilkie Collins felt confident enough to register his son William Charles fraudulently under the surname Dawson, he refused to lie in his will, and acknowledged all three of his children with Martha Rudd. In 1897, Charles Draycott noted that wills "reveal many curious phases of human nature," signaling, on the one hand, the evolving form of the document throughout the subject's life, while on the other the different facets of personal identity, the material and symbolic signifiers that make up the self.[76] Most intriguing, in 1901, *The Spectator* ran an article titled "The Degeneracy of Wills," which argued that "graceful personal touches are not to be found in the wills of the present day."[77] At a time when the potential degeneracy of the species was a pervasive cultural anxiety, this writer seems to suggest that the increasingly invasive bureaucracy of wills robbed the documents of their humanity. But the greater issue was that wills could rob humans of their humanity, reforming personal identity into certified paperwork filled with legal jargon.

Modern attention to the significance of wills might have started with William Hazlitt, who argued that "[f]ew things shew the human character in a more ridiculous light than the circumstance of will-making."[78] Hazlitt criticized rather than fetishized wills, seeming to understand them as bureaucratic nightmares that represented the worst of humanity's impulses. "All that we seem to think of," he argues, "is to manage matters so . . . as to do as little good, and to plague and disappoint as many people as possible."[79] Hazlitt's most intriguing remark, however, concerns the way that the will "privileges of an abstract idea, so that the project has the air of a fiction or of a story in a novel."[80] Hazlitt, whose notions of personal identity anticipated twentieth-century claims, was also prescient about the role that the will would play in the nineteenth-century novel. Nowhere is this focus more prominent than in Charles Dickens's *Bleak House* (1852–53), which bookends with the interminable Jarndyce and Jarndyce suit. Seemingly every character is "insensibly tempted" by the "scarecrow of a suit," and Dickens bases each character's virtue on their ability to resist entering Chancery.[81] In the end, "great bundles of paper . . . , immense masses of papers of all shapes and no shapes," are brought in, only for the suit to be "absorbed in costs."[82]

Just two years before *Bleak House* began its serial run in *Household Words*, Dickens, initially alongside the aptly named William Henry Wills, began a series in the same periodical under the title "The Doom of English Wills." The series unfolds in four "cathedrals," wherein the fictional reporter William Wallace visits various church holdings to understand the state of English wills. Dickens (who stopped contributing after the second cathedral) and Wills criticize the arrangement of the first cathedral's holdings, which alphabetized items by forename, greatly complicating search attempts. More problematic was "the dilapidative neglect, the hideous disorder, the willful destruction of documents."[83] The lack of a legislated system of restoration, copying, and containment invited imposture. Although the institution of the Principal Probate Registry in 1858 would obviate some of these issues, providing a centralized site for the storage of new wills, sensation novelists continued not only to suggest that wills were particularly susceptible to imposture but also to represent the ways that wills affect and potentially transform personal identity.

In the early Victorian period, criminal cases predicated on will forgery caused media spectacles, potentially influencing sensation novelists in the coming decades to compose complex plots involving missing, counterfeit, or fraudulent wills. The most significant case began in 1856 and extended into the 1860s. The *Annual Register* noted its "marvels and confusion," and predicted that the case "seems likely to end—like the great case of *Jarndyce v. Jarndyce*—in costs."[84] One of the judges, the *Saturday Review* reported, "declared [the case] to be one of the most important and interesting with which he had ever been connected."[85] The trial concerned events that transpired following the death of George Nuttall in 1856. Nuttall, described as a solitary man, never married, and left the majority of his considerable estate to John Nuttall, his cousin, who died just a month later. Upon George's death, witnesses broke open his desk and retrieved his will. But a week later, a duplicate will was produced, replete with emendations and the notation "This is my *rigt* (*sic*)."[86] This revised will left more property to John Else, the husband of one of Nuttall's other cousins. *The Spectator* claimed that Else had "not yet fully developed his special faculty, but his greatness was descending on him."[87] Else subsequently discovered a "gummed envelope" that acted as a codicil, allocating him even more of the estate.[88] Shortly thereafter, Else produced a second codicil, once again adding to his share. But the "crowning discovery" of a third codicil occurred under the most remarkable circumstances yet.[89] Having taken control of Nuttall's house, Else turned to cleaning what one writer called a "lumber-room" and another an "out-house."[90] Else enlisted a boy to clean the windows, during which they discovered a hole in the wall that contained a jar, some money, and the most recent codicil, leaving Else majority control of Nuttall's estate.

At this point, "[t]he suspicions of . . . [the] trustees were now thoroughly aroused," and John Nuttall's family took Else to court, eventually resulting in three separate trials of increasing publicity.[91] Else's case was aided by witness testimony, but lawyers for the opposition remained incredulous. One barrister's statement, which served as the initial sway for jurors, establishes the absurdity of the case:

> What's that in the jar? Why, a codicil to be sure! What else could it be? In a jar, in a hole in the wall, covered with cobwebs. What could it be but a codicil! This finder of codicils, who found nothing but codicils—what should it be but a codicil, and a codicil in his favor! In a hole in the wall! Why, it might not but for this miraculous discovery have ever been discovered at all! What a place for a man of business to put his last will in![92]

George Nuttall's physical ailments added suspicion to the intricate and nearly unreachable location of the third codicil. Jurors were most influenced, however, by the deposition of Chabot, a "Huguenot by descent and a lithographer by trade."[93] Chabot demonstrated that the handwriting specimens from the wills and the codicils were similar, but differing in one respect—the propensity for the writers to cross the letter "t." Jurors were able to follow along with Chabot's testimony because he produced photographs of the handwriting that were enhanced "by the aid of powerful magnifying glasses."[94] The corresponding guilty verdict was "received with great applause by the spectators."[95] After the trial concluded, *Punch* ran a satirical article that reported six more codicils—discovered in a bird cage, in a mine-shaft, in a bottle inside "an enormous large turnip," in a magpie nest, in a saucepan, and under the cushion of a church-pew.[96] More serious publications noted the significance of the case. The *Saturday Review*, for example, ended its article with a plea for the regulation of wills under the "unlimited power which the law of England confers."[97]

The Nuttall case seems to have sprung straight out of the sensation novel. Yet Else's initial codicil claims, which were reported in newspapers beginning in August 1859, predated the first serial number of *The Woman in White*, which has often, though perhaps too hastily, been accepted as the genesis of sensation fiction. Following Collins's example, in which the villains work tirelessly to access Laura's "comfortable little fortune" (146), sensation writers composed increasingly complex inheritance plots, wherein wills become signifiers of the self that can be destroyed, counterfeited, and forged. The potential for wills fully to transpose personal identity is the primary focus of Ellen Wood's *Verner's Pride* (1862–63), which features a personation plot performed by a character acting largely on a whim. The novel centers on a missing, or rather stolen, codicil to a will that restores a substantial inheritance to the protagonist, Lionel Verner. The existing will functions to alter the financial prospects of a number of characters, elevating some to riches while consigning others to poverty. But *Verner's Pride*, attuned to the modern world controlled by capital rather than ancestry, also suggests that finances structure subjectivity. Lionel's personal identity, in particular, vacillates in extremes, depending on the authority of paperwork to determine his place in the world as either the head of a prosperous estate or a dispossessed wanderer without name or home. Although Wood demonstrates how various forms of imposture threaten documentary identity, she ultimately villainizes Mormonism, which she sees as a particularly threatening species of fraud.[98]

By the time that *Verner's Pride* concluded its serial run in the periodical *Once a Week*, critics had equipped themselves with an arsenal of complaints against sensation novels. The *London Review* led with the hope that "people will soon get tired of the sensation novel, and young ladies will cease to thrill over bigamy and murder."[99] The reviewer, asserting the derivative nature of the sensation genre, labels *Verner's Pride* as "Renaissance Newgate," and upbraids Wood for "abandon[ing] . . . evangelical teaching" in favor of being "confined to crime."[100] The model that Wood should follow, the reviewer claims, is to be found in the "artistic handling of the plot or delicate finish of detail" in George Eliot's *Adam Bede* (1859), "almost a perfect novel."[101] Other reviews acknowledged the merits of *Verner's Pride* but ultimately criticize Wood for "hasty writing" in which "too many vicissitudes occur to the actors . . . even for this world of change and chance."[102] The *Examiner* makes the most interesting point, describing the novel's "sly villain" as possessing a "sensation mark upon his face."[103] The personation plot in *Verner's Pride* relies on a distinct facial mark that allows John Massingbird to personate his younger brother Frederick. That the reviewer identifies this feature as a "sensation mark" demonstrates how this device was pervasive enough in sensation novels to warrant its own idiom. The phrase also suggests a connection between bodies and texts wherein the reviewer can identify the genre of the novel through a particular device that it employs. But this connection more specifically associates the body with the will, in that John Massingbird's counterfeit mark, made with "Indian-Ink," vies for authority with a missing codicil to establish and to divest various characters' documentary identities.[104]

Verner's Pride begins by establishing the new-money actors who populate its titular estate. The Verner family became rich via the discovery of "valuable mines" (2), directly linking the Verners with industrial modernity. Mr. Verner, the first owner of the house, had two sons, Lionel and Stephen. Lionel's death in India tasked Stephen with raising his nephew, also named Lionel. When Stephen's wife and daughter died, the younger Lionel became the closest relation to inherit Verner's Pride. Stephen remarried, however, complicating the line of inheritance, as his new wife's two sons, John and Frederick Massingbird, came to live at the house. The latter possesses "a strange, very ugly mark upon his cheek. A very strange mark indeed, as large as a pigeon's egg, with what looked like radii shooting from it on all sides" (4). Villagers call it variously a "hedgehog" and a "porkypine," but the narrator settles on a "black star-fish" (4). Notwithstanding the animal comparisons, the mark is "black as jet; and his pale cheek . . . made it more conspicuous" (4). Fred's mark acts as text on his white face, making his body both legible and able to be forged. That Fred has the habit of rubbing his finger "round and round the mark upon his cheek" (7) draws even more attention to his unique feature, as if it is constantly being reinscribed. When John personates Fred later in the novel, the success of the performance relies almost exclusively on the duplication of this mark. Only one year apart, the brothers possess a "great likeness . . . in figure and feature," but the "strange black mark" (8) distinguishes them.

The cardinal intrigue of the novel concerns the existence of a missing codicil. Mr. Verner earlier rushed to compose the codicil because he "beg[a]n to think I have not the right" (95) to disinherit Lionel, suggesting the dispossession would affect Lionel's very personhood. Although the lawyer Matiss knows Lionel is the rightful owner of Verner's Pride, the missing codicil prevents further legal action. "A will is a will," he admits, "and must be acted upon" (101). With Lionel "displaced" (102), his "independence seemed to have gone out with the blow, and a slight seemed to have fallen upon him, if not upon his name" (102). His authority both on the estate and in the nearby village changes. "From being a landed country gentleman," Lionel complains, "I descend down to a poor fellow who must work for his bread and cheese before he eats it" (109). This transformation affects his health, and he suffers a "sun stroke" that was not quite "brain fever, though bordering closely upon it" (126). Lionel is debilitated from the illness, made worse by intentionally inadequate medical attention.

Lionel, now also implicated in murder, plans to leave town, but learns at the last second that Fred Massingbird has died. Since Lionel is third in line after John and Fred, he experiences another transformation of identity, or perhaps a reconstitution of his previous self. Now the "master of Verner's Pride," Lionel "could scarcely believe in his own identity" (160). Lionel experiences "tumultuous thought" and "felt as if some fairy must have been at work with a magic wand" (160). Lionel's dream turns into a nightmare, however, when various townspeople report seeing Fred roaming about Willow Pond: "There never was another face like Mr. Frederick Massingbird's. Other features may have been made like his . . . but whose else would have the black mark upon it?" (276). Mr. Bourne, the local rector, asserts that "some person, from evil design or love of mischief, must be personating Frederick Massingbird. It was a natural conclusion to come to" (278). Lionel, faced with evidence that Fred did not die, experiences another identity crisis, suffering a "fevered dream" (301). When Lionel sees the ghostly figure himself, a "stifled cry, suppressed instantly, escaped his lips; his pulses stood still, and then throbbed on with painful violence" (310). The man with the "Indian-Ink" on his cheek becomes a sort of corporeal codicil that has reemerged after having gone missing.

The figure's identity turns out to be what Bourne suggested. Fred has been personated by his brother John, who never actually died in Australia: "And so the mystery was out. And the ghost proved to be no ghost at all, . . . come to disturb her peace and that of Lionel; but *John* Massingbird in real flesh and blood" (351). This revelation is as frustrating as it is senseless. John could merely have returned to England and claimed Verner's Pride as his own. Asked why he went to such trouble, John reveals that he personated Fred on a whim: "The fun it has been!" (351). The only true motive that John admits is that Fred "had neither creditors nor enemies round Deerham" (356), meaning he could return without addressing his financial and personal responsibilities. Installed as the owner of Verner's Pride, John awards Lionel a position as manager. The reemergence of the codicil, however, triggers one last identity crisis. Lionel is restored as the head of Verner's Pride, and John, ever "restless" (351), makes plans to leave, revealing beforehand that Fred had impregnated Rachel Frost, having wooed her with promises of marriage.

The novel concludes with a group of Deerham residents returning from "New Jerusalem," a Mormon outpost at Salt Lake City, "now in humility and poverty" (503), having been deceived by "an awful impostor" (504) named Brother Silas Jarrum. Promised salvation through bigamy, residents of Deerham, "famous for old maids" (204), had flocked to Jarrum, who asserted, "*I'm* no impostor" (203). Susan Peckaby, a particularly credulous resident, catches the "Mormon fever" (220), but gets left behind, staying ever hopeful she will be sent a white donkey to make her solitary journey. Jarrum, who marries several Deerham women, is also blamed for the conversion of a fifteen-year-old girl, who becomes his "thirteenth wife" (504). Yet Fred escapes even posthumous condemnation, even though he abandoned Rachel, which led directly to her suicide. John likewise suffers no punishment, the imposture being "the primest fun he ever had in his life" (360). Even Dr. West, who hid the codicil with the hope of enriching his family, escapes with impunity, largely ignoring his role in his daughter's death. Instead, Jarrum becomes the true villain. Wood ultimately sides with the devious philanderer, the "harum-scarum fellow" (9), and the "false one" (402) over the religious zealot. "[T]hem Mormons deceived with their tales" (505), one victim complains, while ignoring the false tales, both interpersonal and legal, that permeate Deerham society.

Chapter 6

That Mysterious Paper Currency

Refuse and Photographs

In Charles Dickens's *A Tale of Two Cities* (1859), Sydney Carton infiltrates Charles Darnay's prison cell, drugs him, exchanges their clothes, and later becomes the day's twenty-third victim of the guillotine. Darnay, meanwhile, narrowly escapes France using Carton's identification documents. The exchange succeeds because Carton and Darnay are "sufficiently like each other to surprise . . . when they were thus brought into comparison."[1] On page ninety-five of the November 26, 1859, number of *All the Year Round*, *A Tale of Two Cities* concluded and Wilkie Collins's *The Woman in White* began. Dickens introduces Collins's novel as "[t]he second story of our series" that will "produce . . . sustained works of imagination that may become a part of English Literature."[2] The reference to a "series" is perhaps more telling of the relationship between the novels than Dickens intended. Both novels, of course, center on personation—the first between Carton and Darnay, and the second between Laura Fairlie and Anne Catherick. In spite of Dickens's French Revolution setting, both novels also confront specifically Victorian concerns over the effects of industrial mechanization. *A Tale of Two Cities* portrays what Daniel Stout has called an "indifference to individual distinction."[3] Carton and Darnay's resemblance is part of a novel-wide theme wherein subjects are reduced to numbers, masses, or anonymous "Jacques." But ultimately clothes—and papers—make the man. Collins offers a similar premise in *The Woman in White*, in which characters are (mis)identified by marked clothing and registration documents. Thus, the novels' attention to imposture does not stop at the supernatural novelty of the doppelgänger but rather signals the relentless economy of duplication installed by industrialization.

Sensation fiction's ubiquitous inclusion of personation plots reflects the material conditions of industrial Britain, which produced undifferentiated products that no longer counterfeited an original model. The increasing mechanization of society forewarned inescapable objectification, threatening subjectivity through what Karl Marx terms reification. At the same time, the proliferation of material signifiers, the products of industrialization, progressively came to represent an individual's identity. Charles Darnay and Laura Fairlie, for example, respectively become Sydney Carton and Anne Catherick due as much to clothes and documents as to resemblance. Numerous sensation novels, moreover, stage personation plots between characters that lack any likeness, indicating that imposture could be achieved entirely through documentary means.[4] This chapter demonstrates how the influx of signifying things in Victorian society, particularly refuse and photographs, challenged corporeal definitions of personal identity by functioning as segments of the self that could be discarded, discovered, circulated, and sold. As in the previous chapter, paper best exemplifies this process. The combined influence of tax repeals and production advances meant that paper, for the first time, became affordable and dispensable. The explosion of various forms of cheap paper, occurring concomitantly with the rise of the sensation novel, created floating, discarded, lost, and hoarded signifiers of identity. Victorians were the first people who had to worry about two threats that have plagued modernity: what they threw away, and who possessed their image. In the twenty-first century these concerns have become largely digital, though no less threatening. But in the second half of the nineteenth century, they were matters of paper.

In an August 1850 article in *Household Words*, Dickens describes his visit to a papermill in Dartford, Kent. What was once an area used for gunpowder mills now produces paper, underscoring the article's promotion of paper as a pacifying agent, and offering an industrial analogue to the pen and sword idiom. During the tour, which resembles a fairytale, Dickens follows the process of reclaiming rags into paper by becoming a rag himself: "I am to suppose myself a bale of rags. I *am* rags."[5] As Michelle Allen notes, Dickens "represents the process of paper making explicitly as a process of purification, of cleansing."[6] In addition to the racial and xenophobic implications, Dickens draws attention to the way that paper reconstitutes waste, as the "dusty rags, native and foreign, of every color and of every kind" exit their journey as "[w]hite, pure, spick and span new paper."[7] But of all the wonders Dickens experiences, the machine stands foremost. During the "astounding transformation," the machine "receives me, at one end of a long room, gruel, and dismisses me at the other, paper!"[8] Unlike the foul furnaces of England's other manufacturing plants, the paper machine remains bucolic, a picturesque prospect dotting the industrial landscape.

The dawn of the nineteenth century witnessed the first paper-making machine, invented in France by Louis Nicholas Robert, and then installed in England under the supervision of brothers Sealy and Henry Fourdrinier. Mechanization quickly transformed the landscape of paper production, and by 1830 half of British paper was produced by machine. Three decades later, during the rise of the sensation novel, the number had increased to 95 percent.[9] The change from rags to esparto grass and finally to wood pulp marked the other important factors in paper's Victorian development. As Richard Menke observes, "[w]ood pulp broke the logjam in the nineteenth-century paper supply."[10] What is more, advances in "economical presses and imposition schemes" increased the production efficiency of print material.[11] These developments also affected photography, since photographs were produced from chemically treated paper. Although professional photographers tended to prefer rag paper made of linen or cotton over pulp or grass (which could yellow), new refining technologies continued to enhance the purity of all forms of paper used for photography.[12]

In 1894, a reporter for *All the Year Round* observed that "the enormous increase in the consumption of paper" was "[o]ne of the most remarkable features of modern times."[13] Cheap, machine-made paper was affordable for the masses and displaced rag and linen production, which was reserved for "editions de lux" and "similar high-class book work."[14] The writer also notes that paper possesses the "unique position" of being a "plastic and adaptable material" that can satisfy an "ever-increasing multitude of uses."[15] The article ends on a sour note, however, addressing the concern that cheap paper "will bring on rapid decay."[16] Of the mountains of print material produced in the latter half of the nineteenth century, "[o]nly remnants . . . will survive for the information of future generations," and the "literary historian of . . . the twenty-first century" will encounter a "heterogeneous mass of rubbish."[17] On the surface, this prediction has proved inaccurate: much of what the twenty-first century knows about the Victorian period is testament to the endurance of paper, thanks to the improved collection and storage of civil records and the efforts of librarians and private collectors. Yet researchers have also benefited from the "mass of rubbish," the signifiers of personal identity that survived the dustbin of history. As Leah Price observes, "[m]odernity can be defined not just by what's produced, but by what's discarded, and when."[18] Victorian life, in other words, has been reconstructed, in no small part, by what people threw away.

Refuse in *Our Mutual Friend*

Trash is an inescapable byproduct of modernity, the consequence of industrial capitalism's myopic devotion to increasingly efficient manufacturing processes that use cheaper, less durable materials without decreasing consumer spending. The twenty-first century has begun to experience the environmental effects of what Igor Kopytoff has termed "terminal commodities," exemplified by single-use plastics, which "make only *one* journey from production to consumption."[19] As the first people forced to cope with the fully realized effects of industrial mechanization, the Victorian period, Natalka Freeland has argued, developed an "uneasy consciousness of itself as a period of transition."[20] Thus, the problem of refuse—where it collected and where it should go—triggered sweeping social, political, and domestic reforms, transforming not only the civic landscape but also everyday Victorian life. The accumulation and disposal of refuse forced Victorians to be discerning about what they threw away, which is a particularly modern outcome that survives today. We are what we eat, of course, but we are also what we discard. Aspects of our personal identity often wind up in our trash, both materially in garbage cans and virtually online. And this information, whether physical or digital, can be stolen, used to counterfeit or to blackmail, or sold to the highest bidder.

Victorian reactions to refuse helped to shape modernity. The association between filth and disease, prescribed initially through a series of cholera outbreaks, educated nineteenth-century reformers to treat waste as a social evil that should be eliminated promptly and efficiently. As Pamela K. Gilbert observes, waste became "evidence of a vicious, even murderous, disregard for life."[21] But the removal of refuse also contained a symbolic message. For Mary Douglas, "dirt is essentially disorder," and its elimination is a "positive effort to organize the environment."[22] Removing waste from everyday life creates a "semblance of order" that is predicated on "exaggerating the difference" between a series of binaries, including "order to disorder, being to non-being, form to formlessness, life to death."[23] We tend to consider the matter that we discard as no longer useful, if not dead, and the disposal of this antimatter thus affirms usefulness and life. Yet Victorian rubbish-scavengers signal the economic energy that waste maintains. Michael Thompson's "rubbish theory" complicates simple distinctions between valued objects and rubbish, positing that the labels "transient" and "durable" are "socially imposed," defined by certain upper-class gatekeepers.[24] But Thompson adds a third category, "rubbish," which "provides the one-way route" from transient to durable.²⁵ This transition demonstrates the way that waste can be utilized by people across the class spectrum. One man's trash is another man's treasure becomes literal for both scavengers and "creative and upwardly-mobile individual[s]."²⁶ But the potential value in waste also attracts another forward-thinking type—impostors who discover and exploit items discarded by unwary subjects, whose search for order meant disposing seemingly disordered pieces of personal identity.

In an April 3, 1872, stump speech, Benjamin Disraeli argued that "public attention . . . ought to be concentrated upon sanitary legislation."²⁷ As part of Disraeli's call to rally conservative votes, he drew attention to the "kindred matters" of "[p]ure air, pure water, the inspection of unhealthy habitations, [and] the adulteration of food."²⁸ Decrying the failures of William Gladstone's liberal government in regard to sanitation, Disraeli concluded that "the first consideration of a minister should be the health of the people."²⁹ By the time of this speech, England, and especially London, had already undergone dramatic improvements in sanitation. Built into the 1837 Births, Deaths, and Marriages Act, which was run through the structure of the Poor Law commission, were provisions to study mortality rates and causes of death, with the goal to understand and to promote the health of the nation. In 1839, Edwin Chadwick began compiling the results of a nationwide questionnaire, which he later published as *The Sanitary Condition of the Labouring Population of Great Britain* (1842). The report, clear in its recommendations and unyielding in its accusations, delineates the nation's sanitary problems that are "attendant on removable circumstances."³⁰ Chadwick saw proper circulation, in terms of air, water, and sewage, as the most significant means to improve the population's health.³¹

Chadwick excoriated London's obsolete sewage system, which was a "vast monument of defective administration, of lavish expenditure, and extremely defective execution."³² His advocacy for proper drainage included domestic spaces, where "the present mode of retaining refuse . . . in cesspools and privies is injurious to the health and often extremely dangerous."³³ The cost of paying for the removal of human waste from households was prohibitive for a large percentage of the population, and laborers called "night soil men" often refused to enter poorer homes because they did not expect to earn a tip.³⁴ Chadwick saw indoor water-closets, recently installed in "the wealthy and newly-built districts," as the solution, because they "discharge . . . refuse at once from the house through the drain into the sewers."³⁵ Under the influence of sanitary advocates, the Metropolitan Board of Works was founded in 1855, and Joseph Bazalgette was tasked with improving the sewers, and later commissioned to oversee the construction of the Thames embankment. As Michelle Allen notes, sanitary reform "altered [London's] social and symbolic meanings."[36] Bazalgette's mark on London's civic structures is unparalleled. By the last decades of the nineteenth century, Sally Mitchell notes, "virtually all municipalities built reservoirs, provided adequate water supplies, and established sanitary drainage."[37] These civic improvements had a gradual, but significant, influence not only on the daily lives of London's inhabitants but also on quantifiable measures, such as the death rate, which decreased by almost 4 percent by the end of the century.

Chadwick's plan to eliminate human waste from London homes was not limited to excrement. The accumulation of rubbish, both in houses and on the streets, "fosters habits of the most abject degradation and tends to the demoralization of large numbers of human beings."[38] The 1875 Public Health Act required the use of a dustbin for every household, which was to be emptied by municipal entities and either taken to a landfill or incinerated. But this measure seems to have done little to improve the lives of London's poor. In 1883, George R. Sims noted the "dark continent" of the city's slums, which are "full of refuse, heaps of dust and decaying vegetable matter [that] lie about here and there, under the windows and in front of the doors of the squalid tumble-down houses."[39] Henry Mayhew earlier noted of the poor that "[d]irt is the rule with them, and cleanliness the exception."[40] On the one hand, the seeming permanence of refuse that spilled out of homes and clogged alleyways meant the threat of disease was never at bay. But on the other hand, this environment of unrelenting rubbish led to a veritable economy of reclamation, some of which was devoted to the search for and the offloading of paper.

In his portraits of London's lower-class laborers, Mayhew observes that "the street-purchase of waste paper is the most curious."[41] These "waste-men" visited domiciles ranging from publishers and attorneys to restaurants and pubs, and then sold their supply to "cheesemongers, buttermen, butchers, fishmongers, poulterers, pork and sausage-sellers, sweet-stuff sellers, tobacconists, chandlers."[42] Leah Price notes the diverse afterlives of printed material in the early Victorian period, arguing that "loose sheets accreted scars and bruises as telling as any it-narrator."[43] Increasingly inexpensive paper made from wood-pulp rather than rags curtailed such reclamation efforts. Yet paper-recycling programs endured, albeit bureaucratically. In 1886, *Chambers's Journal* ran an article titled "Government Waste-Paper" that exposed the inner-workings of "Her Majesty's Stationary Office," which "takes in a constant stream of material from paper-mills, and factories, and printing-offices, and distributes it to over three hundred government establishments in all parts of the kingdom."[44] Paper of various kinds, escalated by the institution of halfpenny postage, arrived at the processing department, where it was unloaded by "forty or fifty girls" employed "in turning and sorting and cutting up and re-packing into bags."[45] Although the article writer does not mention novels or other forms of printed fiction under the "many various kinds of things [that] come under the general heading of 'waste-paper,'" surely the stationary office workers sorted through a fair share of penny dreadfuls and shilling shockers, so called for both their affordability *and* their disposability.[46]

Given the rhetoric of many Victorian reviews, we might add sensation fiction to the list of wastepaper. In 1863, Henry Mansel, as part of his scathing attack on the genre, lamented that "the public appetite can occasionally descend from trash to garbage."[47] Three years later, another reviewer criticized "that abomination of abominations," whose "approximate result must be worthless trash."[48] Sensation characters could not escape similar charges. In its review of Collins's *Armadale* (1864–66), *The Spectator* described Lydia Gwilt as "fouler than the refuse of the streets."[49] The most intriguing criticism, however, comes from the *Saturday Review*'s article on Collins's *The Law and the Lady* (1875), which closes by suggesting that the novel itself belongs in the trash: "With the dust-heap, and its contents of paper rubbish, we shall take leave of Mr. Collins and his novel."[50] In the novel, Sara Macallan's suicide confession is painstakingly reconstructed from a dust-heap containing a "small attendant litter of waste paper and frowsy rags."[51] At the very least, this conclusion draws attention to the significance of the novel's interrelation of refuse and identity. Not only does the illustration of Sara's true self, depressed and suicidal, become rubbish but so too does the evidence of Eustace Woodville's innocence.

In many sensation novels, paper refuse performs as a detached material signifier of personal identity.[52] There is no better specimen of this model than Dickens's *Our Mutual Friend* (1864–65), in which dust-mounds contain the will that Silas Wegg uses to blackmail the Golden Dustman Nicodemus Boffin. This will, hidden among an amorphous assortment of trash and treasure, awards the majority of the Harmon estate to the Crown, seeming to spoil Boffin's increasingly miserly ownership. For J. Hillis Miller, the dust-mounds, together with a host of other matter, support an "immense network of interrelations" that "liberate[] all of the characters from the prison of their subjectivity."[53] Indeed, rubbish embodies the fractured personal identity of every character, not the least Boffin, whose livelihood was already constructed from dust. "I should *not* like," Boffin declares, "to be what I may call dispersed."⁵⁴ But rubbish most significantly shapes Harmon, who performs two separate impostures that are dictated by intentionally lost or misplaced paperwork. Sean Grass emphasizes the novel's "textualization and commodification of subjectivity," which "belong[s] to an ecological economics that reduces all things and subjects to the . . . wealth-giving dust."⁵⁵ The dust-mounds act as a collective memory, a material record of the past, whose items retain the energy to shape the future. As Jessica Kuskey observes, "the images of trash in the novel emblematize wasted energy as both a moral and a material phenomenon."⁵⁶ That the dust-mounds retain value demonstrates the wastefulness of industrial society, the "emptying out of human beings," which depletes and discards both objects and subjects.⁵⁷

Above all, *Our Mutual Friend* resolves, or rather dissolves, one of the central themes of *Bleak House*. As one reviewer remarked in 1865, Dickens has "for sixteen years been haunted by a great Dust Heap[,] . . . industriously engaged in attempting to ferret out the bright things in dirty places."⁵⁸ Following Krook's death in *Bleak House*, "a dustman is called in to carry off a cartload of old paper, ashes, and broken bottles."⁵⁹ Krook's gelatinous remains are among this refuse, which supports the narrator's words concerning Tulkinghorn's "lowering magazine of dust, the universal article into which his papers and himself, and all things of earth, animate and inanimate, are resolving."⁶⁰ While dust-mounds dot the landscape of the Harmon estate, inside the house "the dust into which they were all resolving would have lain thick on the floors" (232). Dust, in *Our Mutual Friend*, contains not only various forms of rubbish—and most significantly the "mysterious paper currency which circulates in London" (191)—but also the waste of bodies, remnants of corporeal personal identity, testifying to what one reviewer called a "marvellous liking for whatever is physically offensive."⁶¹ The imposture performed by John Harmon means assuming two alternate identities—constantly "resolving," shedding waste, becoming new.

In the extraordinary opening scene of *Our Mutual Friend*, Gaffer Hexam and his daughter Lizzie fish a corpse from the Thames. This is no remarkable occurrence for the "bird of prey," whose sole occupation is to drag the river for valuables. "How can money be a corpse's" (47), he reasons, suggesting that the dead lose all subjectivity. The authorities manage only to secure the quick testimony of Julius Handford regarding the body's identity. Handford thereafter disappears, frustrating the court's attempt to subpoena him for an official inquest. With no further leads, officials register the body as John Harmon, who was reported missing from a boat traveling into London. Mortimer Lightwood, a listless attorney, provides some necessary exposition concerning the Harmon family. "[A] tremendous old rascal," Harmon's father "made his money by Dust" (55), meaning that he collected "mountains" of refuse at his estate: "Coal-dust, vegetable-dust, bone-dust, crockery dust, rough dust and sifted dust,—all manner of Dust" (56). On the one hand, the dust-mounds act as troves of valuable artifacts and hoarded information. But on the other, they remain waste, a putrid mixture of discarded, useless, toxic ephemera. Virginia Zimmerman observes that the dust-mounds are a "signifier that is a perfect cipher—at once a powerful symbol and a complete nothing."[62] John Harmon's familial association with dust means that his identity also becomes largely symbolic, constructed from empty signifiers that permit his various impostures. For Leslie Simon, the dust-mound "is not *one* body of useless matter, but an accumulation of many bodies."[63] Harmon, similarly, contains multitudes, which conflict to the point that his original identity disappears, only to be restored by Boffin's gift at the end of the novel.

The initial will for the Harmon estate stipulates that John Harmon receives all but one of the dust-mounds, contingent on his marrying Bella Wilfer. The remaining dust-mound passes to Noddy Boffin, a servant at the estate. John Harmon's death, however, transfers the majority of the property to Boffin, who becomes instantly enriched. Like flies to dung, swindlers sense an opportunity to take advantage of Boffin, who puts on airs of simple incredulity. Silas Wegg, who is under Boffin's employ, partners with Mr. Venus, a collector of eccentricities and an articulator of bones, with the plan to scour the dust-mounds for valuables. Venus's taxidermy shop acts as an alternate dust-mound, featuring a "muddle of objects . . . among which nothing is resolvable into anything distinct" (122). For Daniel Novak, Venus's emporium is "literally a site for the convergence of bodies and commodities."[64] Yet its business model pales in comparison to Harmon dust, which boasts value in deconstruction, as opposed to Venus's reconstruction. What Eve Kosofsky Sedgwick has called the "anthropomorphization of capital," the dust-mounds act as both a bank-vault and a goldmine.[65] Like Krook's shop in *Bleak House*, dust-mounds contain rags and riches, and conceal priceless paperwork that signifies identities more than bodies themselves.

Wegg convinces Venus that the Boffin dust contains articles of worth, including "money, valuables, maybe papers" (355). Living by a similar code as Gaffer Hexam, Wegg believes that misplaced or unwanted items are the property of the finder: "Say it was money, or plate, or jewelry, it would be as much ours as anybody else's" (357). But it is paper that proves most enticing. Given the elder Harmon's propensity to punish his relations, it is likely, Venus claims, that he "made a good many wills and codicils" (356). Sean Grass notes that wills in the novel "help[] generally to scatter dust," while also "underwrit[ing] a larger culture that textualizes subjectivity and causes it to circulate."[66] This fragmentation and objectification of personal identity most affects Harmon, whose very selfhood lies buried in dust. Such a "collapse of the Victorian subject into the realm of property" was earlier articulated by R. H. Horne in his 1850 *Household Words* article "Dust; or Ugliness Redeemed."[67] Horne maintains that a sizeable dust-mound "is often worth thousands of pounds" and claims that a "banker's cheque for a considerable sum was found in one of them."[68] As in *Our Mutual Friend*, personal identity becomes tied to paperwork that circulates until it deposits in waste, ready to be (re)claimed.

Wegg searches the dust for a similar prize. In a stroke of luck, he unearths a cashbox, labeled as old John Harmon's, only "temporarily deposited" (556). To determine the dates of the two wills, Wegg "paid a shilling" (556), indicating that he traveled to the Principal Probate Registry to inspect the public record. Dated after the will on file, the new will still guarantees Boffin one mound, but it transfers the remainder of the estate to the Crown. Wegg threatens to publicize the will and extorts Boffin. Under Wegg's terms, he will own anything of value sorted from the dust-mounds, and the remainder of the property will be split three ways, with Venus and Boffin taking two-thirds. Wegg's mistake, however, is that he trusts Venus, who has been recruited and flipped by Rokesmith and Boffin. The precious will is locked away in Venus's shop among the "heterogeneous objects" (126), never to be sold. This paper signifier, forever buried alongside the hamper of "human warious" (126), threatens to certify Harmon's false identity as Rokesmith. Another will exists, however, contained in a "Dutch bottle" that Boffin had earlier discovered. This will still excludes John Harmon from the estate, but it leaves everything to Boffin, who subsequently restores the terms of the original will. Thus, the dust, working its filthy magic, ultimately reinstates Harmon's original identity. And Wegg, embarrassed and ruined, is tossed into a "scavenger's cart" (862), becoming decidedly worthless detritus of the dust he treasures.

Our Mutual Friend contours villains with little gray area. As J. Hillis Miller observes, "[t]here is no central protagonist."[69] Like wills in a dust-mound, however, one of the novel's antagonists might be hidden beneath the novel's mountain of narrative matter. For John Harmon, the eponymous "Our Mutual Friend" (157), is perhaps Dickens's most devious identity thief.[70] In fact, Harmon adds another identity to his repertoire, the mysterious captain who attempts to wring a confession from Rogue Riderhood. Dickens withholds the events that led to Harmon's various impostures until they emerge through Harmon's first-person narrative, which one reviewer derisively termed a "mental soliloquy."[71] Natalka Freeland observes that Dickens "describes a world of fragmentary dust and rubbish by fracturing the text into a disconnected multiplicity of plots and voices."[72] Harmon's embedded account destabilizes the novel's third-person narration, reflecting Harmon's own fragmented identity. Following a fight with his father as an adolescent, Harmon left England for fourteen years. Aboard the ship home, he became acquainted with George Radfoot, a crewmember whom he somewhat resembled. The pair hatched a plan, based on Harmon's uneasiness with his arranged marriage, to disguise themselves to test Bella's resolve. Searching for lodging, they happened upon Riderhood's pawnshop. Harmon pieces together his fragmentary memories thereafter, but he surmises that Riderhood supplied Radfoot with poison, which Harmon ingested with some coffee. Incapacitated, Harmon recalls hearing a scuffle and then being dropped into the Thames. Miraculously, he survived, recovered in a public-house, and eventually identified Radfoot's corpse as himself under the alias Julius Handford.

Although details of the incident remain murky, it seems that Radfoot was double-crossed in much the same way that he betrayed Harmon. We must recall, however, that Harmon's memory is, at best, hazy, and that his first reaction upon being drugged is "to rush at" Radfoot (426). That Harmon and Radfoot plunge into the Thames together, moreover, might purposefully parallel the later scene in which Bradley Headstone seizes Riderhood and drowns with him under rushing water. Regardless, the novel's identity exchange darkens the terms of the heroic act that concludes *A Tale of Two Cities* (1859). For one reviewer, "The likeness between George Radfoot and John Harmon, with its results, is an infelicitous travesty of Sydney Carton's story."[73] The fact remains that Harmon adopts the identities of Handford and Rokesmith because he steals and then ostensibly erases Radfoot's identity. As Gwen Watkins remarks, "Radfoot is not a willing victim."[74] If the London of *Our Mutual Friend* is, as Ellen Handy argues, a "functioning organism," then Radfoot becomes Harmon's prey.[75] When Rokesmith "heap[s] mounds upon mounds of earth over John Harmon's grave" (435), he simultaneously submerges Radfoot's memory. No mention is made to Bella of this sordid detail when Harmon comes clean. Rokesmith "buries" his previous identity "under mountains" (443), but it is Radfoot who becomes dust.

Photographs in *Unconditional*

In 1841, Dickens sat for a daguerreotype portrait in the studio of the litigious photographer Richard Beard. He subsequently reported his experience to Angela Burdett-Coutts: "If anybody should entreat you to go to the Polytechnic Institution and have a Photographic likeness done—don't be prevailed upon, on any terms. The Sun is a great fellow in his way, but portrait painting is not his line. I speak from experience, having suffered greatly."[76] Over a decade later, in a *Household Words* article, Henry Morley and William Henry Wills referred to photographers as "modern priests of Apollo, the old sun god."[77] In the years between these pronouncements, the technology and popularity of photography had flourished. Morley and Wills begin their article by entering the studio of the "necromancer" John Jabez Edwin Mayall, who would take Queen Victoria's daguerreotype portrait in 1860. They subsequently encounter a "thousand images of human creatures" and inquisitively wonder: "The innumerable people whose eyes seemed to speak at us, but all whose tongues were silent; all whose limbs were fixed. . . . [W]hat people were these?"[78] Morley and Wills proceed to detail the intricacies of the photographic process, including Mayall's retreat into his "den," the "very head quarters of spectredom."[79] But arguably the most significant event in the article occurs at the beginning, when Mayall reportedly remarked: "they have all been executed here. If you mount farther up you also may be taken."[80] Thereafter, Morley and Wills refer to the photographer as "the taker of men."[81] The language of photography, including being "posed," suggests artificiality, and being "executed" and "taken"—not to mention "captured"—invokes violence and violation, as if the performance disturbs or drains some part of the sitter's personal identity.

During Victorian colonial exploits in Africa, British travelers frequently noted the aversion some communities expressed toward photography, which was seen as tantamount to stealing a part of the soul.[82] This discomfort persists today, even in industrialized nations. Susan Sontag, for example, asserts that photographs keep humanity fettered in Plato's cave, gazing upon "mere images of truth," which have altered our perception of reality.[83] "To photograph," Sontag writes, "is to appropriate the thing photographed."[84] At stake here is not only a corollary to the anxieties of various indigenous cultures but also a portrayal of what Morley and Wills referred to as being "taken." Sontag lingers over the destructive properties of photography, which is "as much an interpretation of the world as paintings and drawings are."[85] This understanding of photography's artistic features, which offer a glimpse of the world that has been manipulated both by the photographer and by the technology itself, echoes nineteenth-century concerns over the trustworthiness of photographs in criminal cases. But Sontag's most intriguing claims regard photography as a "tool of power" that "violate[s]" and "turns people into objects that can be symbolically possessed."[86]

Roland Barthes expresses similar unease over these objectifying properties, noting that photography "transform[s] subject into object," and even "into a museum object."[87] This objectification suggests a violative display for the consumer gaze and carries colonial implications. "A specific photograph," Barthes continues, "is never distinguished from its referent. . . . It is as if the Photograph always carries its referent with itself."[88] Since "the referent adheres," the subject becomes a "kind of little simulacrum," causing a "cunning dissociation of consciousness from identity."[89] Photography thus "captures" a piece of personal identity, freezing the moment in time, so that the subject who looks upon his own image "feels he is becoming an object. . . . I am truly becoming a specter."[90] As the result of photography's technology of simulation, the object displaces the subject, and personal identity transmogrifies into the material product that spectators crown as reality.[91]

The Victorian culture of imposture spurred contentious debates over the legitimacy of photographs as evidence during trials. Many legal authorities and photography experts advocated the particular faculty of photography to illuminate details that were not present to the naked eye. For example, one photographer used different color-sensitive plates to identify fraudulent and falsified paperwork. "[T]he photograph had revealed the truth," the writer boasted.[92] In 1866, another writer argued that photography, "as the auxiliary of the detective in tracking the criminal flying from justice, renders most important service."[93] And several writers expressed excitement over "telegraphic photographs" being developed in France, which promised to " 'wire' [the suspect's] likeness."[94] But other parties were less convinced, and several of these arguments coalesced during the trial of the Tichborne Claimant. During the trail, William Matthew promoted his invention called the Identiscope, which overlaid two photographs to ascertain whether the same subject appeared in both. Matthew claimed it was a "process that cannot err" and showed that Arthur Orton's and Roger Tichborne's features matched exactly.[95] Francis Galton ridiculed Matthew's claims, arguing that "[t]he reason why photographic portraits blend so well together is that they contain no sharp lines, but only shades."[96] The dubious nature of photography came up again at the trial in regard to two daguerreotypes, one of which had been damaged during transport. The defense, led by Edward Kenealy, argued that the image displayed Tichborne's "very peculiar thumb," which Orton shared.[97] That each piece of photographic evidence, including the infamous grotto image, ultimately hurt the defense's case demonstrates the contradictory position photography held in legal proceedings.

In 1880, Francis Wharton, an American legal expert, noted that photographs "may be used as instruments of fraud."[98] Sensation novelists were the first writers to understand the potential for photography to be exploited in personation plots.[99] The most significant of these plots occurs in Thomas Hardy's *Desperate Remedies* (1871). The novel's central mystery settles on the whereabouts of Aeneas Manston's first wife, Eunice, who was reported to have died in a fire but then miraculously reappears. As it turns out, Manston convinced an acquaintance, Anne Seaway, to personate Eunice, whom he had murdered. In a remarkable scene, Manston suddenly becomes "impregnated with a bright idea."[100] He searches through a photograph album, finds a few likenesses of Seaway, and selects the one that most resembles Eunice's photograph in "tone, size, and attitude."[101] He then submerges them in shallow water and "found that each photograph would peel from the card on which it was mounted."[102] Finally, he "stuck upon the original card the recent likeness from the album, dried it before the fire, and placed it in the envelope with the other scraps."[103] Through this remarkably inventive process, Manston performs photographic identity fraud, committing a crime that resembles the more modern manipulation of IDs and passports.[104]

The focus on photography in *Desperate Remedies* pales in comparison to Thomas Sutton's *Unconventional* (1866), which features the most apposite title in the entire genre of sensation fiction.[105] Not only that, but the novel is easily one of the strangest and most frustrating texts of the Victorian period. Sutton completed only one novel, and the overt reference to a sequel at the end of *Unconventional*, understandably, never came to fruition. Contemporary reviewers, irrespective of their level of scorn, emphasized that the novel's plot hinged on photography. "[T]he leading element of the novel is *photography!*" *The Athenaeum* declared: "Everybody is engaged in photography, either for business or pleasure."[106] And *The Reader* similarly explained: "Photography, and its application to good or evil purpose, is . . . discussed in details, which reveal scenes of vice as painful as we know them to be true."[107] Indeed, the novel's "scenes of vice" occur during its most shocking subplot, which features the threat of a sexual violation perhaps unmatched in sensation fiction. The novel's heroine, Nelly May, is abducted and imprisoned under the condition that her captors will take nude photographs of her to be distributed among aristocrats who have bankrolled the operation. Although Nelly manages to escape before being photographed, her experience demonstrates the danger of new and affordable camera technology placed in the wrong hands. These photographs threaten Nelly's personal identity, as signifiers of her most private self very nearly circulate among strangers.

Throughout *Unconventional*, Sutton suggests that the rise of photography to a respectable artform was threatened by both pornography and counterfeiting, the latter of which is another plot introduced by the novel's villains. These dual threats merge along the lines of reproduction, which could be considered the primary concern of the novel. Sutton wanted photography to claim a place alongside painting as high art, but reproduction did not necessarily equal representation. As Elazar Barkan notes, "[t]he photographer was regarded less as an artist than as a technician."[108] Sutton vocally criticized similar assessments, writing that good photography was not merely "mechanical, but purely the work of human intelligence."[109] At issue, as well, was the ability for photographers to produce multiple copies, duplicates that ultimately lessened the value of the original. The antagonists of *Unconventional* engage photography either to manufacture counterfeit banknotes, or to produce nude photographs—idealized with bondage positions and accessories—distributed on cards. Respectively, the individual object and subject lose value in the copying and the circulation of fraudulent images. As with the "mysterious paper currency . . . gyrated here and there and everywhere" (191) in *Our Mutual Friend*, the pornographic cards can be "picked up in the neighboring fields, or be found floating down on the river beneath the walls, having been blown there by the wind."[110]

Unconventional begins with a shipwreck, but the true intrigue commences when the hero, Mark Levisne, takes lodgings at the house of an "unconventional being" (2.141) named Signor Caitiff Xenosthes. Indeed, the novel's title appears directly to refer to Xenosthes, whose "mode of life is solitary and unconventional" (2.199). In spite of his misgivings, Mark agrees to stay at the house, which is supervised by a Frenchman named Adolphe and his niece Giovanna. Xenosthes's wealth derives from "something called ART, and a black art too" (1.265). But Xenosthes is no artist and instead uses his camera to produce counterfeit banknotes. "They have set up a lot of machinery there," one character explains, "and the whole crew of them work away at paper making till the spring; when they come back to us. Of course it wouldn't do to make everything here. They only do the photographic part here, and the printing" (2.33). In spite of the originality of this crime, the novel's primary antagonist remains Adolphe, disguised and plotting from within Xenosthes's employ. The confusion between potential antagonists puzzled at least one contemporary reviewer, who transposed Adolphe's crimes to Xenosthes. Adolphe is actually a French marquis living under an assumed name to escape from an unnamed enemy, and he plans to rob Xenosthes of some "curiosities" (1.263), deeds, and jewels, which Xenosthes keeps boobytrapped in his bedroom. As with everything associated with Xenosthes, however, these jewels are fake, valueless duplicates that debase the original objects, much like the counterfeit money and the pornographic cards.

While absent on his hunt for Giovanna, Xenosthes's house burns down, revealing his crimes to the public. Newspapers run the story: "his name and supposed wealth are an entire myth, and the premises were, in fact, occupied by a swindling Firm, engaged in the nefarious practice of manufacturing bank notes by photography" (2.209). Not surprisingly, the arsonist is Adolphe, who also managed to steal blank checks meant for Mark. The detective on the scene reiterates the earlier approach to using photography in criminal justice: "If I had but a photographic portrait of them, it would assist me greatly in the search. I have found photography extremely useful in my profession, and it is a great safeguard to the public" (2.222). With no photographs to verify identity, Adolphe moves freely under his assumed name. He already established his den of iniquity, where he photographs nude women and distributes copies to elite customers. Through a series of deceits, Adolphe imprisons Nelly at his chateau, where "[r]eport said that a black art was carried on within its dingy walls, for a black and an infamous purpose" (3.174). Nelly eventually learns that she is to be photographed nude and that her image will become one of the "scraps of paper . . . , which bore hideous and strange pictures that raised a blush on modest cheeks" (3.175). Rather than be subjected to this invasion, Nelly courageously jumps out of a window, swims down a river, and disguises herself in peasant clothes. She begins an arduous journey away from the chateau, where she serendipitously reunites with Mark.

Sutton's goals to rehabilitate photography and to claim its position as high art become clear as the novel progresses. In the right hands—those of trained artists and detectives—photography could reach both aesthetic and moral heights in Victorian society. But when placed in the hands of amateurs and criminals, photography was a dangerous technology. In Adolphe's chateau, "one of the brightest discoveries of modern science was being prostituted to a vile purpose, on a large scale. Photography has originated a new and obscene traffic" (3.175). Sutton urges consumers of such photographs to "reflect on the scenes which must accompany the taking of the negatives, and the wholesale printing of the proofs" (3.175). That Adolphe's business is lascivious and a violation of either desperate or unwilling women is not up for debate. But his method nevertheless displays some artistry, however immoral and illegal. For Nelly's nude body is not subjected to mere copying; she is posed and idealized for sexual fetish. As part of Adolphe's explanation of the forthcoming process, he opens an "ottoman, and expose[s] to view some pieces of rope, a riding whip, and various old tools and leathern straps" (3.186). Nelly later acknowledges that she was "to be tied down upon the ottoman by the rings in its two ends" (3.226–27). Bondage scenes will idealize Nelly's form and justify Adolphe's occupation. "It is but a small favor I ask of you," Adolphe implores, "as a boon to ART. . . . Your charms, exhibited on the truthful carte, will be the admiration of crowned heads, and of the first artists in the world, who will sign over perfections which neither their brush nor their chisel could so truthfully portray" (3.190). Measured against his disapproval of the counterfeiting employed by Xenosthes, Sutton seems, however unintentionally, to champion the artistry of Adolphe's pornography.[111]

Afterword

Reverse Personation

Sensation fiction conspicuously reveals its Gothic roots.[1] Foreign horrors become domestic intrigues, and supernatural phenomena, for the most part, become natural occurrences. "Instead of the terrors of 'Udolpho,'" Henry James observes, "we are treated to the terrors of the cheerful country house and the busy London lodgings."[2] But as the sensation genre finally succumbed to the weight of criticism and to the whims of popular culture, it was absorbed into the Gothic's revival. One way to identify this absorption is through personation plots. The late-Victorian Gothic obsessed over personal identity, exploring the ways that it could be split, transferred, or duplicated. Whereas personation was a crime of body, mind, and matter in sensation novels, it became supernatural in the Gothic. This is not to say that personation became fantasy, but rather that Gothic novels extended the horror of personation to fantastic ends, demonstrating how the modern world split, transposed, and multiplied the self.

In *Alice's Adventures in Wonderland* (1865), Lewis Carroll's eponymous heroine is "very fond of pretending to be two people."[3] Throughout the novel, Carroll taps into a cultural fascination with identity (de)construction that contemporaneous sensation fiction pursued obsessively. Two decades later, Robert Louis Stevenson's *The Strange Case of Dr. Jekyll and Mr. Hyde* (1886) reanimated Gothic fiction, taking a cue from Carroll by introducing a character who *is* two people. The identity struggle between Jekyll and Hyde has inspired an extraordinarily rich bounty of interpretations mined from the novella's frustrating and fascinating ambiguity. One such reading might arise from the text's links to sensation fiction: *Jekyll and Hyde* articulates the horror, indeed the monstrosity, of personation. Jekyll's desire to experience new freedoms through the "evil side of [his] nature" begins as an imposture.[4] The salty potion he concocts causes him "to doff at once the body of the noted professor, and to assume, like a thick cloak, that of

Edward Hyde" (64). Stevenson suggests that identity is a "fleshly vestment" (61) that can be removed in favor of another "hide."

Imposture in *Jekyll and Hyde* is not limited to the supernatural, but also becomes a matter of paperwork. When Jekyll draws a check as part of the payment for running "Juggernaut" (9) over a young girl, he forges Hyde's handwriting: "by sloping my own hand backward, I had supplied my double with a signature" (66). At the end of the novel, however, the tables have turned. Hyde personates Jekyll, taking control of their shared identity. After Jekyll begins to "leap almost without transition" (74) into his "polar twin" (61), Hyde begins to forge Jekyll's handwriting, "scrawling in my own hand blasphemies on the pages of my books" (75). Jekyll becomes a "stranger in [his] own house" (63), having "lost [his] identity beyond redemption" (64). Poole, Jekyll's butler, thinks that his "master's [been] made away with," and wonders: "*who's* in there instead of him" (44). Poole's "theory," *The Century* noted, is that someone has been "personating [Jekyll] with a sort of clumsy diabolism."[5] But this personation involves both the potion *and* the participation of Gabriel Utterson, Jekyll's prying lawyer.

Utterson's unsavory character gradually emerges through his role as the novella's lead detective. He is "the last reputable acquaintance and the last good influence in the lives of down-going men" (7), and later he is "humbled to the dust by the many ill things he had done" (21). Utterson's most outwardly duplicitous act is to ensure that he becomes the inheritor of Jekyll's estate. Carol Margaret Davison argues that Utterson "seems to have a monomania about the will, a signature characteristic of the traditionally excessive gothic hero-villain."[6] Initially, Jekyll's will ensures that "Edward Hyde should step into the said Henry Jekyll's shoes without delay" (14). Jekyll recertifies his instructions to Utterson, his trusted friend: "I wish you to promise me that you will bear with him and get his rights for him" (23). But by the end of the novella, the will has been revised: "in the place of the name of Edward Hyde, the lawyer, with indescribable amazement, read the name of Gabriel John Utterson" (51). In triumph, Utterson remarks: "he must have raged to see himself displaced" (51). Stevenson may have warned readers of Utterson's scheme through the lawyer's surname. Sara Malton observes that "[t]he ultimate positioning of the utterer, the circulator of forgeries, as the proper inheritor in *Jekyll and Hyde* shows how the copy's ascension cannot finally be seen as a triumph, but a miserable loss."[7] Utterson succeeds not only because he allows the full personation of Jekyll to occur, thus ensuring himself the inheritance, but also because he covers up the crime, collecting documentary evidence, and "locking the door of the theater behind [him]" (52).

Contemporary reviewers took issue with the novella's conclusion. *The Athenaeum* noted that Stevenson "overlooked the fact that a man's will does not come into force until he is dead, and . . . the fact that he has not been heard of for three months would not enable his executor to carry out his testamentary directions."[8] Indeed, when Utterson breaks into the laboratory, he observes "the body of man sorely contorted and still twitching . . . and beheld the face of Edward Hyde. He was dressed in clothes far too large for him, clothes of the doctor's bigness" (49). For Utterson to acquire Jekyll's estate, he would have to prove that Jekyll was dead. But only Hyde's body remains. The *Saturday Review* ran a satirical article, featuring characters from the text in court proceedings. Utterson attempts to circumvent the "ambiguous remains of the enigmatic sufferer" and worries that the coroner will hold an inquest "[o]n *him*—on *whom*? That is just what they will insist on knowing."[9] The article taps into the ambiguity of the victim's identity. "If it's *not* Dr. Jekyll," Poole inquires, "where is Dr. Jekyll?"[10] Utterson claims that the dead body is Jekyll "bar none!" because he possesses "documents—holographs every one of them."[11] The authentic handwriting specimens of Jekyll's "full statement," together with Hastie Lanyon's "narrative," offer enough proof of what transpired that Utterson is awarded the estate. This conclusion demonstrates the power of paperwork in determining personal identity. The body is cursory, while cursive is confirmation.

Although Jekyll manages to access his "second self" (67), the split identity can occupy only one body. As the *Dublin Review* observed, "a complete bodily transformation accompanies his change of identity."[12] Jekyll's laboratory is located in an "old dissecting room" (20), but he never succeeds in the "separation of these elements" (61). In *The Picture of Dorian Gray* (1891), Oscar Wilde navigates a similar division, but his interest is in body and soul rather than good and evil. Dorian's portrait becomes an "emblem of conscience" designed "to bear the burden of his shame."[13] As in *Jekyll and Hyde*, personation plays into Wilde's novel. The division of Dorian's body from his soul means that Dorian attains physical permanence, while the portrait ages and decays under the weight of his sins. In a sense, the portrait personates Dorian, while Dorian personates the portrait. Thus, Dorian personates himself, much like the struggle between Jekyll and Hyde. But this identity exchange is not triggered by a potion in a solitary room; it directly involves the participation of Basil Hallward and Lord Henry Wotton, who incorporate themselves into the personation plot. For Kathryn Humphreys, the "interchangeability of character and portrait and of individual qualities between characters set up chains of substitutions that undermine not only the concept of an individuated character but also that of an individuated reader."[14] Acts of absorption and influence in *Dorian Gray* initiate mergers between characters (and the titular picture), with the result that only one character retains his original identity—the novel's ostensible villain, Lord Henry.

During his final brushstrokes, Basil admits: "I have put too much of myself into it" (6). He then remarks that "every portrait that is painted with feeling is a portrait of the artist, not of the sitter" (8). Dorian's portrait, then, consumes Basil's identity. Dorian acts as a seductive succubus of Basil's soul during their first interaction: "When our eyes met, I felt that I was growing pale. A curious sensation of terror came over me. I knew that I had come face to face with some one whose mere personality was so fascinating that, if I allowed it to do so, it would absorb my whole nature, my whole soul, my very art itself" (9). Basil follows through with this absorption, inventing a "new medium for art" that allows him to "recreate life" (12). Like a decadent Victor Frankenstein, however, regret sets in. "There is too much of myself in the thing" (13), he repeats. When Basil finishes the portrait, he seems to acknowledge the splitting of Dorian's identity: "as soon as you are dry, you shall be varnished, and framed, and sent home. Then you can do what you like with yourself" (27). There are now two Dorians, one of which has absorbed Basil's "whole soul" (14). When the corporeal Dorian separates entirely, choosing Lord Henry's company and plunging into a netherworld of sin, Basil experiences a "strange sense of loss" (69). Stabbed by Dorian and dissolved by Alan Campbell, Basil—having increasingly faded from the novel since he reluctantly remitted the portrait—finally disappears. The portrait's personation completes.

Lord Henry's intentions are far more malicious. His attraction to Dorian centers more on Dorian's mind, or the lack thereof. Lord Henry remarks that Dorian "never thinks" (6), suggesting that Dorian's mind is a blank canvas on which Lord Henry can paint his own portrait. Whereas the portrait absorbs Basil, Lord Henry influences Dorian. "[T]o influence a person," Lord Henry warns, "is to give him one's own soul" (19). Although Lord Henry knows that influence is "immoral," causing the subject to be "an echo of some one else's music, an actor of a part that has not been written for him" (19), he continues to spread his philosophical contagion. This influence, initially supplied through indolence and aphorism, impels

Dorian to personate Lord Henry: "There was something terribly enthralling in the exercise of influence. No other activity was like it. To project one's soul into some gracious form, and let it tarry there for a moment" (33). Dorian initially basks in Lord Henry's "fresh influences" (19), but eventually comes to understand the "poisonous theories" (79). Just when Lord Henry begins to lose his hold on Dorian—as the latter's dissipation exceeds that of his most dissolute associates—he sends Dorian a book that reinstalls his authority: "For years, Dorian Gray could not free himself from the influence of this book" (108). Lord Henry's influence severs Dorian from the portrait, and his interest in "vivisecting others" (50) suggests that the operation to separate the conjoined twins was as precise as it was poisonous. As much as Basil brings the portrait to life, Lord Henry creates Dorian: "To a large extent the lad was his own creation," but he errs in being too hasty; his monster is "premature" (51).

The various personations in *Dorian Gray* form a complex structure, resembling an uroboros. The portrait personates Basil; Dorian personates Lord Henry; and Dorian and the portrait personate each other. The result is that Basil and Lord Henry personate each other through their versions of Dorian, which also function as the binary of realism and romanticism that Wilde defines in the novel's preface. This closed circuit unleashes a direct current via Lord Henry's ominous last words: "I don't think there have been such lilacs since the year I met you" (184). The allusion to Walt Whitman's "When Lilacs Last in the Dooryard Bloom'd" (1865) might not only spell Dorian's doom but also indicate that Lord Henry has chosen another victim.[15] The curtain falls on *Dorian Gray* like a Shakespearean tragedy, with murder, suicide, and manslaughter leaving bodies strewn about (or dissolved). But Lord Henry survives. J. Halberstam notes that Lord Henry "revels in the beauty of the superficial" and survives because "he has no conscience."[16] But Wilde may be indicating something more sinister and perhaps more supernatural. Andrew Eastham has read both Lord Henry and Dorian as vampires who practice an aestheticism that "literally embrace[s] the inhuman."[17] Although Lord Henry describes himself as "wrinkled, and worn, and yellow" (181), he never changes, remaining typeset and jaundiced like the book he gives Dorian. Just before he parts with Dorian for the last time, Lord Henry remarks: "You and I are what we are, and will be what we will be" (183). Lord Henry will continue to spread his contagion, personating himself throughout London.

The threat of Lord Henry's survival lies in the potential continuation of his "fascinating, poisonous, delightful theories" (67), which suggests a transition at the *fin de siècle* from a fear of being copied to a fear of being a copy. Bram Stoker's *Dracula* (1897) represents this latter fear through the logic of vampirism. Dracula's relocation from Transylvania to England demonstrates what Stephen Arata has termed "reverse colonization," in which the "'civilized' world is on the point of being overrun by 'primitive' forces."[18] I would like to revise Arata's term to suggest that Stoker also explores "reverse personation," the overwriting of one identity onto others. Well into his stay at Dracula's castle, Jonathan Harker becomes aware of his firm's dangerous client: "This was the being I was helping to transfer to London, where, perhaps, for centuries to come, he might, amongst its teeming millions, satiate his lust for blood, and create a new and ever-widening circle of semi-demons to batten on the helpless."[19] Dracula's plan is not just to invade, conquer, and subjugate, but also to erase human identities and to replace them with his vampire prototype.

The Transylvanian setting reflects the repetitive nature of Dracula's vampirism. As Harker travels eastward, he describes the feeling of "simply going over and over the same ground again" (19). Dracula first appears to Harker "clad in black from head to foot, without a single speck of color about him anywhere" (21). He is the reverse of Anne Catherick in *The Woman in White*, whose complete whiteness allows the villains to write Laura Fairlie's identity onto to her. Dracula is all text, his blood the ink that he uses to inject his own identity into other subjects.[20] That Dracula neither owns a mirror nor produces a reflection might indicate that he already sees himself mirrored in his victims. But Dracula's personation plot is not just supernatural; he also practices traditional means of assuming identities. Harker, having already witnessed Dracula shuffle like a lizard down the castle wall, is perhaps most disturbed by his host's more natural maneuver: "It was a new shock to me to find that he had on the suit of clothes which I had worn whilst travelling here. . . . [H]e will allow others to see me, as they think, so that he may both leave evidence that I have been seen in the towns or villages posting my own letters, and that any wickedness which he may do shall by the local people be attributed to me" (47). This scene demonstrates that Dracula can act as a villain in a sensation novel, with sartorial rather than supernatural schemes.

Dracula thereafter relies on paranormal plots to spread his terror, taking the form of animals, dispersing as mist, and toying with his zoophagous protégé Renfield. When he feeds on Lucy Westenra, she begins to replicate her attacker. Dr. Seward observes her "awful, waxen pallor" (124), but when Lucy begins to feed on children as the "bloofer lady," she transforms into a "dark-haired woman" (187). The vampire hunters make a distinction between the "true Lucy" (269) and the "foul Thing which had taken Lucy's shape" (190). Seward seems to suggest that a personation has transpired, describing the vampire as a "devilish mockery" (190). Similarly, Mina begins to transform into Dracula's counterpart after he forces her into his "Vampire baptism" (315). Harker remarks that "she did not seem the same woman" (271), and Seward records that he "can see the characteristics of the vampire coming in her face" (280). Mina and Dracula become linked both mentally—via Van Helsing's hypnotism—and physically, bearing matching forehead scars, which act as corporeal signifiers for vampirism. "It is that we become as him" (209), Van Helsing warns. Dracula's victims gradually lose their identities as they personate their assailant.

The main weapon against Dracula—as crosses, wafers, garlic, and hypnotism play secondary roles—is the textual evidence that the group builds. The double meaning of Mina as a "Recording Angel" (284) indicates, on the one hand, that her body becomes a record of vampiric taint. But on the other hand, she records and re-records all of the documents that prove Dracula's crimes. Although Dracula burns whatever paperwork he can, Mina has been using a "manifold" to take "three copies of the diary, just as I had done with all the rest" (198). Jennifer Wicke has read *Dracula* as staging "the collision of ancient mythologies with contemporary modes of production."[21] Mina's transcribing and copying, together with the novel's other technologies of mass production, produce a "social force most analogous to Count Dracula's."[22] The vampire hunters fight fire with fire. Combatting vampire blood with a "brave man's blood" (136) fails, but combatting vampire blood with a "brave and gallant" (326) woman's ink succeeds. However paradoxically, mass media arrests Dracula's reverse personation. The collection of inauthentic documents that supply "no proofs" (326) keep the "whirl and rush of humanity" (26) authentic.

Notes

Introduction

1. "Mistaken Identity: A Marvellously Strange Case," *Bangor Whig* 17, no. 66 (8 February 1849): 4. The young man correctly, though hesitantly, chose Rowland's bedroom in the house. He was also able to recall parts of a "negro vision" and to remember a trip he made to Harmony, Maine, with James Hause to sell oxen (4).

2. "Mistaken," *Bangor*, 4.

3. "Cases of Mistaken Identity," *Dublin University Magazine* 498, no. 83 (June 1874): 738.

4. "A Strange Case—A Family Deceived as to the Identity of a Son and Brother," *Saturday Evening Post* 28 (3 February 1849): 2.

5. "Mistaken," *Bangor*, 4.

6. "Cases," *Dublin*, 738.

7. "Cases," *Dublin*, 738.

8. "Cases," *Dublin*, 738.

9. "Cases," *Dublin*, 740.

10. Allan McLane Hamilton and Lawrence Godkin, *A System of Legal Medicine*, vol. 1 (New York: E. B. Treat, 1894), 222.

11. "Cases," *Dublin*, 736. Edward Higgs notes that Arthur Orton's body "became a site for contestation over identification" (*Identifying the English: A History of Personal Identification 1500 to the Present* [London: Continuum, 2011], 30). Orton, as David Wayne Thomas observes, also became a "kind of literary object" (*Cultivating Victorians: Liberal Culture and the Aesthetic* [Philadelphia: University of Pennsylvania Press, 2004], 82). Rebecca Stern similarly observes that Arthur Orton quite literally "t[ook] a page out of a Victorian novel" (*Home Economics: Domestic Fraud in Victorian England* [Columbus: The Ohio State University Press, 2008], 19, 34). Lord Chief Justice Alexander Cockburn, who read *Aurora Floyd* while preparing his closing remarks, having been sent a copy of the novel by Braddon herself, diagnosed the body as an "embarrassingly ambiguous site," and instead focused on

a "discursive construction of the soul" (Sara Murphy, "'No Two Men Were Ever Alike Within': The Tichborne Trial, The Lord Chief Justice, and the Narration of Identity," *Law, Culture and the Humanities* 13, no. 2 [2017]: 259, 260).

12. According to Rebecca Stern, "[t]he Claimant's body was . . . a source of sensational thrill," as various marks and measures, including the infamous "malformation," became "hotly contested points of evidence" (*Home*, 44). Charles Reade laid out his own case against Orton, much of which hinged on physical discrepancies. Reade admits that both Tichborne and Orton were proved to be "in-kneed," but other bodily comparisons presented a "falling off in the evidence" ("The Doctrine of Coincidences," in *Readiana: Comments on Current Events* [London: Chatto and Windus, 1883], 88).

13. Pamela K. Gilbert, *Victorian Skin: Surface, Self, History* (Ithaca, NY: Cornell University Press, 2019), 1.

14. Although attention to the materiality of identity began far earlier than the mid–nineteenth century, I argue that this type of corporeal forensics reached its height during the decades that the sensation novel developed and flourished. One might trace this development through Dickens's *Pickwick Papers* (1836–37), in which Pickwick must "sit[] for [his] portrait" in prison so that the turnkeys, who take only a mental image of his likeness, "might know prisoners from visitors" (*The Posthumous Papers of the Pickwick Club*, vol. 1 [London: Chapman and Hall, 1837], 433–434).

15. Rebecca Stern, "'Personation' and 'Good Marking-Ink': Sanity, Performativity, and Biology in Victorian Sensation Fiction," *Nineteenth-Century Studies* 14 (2000): 35.

16. Anna Maria Jones has argued that one of the "problems" sensation novels pose is that they "invite [readers] to consider the process of their own subject formation," by "theorizing 'problematic' versions of subjectivity" (*Problem Novels: Victorian Fiction Theorizes the Sensational Self* [Columbus: The Ohio State University Press, 2007], 6, 15).

17. "Personate" is the older and more accurate word for identity fraud than "impersonate," which is more widely used today. As a verb, the former is defined as "[t]o assume the person or character of (another person), *esp.* for fraudulent purposes; to pretend to be; to act the part of" (OED).

18. In the 1880s, Alphonse Bertillon developed the "signaletic system" of anthropometry, which consisted of three categories of corporeal study: anthropometrical, descriptive, and pathological, with the ear representing "the jewel of [his] morphological vocabulary" (Simon A. Cole, *Suspect Identities: A History of Fingerprinting and Criminal Identification* [Cambridge, MA: Harvard University Press, 2001], 40). "[S]ignalment," Bertillon boasted, "is the instrument, by excellence, . . . which necessarily implies the *proof of identity*" (*Signaletic Instructions* [Chicago: The Werner Company, 1896], 11). According to Simon A. Cole, anthropometry "reduced the

body to language and then to code," ensuring that the individual subject "began and ended at its skin and bones" (*Suspect*, 48, 53).

19. William A. Cohen examines "embodied experience," which he understands through materialist efforts "to locate a unique essence of the human in the physical existence of the body" (*Embodied: Victorian Literature and the Senses* [Minneapolis: University of Minnesota Press, 2009], xi). Embodiment, Cohen argues, "came to be the untranscendable horizon of the human" (xii). During debates over the constitution of subjectivity, "the material ultimately prevails," with the result that the body functions as a "concrete means of giving form to intangible thoughts and feelings" (16, 27).

20. Dallas Liddle notes that sensation novels "implied that both personal and class identity . . . were fluid and unstable rather than secure, and thus potentially subject to manipulation, misrepresentation, and outright theft" (*The Dynamics of Genre: Journalism and the Practice of Literature in Mid-Victorian Britain* [Charlottesville: University of Virginia Press, 2009], 133).

21. According to Kelly A. Gates, "key nineteenth-century developments in identification systems evidence a perceived need to use the body itself as a marker of identity at the time of modern state expansion" ("Biometrics and Post-9/11 Technologies," *Social Text* 83 [2005]: 39).

22. One of the first ways that the body was used as a marker for personal identity was through the pseudo-scientific theories of physiognomy and phrenology. Joseph Pugliese argues that these theories "must be seen as proto-biometric technologies, as they are fundamentally concerned with the measurement, calibration, classification, and identification of bodily and behavioral features" (*Biometrics: Bodies, Technologies, Biopolitics* [New York: Routledge, 2010], 26). Johann Kaspar Lavater first outlined his theories on physiognomy in 1775, claiming that "[a]ll countenances, all forms, all created beings, are not only different from each other in their classes, races, and kinds, but are also individually distinct" (*Physiognomy* [London: Cowie, Low, and Co., 1826], 3). Theories of phrenology followed in the wake of Lavater's physiognomy and were inspired by Franz Joseph Gall's pioneering work on brain localization in the late eighteenth century. According to George Henry Lewes, Gall "rescued the problem of mental functions from Metaphysics and made it one of Biology" (*The History of Philosophy from Thales to Comte*, vol. 2 [London: Longmans, Green, and Co., 1867], 407).

23. In the early nineteenth century, Charles Bell and François Magendie simultaneously determined the cerebral division between sensory and motor nerves, inaugurating a "modern view of the brain" (Gilbert, *Victorian*, 35–36). As Robert M. Young explains, the mind "ceased to be viewed as an isolated substance," and became a "biological science concerned with an important function of the organism" (*Mind, Brain, and Adaptation in the Nineteenth Century* [Oxford: Oxford University Press, 1990], 7). Jenny Bourne Taylor and Sally Shuttleworth similarly note that mental

physiology "aimed to wrest away" questions of the self "from the abstract realm of metaphysics, and to subject them to empirical criteria and practical application based on the study of physiology" (Introduction, *Embodied Selves: An Anthology of Psychological Texts 1830–1890* [Oxford: Clarendon Press, 1998], xiv). For Anne Stiles, Victorian advances in brain science were controversial because they "challenged the possibility of free will or an extra-corporeal soul" (*Popular Fiction and Brain Science in the Late Nineteenth Century* [Cambridge: Cambridge University Press, 2012], 2).

24. Peter Garratt, *Victorian Empiricism: Self, Knowledge, and Reality in Ruskin, Bain, Lewes, Spencer, and George Eliot* (Madison, NJ: Fairleigh Dickinson University Press, 2010), 18.

25. In 1859, Karl Marx posited a materialist model of personal identity. "Just as our opinion of an individual is not based on what he thinks of himself," Marx writes, "so can we not judge of such a period of transformation by its own consciousness; on the contrary, this consciousness must rather be explained from the contradictions of material life, from the existing conflict between the social forces of production and the relations of production" (*A Contribution to the Critique of Political Economy* [Chicago: Charles H. Kerr & Company, 1904], 12). Marx's earlier comments in *The German Ideology* (1846) also center on personal identity. "As individuals express their life," he explains, "so they are. What they are, therefore, coincides with their production, both with *what* they produce and with *how* they produce" (ed. C. J. Arthur [New York: International Publishers, 1970], 42).

26. Cohen, *Embodied*, 1. By the nineteenth century, as Simon A. Cole observes, "[t]he informal system of personal acquaintance and collective memory began to collapse" (*Suspect*, 8). Population increases that amassed primarily in cities created the potential for corporeal duplication. Between 1751 and 1851, the urban population grew from one-quarter to one-half. By 1901, three-quarters of the population amassed in urban centers (Robert Woods, *The Demography of Victorian England and Wales* [Cambridge: Cambridge University Press, 2000], 360). In 1861, perhaps not coincidentally the same year as a particularly influential census, an essay in Charles Dickens's *All the Year Round* tackled the subject of "striking likenesses," and reminded readers that "[n]ature has patterns which she sometimes repeats in her work; jacquard looms of her own, where she weaves two or three pieces of humanity, varied perhaps in material and color, but of identical style and arrangement—pieces so much alike, indeed, they can hardly be known apart" ("Striking Likenesses," *All the Year Round* 6, no. 127 [28 September 1861]: 19).

27. Jane Caplan and John Torpey observe "the drift toward techniques of identification anchored in the body itself," in which "[w]riting on the body gave way to reading off it" ("Introduction," in *Documenting Individual Identity: The Development of State Practices in the Modern World*, ed. Jane Caplan and John Torpey [Princeton, NJ: Princeton University Press, 2001], 12, 8). Jeremy Bentham marks a potential starting point for legal attention to corporeal identity. "To facilitate the [r]ecognition and the finding of individuals," Bentham suggested tattooing names

upon bodies, the outcome of which "would be a new spring for morality, a new source of power for the laws, an almost infallible precaution against a multitude of offences, especially against every kind of fraud in which confidence is requisite for success" (*Principles of Penal Law*, in *The Works of Jeremy Bentham*, part II [Edinburgh: William Tait, 1838], 557).

28. Étienne Balibar, *Identity and Difference: John Locke and the Invention of Consciousness*, ed. Stella Sandford (London: Verso, 2013), 1. Locke added the chapter to the second edition of *An Essay Concerning Human Understanding* (1694). Most models of personal identity begin with Locke, for whom "consciousness and only consciousness matters" (Raymond Martin and John Barresi, *Naturalization of the Soul: Self and Personal Identity in the Eighteenth Century* [London: Routledge, 2000], 16). Locke differentiates between the "human" or "man" and the "person," the former defined by the physical body, while the latter is the "thinking intelligent being, that has reason and reflection, and can consider itself as itself . . . only by that consciousness which is inseparable from thinking, and . . . essential to it" (*An Essay Concerning Human Understanding* [Philadelphia: Kay & Troutman, 1849], 210). Thus, personal identity consists only of the continuity of consciousness that "can be extended backwards to any past action or thought" (210). Locke's most persistent eighteenth-century critic was David Hume, who introduced the "bundle" theory of personal identity, which posits that "self or person is not any one impression, but that to which our several impressions and ideas are suppos'd to have reference" (*A Treatise of Human Nature*, vol. 1 [London: Longmans, Green, and Co., 1878], 533). Personal identity is "nothing but a bundle or collection of different perceptions, which succeed each other with an inconceivable rapidity, and are in a perpetual flux and movement" (534). When one sleeps or dies, these impressions cease, and thus one "may truly be said not to exist" (534). Discrete personal identity theory largely died out in the Victorian period and was "rediscovered and debated anew" in the twentieth century (Martin and Barresi, *Naturalization*, xi).

29. What I term "the self," Ronald R. Thomas terms "character," which is "the romantic-autonomous individual of a revolutionary period" (*Detective Fiction and the Rise of Forensic Science* [Cambridge: Cambridge University Press, 1999], 11). "Identity," in contrast is "the alienated, bourgeois agent of the state in the industrial and post-industrial age of capital" (11). In an 1889 story, titled "A Stolen Identity," Henry North usefully differentiates between these terms. Aldon Stassart, through the mesmeric power of a Japanese doctor, switches souls with his romantic rival, Stanton Kingsford. North distinguishes between a "man's self—his ego, his psychical side" and the body, which he associates with identity (*Belgravia* 69 [July 1889]: 46).

30. Thomas, *Detective*, 63; Ronald R. Thomas, "Wilkie Collins and the Sensation Novel," in *The Columbia History of the British Novel*, ed. John Richetti (New York: Columbia University Press, 1994), 501.

31. Simon A. Cole remarks that a "wide variety of new technologies" in twenty-first-century biometrics . . . all point toward the demise of the nineteenth-century

notion of the body as solid, stable entity and the advent of some new conception of bodies as mutable and flexible" (*Suspect*, 310).

32. J. Hillis Miller, *Victorian Subjects* (Durham, NC: Duke University Press, 1991), vii.

33. Miller, *Victorian*, viii.

34. Miller, *Victorian*, viii.

35. Jacques Derrida, "Structure, Sign and Play in the Discourse of the Human Sciences," in *Writing and Difference*, trans. Alan Bass (Chicago: University of Chicago Press, 1978), 279.

36. Kelly Hurley, *The Gothic Body: Sexuality, Materialism and Degeneration at the* Fin de Siècle (Cambridge: Cambridge University Press, 1996), 3. Hurley examines a form of "grotesque realism" in her study of the *fin-de-siècle* Gothic, which "offers the spectacle of a body metamorphic and undifferentiated" (3). Hurley's concept of the abhuman emerges from the Gothic's "relentless destruction of 'the human' " that then heralds its "violent reconstitution" (3, 4).

37. Stern, "Personation," 39.

38. Henry Mansel, "Sensation Novels," *Quarterly Review* 113 (April 1863): 489.

39. Susan D. Bernstein observes that natural selection "hinges on categorical uncertainty," and that sensation fiction "operates as a sign for this edginess" ("Ape Anxiety: Sensation Fiction, Evolution, and the Genre Question," *Journal of Victorian Culture* 6, no. 2 [January 2001]: 251–52). Darwin's *On the Origin of Species* was published 24 November 1859, while Collins's *The Woman in White* began its serial run two days later. Margot Norris observes that "Darwin's theories are so immense that they strike at the most fundamental oppositions at the heart of Western culture," which include "[t]he abolition of the subject and the consequent collapse of the intentional fallacy in the study of Nature" (*Beasts of the Modern Imagination* [Baltimore: Johns Hopkins University Press, 1985], 37, 32). George Levine similarly notes that Darwinian evolution "thrust the human into nature and time, and subjected it to the same dispassionate and material investigations hitherto reserved for rocks and stars" (*Darwin and the Novelists: Patterns of Science in Victorian Fiction* [Chicago: University of Chicago Press, 1991], 1). At the very same time that criminologists formed identity through corporeal particularities, evolution emphasized a world in which matter was always in flux. Jenny Bourne Taylor notes sensation fiction's interest in the Darwinian "process of continual transformation and exchange" (*In the Secret Theatre of Home: Wilkie Collins, Sensation Narrative, and Nineteenth-Century Psychology* [London: Routledge, 1988], 20). For Kelly Hurley, "Darwinism opened up a space wherein hitherto unthinkable morphic structures could emerge" (*Gothic*, 7). And Cannon Schmitt notes that evolution promotes a "chance-driven, constantly shifting scene of competition" ("Evolution and Victorian Fiction," in *Evolution and Victorian Culture*, ed. Bernard Lightman and Bennett Zon [Cambridge: Cambridge University Press, 2014], 20).

40. Nicholas Daly, *Sensation and Modernity in the 1860s* (Cambridge: Cambridge University Press, 2009), 10.

41. Norris, *Beasts*, 37.

42. Andrew Radford, *Sensation Fiction* (New York: Palgrave Macmillan, 2009), 65.

43. Sean Grass, *The Commodification of Identity in Victorian Narrative: Autobiography, Sensation, and the Literary Marketplace* (Cambridge: Cambridge University Press, 2019), 10, 7.

44. Kylee-Anne Hingston's work on "slippery," "illusory" bodies in sensation novels comes closest to the aims of the present study. According to Hingston, sensation fiction was "inextricably related to identity and the body," and Victorian criticism on the genre "connected anxieties about the body to fears about the instability of social identity" ("'Skins to Jump into': The Slipperiness of Identity and the Body in Wilkie Collins's *No Name*," *Victorian Literature and Culture* 40 [2012]: 117). Pamela K. Gilbert studies corporeality as a site of dynamic cultural engagement, arguing that the body is a "text in which th[e] drama of colliding and blending surfaces is written and read" (*Disease, Desire, and the Body in Victorian Women's Popular Novels* [Cambridge: Cambridge University Press, 1997], 2). At the same time, the body "practices and signifies identity," performing as "the fundamental trope of human experience" (15). The sensation novel is "particularly concerned with violation of the domestic body," but the novels themselves also fixate on women's bodies, which are "defined by degrees of openness and contamination" (4, 13). The contamination of texts implies the simultaneous "disintegration of the physical and social body," with the result that the body becomes a "discursive" site, "into which collapses other discourses—legal, political, moral, etc." (18, 47). Laurie Garrison examines the way that Victorian reviewers "theorize[d] the effects of the sensation novel in scientific, specifically physiological terms" (*Science, Sexuality and Sensation Novels: Pleasures of the Senses* [London: Palgrave Macmillan, 2011], xii). For Garrison, the sensation novel not only "powerfully reinvigorated the writing of fiction," but also "inspired a new form of reading, one that depended first on the physical effects it inspired in the reader and secondly on the psychological effects that occurred as a result of this form of reading" (184, xii). Laurence Talairach similarly examines Victorian materialism, noting that "advances of science from mid-century onwards could provide brand new plot devices for novelists and readers in search of more sensational thrills" (*Wilkie Collins, Medicine, and the Gothic* [Cardiff: University of Wales Press, 2009], 2). The development of mental physiology, which "increasingly constructed the mind in its most materialistic aspect," served to "reduce[] man to 'matter'" (4, 5).

45. Gilbert, *Victorian*, 101.

46. Gilbert, *Victorian*, 22.

47. "Novels Past and Present," *Saturday Review* 21, no. 546 (14 April 1866): 439.

48. I count well over 150 plots that concern identity in Andrew Maunder's bibliography of sensation fiction (*Varieties of Women's Sensation Fiction: 1855–1890*, vol. 1 [London: Pickering & Chatto, 2004], 279–392). And this is not to mention plots about forgery or other types of fraud.

49. Winifred Hughes was the first modern critic to note sensation fiction's "recurrent preoccupation with the loss or duplication of identity" (*The Maniac in the Cellar: Sensation Novels of the 1860s* [Princeton, NJ: Princeton University Press, 1980], 21). Patrick Brantlinger subsequently analyzed the phenomenon of "character splitting" in the genre, which "hark[s] back to the patterns of doubling" in early Gothic novels ("What is 'Sensational' about the 'Sensation Novel'?" *Nineteenth-Century Fiction* 37 [June 1982]: 23–24). Doubling in the realist novel, for Brantlinger, remains metaphoric, while it takes on a "much more literal expression" in sensation novels (24).

50. Jonathan Loesberg, "The Ideology of Narrative Form in Sensation Fiction," *Representations* 13 (Winter 1986): 117.

51. Loesberg, "Ideology," 134. Peter Stallybrass and Allon White's work on transgression derives from their "intellectual curiosity about the production of identity and status through a repudiation of the 'low'" (*The Politics and Poetics of Transgression* [Ithaca, NY: Cornell University Press, 1986], ix). Engaging Mikhail Bakhtin's carnivalesque, Stallybrass and White seek to understand how the "top" performatively rejects the "bottom" but ultimately discover that it "*includes* that low symbolically, as a primary eroticized constituent of its own fantasy life" (3, 5). Winifred Hughes has argued that the sensation novel was "drawn to the borderlands; it compulsively blurred and transgressed boundaries and knocked down established barriers" ("The Sensation Novel," in *A Companion to the Victorian Novel*, ed. Patrick Brantlinger and William B. Thesing [Malden, MA: Wiley-Blackwell, 2002], 264).

52. Loesberg, "Ideology," 117. In his most tenuous claim, Loesberg remarks that sensation fiction's interest in identity manifests in "its legal and class aspects rather than in its psychological aspect" (117). I would counter that the identity exchange in Dickens's *A Tale of Two Cities* (1859), surely among Loesberg's "other works of fiction" (117), is far more legal than psychological.

53. Anxieties over the sensation novel were often based on its transgressions of class boundaries. In 1866, the *Westminster Review* claimed that "we now have a Sensation Mania," which was an "epidemic . . . [but] has lately changed into an endemic. Its virus is spreading in all directions, from the penny journal to the shilling magazine, and from the shilling magazine to the thirty shillings volume" ("Belles Lettres," *Westminster Review* 86 [July 1866]: 126). Another 1866 reviewer similarly conflated popularity with pathology, noting that "[t]wenty years ago stories of this kind were only to be found in magazines which circulated in a lower stratum of society, but they have gradually crept upwards" ("A Casual Acquaintance," *Times* 25,462 [3 April 1866]: 4).

54. Laura Fairlie's "loss of legal identity," for Loesberg, "entails loss of class identity, which in turn leads to a frightening immersion in a world without common boundaries" ("Ideology," 119). I argue, conversely, that the "essentially legal status" of Laura's identity should draw our attention back to the instability of her body, which allowed the personation plot to commence in the first place. Andrew Rad-

ford argues that Collins's novels, "[r]ather than seeking to enshrine traditional class boundaries, . . . show that those boundaries have already been reconfigured through financial means" (*Victorian*, 80). Walter Hartright, trained as an art teacher, finishes the novel "situated within the gentry and father to the heir of Limmeridge estate" (80). Mariaconcetta Costantini similarly studies Hartright's ascension to speculate on "the loss of identity resulting from the collapse of class barriers. Sensation fiction encodes these fears in its obsessive handling of plots of lost identity" ("Sensation, Class and the Rising Professionals," in *The Cambridge Companion to Sensation Fiction*, ed. Andrew Mangham [Cambridge: Cambridge University Press, 2013], 100). In this sense, Hartright "violates various boundaries in the course of the narration," becoming a principal actor in the novel's drama of identity fraud (*Sensation and Professionalism in the Victorian Novel* [Bern: Peter Lang, 2014], 16, 165).

55. Tara MacDonald takes issue with Loesberg's claims: "While class identity may indeed motivate the majority of sensation plots, most novels interrogate a variety of identity categories" ("Sensation Fiction, Gender, and Identity," in *The Cambridge Companion to Sensation Fiction*, ed. Andrew Mangham [Cambridge: Cambridge University Press, 2013], 129). MacDonald emphasizes sensation fiction's interest in gender identity and argues that false identities for women characters not only "revel possibilities of empowerment" but also are "often the result of a desperate need for concealment, a need that lays bare women's precarious social position" (128).

56. Taylor, *Secret*, 1.

57. Kathleen Tillotson, "Introduction: The Lighter Reading of the Eighteen-Sixties," in *The Woman in White*, by Wilkie Collins (Boston: Houghton, 1969), xv; Taylor, *Secret*, 7. Alexander Welsh's study of blackmail—the threat of exposing secrets—centers on the observation that Victorian novels prefigured, if not invented, the modern understanding of the crime. Victorians were "increasingly dependent on information," and the "rise of publicity" resulted in a "real or imagined need for secrecy" (*George Eliot and Blackmail* [Cambridge, MA: Harvard University Press, 1985], vi). Welsh reads blackmail plots as "the translation of reputation into information" and notes that Braddon's *Lady Audley's Secret* is a "story in which the secrets of the past threaten the tranquility of the present" (22).

58. Taylor, *Secret*, 8.

59. Daly, *Sensation*, 4, 7. Daly elsewhere examines how the sensation novel contributed to industrial modernity through "the creation of mechanic readers" (*Literature, Technology, and Modernity, 1860–2000* [Cambridge: Cambridge University Press, 2004], 7). In fact, sensation fiction "acclimatize[s] its readers to railway time and space" through the "deployment of nervousness" (7). Sensational affect "provides a species of temporal training," which serves to "synchronize[] its readers with industrial modernity" (37). Natalie Houston similarly observes that sensation novels "reflect an increasing instability in the concepts of privacy and personal identity in a newly urban and technological society" (Introduction, *Lady Audley's Secret* [Peterborough, Ontario: Broadview Press, 2003], 29).

60. Daly, *Sensation*, 37.
61. Thomas, *Detective*, 17.
62. Thomas, *Detective*, 59.
63. Thomas, *Detective*, 63.
64. Thomas, *Detective*, 60.
65. Mary Elizabeth Braddon, *Lady Audley's Secret*, ed. Lyn Pykett (Oxford: Oxford University Press, 2012), 331.
66. Kylee-Anne Hingston studies how "medicine and literature overwhelmingly conflated text and body" (*Articulating Bodies: The Narrative Form of Disability and Illness in Victorian Fiction* [Liverpool: Liverpool University Press, 2019], 2). Both representations of disabled bodies and the narrative structures of novels, Hingston argues, reflect "the Victorian sense of instability" (8). Narrative focalization, in particular, "articulates bodies," which, in the case of sensation fiction, "enact[s] the anxiety with which Victorians were determining the body's connection to identity and illustrate[s] how that connection threatened established views of normalcy" (82).
67. Grass, *Commodification*, 6.
68. Grass, *Commodification*, 6.
69. Grass, *Commodification*, 7.
70. Grass, *Commodification*, 13.
71. Grass, *Commodification*, 71, 74.
72. Grass, *Commodification*, 75.
73. Grass, *Commodification*, 112, 182.
74. Sara Malton reads forgery, "an act of intensely dangerous social and economic disruption," as one of the primary outcomes of the credit economy (*Forgery in Nineteenth-Century Literature and Culture: Fictions of Finance from Dickens to Wilde* [New York: Palgrave Macmillan, 2009], 2). Malton highlights the increase in forgery during the Restriction Period (1797–1821), examining the cultural anxiety over "the susceptibility of the economic health of both the state and individual" (4). New possibilities for "self-making" led to "concerns about the legibility of an individual's moral and economic legitimacy" (2, 6). Forgery is thus "centrally implicated in changing ideas of selfhood," becoming "the emblem of the disruption of social and political order and representative of the potential violation of authorized origins" (8, 7).
75. In *Lady Audley's Secret*, for example, Helen Talboys's bodily personation of Matilda Plowson precedes—and indeed permits—her many documentary frauds. And Isabel Vane's reemergence as Madame Vine in Ellen Wood's *East Lynne* depends on facial disfigurement, a limp, a lisp, and a pair of "disfiguring green spectacles" (ed. Elisabeth Jay [Oxford: Oxford University Press, 2008], 389).
76. The institution of the police force in 1829, together with the formation of the detective police in 1842, "focused attention on issues of law enforcement and the tracking, capture, and taxonomy of the criminal" (Andrew Maunder and Grace Moore, Introduction, *Victorian Crime, Madness, and Sensation* [Aldershot,

Hampshire, UK: Ashgate, 2004], 1). The Police Act of 1856 further mobilized a nationwide corps that sought to purify the social body by identifying criminal bodies.

77. James Appleton Morgan, "Personal Identity," *Sanitarian* 5, no. 46 (January 1877): 22.

78. Morgan, "Personal," 26.

79. Morgan, "Personal," 26.

80. Francis Wharton, *A Treatise on the Law of Evidence in Criminal Issues* (Philadelphia: Kay and Brother, 1880), 675–76.

81. Robert Travers, "Essay on Personal Identity, and its Proof from Physical Signs," *Dublin Quarterly Journal of Medical Science* 52 (1871): 377.

82. Travers, "Essay," 382.

83. Travers, "Essay," 382. In an 1874 pamphlet, Aubrey Moriarty attempted to outline the concept of "disputed identity" as it played out in the court system. Moriarty was particularly interested in the crime of personation, "a subject of considerable difficulty" (*On Personation and Disputed Identity, and Their Tests* [London: Stevens and Haynes, 1873], 3). Although the "combination" of physical and memorial signs often provides enough evidence to identify impostors, this method is far from foolproof, since "no amount of resemblance, and hardly any amount of similitudes in combination, can be safely received as proofs of identity" (20).

84. Higgs, *Identifying*, 23.

85. In "The Organ of Mind" (1879), David Ferrier makes several important distinctions that help to elucidate the mind/body dilemma that enraptured Victorian science. Ferrier emphasizes the "sentiment of hostility" between physiologists and psychologists, and then differentiates between "the psychologist, alienist, and physiologist," who have "for their substratum a single organ" (*Princeton Review* 55 [1879]: 98). Alienism, which Ferrier also refers to as "medical psychology," bridges "subjective" psychology and "objective" physiology (99). Ferrier subsequently constructs a materialist model of personal identity, arguing that "every thing which forms a part of our subjectivity must be represented in the cerebral hemispheres" (112).

86. Laurence Talairach-Vielmas, "Sensation Fiction: A Peep Behind the Veil," in *The Victorian Gothic: An Edinburgh Companion*, ed. Andrew Smith and William Hughes (Edinburgh: Edinburgh University Press, 2012), 30.

87. Malton, *Forgery*, 151.

88. In 1879, John J. Reese concluded that "[p]*hotographs* and other *portraits* of the suspected person are sometimes useful aids in the identification of the living as well as of the dead" ("The Personal Identity of the Living and the Dead," *Medical Record* 15, no. 19 [10 May 1879]: 434).

89. Charles Neaves's "How to Make a Novel. A Sensational Song" instructs readers to "Choose adventures strange / Of fraud and personation" (in *Songs and Verses: Social and Scientific* [Edinburgh: William Blackwood and Sons, 1869], 83).

90. "Henry Dunbar," *Saturday Review* 18, no. 454 (9 July 1864): 64; "Sir Jasper's Tenant," *Saturday Review* 20, no. 521 (21 October 1865): 521. Both big-

amy and "near-bigamy," Maia McAleavey observes, "confound the Victorian novel's tendency to depict personal identity as a single, coherent narrative, concluding in marriage or death" (*The Bigamy Plot: Sensation and Convention in the Victorian Novel* [Cambridge: Cambridge University Press, 2015], 4). The act of fraudulently repeating the civil contract of marriage, resembling a form of forgery, took on a new textual life in the 1860s, often lifted from actual cases, such as the Yelverton trial.

91. "Casual," *Times*, 4.

92. "Personation," *Spectator* 37, no. 1875 (4 June 1864): 656.

93. "Personation," *Spectator*, 656.

94. For several prominent sensation writers, this condemnation of imposture was profoundly hypocritical. Charles Dickens used variations of the surname Tringham to conceal his relationship with Ellen Ternan, whom he met in 1857. Mary Elizabeth Braddon used the stage name Mary Seyton from the ages of seventeen to twenty-five, the point at which she became a professional writer. Braddon also used the pseudonyms Lady Caroline Lascelles and Babington White, and faced accusations of plagiarism under the latter. Hall Caine, author of the enormously popular novel *A Son of Hagar* (1886), falsified his son's birth register, fraudulently recording that he was married to "Mary Alice Caine." Wilkie Collins fraudulently registered his son, William Charles Collins, under the surname Dawson in February 1875. Collins's three children with Martha Rudd lived under the surname Dawson their entire lives, though the daughters were never registered.

95. The development of fingerprinting in the late nineteenth century "embedded firmly within our culture the notion that personhood is biological" (Cole, *Suspect*, 5). As Jane Caplan observes, the fingerprint became "the unofficial emblem of modern identity culture" ("This or That Particular Person: Protocols of Identity in Nineteenth-Century Europe," in *Documenting Individual Identity: The Development of State Practices in the Modern World*, ed. Jane Caplan and John Torpey [Princeton, NJ: Princeton University Press, 2001], 53). In 1891, Francis Galton, the technology's leading advocate, observed that "every one bears on his body a visible token of identity which has the unique value of persisting throughout his whole life" ("Identification by Finger-Tips," *The Nineteenth Century: A Monthly Review* 30, no. 174 [August 1891]: 303). This "token of identity" could "settle questions of personation" and apprehend the "alien scoundrel from foreign parts [who] may assert himself to be the long lost right claimant to an estate" (303–304).

96. Anne-Marie Beller, "Sensation Fiction in the 1850s," in *The Cambridge Companion to Sensation Fiction*, ed. Andrew Mangham (Cambridge: Cambridge University Press, 2013), 8.

97. As John Cyril Barton and Jennifer Phegley have noted, sensation "cross-pollinated over the long nineteenth century through transatlantic exchanges" that "developed in a reciprocal relation" (Introduction, *Transatlantic Sensations*, ed. Jennifer, Phegley, John Cyril Barton, and Kristin N. Huston [Burlington, VT: Ashgate, 2012], 13, 16). The chronological bookends for the genre have also

widened. For Alberto Gabriele, "sensationalism becomes a constant transhistorical presence, a trope of the emergence of modernity, which can be charted over a very long period" ("Transnational Currents, Intermedial Trajectories—A Global Nineteenth-Century Approach," in *Sensationalism and the Genealogy of Modernity: A Global Nineteenth-Century Perspective*, ed. Alberto Gabriele [New York: Palgrave Macmillan, 2017], 4). David S. Reynolds even claims that "[s]ensationalism is as old as literature itself" (Preface, *Transatlantic Sensations*, ed. Jennifer Phegley, John Cyril Barton, and Kristin N. Huston [Burlington, VT: Ashgate, 2012], xiii).

98. In 1868, George Augustus Sala, frequent contributor to *Household Words* and *All the Year Round*, wrote that Dickens is "perhaps the most thoroughly, and has been from the very outset of his career the most persistently 'sensational' writer of the age" ("On the 'Sensational' in Literature and Art," *Belgravia* 4 [February 1868]: 454. Anne-Marie Beller notes that Dickens "provided a blueprint for sensationalizing everyday life and domestic relations" ("Sensation," 9).

Chapter 1

1. A. T. Thomson, *Lectures on Medical Jurisprudence*, *The Lancet* 1 (26 November 1836): 315.

2. François Crouzet, *The Victorian Economy*, trans. Anthony Forster (London: Routledge, 1982), 190.

3. Thomas Richards, *The Commodity Culture of Victorian England: Advertising and Spectacle, 1851–1914* (Stanford, CA: Stanford University Press, 1990), 3.

4. Laurence Talairach-Vielmas, *Moulding the Female Body in Victorian Fairy Tales and Sensation Novels* (London: Routledge, 2007), 133.

5. Mary Eliza Haweis, *The Art of Beauty* (New York: Harper & Brothers, 1878), 3.

6. Rebecca Stern, "'Personation' and 'Good Marking-Ink': Sanity, Performativity, and Biology in Victorian Sensation Fiction," *Nineteenth-Century Studies* 14 (2000): 35.

7. Karl Marx, "Theses on Feuerbach," in *The German Ideology*, ed. C. J. Arthur (New York: International Publishers, 1970), 122.

8. Karl Marx, *The German Ideology*, ed. C. J. Arthur (New York: International Publishers, 1970), 39–40.

9. Marx, *German*, 46.

10. Mary Poovey, *Making a Social Body: British Cultural Formation, 1830–1864* (Chicago: University of Chicago Press, 1995), 4.

11. Mary Elizabeth Braddon, *Henry Dunbar: The Story of an Outcast*, 2 vols. (Leipzig: Bernhard Tauchnitz, 1864), 1.50–52.

12. Katherine Montwieler, "Marketing Sensation: *Lady Audley's Secret* and Consumer Culture," in *Beyond Sensation: Mary Elizabeth Braddon in Context*, ed.

Marlene Tromp, Pamela K. Gilbert, and Aeron Haynie (Albany, NY: SUNY Press, 2000), 43–44.

13. Kimberly Harrison, "'Come Buy, Come Buy': Sensation Fiction in the Context of Consumer and Commodity Culture," in *A Companion to Sensation Fiction*, ed. Pamela K. Gilbert (Malden, MA: Wiley-Blackwell, 2011), 535.

14. Greta Depledge notes that Leona, when dressed in men's clothing, "is granted a freedom without any cultural anxieties about the propriety of a woman traveling alone and sleuthing" ("Sensation Fiction and the New Woman," in *The Cambridge Companion to Sensation Fiction*, ed. Andrew Mangham [Cambridge: Cambridge University Press, 2013], 199).

15. "Ingenious Impostor," *John Bull* 5, no. 27 (4 July 1825): 215.

16. "Ingenious," *John*, 215.

17. "Ingenious," *John*, 215.

18. "Ingenious," *John*, 215.

19. "Ingenious," *John*, 215.

20. "Ingenious," *John*, 215.

21. "Literary Notices," *Public Opinion* 3, no. 69 (17 January 1863): 74.

22. A. M. Barnard [Louisa May Alcott], *Behind a Mask, or A Woman's Power*, in *Alternative Alcott*, ed. Elaine Showalter (New Brunswick, NJ: Rutgers University Press, 1988), 100.

23. Barnard, *Behind*, 106.

24. Barnard, *Behind*, 103.

25. Barnard, *Behind*, 147.

26. Barnard, *Behind*, 123.

27. Barnard, *Behind*, 155.

28. Tara MacDonald, "Sensation Fiction, Gender, and Identity," in *The Cambridge Companion to Sensation Fiction*, ed. Andrew Mangham (Cambridge: Cambridge University Press, 2013), 129. Jessica Cox observes that "[w]omen's bodies are construed as potentially dangerous, because they are too easily disguised" (*Victorian Sensation Fiction* [London: Red Globe Press, 2019], 65). And Laurence Talairach notes: "sensation fiction capitalized on the artificiality of the modern world and the rise of consumer culture, enticing women to play parts and conceal themselves beneath layers of make-up and fashionable clothes" ("Sensation Fiction: A Peep Behind the Veil," in *The Victorian Gothic: An Edinburgh Companion*, ed. Andrew Smith and William Hughes [Edinburgh: Edinburgh University Press, 2012], 30).

29. An 1863 review associates sensation fiction with "sexual immorality" and specifically argues that "the decline of female (and consequently of male) virtue, has been . . . due to no less a cause than *crinoline*," which offers an "exhibition of legs" ("Sensation Novels," *Medical Critic and Psychological Journal* 16 [July 1863]: 516–17).

30. "An M. D.," *The Pocket Magazine*, vol. 2 (London: James Robins & Co., 1829), 87.

31. Thomas Carlyle, *Sartor Resartus*, ed. Rodger L. Tarr (Berkeley: University of California Press, 2000), 27.

32. In "Signs of the Times" (1829), Carlyle describes the decline of metaphysical and moral science attendant to the rise of "the Physical," which is "engrossing, every day, more respect and attention" (*Edinburgh Review* 49, no. 98 [July 1829], 442). The "Science of Mind," in other words, has been displaced by "advancement in the general science, or the special sciences, of matter" (444). Carlyle reiterates his claim that "the Body-politic [is] more than ever worshipped and tendered; but the Soul-politic less than ever" (448).

33. *Secrets in the Art of Dress* (London: Jas. Gilbert, 1849), 8.

34. Haweis, *Art*, 11.

35. In *Desperate Remedies* (1871), Thomas Hardy writes: "clothes are something exterior to every man; but to a woman her dress is part of her body. Its motions are all present to her intelligence if not to her eyes" ([London: Ward and Downey, 1889], 129).

36. William James, *The Principles of Psychology*, vol. 1 (London: Macmillan and Co., 1891), 292.

37. Rosey Aindow, *Dress and Identity in British Literary Culture, 1870–1914* (Burlington, VT: Ashgate, 2010), 8. Stefanie Lethbridge observes that clothes in Gothic and sensation novels are "used specifically to signal moments of social order disruption; instead of expressing the self, clothes here frequently indicate disjunctions between subject and object and on occasion a disquieting domination of the material over the spiritual" ("The Horror of Clothing and the Clothing of Horror: Material and Meaning in Gothic and Sensation Fiction," in *Sensationalism and the Genealogy of Modernity*, ed. Alberto Gabriele [London: Palgrave Macmillan, 2017], 50).

38. In 1851, Matilda Eliza Lyle, under the assumed names Chippendale and Tremaine, gained notoriety as the "Norwich Impostor." Among other exploits, Lyle claimed to have run away from home in disguise. She kept an embroidered handkerchief lent to her by a respectable gentleman to prove her status, and she asserted that her servants' clothes were part of her disguise. She succeeded in borrowing a "suit of apparel" from a woman, claiming she was about to be married, but she never returned the new clothes, using them in further impostures ("The Norwich Impostor," *Daily News* 1,990 [7 October 1852]: 6). In 1867, a woman named Mary Bland Ballantine arrived at a lawyer's office "attired in mourning," claiming to be a relative of a man who had recently died in a lunatic asylum ("Obtaining Money Under False Pretences," *Leeds Mercury* 9,324 [2 March 1868]: 3). Fooled by a forged document, the lawyer forwarded her some money, and she departed, only to return "differently attired" (3), begging for more money. Once Ballantine was apprehended, having swindled another firm, a witness was able to identify her, "although she now wore different clothes" (3).

39. Two other types of sartorial imposture are worth mentioning. The first occurs when an impostor discards clothes to obscure an identity. In Mary Elizabeth Braddon's *Henry Dunbar* (1863–64), for example, Joseph Wilmot murders the eponymous character, strips the body, and submerges the clothes that bear Dunbar's name. The second occurs when an impostor wears various clothes to

assume a new identity. In Florence Warden's *A Prince of Darkness* (1885), Louis de Breteuil dresses in layers of clothes to become the enfeebled character Martin Beresford. And while de Breteuil oversees business in Paris, Robert Meredith, alias Smith, personates Beresford.

40. In Wilkie Collins's *The Dead Secret* (1856), Mrs. Treverton and Sarah Leeson trade clothes on the day that Sarah gives birth, allowing Mrs. Treverton to claim the child as her own. And in Mary Elizabeth Braddon's *The Trail of the Serpent* (1860), Jabez North exchanges clothes with his twin brother Jim to fake his own death.

41. Stern, "Personation," 40.

42. Collins uses the trope frequently: in *Armadale* (1864–66), Lydia Gwilt exchanges clothes with a maid; in *The New Magdalen* (1872–73), Mercy Merrick exchanges clothes with Grace Roseberry to assume her identity; and in *The Law and the Lady* (1875), Helen dresses in a maid's clothes to sneak from the house to attend a ball. Additionally, in Marcus Clarke's *His Natural Life* (1874), Rufus Dawes (formerly Richard Devine) swaps clothes with Reverend North to escape prison; and in Hall Caine's *A Son of Hagar* (1886), Paul Drayton exchanges clothes with Paul Ritson, and the latter is arrested.

43. "Novels of the Week," *Athenaeum* 2,307 (13 January 1872): 48.

44. "Novels," *Athenaeum*, 48.

45. John Cordy Jeaffreson, *A Woman in Spite of Herself*, 2 vols. (Leipzig: Bernhard Tauchnitz, 1872), 1.14, 43; subsequent references to this edition provided in the text.

46. "A Woman in Spite of Herself," *Examiner* 3,339 (27 January 1872): 103.

47. "New Novels," *Graphic* 112 (20 January 1872): 13.

48. "A Woman in Spite of Herself," *Spectator* 45, no. 2,277 (17 February 1872): 214.

49. Judith Butler, *Gender Trouble: Feminism and the Subversion of Identity* (New York: Routledge, 1999), 136.

50. Butler, *Gender*, 136.

51. Laurence Talairach-Vielmas, "Victorian Sensational Shoppers: Representing Transgressive Femininity in Wilkie Collins's *No Name*," *Victorian Review* 31, no. 2 (2005): 62.

52. Such cosmetic subtlety was often juxtaposed against French preferences. "In France," one 1870 writer claimed, "old ladies are even being made up into 'young ones' at the cost of half their fortunes" ("Beauty," *Reynolds's Newspaper* 1,023 (20 March 1870): 2.

53. *The Art of Beauty* (London: Knight and Lacey, 1825), 90, 187.

54. Mrs. A. Walker, *Female Beauty, as Preserved and Improved by Regimen, Cleanliness and Dress* (New York: Scofield and Voorhies, 1840), 5.

55. "Paint, and No Paint," *All the Year Round* 7, no. 172 (9 August 1862): 521.

56. Nadine Bérenguier, *Conduct Books for Girls in Enlightenment France* (London: Routledge, 2016), 223; Baroness Staffe, *My Lady's Dressing Room*, trans. Harriet Hubbard Ayer (New York: Cassell Publishing Company, 1892), 349.

57. Carolyn A. Day, *Consumptive Chic: A History of Beauty, Fashion, and Disease* (London: Bloomsbury, 2017), 97.

58. Walker, *Female*, 39. In 1876, Marie Bayard noted: "Although we have given numerous reliable recipes for those ladies who would like to prepare their own cosmetics, &c., we would advise that they should be made up by a respectable chemist or purchased from a skilled perfumer" (*The Art of Beauty or Lady's Companion to the Boudoir* [London: Weldon & Co., 1876], 4).

59. One 1893 writer observed that Collins "got hold of the Madeline Smith and Pritchard trial, and concocted his account by skilfully combining the two" ("English Fiction and Scottish Law," *Scottish Law Review* 9, no. 104 [August 1893]: 177). In *The Law and the Lady* (1874–75), Valeria Woodville applies cosmetics before she meets with Major Fitz-David. Aviva Briefel observes that "[c]osmetics endow Valeria with a properly feminine attitude" ("Cosmetic Tragedies: Failed Masquerade in Wilkie Collins's *The Law and the Lady*," *Victorian Literature and Culture* 37, no. 2 [2009]: 467). Tara MacDonald argues that Valeria "reveals the way in which Victorian women constantly falsified their appearances, whether for sensation purposes or for everyday interactions" ("Sensation," 130).

60. John Scoffern, "Cosmetics," *Belgravia* 4 (December 1867): 208.

61. Scoffern, "Cosmetics," 208. Personation plots in sensation novels frequently hinge on men using cosmetics. In the anonymous novel *The Old Roman Well* (1861), George Messenger studies the cosmetic arts in London's criminal underworld, learning how to disguise his body "with a mixture of acids and gunpower" to feign "terrible accidents" (3 vols. [London: Saunders, Otley, and Co., 1861], 1.109); Ellen Wood's *Verner's Pride* (1862–63) shows how a cosmetic applications can counterfeit a peculiar bodily signifier, as John Massingbird fabricates his brother Frederick's large facial birthmark using "Indian-Ink" ([Macmillan and Co., 1900], 352); Wilkie Collins's *The Moonstone* (1868) concludes with the revelation of Godfrey Ablewhite's disguise, a process that involves "washing off his complexion" (ed. John Sutherland [Oxford: Oxford University Press, 2008], 444); in Fortuné Du Boisgobey's *Where's Zenobia?* (1880), the spy Saint-Privat possesses "disguises of all sorts" and "various cosmetics" (vol. 1 [London: Vizetelly & Co. 1888], 119); and Frank Barrett's *Under a Strange Mask* (1889) illustrates how intricate and expert cosmetic use can produce a full-scale facial personation, when Lestrange, who was "rigid and shining with the enamels and fards employed to conceal that mark of Time's finger," is ultimately revealed as "grotesquely ludicrous" under his melting make-up ([London: Cassell & Company, 1890], 162, 303).

62. "The Park-Lane Murder," *Daily News* 8,103 (17 April 1872): 3.

63. "The Belgian Murder Trial," *Bristol Mercury* 10,781 (2 December 1882): 5.

64. "Belgian," 5.

65. Rebecca Kling, "'It is only colour that you want': *Lady Audley's Secret* and Cosmetics as Discursive Fantasy," *Victorian Periodicals Review* 50, no. 3 (Fall 2017): 564.

66. Walker, *Female*, 201.

67. Wilkie Collins, *The Woman in White* (New York: Barnes & Noble, 2005), 24.

68. Collins, *Woman*, 215.

69. Deborah Wynne notes that a serial part of *No Name* ran adjacent to an article on makeup in *All the Year Round* and argues that Magdalen's "deceptive strategies [are] . . . not so much a characteristic of the sensation novel's heroine but a normal part of feminine behavior" (*The Sensation Novel and the Victorian Family Magazine* [New York: Palgrave, 2001], 110).

70. Wilkie Collins, *No Name*, ed. Mark Ford (London: Penguin, 2004), 8; subsequent references to this edition provided in the text.

71. Kylee-Ann Hingston, "'Skins to Jump into': The Slipperiness of Identity and the Body in Wilkie Collins's *No Name*," *Victorian Literature and Culture* 40 (2012): 118.

72. Jessica Cox notes that *No Name* "represents the pinnacle of [Collins's] attack on the Victorian legal and social system that condemned illegitimacy" ("Representations of Illegitimacy in Wilkie Collins's Early Novels," *Philological Quarterly* 83, no. 2 [Spring 2004]: 151).

73. Slavoj Žižek explains that the voice, together with the gaze, is "the object of psychoanalysis, the celebrated *objet petit a*," and observes that "the voice, for example of the superego, addressing me without being attached to any particular bearer, floating freely in some horrifying interspace, functions again as a stain or blemish, whose inert presence interferes like a foreign body and prevents me from achieving self-identity" ("The Undergrowth of Enjoyment: How Popular Culture Can Serve as an Introduction to Lacan," in *The Žižek Reader*, ed. Elizabeth Wright and Edmond Wright [Oxford: Blackwell, 1999], 14, 15).

74. Jacques Derrida, *Writing and Difference*, ed. Alan Bass (Chicago: University of Chicago Press, 1978), 230.

75. Magdalen early on displays cosmetic "habits of mimicry" (11) during an evening of "theatrical entertainment" (35), effecting a "cool appropriation of Norah's identity to theatrical purposes" (48). Magdalen's reappearance, "with false hair and false eyebrows, with a bright-red complexion and patches on her cheeks" (48), floors the audience.

76. Talairach-Vielmas, *Moulding*, 137.

77. Magdalen leaves a "blank space" (397) instead of a signature in a letter to Norah; Lecount leaves a "blank space" (244) in the advertisement for Noel to fill and later experiences a "momentary blank" (308) before she realizes that Miss Bygrave is actual Magdalen; there are "blank spaces" (458) in the new will Noel composes; and Norah leaves Miss Garth a "blank space" (597) in a letter to Magdalen.

78. Lecount's actual name is Lecompte. The anglicization demonstrates that the perceptive housekeeper, ever Magdalen's equal, also practices a form of imposture.

79. Andrew Mangham, *Violent Women and Sensation Fiction: Crime, Medicine and Victorian Popular Culture* (New York: Palgrave Macmillan, 2007), 190.

80. Tatiana Kontou, "Parallel Worlds: Wilkie Collins's Sensationalism and Spiritualist Practice," in *Wilkie Collins: Interdisciplinary Essays*, ed. Andrew Mangham (Newcastle UK: Cambridge Scholars Publishing, 2007), 50.

81. Victorian readers would have known about the potential hazards of meddling with moles. In 1825, one beauty manual warned that "any tampering with them is extremely apt to produce cancer" (*The Duties of a Lady's Maid* [London: James Bulcock, 1825], 256). Fifty years later, Marie Bayard noted that "it will be found very dangerous to apply depilatories for eradicating the tufts of hair on moles, as cancer is not an unfrequent consequence of such empirical applications" (*Art*, 35). Wragge's dubious cosmetic formula, then, would have been considered particularly dangerous, and Magdalen's acceptance of the application further demonstrates her myopic ambition that ignores the potentially mortal risk of concealing her moles with quack applications.

82. Alison Milbank notes that Collins "wishes to present Magdalen as a heroine, however errant, and he uses a variety of devices to preserve her character from corruption" (*Daughters of the House: Modes of the Gothic in Victorian Fiction* [London: Palgrave Macmillan, 1992], 33). But Magdalen's entrance into a "new and nobler life" (590) riled contemporary critics. Although "the characters are moral monstrosities," according to the *London Review*, Collins permits both Magdalen and Wragge to find happiness ("No Name," *London Review* 6, no. 132 [10 January 1863]: 46). *The Spectator* outlined Magdalen's "legalized prostitution" and wondered "why leave the guilty always so successful?" ("No Name," *Spectator* 36, no. 1,802 [10 January 1863]: 1501–1502). Margaret Oliphant, reviewing *No Name* in *Blackwood's*, argued that Magdalen's redemption was a "great mistake in art, as well as a falsehood to nature" ("Novels," *Blackwood's Edinburgh Magazine* 94 [August 1863]: 170).

Chapter 2

1. Francis Wharton, *A Treatise on the Law of Evidence in Criminal Issues* (Philadelphia: Kay and Brother, 1880), 676.

2. Wharton, *Treatise*, 676.

3. Alfred Swaine Taylor, "Medico-Legal Observations on Tattoo-Marks as Evidence of Personal Identity. Remarks on the Tichborne Case," in *Guy's Hospital Reports*, ed. H. G. Howse, vol. 19 (London: J. & A. Churchill, 1874), 442.

4. Taylor, "Medico," 449–50.

5. In 1868, William Augustus Guy noted a Belgian case in which prison physicians "stat[ed] that prisoners are in the habit of effacing scars by applying a

salted herring to them" (*Principles of Forensic Medicine* [London: Henry Renshaw, 1868], 3).

6. William Bathurst Woodman and Charles Meymott Tidy, *A Handy-Book of Forensic Medicine and Toxicology* (London: J. A. Churchill, 1877), 638.

7. In Mary Elizabeth Braddon's *The Captain of the Vulture* (1861–62), James Duke murders and personates his twin brother George but is revealed as an impostor during a trial because he does not possess "the mark of the branding-iron on his back" [London: John and Robert Maxwell, 1868], 310). And in John Berwick Harwood's *One False, Both Fair* (1883), twins Cora and Clare can only be distinguished by a nurse who identifies a "little, dull, bluish-white mark" on Cora's wrist that resulted from a childhood accident ([New York: John W. Lovell, 1885], 204). Scars also figure into the personation plots in several other sensation novels. In Braddon's *The Trail of the Serpent* (1860), Jabez North can be identified by a forehead scar, inflicted by the mother of his child, who throws coins into his face "with such a strong and violent hand, that one of them, striking him above the eyebrow, cut his forehead to the bone" (ed. Chris Willis [New York: Modern Library, 2003], 38). And in Charlotte Evans's *Over the Hills and Far Away* (1874), Beatrice fails to personate her sister Laura because she does not possess a scar from a dog bite. Rylston Dacre, Laura's estranged husband, finally observes Beatrice's exposed neck: "[t]he velvet band was gone!" ([London: Sampson Low, Marston, Low, & Searle, 1874], 299).

8. Mary Elizabeth Braddon, *Sir Jasper's Tenant*, 2 vols. (Leipzig: Bernhard Tauchnitz, 1866), 1.164.

9. Wilkie Collins, *No Name*, ed. Mark Ford (London: Penguin, 2004), 263.

10. Braddon, *Sir Jasper*, 1.164.

11. W. J. Bishop, *The Early History of Surgery* (New York: Barnes & Noble, 1995), 131.

12. The Roman medical writer Celsus reportedly repaired deformed lips and ears. Perhaps the most renowned innovator in rhinoplasty in late nineteenth century was Tribhovandas Motichand Shah, an Indian surgeon who aided a great number of patients whose noses (and sometimes upper lips and teeth) were removed by punitive or criminal sword strikes. Shah, according to a contemporary account, would perform rhinoplasty "by removing a flap of skin from the forehead or cheek of the patient, and uniting this with the help of sutures to the remaining portion of the mutilated nose until the junction is complete" ("The Renewing of Noses," *Birmingham Daily Post* 9,965 [2 June 1890]: 8). Sander L. Gilman notes that Shah's practice "is one in which defending the civilization of India . . . demanded the medical intervention of the surgeon, as opposed to the use of similar interventions in the diseased and sexually corrupt West" (*Making the Body Beautiful: A Cultural History of Aesthetic Surgery* [Princeton, NJ: Princeton University Press, 1999], 82).

13. "The Female Form Divine," *Women's Penny Paper* 7, no. 211 (12 November 1892): 16.

14. Baroness Staffe, *My Lady's Dressing Room*, trans. Harriet Hubbard Ayer (New York: Cassell Publishing Company, 1892), 204–205.

15. Staffe, *My Lady's*, 204.

16. David Tolhurt, *Pioneers in Plastic Surgery* (London: Springer, 2015), 5.

17. Gilman, *Making*, 12.

18. "Analytical and Critical Review," *British Foreign Medical Review* 21 (April 1846): 292.

19. J. M. Chelius, "Organic Restoration of Lost Parts," in *A System of Surgery*, vol. 3 (Philadelphia: Lea & Blanchard, 1847), 578.

20. Chelius, "Organic," 579.

21. Ellen Wood, *East Lynne*, ed. Elisabeth Jay (Oxford: Oxford University Press, 2008), 321.

22. Wood, *East*, 388.

23. Wood, *East*, 389.

24. Audrey Jaffe, *Scenes of Sympathy: Identity and Representation in Victorian Fiction* (Ithaca, NY: Cornell University Press, 2000), 113.

25. "Novels," *Saturday Review* 67, no. 1741 (9 March 1889): 286.

26. Vere Clavering, *Barcaldine*, 3 vols. (London: Hurst and Blackett, 1889), 3.201.

27. "New Novels," *Examiner* 3,288 (4 February 1871): 130. "Taliacotian" refers to Gaspare Tagliacozzi's procedure for rhinoplasty.

28. "Checkmate," *Saturday Review* 31, no. 803 (18 March 1871): 352.

29. Anna Maria Jones, "Sheridan Le Fanu," in *A Companion to Sensation Fiction*, ed. Pamela K. Gilbert (Malden, MA: Blackwell, 2011), 269.

30. "New Books," *Penn Monthly* 6 (March 1875): 234.

31. Sheridan Le Fanu, *Checkmate* (Philadelphia: Evans, Stoddard & Co., 1871), 5; subsequent references to this edition provided in the text.

32. Jones, "Sheridan," 269.

33. "Checkmate," *British Quarterly Review* 54, no. 107 (July 1871): 248. *The Spectator* noted the "utterly trashy . . . sensation element," but admitted that *Checkmate* was better than "the Braddon school of fiction" ("Checkmate," *Spectator* 44, no. 2,226 [25 February 1871]: 224).

34. Wharton, *Treatise*, 677.

35. A. B. McEachin, "Personal Identity," *Law Journal and Reporter* 1, no. 6 (May 1880): 395.

36. Douglas Starr, *Blood: An Epic History of Medicine and Commerce* (New York: Alfred A. Knopf, 1998), xiii.

37. Holly Tucker, *Blood Work: A Tale of Medicine and Murder in the Scientific Revolution* (New York: Norton, 2011), xxiv.

38. James Blundell, *Researches Physiological and Pathological* (London: E. Cox and Son, 1824), 92.

39. "Monthly Synopsis of Practical Medicine," *London Medical and Surgical Journal* 1, no. 2 (1 August 1828): 173.

40. Harold A. Oberman, "Organization, Functions, Regulation, and Legal Concerns of Blood Banks," in *Clinical Laboratory Medicine*, ed. Kenneth D. McClatchey (Philadelphia: Lippincott, Williams, & Wilkins, 2002), 1,517.

41. "Blood Transfusion," *Our Young Folk's Weekly Budget* 26, no. 748 (4 April 1885): 16.

42. "The Fatal Case of Blood Transfusion," *Liverpool Mercury* 9,159 (24 May 1877): 8.

43. In 1889, a laborer was injured by a thrashing machine, "one of his legs being torn off" ("Bravery of a Surgeon," *Morning Post* 36,628 [7 November 1889]: 3). One of the surgeons volunteered his own blood for a transfusion, but the man died shortly thereafter.

44. George Henry Lewes, *The Physiology of Common Life*, vol. 1 (Edinburgh: William Blackwood and Sons, 1859), 277.

45. Jules Law, *The Social Life of Fluids: Blood, Milk, and Water in the Victorian Novel* (Ithaca, NY: Cornell University Press, 2010), 93.

46. "Blood Transfusion," *Freeman's Journal* 107 (31 July 1874): 4.

47. Ann Louise Kibbie, *Transfusion: Blood and Sympathy in the Nineteenth-Century Literary Imagination* (Charlottesville, VA: University of Virginia Press, 2019), 7.

48. Kibbie, *Transfusion*, 2.

49. George Eliot, *The Lifted Veil* and *Brother Jacob*, ed. Sally Shuttleworth (London: Penguin, 2001), 21.

50. Eliot, "Lifted," 19.

51. Eliot, "Lifted," 38.

52. Eliot, "Lifted," 39.

53. Eliot, "Lifted," 39.

54. Kate Flint, "Blood, Bodies, and *The Lifted Veil*," *Nineteenth-Century Literature* 51, no. 4 (March 1997): 470.

55. In the anonymous novel *Martha and Mary* (1880), the villain Alfred Burnaby receives a blood transfusion from Dr. Charteris, which had "only been tried once before in this hospital, and both died" ([London: Smith, Elder, and Co., 1880], 289). An even more interesting scene occurs in William Westall's *Red Ryvington* (1882). Sergius Kalougia, a Russian exile, is stabbed in the back by mercenaries, and his wife Dora recalls her desperate solution: "like a flash, there came into my mind something that Sergius had said only the day before about the transfusion of blood. There was a surgeon at Geneva he told me—in this very street—whose writings on the best methods of transfusing blood had won him a European reputation, and who had invented the best apparatus for the purpose in existence" ([London: Cassel & Company, 1885], 362). Dora's blood restores Sergius, and the heroic exile survives.

56. Mary Elizabeth Braddon, "Good Lady Ducayne," *Strand Magazine* 11 (1896): 198.

57. Charles Reade, "The Prurient Prude," in *Readiana: Comments on Current Events* (London: Chatto and Windus, 1883), 319.

58. Charles Reade, *Griffith Gaunt; or, Jealousy* (Boston: Ticknor and Friends, 1866), 181.

59. Reade, *Griffith*, 209.

60. Reade, *Griffith*, 209.

61. Bram Stoker, *Dracula*, ed. Nina Auerbach and David J. Skal (New York: Norton, 1997), 158.

62. Reade, *Griffith*, 209.

63. Kibbie, *Transfusion*, 101.

64. "New Novels," *The Literary World* 37 (27 January 1888): 73.

65. "Six Stories," *Saturday Review* 64, no. 1,678 (24 December 1887): 856.

66. "Belles Lettres," *Westminster Review* 129, no. 1 (January 1888): 124.

67. Kibbie, *Transfusion*, 121.

68. In *An Essay on the Principles of Human Action* (1805), William Hazlitt argues that "personal identity neither does, nor can imply any positive communication between a man's future, and present self" ([London: J. Johnson, 1805], 20). Drawing on David Hume, Hazlitt understands personal identity as a bundle of impressions, thus negating any connection to a future beyond present sensations. "For Hazlitt," Tim Milnes writes, "the *known* self, like any other category, is an abstraction, a projection or construction of the mind" (*The Testimony of Sense: Empiricism and the Essay from Hume to Hazlitt* [Oxford: Oxford University Press, 2019], 209). Modern philosophers have been most interested in Hazlitt's concept of what has now been termed "fission," which refers to the possibility of the brain being divided or transplanted into new subjects.

69. William Delisle Hay, *Blood: A Tragic Tale* (London: Swan Sonnenschein, Lowrey & Co., 1888), 1; subsequent references to this edition provided in the text.

70. Stoker, *Dracula*, 26.

71. Wharton, *A Treatise*, 682.

72. Kibbie, *Transfusion*, 121.

73. Jolene Zigarovich, "'A Strange and Startling Creature': Transgender Possibilities in Wilkie Collins's *The Law and the Lady*," *Victorian Review* 44, no. 1 (Spring 2018): 99.

First Interlude

1. "Eastern Counties," *Herpath's Railway and Commercial Journal* 18, no. 869 (2 February 1856): 108.

2. J. L., "Female Impostors.—A Parallel," *Morning Post* 25,540 (12 November 1855): 3.

3. "London, Thursday, November 1, 1855," *Times* 22,200 (1 November 1855): 6.

4. "London," *Times*, 6; "Alice Grey, the Impostor," *Annual Register* (London: F. & J. Rivington, 1856), 165.

5. "Alice Grey's Continental Double," *Examiner* 2,499 (22 December 1855): 2.

6. T. B. M., *The Ballad of Alice Grey and the Grand Jury: A Lay of Modern Staffordshire* (Wolverhampton: Joseph York, 1856), 8.

7. In 1855, Lewis Carroll's parody of Mee's poem, titled "She's All My Fancy Painted Him," was published in the *Comic Times*. Carroll subsequently included a revised version of the poem (without its first stanza, which contains the only clear link to Mee) in *Alice's Adventures in Wonderland* (1865).

8. Grey's forename varies between Annistatia, Annastasea, and Anastasia, and her surname between Huggard, Haggett, and Haggart.

9. C. L. McCluer Stevens, *Famous Crimes and Criminals* (New York: Duffield & Company, 1924), 205; Charles Kingston, *A Gallery of Rogues* (London: Stanley Paul & Co., 1924), 124.

10. Brazil's surname varies between Brassill, Brussil, and Brussell.

11. "The Extraordinary Impostures," *Morning Post* 25,544 (16 November 1855): 4.

12. "Singular Case of Imposture," *Cheshire Observer and General Advertiser* 77 (27 October 1855): 3.

13. "The Extraordinary Impostures of 'Miss Alice Grey,'" *Lady's Newspaper* 461 (27 October 1855): 256.

14. "Singular," *Cheshire*, 3.

15. "Extraordinary Case of Imposture and Perjury," *Huddersfield Chronicle* 293 (27 October 1855): 7; "Women in Prison," *London Review* 5, no. 115 (13 September 1862): 240.

16. "Extraordinary Case of Perjury," *Northampton Mercury* 51 (3 November 1855): 4.

17. "Latest Intelligence," *Bell's Life in London and Sporting Chronicle* (18 November 1855): 8; "Alice Grey, Actress," *Port Pirie Recorder and North Western Mail* 671 (7 January 1905): 1.

18. "Extraordinary Imposture and Systematic Perjury," *Bell's Life in London* (4 November 1855): 7.

19. "A Case in Point," *Law Times* 26 (10 November 1855): 90.

20. "Alice Grey, the Impostor," *Standard* 9,774 (10 December 1855): 1.

21. "Eastern," *Herpath's*, 108.

22. "Alice," *Examiner*, 1–2.

23. "Alice," *Port*, 1.

24. "Alice Grey," *Leader* 6, no. 300 (22 December 1855): 1218.

25. "Alice," *Annual*, 165.

26. "The Female Impostor at Wolverhampton," *Cork Examiner* 15, no. 2,104 (7 November 1855): 4; "The Female Impostor at Wolverhampton," *Times* 22,206 (8 November 1855): 10.

27. "Extraordinary," *Lady's*, 256.
28. "The Female Impostor at Wolverhampton," *Morning Chronicle* 27,722 (1 November 1855): 7.
29. "The Impostures of 'Alice Grey,' " *Lady's Newspaper* 462 (3 November 1855): 284.
30. "The Case of Imposition by a Female in Wolverhampton," *Morning Post* 25,531 (1 November 1855): 2.
31. "Extraordinary," *Huddersfield*, 7.
32. "Case," *Morning*, 2.
33. "Case," *Morning*, 2; "Extraordinary Case of Imposture at Wolverhampton," *John Bull* 35, no. 1,821 (3 November 1855): 15; "Extraordinary Series of Frauds and Perjury," *Essex Standard* 25, no. 1,299 (7 November 1855): 4.
34. "Narrative of Law and Crime," *Household Narrative of Current Events* (November 1855): 247.
35. "Alice Grey, The Impostor," *Lady's Newspaper* 463 (10 November 1855): 301.
36. "A Scottish Maiden," *Leader* 6, no. 292 (27 October 1855): 1025; "Impostures," *Lady's*, 283.
37. "The Extraordinary Case of Imposture at Wolverhampton," *Examiner* 2,492 (3 November 1855): 13.
38. "Extraordinary Imposture," *Sheffield & Rotherham Independent* 1,882 (3 November 1855): 12.
39. "Alice Grey," *Morning Post* 25,552 (26 November 1855): 8.
40. "Female," *Standard*, 1.
41. "Female," *Standard*, 1.
42. "The Female Impostor at Wolverhampton," *Standard* 9,747 (8 November 1855): 1.
43. "Alice," *Lady's*, 301.
44. "Alice Grey the Impostor," *Morning Advertiser* (9 November 1855): 3.
45. "Alice Grey," *Times* 22,242 (20 December 1855): 10.
46. "Grey," *Times*, 10.
47. "To the Editor of the Times," *Times* 22,203 (5 November 1855): 5.
48. "To the Editor," *Times*, 5.
49. "To the Editor," *Times*, 5.
50. "To the Editor," *Times*, 5.
51. "To the Editor," *Times*, 5.
52. "Alice Grey," *Leeds Times* 22, no. 1,185 (8 December 1855): 7.
53. "Alice Grey, the Impostor," *Daily News* 2,980 (6 December 1855): 3.
54. "Alice," *Daily*, 3.
55. "Alice Grey, &c. &c. &c. &c. &c.," *Times* 22,204 (6 November 1855): 10.
56. "The Female Impostor at Wolverhampton," *Northampton Mercury* 135, no. 43 (10 November 1855): 3.
57. "Extraordinary," *Lady's*, 256.

58. "Female," *Standard*, 1.
59. "The Extraordinary Case of Imposture at Wolverhampton," *Leicester Chronicle* 45 (3 November 1855): 1.
60. "Extraordinary," *Lady's*, 256.
61. "District News," *Birmingham Gazette* 114, no. 5,948 (19 November 1855): 2.
62. "District," *Birmingham*, 2.
63. "Notes from Our Diary," *Lady's Newspaper & Pictorial Times* 465 (24 November 1855): 13.
64. "Notes," *Lady's*, 13.
65. "District," *Birmingham*, 2.
66. "The Provinces," *Spectator* 1,427 (3 November 1855): 1128.
67. "Extraordinary," *Bell's*, 7.
68. "Female," *Morning*, 7.
69. "Alice," *Annual*, 163.
70. "Female," *Morning*, 7.
71. "London," *Times*, 6.
72. The most noteworthy of these impostors was Amelia Eliza Tremaine, known as "the Yorkshire Alice Grey." Tremaine went by several names, including Emma Smith, Mary Eliza Teale, Mary Eliza Field, and Mary Eliza Chippendale.
73. "Alice," *Lady's*, 301.
74. "Alice," *Lady's*, 301.
75. "Alice Grey in Ireland," *Morning Post* 25,549 (22 November 1855): 3.
76. "Conviction of Alice Grey," *John Bull* 1,841 (22 March 1856): 190.
77. "A Daring Female Impostor," *Albion* 13, no. 37 (24 November 1855): 557.
78. "Conviction," *John*, 190.
79. Henry Mayhew and John Binny, *The Criminal Prisons of London and Scenes of Prison Life* (London: Griffin, Bohn, and Company, 1862), 272.
80. Frederick William Robinson, *Female Life in Prison*, vol. 2 (London: Hurst and Blackett, 1862), 18.
81. "Literature," *Athenaeum* 1,807 (7 June 1862): 782.
82. Robinson, *Female*, 29.
83. "Female Life in Prison," *Christian Remembrancer* 44 (1863): 383.
84. Arthur Griffiths, *Memorials of Millbank, and Chapters in Prison History*, vol. 2 (London: Henry S. King & Co., 1875), 159. In another prison retrospective, Julian Hawthorne, who claims to have edited an anonymous manuscript sent to him by a prisoner, describes Grey as an "unusual, and in some respects picturesque, prison character" (*The Confessions of a Convict* [Philadelphia: Rufus C. Hartranft, 1893], 267).
85. Robinson, *Female*, 32. Under the stewardship of W. Bayne Ranken, the Royal Society for the Assistance of Discharged Prisoners was founded in 1857

and located at 32 Charing Cross, London. The society would oversee the reentry of "ticket-of-leave" men and women into society, assisting with employment and finances. Subjects accepted into the program would be furnished with a respectable outfit, and their earnings would be controlled by the society. They were required to check in monthly with the central office and were also monitored by special investigators. The society's success, according to William Gilbert, meant that, "out of every hundred convicts discharged with tickets-of-leave, ninety-three remain honest" (*Our Discharged Convicts* [London: Thomas Brettell & Co., 1870], 3).

86. Robinson, *Female*, 32.

87. Charlotte Ward, *Lending a Hand: Or, Help for the Working Classes* (London: Seeley, Jackson, and Halliday, 1866), 286.

88. Ward, *Lending*, 287.

89. Ward, *Lending*, 289.

90. "Alice," *Port*, 1; see also "Made Her Living by Sending Innocent Men to Prison," *Albury Banner and Wondonga Express* 16 (18 March 1938): 16.

91. Stevens, *Famous*, 205.

92. Stevens, *Famous*, 207, 209.

93. Kingston, *Gallery*, 120.

94. Kingston, *Gallery*, 120, 122.

95. Kingston, *Gallery*, 128.

96. Stevens, *Famous*, 210; Kingston, *Gallery*, 130.

97. Kingston, *Gallery*, 128.

98. Hawthorne, *Confessions*, 270.

Chapter 3

1. Charlotte Brontë, *Jane Eyre*, ed. Stevie Davies (London: Penguin, 2006), 15.

2. Brontë, *Jane*, 19.

3. Brontë, *Jane*, 22.

4. Brontë, *Jane*, 24.

5. Brontë, *Jane*, 24.

6. Brontë, *Jane*, 24.

7. Brontë, *Jane*, 25.

8. Leonard Guthrie, "Night Terrors, Symptomatic and Idiopathic, with Associated Disorders in Children," *Clinical Journal* 14, no. 7 (7 June 1899): 107.

9. Brontë, *Jane*, 337.

10. Jill L. Matus observes the scene's "poignant representation of the aftermath of overwhelming emotional shock" (*Shock, Memory and the Unconscious in Victorian Fiction* [Cambridge: Cambridge University Press, 2009], 1).

11. James Crichton Browne, "Personal Identity, and Its Morbid Modifications," *Journal of Medical Science* 8, no. 43–44 (October 1862–January 1863): 386.

12. Browne, "Personal," 386. Henry Maudsley, with particular vigor, sought to restore the vital connection between mind and body through physiological study, rather than "disdaining [the body], as metaphysicians, religious ascetics, and maniacs have done" (*Body and Mind* [London: Macmillan, 1873], 4).

13. Browne, "Personal," 387.

14. Browne, "Personal," 387–88.

15. Browne, "Personal," 388.

16. Browne, "Personal," 389.

17. Browne, "Personal," 390.

18. Browne, "Personal," 395, 536.

19. Browne, "Personal," 536–37.

20. Browne, "Personal," 535.

21. Brontë, *Jane*, 339.

22. Brontë, *Jane*, 494.

23. Margaret Oliphant, "Modern Novelists—Great and Small," *Blackwood's Edinburgh Magazine* 77, no. 475 (May 1855): 557.

24. Jenny Bourne Taylor, *In the Secret Theater of Home: Wilkie Collins, Sensation Narrative, and Nineteenth-Century Psychology* (New York: Routledge, 1988), 4.

25. "Waiting for the Verdict," *Saturday Review* 15, no. 389 (11 April 1863): 478.

26. Mariaconcetta Costantini emphasizes the dual pressures of sensation writing: "Defensive, ironic and sometimes provocative in their strategies of self-representation, [sensation writers] laid stress on their heteronomous position as professionals aiming at artistic independence but also resolved to sell the products of their labour to a cross-class readership" ("Sensation, Class and the Rising Professionals," in *The Cambridge Companion to Sensation Fiction*, ed. Andrew Mangham [Cambridge: Cambridge University Press, 2013], 106).

27. "The Doctor's Wife," *Saturday Review* 18, no. 471 (5 November 1864): 571. In 1865, Henry James noted that Mary Elizabeth Braddon composed "stories of action" rather than "stories of passion," suggesting that her novels elevated plot over character ("Miss Braddon," *Nation* 1.19 [9 November 1865]: 594). In 1866, H. F. Chorley wrote that "[t]hose who make plot their first consideration and humanity the second . . . have placed themselves in a groove which goes, and must go, in a downward direction, whether as regards fiction or morals" ("Armadale," *Athenaeum* 2,014 [June 1866]: 732). Even T. S. Eliot, arguably the sensation novel's sole Modernist defender, observed that Collins was "not usually strong in the creation of character, but he was a master of plot and situation" ("Wilkie Collins and Dickens," in *The Victorian Novel*, ed. Harold Bloom [New York: Chelsea House, 2004], 308).

28. "John Marchmont's Legacy," *Ladies' Companion* 25 (1864): 278.

29. "Madness in Novels," *Spectator* 39, no. 1,962 (3 February 1866): 134.

30. "Madness," *Spectator*, 135.

31. "Madness," *Spectator*, 135.

32. Jessica Cox, *Victorian Sensation Fiction* (London: Red Globe Press, 2019), 113.

33. "St. Martin's Eve," *Saturday Review* 21, no. 544 (31 March 1866): 387.

34. John Conolly, *An Inquiry Concerning the Indications of Insanity* (London: John Taylor, 1830), 8.

35. "Nothing Can Be More Slightly Defined," *Times* 21,800 (22 July 1854): 8.

36. "Nothing," *Times*, 8.

37. Mary Elizabeth Braddon, *Lady Audley's Secret*, ed. Lyn Pykett (Oxford: Oxford University Press, 2012), 176; subsequent references to this edition provided in the text. Sally Shuttleworth observes that sensation fiction illustrates a world where "the boundaries of normality are no longer in place" (" 'Preaching to the Nerves': Psychological Disorder in Sensation Fiction," in *A Question of Identity: Women, Science, and Literature*, ed. Marina Benjamin [New Brunswick, NJ: Rutgers University Press, 1993], 221). And Laurence Talairach argues that *The Woman in White* "uses mental disease to shatter the frontier between sanity and insanity" (*Wilkie Collins, Medicine and the Gothic* [Cardiff: University of Wales Press, 2009], 22).

38. Thomas Laycock, *Mind and Brain: Or, The Correlations of Consciousness and Organization*, vol. 1 (London: Simpkin, Marshall, and Co., 1869), viii.

39. Andrew Wynter, "First Beginnings," *Cornhill Magazine* (April 1862): 481.

40. The Lunacy Commission was established in 1845. In February 1859, less than a year before the first serial number of *The Woman in White*, the British Parliament created a committee for "the care and treatment of lunatics and their property."

41. Lewis Carroll, *Alice's Adventures in Wonderland and Through the Looking-Glass*, ed. Peter Hunt (Oxford: Oxford University Press, 2009), 58.

42. "Thoughts upon Insanity, Dreams, Hallucinations, and Self-Control," *Metropolitan* 4 (1856): 536.

43. Joshua Burgess, *The Medical and Legal Relations of Madness* (London: John Churchill, 1858), 33.

44. *The Cyclopedia of Practical Medicine*, vol. 3, ed. John Forbes, Alexander Tweedie, and John Conolly (Philadelphia: Henry C. Lea, 1867), 38.

45. George Combe, *A System of Phrenology*, vol. 1 (Edinburgh: Maclachlan, Steward & Co., 1848), 172.

46. Combe, *System*, 172.

47. James F. Duncan, *The Personal Responsibility of the Insane* (Dublin: Fannin and Co., 1865), 24.

48. Duncan, *Personal*, 25.

49. W. T. Gairdner, *Insanity: Modern Views as to Its Nature and Treatment* (Glasgow: James MacLehose & Sons, 1885), 34.

50. In the preface to the second edition of *Mind and Brain* (1869), Thomas Laycock noted that "no change occurs in the consciousness without a corresponding

change in the encephalon" (*Mind and Brain: Or, The Correlations of Consciousness and Organization*, vol. 1 [London: Simpkin, Marshall, and Co., 1869], iv). Alexander Bain, who described the human being as an "extended and material mass," was less welcoming: "there is, in company with all our mental processes, *an unbroken material succession*. From the ingress of a sensation, to the outgoing responses in action, the mental succession is not for an instant dissevered from a physical succession" (*Mind and Body: The Theories of Their Relation* [New York: D. Appleton & Company, 1874], 137, 130–31). Elsewhere, Bain denies the existence of "an 'ego' or 'self,'" which is a "pure fiction, coined from non-entity" (*Logic* [London: Longmans, Green, & Co., 1879], 262). This assertion suggests that, at least for Bain, subjectivity is entirely corporeal, whether understood through the body or through the mind.

51. L. S. Jacyna, "Somatic Theories of Mind and the Interests of Medicine in Britain, 1850–1879," *Medical History* 26 (1982): 233.

52. Elaine Showalter, *The Female Malady: Women, Madness, and English Culture, 1830–1980* (New York: Pantheon Books, 1985), 28.

53. Jenny Bourne Taylor, *In the Secret Theatre of Home: Wilkie Collins, Sensation Narrative, and Nineteenth-Century Psychology* (London: Routledge, 1988), 30–31.

54. Jacyna, "Somatic," 233.

55. Wynter, "First," 482.

56. Mary Elizabeth Braddon, *Aurora Floyd*, vol. 1 (Leipzig: Bernhard Tauchnitz, 1863), 185.

57. Benjamin Morgan notes that "the embodied, processual model of the mind . . . shifted attention from abstract faculties toward human corporeality" (*The Outward Mind: Materialist Aesthetics in Victorian Science and Literature* [Chicago: University of Chicago Press, 2017], 136). The mind was increasingly seen as a function of the body located in the specific neurological and locational processes of the material brain. Vanessa Ryan notes that physiological psychologists "claimed that mind and matter were merely two aspects of a single unity" and that "consciousness was not a thing, . . . but a dynamic function" (*Thinking without Thinking in the Victorian Novel* [Baltimore: Johns Hopkins University Press, 2012], 8).

58. Henry Maudsley, *The Pathology of Mind* (London: Macmillan and Co., 1895), 85. In Ella J. Curtis's *A Game of Chance* (1888), George Pottinger, described as a "queer fish," suffers from "severe sunstroke" during a military post in India, and "went clean out of his mind . . . and was removed under restraint and finally sent to England and placed in an asylum for treatment" (3 vols. [London: Hurst and Blackett, 1889], 1.40, 2.93).

59. Rebecca Stern, "'Personation' and 'Good Marking-Ink': Sanity, Performativity, and Biology in Victorian Sensation Fiction," *Nineteenth-Century Studies* 14 (2000): 42–43.

60. Lynn Pykett, *The Nineteenth-Century Sensation Novel* (Devon, UK: Northcote House, 1994), 37.

61. Andrew Mangham, *Violent Women and Sensation Fiction: Crime, Medicine and Victorian Popular Culture* (New York: Palgrave Macmillan, 2007), 174.

62. Wilkie Collins, *The Woman in White* (New York: Barnes & Noble, 2005), 24.

63. John Kucich, *The Power of Lies: Transgression in Victorian Fiction* (Ithaca, NY: Cornell University Press, 1994), 94.

64. Diane Elam, "White Narratology: Gender and Reference in Wilkie Collins's *The Woman in White*," in *Virginal Sexuality and Textuality in Victorian Literature*, ed. Lloyd Davis (Albany, NY: SUNY Press, 1993), 62.

65. Ann Cvetkovich, *Mixed Feelings: Feminism, Mass Culture, and Victorian Sensationalism* (New Brunswick, NJ: Rutgers University Press, 1992), 91.

66. In Mary Eleanor Wilkins Freeman's *Jane Field* (1892), the impostor suffers a "terrible mental impetus" following her confession ([New York: Harper & Brothers, 1902], 260). And in L. T. Meade's *An Adventuress* (1899), Kate Mildmay similarly "got a terrible shock and her mind went" after admitting her imposture ([London: Chatto & Windus, 1899], 394).

67. Ellen Wood followed Braddon's example. In *St. Martin's Eve* (1866), Charlotte Norris, who has experienced "fits of temper" inherited from her father, locks the door on a burning child, and thereafter poses in mourning until Frederick St. John reveals her "incipient madness" ([London: Macmillan and Co., 1901], 48, 387). Pamela K. Gilbert notes the effectiveness of this trope, in which the mad character "seems to outsiders to function normally long after he is in fact quite ill" ("Sensation Fiction and the Medical Context," in *The Cambridge Companion to Sensation Fiction*, ed. Andrew Mangham [Cambridge: Cambridge University Press, 2013], 186).

68. Henry Mansel, "Sensation Novels," *Quarterly Review* 113, no. 226 (April 1863): 489.

69. "The Romance of Wicked Women," *London Review* 6, no. 145 (11 April 1864): 375.

70. "Lady Audley's Secret," *Critic* 25.631 (December 1862): 178.

71. "Lady Audley's Secret," *Athenaeum* 1,826 (25 October 1862): 525.

72. "Miss Braddon's Novels," *Reader* 1.9 (28 February 1863): 211.

73. "Miss," *Reader*, 211.

74. W. Fraser Rae, "Sensation Novelists: Miss Braddon," *North British Review* 43, no. 85 (September 1865): 186.

75. Fraudulent recommendation letters were often used by women who hoped to rise socially. In 1890, for example, a woman who called herself Lady Sinett traveled around England and the continent and "always produced letters of recommendation from well-known personages. These letters were invariably forgeries. . . . Her numerous letters of recommendation caused her to be received with open arms, and she easily gained the confidence of those she intended to dupe" ("'Lady' Sinett and Her Portfolio," *North-Eastern Daily Gazette* [12 August 1890]: 4).

76. When Robert Audley visits Lieutenant Maldon's house, the landlady gives him a "long tress of hair wrapped in silver paper" that she claims to have "cut . . . off when [Helen] lay in her coffin" (41). Robert then finds Helen's actual hair contained within one of George's books.

77. Ann Cvetkovich argues that Robert "becomes simultaneously the representative of dominant ideology and the isolated madman" (*Mixed Feelings: Feminism, Mass Culture, and Victorian Sensationalism* [New Brunswick, NJ: Rutgers University Press, 1992], 65). Pamela K. Gilbert observes that the novel's "duel of narratives . . . replicates the struggle occurring in the popular fiction market between the healthful 'taste' for more elevated reading material . . . and the debasing addition to 'low' fictions like the sensational novel" ("Madness and Civilization: Generic Opposition in Mary Elizabeth Braddon's *Lady Audley's Secret*," *Essays in Literature* 23, no. 2 [Fall 1996]: 219).

78. Jenny Bourne Taylor, Introduction, *Lady Audley's Secret* (London: Penguin, 1998), ii.

79. Braddon establishes the foundation for an identity exchange between Lucy and Phoebe that never comes to fruition; instead, Phoebe is a "person who never lost her individuality" (116), and their connection is a "point of sympathy" (94), perhaps mesmeric in nature, and one that Phoebe breaks by participating in Luke Marks's blackmail plot.

80. Sean Grass, *The Commodification of Identity in Victorian Narrative: Autobiography, Sensation, and the Literary Marketplace* (Cambridge: Cambridge University Press, 2019), 106.

81. Grass, *Commodification*, 107.

82. Immediately following the publication of Darwin's *On the Origin of Species*, T. H. Huxley and Richard Owen engaged in a public feud referred to in the press as the "gorilla wars." Huxley identified a missing link between primates and humans that Owen had not ascertained. In 1861, the *Westminster Review* remarked that the differences between humans and primates are "very great," but "they are differences only of degree, not of kind" ("Equatorial Africa, and Its Inhabitants," *Westminster Review* 20 [1861]: 166).

83. Elaine Showalter, "Desperate Remedies: Sensation Novels of the 1860s," *Victorian Newsletter* 49 (Spring 1976): 4. D. A. Miller similarly notes that "the text leaves ample room for doubt on the score of Lady Audley's 'madness'" (*The Novel and the Police* [Berkeley: University of California Press, 1988], 169). Heidi Logan argues that "Lady Audley is not so much biologically preconditioned toward madness as preconditioned to think of herself within the framework of psychiatry's emphasis on heredity" (*Sensational Deviance: Disability in Nineteenth-Century Sensation Fiction* [New York: Routledge, 2019], 195).

84. Maia McAleavey, *The Bigamy Plot: Sensation and Convention in the Victorian Novel* (Cambridge: Cambridge University Press, 2015), 136.

85. Pamela K. Gilbert, *Disease, Desire, and the Body in Victorian Women's Popular Novels* (Cambridge: Cambridge University Press, 1997), 8–9.

86. Jill L. Matus, "Disclosure as 'Cover-up': The Disclosure of Madness in *Lady Audley's Secret*," *University of Toronto Quarterly* 62, no. 3 (Spring 1993): 334.

87. Simon Petch notes that Robert's "pursuit of Lady Audley's past is also his own quest for a professional future" ("Robert Audley's Profession," *Studies in the Novel* 32, no. 1 [Spring 2000]: 1). Robert's developing "sense of obligation" and "moral trustworthiness" are "the basis of contract and of trust" (3), the keystones of his profession.

88. Leila Silvana May, *Secrecy and Disclosure in Victorian Fiction* (Burlington, VT: Ashgate, 2016), 110.

89. "The Romance of Babington White," *Saturday Review* 24, no. 622 (28 September 1867): 399.

90. Thomas Arnold, "Recent Novel Writing," *Macmillan's Magazine* 13 (January 1866): 208.

91. Mansel, "Sensation," 483.

92. Henry Maudsley, *Responsibility in Mental Disease* (New York: D. Appleton and Company, 1892), 243.

93. Miller, *Novel*, 146. Ann Cvetkovich similarly argues that sensationalism became "the vehicle for the politics of affect" (*Mixed Feelings: Feminism, Mass Culture, and Victorian Sensationalism* [New Brunswick, NJ: Rutgers University Press, 1992], 2). Cvetkovich also notes that "[t]he reader's body becomes a machine hooked into the circuit of production and consumption, rather than a disinterested entity floating above economic exigencies in search of aesthetic or moral truth" (20).

94. Other important figures include Jean-Étienne Dominque Esquirol, who classified types and levels of epileptic activity; Jules Falret, who advanced categorization efforts; and Bénédict Morel, who made strides in understanding "masked epilepsy," meaning "forms of epilepsy" that could be "made in the absence of a history of convulsions" (German E. Berrios, "Memory Disorders and Epilepsy during the Nineteenth Century," in *Epilepsy and Memory*, ed. Adam Zeman, Narinder Kapur, and Marilyn Jones-Gotman [Oxford: Oxford University Press, 2012], 55).

95. Lynn M. Voskuil, "Acts of Madness: Lady Audley and the Meanings of Victorian Femininity," *Feminist Studies* 27, no. 3 (Autumn 2001): 628.

96. Berrios, "Memory," 58.

97. Today, epilepsy is defined as "recurrent episodes of neurological dysfunction—epileptic seizures—capable of affecting either or both behavior and experience, due to the abnormally synchronized electrical discharges of large groups of neurons" (Adam Zeman, Narinder Kapur, and Marilyn Jones-Gotman, Introduction, *Epilepsy and Memory*, ed. Adam Zeman, Narinder Kapur, and Marilyn Jones-Gotman [Oxford: Oxford University Press, 2012], 1).

98. Zeman, Introduction, 1.

99. Zeman, Introduction, 1.

100. Joel Peter Egan, *Unconscious Crime: Mental Absence and Criminal Responsibility in Victorian London* (Baltimore: Johns Hopkins University Press, 2003), 17.

101. John Hughlings Jackson, "A Study of Convulsions," in *Transactions*, vol. 4 (London: John Churchill and Sons, 1870), 162.

102. John Hughlings Jackson, *On Convulsive Seizures* (London: British Medical Association, 1890), 2.

103. Henry Maudsley, *The Physiology and Pathology of Mind* (London: Macmillan and Co., 1868), 421.

104. See *Traité des dégénerescenses physiques, intellectuelles, et morales de l'espèce humaine* (1857) and *Traité des maladies mentales* (1860).

105. Laurence Talairach-Vielmas, *Wilkie Collins, Medicine, and the Gothic* (Cardiff: University of Wales Press, 2009), 94.

106. Gillian Beer, *Darwin's Plots: Evolutionary Narrative in Darwin, George Eliot, and Nineteenth-Century Fiction* (Cambridge: Cambridge University Press, 2000), 12.

107. Richard Von Krafft-Ebing, *Psychopathia Sexualis* (New York: Rebman Company, 1906), 470.

108. Mary Gibson and Nicole Hahn Rafter, Introduction, *Criminal Man*, trans. Mary Gibson and Nicole Hahn Rafter (Durham, NC: Duke University Press, 2006), 11.

109. Cesare Lombroso, *Criminal Man*, trans. Mary Gibson and Nicole Hahn Rafter (Durham, NC: Duke University Press, 2006), 264.

110. Henry Maudsley, *The Pathology of Mind* (New York: D. Appleton and Company, 1886), 447.

111. Maudsley, *Pathology*, 447.

112. Maudsley, *Pathology*, 447–48.

113. Maudsley, *Responsibility*, 227.

114. Maudsley, *Responsibility*, 227.

115. Egan, *Unconscious*, 9–10.

116. In 1843, Daniel M'Naughten murdered Edward Drummond, whom he mistook for Prime Minister Robert Peel. M'Naughten blamed the Tory government for having "entirely destroyed my peace of mind," and he was acquitted (R. M. Bousfield and R. Merrett, "Report of the Trial of Daniel M'Naughton," *Law Magazine* 29 [1843]: 385). The effects of alleged madness on personal identity implicitly emerged in the case because M'Naughten claimed that "I am sure I shall never be the man I formerly was" (385). As Joel Peter Egan notes, M'Naughten's case led directly to the commission of the M'Naughten Rules, which "affirmed the common law's traditional construction of the forensic *person*: a rational, purposeful being capable of perceiving the consequences of his acts" (*Unconscious*, 7).

117. Maudsley, *Responsibility*, 228.

118. Maudsley, *Responsibility*, 228.

119. Maudsley, *Responsibility*, 230.

120. Maudsley, *Responsibility*, 263.
121. Maudsley, *Responsibility*, 265.
122. Maudsley, *Responsibility*, 265.
123. In Wilkie Collins's "Mad Monkton" (1859), the Monkton family suffers from "the horrible affliction of hereditary madness" (in *A Plot in Private Life and Other Tales* [Leipzig: Bernhard Tauchnitz, 1859], 91). In Charles Reade's *Hard Cash* (1863), Dr. Wycherly, an asylum manager, suffers from epileptic fits. And in Matilda Houston's *Done in the Dark* (1877), Augusta "Gussie" Cuthbert suffers from "illnesses, periodical and severe, the result of an accident in early childhood" (vol. 1 [London: Samuel Tinsley, 1877], 51). *The Athenaeum* took issue with this storyline: "we object to epilepsy being utilized for the purposes of romance" ("Novels of the Week," *Athenaeum* 2,578 [24 March 1877]: 382).
124. Wilkie Collins, *Poor Miss Finch* (New York: Harper & Brothers, 1872), 45–46.
125. Collins, *Poor*, 51.
126. Peter Wolf, "Epilepsy and Catalepsy in Anglo-American Literature between Romanticism and Realism: Tennyson, Poe, Eliot, and Collins," *Journal of the History of the Neurosciences* 9, no. 3 (2000): 292. Laurence Talairach observes that Oscar's particular spasms "bear witness to Collins's resort to contemporary medical sources," particularly the work of John Hughlings Jackson (*Wilkie*, 104).
127. In *Griffith Gaunt*, Griffith, presented with false news of his wife's infidelity, begins to seizure: "Griffith's features were horribly distorted, his eyes rolled fearfully, and he fell to the ground, grinding his teeth, and foaming at the mouth. An epileptic fit!" ([Boston: Ticknor and Friends, 1866], 106).
128. "Poor Miss Finch," *Athenaeum* 2,312 (17 February 1872): 202.
129. Collins, *Poor*, 56, 61.
130. George Eliot, *Silas Marner*, ed. George Levine (New York: Barnes & Noble, 2005), 8.
131. Eliot, *Marner*, 8.
132. *The Speaker* pointed to Braddon's "unrivalled art of constructing clever plots" ("Fiction," *Speaker* 10 [28 July 1894]: 109). *The Spectator*, in contrast, claimed that Braddon was "far below her best," and questioned "the chapter of accidents" that follow the murder ("Recent Novels," *Spectator* 73, no. 3,448 [28 July 1894]: 118).
133. "Novels," *Saturday Review* 78, no. 2,039 (24 November 1894): 566.
134. Mary Elizabeth Braddon, *Thou Art the Man*, ed. Laurence Talairach-Vielmas (Kansas City: Valancourt, 2008), 5; subsequent references to this edition provided in the text.
135. Heidi H. Johnson observes the "redefinition of Coralie's identity in opposition to her father," which triggers a "near-erasure of self" ("Electra-fying the Female Sleuth: Detecting the Father in *Eleanor's Victory* and *Thou Art the Man*," in *Beyond Sensation: Mary Elizabeth Braddon in Context*, ed. Marlene Tromp, Pamela K. Gilbert, and Aeron Haynie [Albany, NY: SUNY Press, 2000], 267).

136. Laurence Talairach-Vielmas, Introduction, *Thou Art the Man* (Kansas City: Valancourt, 2008), xv.

137. Courtney A. Floyd, "'Take It When Tendered': M. E. Braddon's *Thou Art the Man* and the *Weekly Telegraph*'s Media Model of Disability," *Victorian Review* 45, no. 1 (Spring 2019): 67. Martha Stoddard Holmes argues that novelists engage disability as "cultural shorthand" to represent "emotional excess" (*Fictions of Affliction: Physical Disability in Victorian Culture* [Ann Arbor: University of Michigan Press, 2009], 3). Rather than understand this connection as natural, Holmes "recast[s] it as naturalized" (4). According to Heidi Logan, sensation novelists represent disability as not just a "biological or mental condition," but also a "life experience influenced by social and legal factors and by medical and psychiatric discourse" (*Sensational Deviance: Disability in Nineteenth-Century Sensation Fiction* [New York: Routledge, 2019], 1). Collins and Braddon, in particular, deploy "empathetic representations" to "convey the experience of disability to their readers" (1).

138. Allen Bauman, "Epilepsy, Crime, and Masculinity in Mary Elizabeth Braddon's *Thou Art the Man*," *Nineteenth-Century Gender Studies* 4, no. 2 (2008). www.ncgsjournal.com/issue42/bauman.htm.

Chapter 4

1. Vanessa Ryan argues that Collins's novels explore the "liminal world between the physical and the psychological, namely the realm of the automatic, reflexive, and unconscious" (*Thinking without Thinking in the Victorian Novel* [Baltimore: Johns Hopkins University Press, 2012], 53).

2. Sharrona Pearl, "Dazed and Abused: Gender and Mesmerism in Wilkie Collins," in *Victorian Literary Mesmerism*, ed. Martin Willis and Catherine Wynne (Amsterdam: Rodopi, 2008), 164.

3. During the serialization of *The Moonstone* (January to August 1868), Collins was in the throes of full-scale opium addiction. Simultaneously, he began a relationship with Martha Rudd, commencing a sort of second life, following his years with Caroline Graves, which would lead him to adopt the surname Dawson for his new family.

4. Wilkie Collins, *The Moonstone*, ed. John Sutherland (Oxford: Oxford University Press, 2008), liii; subsequent references to this edition provided in the text.

5. Gabriel Betteredge notes that he "fell . . . not exactly into a sleep, but into the next best thing to it" (17); asks whether he "hadn't woke up from a dream" (44); and admits "I must have gone clean out of my sense" (133). Betteredge's daughter, Penelope, makes a connection between the Moonstone and intoxicants, claiming that it "gets into my head like liquor, and makes me wild" (143).

6. John Sutherland, Introduction, *The Moonstone* (Oxford: Oxford University Press, 2008), xx.

7. "The Moonstone," *Spectator* 41, no. 2,091 (25 July 1868): 881.

8. Joel Peter Egan, *Unconscious Crime: Mental Absence and Criminal Responsibility in Victorian London* (Baltimore: Johns Hopkins University Press, 2003), 17.

9. What Betteredge considers "hocus-pocus" (19) is clairvoyance, "signifying something like brightness of sight" (49). This detail could identify potentially telepathic connections, such as the "fellow-feeling" (124) Rosanna and Limping Lucy share.

10. "Moonstone," *Spectator*, 882; "The Moonstone: A Novel," *Nation* 7, no. 168 (17 September 1868): 235.

11. William Winter, reminiscing on Collins's anecdotes about the novel, explains that Collins was "almost frenzied with physical torture," moving through several amanuenses. "Opium sometimes hurts," Collins allegedly asserted, "but also, *sometimes*, it helps" (*Old Friends: Being Literary Recollections of Other Days* [New York: Moffat, Yard and Company, 1909], 213). And Mary de Navarro (née Anderson) intriguingly recalled Collins's "personal magnetism," and noted of *The Moonstone* that he "was not only pleased and astonished at the *finale*, but did not recognize it as [his] own" (*A Few Memories* [New York: Harper & Brothers, 1896], 142).

12. Quoted in Catherine Peters, *The King of Inventers: A Life of Wilkie Collins* (Princeton, NJ: Princeton University Press, 1991), 257.

13. Robert Darnton, *Mesmerism and the End of the Enlightenment in France* (Cambridge, MA: Harvard University Press, 1968), 4.

14. Alison Winter, *Mesmerized: Powers of Mind in Victorian Britain* (Chicago: University of Chicago Press, 1998), 3.

15. Winter, *Mesmerized*, 119.

16. John Elliotson, "Letter from Dr. Elliotson," in *Cerebral Physiology and Materialism*, by W. C. Engledue (London: J. Watson, 1842), 27.

17. Elliotson, "Letter," 28.

18. Elliotson, "Letter," 30.

19. Elliotson, "Letter," 30.

20. Chauncy Hare Townshend, *Facts in Mesmerism: With Reasons for a Dispassionate Inquiry into It* (New York: Harper & Brothers, 1843), 208.

21. Townshend, *Facts*, 208–9.

22. Martin Willis and Catherine Wynne, Introduction, *Victorian Literary Mesmerism*, ed. Martin Willis and Catherine Wynne (Amsterdam: Rodopi, 2006), 3.

23. Susan Poznar, "Whose Body? The 'Willing' or 'Unwilling' Mesmerized Women in Late Victorian Fiction," *Women's Writing* 15, no. 3 (2008): 414.

24. John Elliotson, [Untitled], *The Zoist* 10, no. 38 (July 1852): 152.

25. William Gregory, *Animal Magnetism; or, Mesmerism and Its Phenomena* (London: The Psychological Press Association, 1884), 58.

26. Gregory, *Animal*, 59.

27. John Bovee Dods, *The Philosophy of Mesmerism and Electrical Psychology* (London: James Burns, 1886), 185–86.

28. Dods, *Philosophy*, 186.

29. Dods, *Philosophy*, 187.
30. Dods, *Philosophy*, 187.
31. Dods, *Philosophy*, 187–88.
32. Beth Torgerson, "Harriet Martineau, Victorian Sciences of Mind and the Birth of Psychology," in *Harriet Martineau and the Birth of Disciplines: Nineteenth-Century Intellectual Powerhouse*, ed. Valeria Sanders and Gaby Weiner (London: Routledge, 2017), 139.
33. Harriet Martineau, *Letters on Mesmerism* (London: Edward Moxon, 1845), vi–vii.
34. Martineau, *Letters*, viii, 3.
35. Martineau, *Letters*, 21, 31.
36. Martineau, *Letters*, 31.
37. Rachel Ablow, *Victorian Pain* (Princeton, NJ: Princeton University Press, 2017), 70, 71.
38. John Hughes Bennett, *The Mesmeric Mania of 1851* (Edinburgh: Sutherland and Knox, 1851), 3, 4.
39. Bennett, *Mesmeric*, 13.
40. Jane Carlyle, Letter to John Welsh, 13 December 1844, *Carlyle Letters Online*; DOI 10.1215/lt-18441213-JWC-JWE-01.
41. Carlyle, Letter, 13 December 1844.
42. Carlyle, Letter, 13 December 1844.
43. William Benjamin Carpenter, *Mesmerism, Spiritualism, &c.* (London: Longmans, Green, and Co., 1877), v, 5.
44. In Annie Emma Challice's *The Wife's Temptation* (1859), Aurelia Duprez is a practiced mesmerist, and briefly restores Rhoda "to the beauty of untroubled youth" (2 vols. [London: Charles Westerton, 1859], 2.4). Characters in the novel are also unwillingly mesmerized by a mysterious figured called "the Nemesis," who turns out to be Aurelie's aunt. Outside of *The Moonstone*, Collins referred to mesmerism frequently. In *The Woman in White* (1859–60), Dr. Dawson warns that Fosco will "try his quack remedies (mesmerism included)" ([New York: Barnes & Noble, 2005], 359); in *No Name* (1862–63), Michael Vanstone is purported to be "the most powerful mesmerist in Europe" ([New York: Stein and Day, 1967], 305); and Lydia Gwilt, the duplicitous antagonist of *Armadale* (1864–66), remarks: "I believe in mesmerism" (ed. Catherine Peters [Oxford: Oxford University Press, 2008], 465).
45. "Our Library Table," *St. James's Magazine* (1865): 182.
46. "Novelettes," *London Review* 11, no. 267 (12 August 1865): 178.
47. "The Notting Hill Mystery," *Athenaeum* 1,955 (15 April 1865): 520.
48. "Notting," *Athenaeum*, 520. Lara Karpenko calls the novel a "polyphonic page turner, [which] clearly seems inspired by" *The Woman in White* (" 'So Extraordinary a Bond': Mesmerism and Sympathetic Identification in Charles Adams's *Notting Hill Mystery*," in *Strange Science: Investigating the Limits of Knowledge in the Victorian*

Age, ed. Lara Karpenko and Shalyn Claggett [Ann Arbor: University of Michigan Press, 2017], 146). Wieland Schwanebeck argues that the novel's "mosaic arrangement of eyewitness reports, owes a considerable debt to Collins's *The Woman in White*" ("'It's Never Twins?'—It's *Always* Twins: *The Notting Hill Mystery* [1865] and the Specter of Twinship in Early Detective Fiction," *Clues* 36, no. 1 [Spring 2018]: 59).

49. Cheryl B. Price argues that *Notting Hill Mystery* "reveals the uncomfortable link between capitalism and the detective" since readers understand immediately that Henderson's investigation is performed "to avoid paying a claim" ("Probability and Capital Crime: The Rise and Fall of Actuarial Detection in Victorian Crime Fiction," *Clues* 34, no. 2 [Fall 2016]: 9, 13).

50. Charles Felix [Charles Warren Adams], *The Notting Hill Mystery* (London: Saunders, Otley, and Co., 1865), 4; subsequent references to this edition provided in the text.

51. Karpenko, "So Extraordinary," 147.

52. Karpenko, "So Extraordinary," 147, 148.

53. Karpenko, "So Extraordinary," 148.

54. Karpenko, "So Extraordinary," 159.

55. "Mesmerism; Its Dangers and Curiosities," *Punch* 6 (1844): 100.

56. "Mesmerism," *Punch*, 100.

57. "Mesmerism," *Punch*, 100.

58. Samuel Taylor Coleridge, "Kubla Khan," in *The Major Works*, ed. H. J. Jackson (Oxford: Oxford University Press, 2000), 104, ll. 39, 43–44.

59. Coleridge, "Kubla," 104, ll. 42, 46.

60. Coleridge, "Kubla," 102.

61. Samuel Taylor Coleridge, *Collected Letters*, vol. 6, ed. Earl Leslie Griggs (Oxford: Oxford University Press, 1966), 894; Coleridge, "Kubla," 104, l. 54.

62. Arthur Symons, Introduction, *Poems of Coleridge* (London: Methuen & Co., 1905), xxii.

63. Symons, Introduction, xxii.

64. Thomas De Quincey, *Confessions of an English Opium-Eater*, ed. Grevel Lindop (Oxford: Oxford University Press, 1998), 2.

65. Grevel Lindop, "Lamb, Hazlitt, and De Quincey," in *The Coleridge Connection: Essays for Thomas McFarland*, ed. Richard Gravil and Molly Lefebure (New York: St. Martin's, 1990), 129. Nigel Leask notes that "opium in the *Confessions* is a material simulacrum of the agency of imagination in Coleridge's *Biographia* [*Literaria*], controlled by hedonism rather than Christian asceticism" (*British Romantic Writers and the East: Anxieties of Empire* [Cambridge: Cambridge University Press, 1992], 206).

66. John Barrell, *The Infection of Thomas De Quincey: A Psychopathology of Imperialism* (New Haven, CT: Yale University Press, 1991), 18.

67. De Quincey, *Confessions*, 69.

68. De Quincey, *Confessions*, 40.

69. Thomas Laycock, "Researches into the Functions of the Brain," *Journal of Psychological Medicine* 8 (1855): 539.

70. John Elliotson, *Human Physiology* (London: Longman, Rees, Orme, Brown, Green, & Longman, 1835), 366.

71. Elliotson, *Human*, 677.

72. Alonzo Calkins, *Opium and the Opium-Appetite* (Philadelphia: J. Lippincott & Co., 1871), 324–25.

73. "What Shall They Do to Be Saved?" *Harper's New Monthly Magazine* 35, no. 207 (August 1867): 379.

74. "Synopsis of Opium Inebriety," *New York Medical Journal* 55, no. 5 (30 January 1892): 139.

75. Charles Dickens, *The Mystery of Edwin Drood*, ed. Margaret Cardwell (Oxford: Oxford University Press, 2009), 208; subsequent references to this edition provided in the text.

76. Charles Richet, "Opium and Its Antidote," *Pharmacist* 11, no. 6 (June 1878): 177.

77. Richet, "Opium," 177.

78. "M. Richet on Poisons of Intelligence," in *All about Opium*, ed. Hartmann Henry Sultzberger (London: Cannon Street, 1884), 180.

79. *The Works of Charles Dickens: Letters and Speeches*, vol. 2 (London: Chapman and Hall, 1908), 83.

80. Charles Dickens, *Bleak House*, ed. George Ford and Sylvère Monod (New York: Norton, 1977), 124.

81. Dickens admitted to taking laudanum, "the only thing that has done me good," in March 1868, during an arduous reading tour in New England (*The Letters of Charles Dickens*, vol. 12, ed. Graham Storey [Oxford: Clarendon Press, 2002], 85).

82. *Letters of Charles Dickens*, vol. 12, 159.

83. *The Letters of Charles Dickens*, vol. 11, ed. Graham Storey (Oxford: Clarendon Press, 1999), 385.

84. Thomas Dormandy, *Opium: Reality's Dark Dream* (New Haven, CT: Yale University Press, 2012), 155.

85. Ronald R. Thomas, *Dreams of Authority: Freud and the Fictions of the Unconscious* (Ithaca, NY: Cornell University Press, 1990), 223.

86. Lillian Nayder, *Unequal Partners: Charles Dickens, Wilkie Collins, and Victorian Authorship* (Ithaca, NY: Cornell University Press, 2002), 165–66, 186.

87. Barry Milligan, *Pleasures and Pains: Opium and the Orient in 19th-Century British Culture* (Charlottesville: University of Virginia Press, 1995), 113.

88. Miriam O'Kane Mara, "Sucking the Empire Dry: Colonial Critique in *The Mystery of Edwin Drood*," *Dickens Studies Annual* 32 (2002): 234.

89. Stephen Arata, *Fictions of Loss in the Victorian Fin de Siècle: Identity and Empire* (Cambridge: Cambridge University Press, 1996), 107.

90. Mesmerism plays into the novel in other respects. Jasper communicates and controls nonverbally, making Rosa a "slave . . . with his looks" (53), and Helena and Neville Landless, twin exiles from Ceylon, possess a "complete understanding" (48), which Crisparkle refers to as "sympathy" (156).

91. John Forster, *The Life of Charles Dickens*, vol. 2 (London: Chapman and Hall, 1890), 291.

92. "Lazarus, Lotus-Eating," *All the Year Round* 15 (12 May 1866): 422; "East London Opium Smokers," *London Society* 14 (1868): 69.

93. Milligan, *Pleasures*, 104.

94. Jeremy Tambling, *Dickens' Novels as Poetry: Allegory and Literature of the City* (New York: Routledge, 2015), 206.

95. Philip Collins, "Inspector Bucket Visits the Princess Puffer," *Dickensian* 343 (1 May 1964): 89.

96. "Lazarus," *All*, 423.

97. "Lazarus," *All*, 424; "East," *London*, 71. In 1883, John Liggins described "the proprietor" of an opium den as an "Egyptian mummy" (*Opium: England's Coercive Opium Policy and Its Disastrous Results in China and India: The Spread of Opium Smoking in America* [New York: Funk & Wagnalls, 1883], 40). And in 1892, Frederick J. Masters described a "very dried-up pair of mummies" in a San Francisco opium den ("Opium and Its Votaries," *Californian* 1.6 [May 1892]: 637).

98. Jill L. Matus observes that Dickens avoids the use of free indirect speech with Jasper so that "the authorial presence is not implicated in or accountable for merging with his consciousness" (*Shock, Memory and the Unconscious in Victorian Fiction* [Cambridge: Cambridge University Press, 2009], 110).

99. Francis Wharton, *Philosophy of Criminal Law* (Philadelphia: Kay & Brother, 1880), 95.

100. Wharton, *Philosophy*, 5.

101. Stephanie Peña-Sy, "Intoxication, Provocation, and Derangement: Interrogating the Nature of Criminal Responsibility in *The Mystery of Edwin Drood*," *Dickens Studies Annual* 40 (2009): 225.

102. Peña-Sy, "Intoxication," 228.

103. John Milton, *Paradise Lost*, ed. Gordon Teskey (New York: Norton, 2005), 83, ll. 181–82.

Second Interlude

1. "The Remarkable Fraud at Birmingham," *Kerang Times and Swan Hill Gazette* (14 April 1882): 2.

2. "The Trial of Mary Jane Fearneaux," *Spectator* 55, no. 2,811 (13 May 1882): 615.

3. "Swindling as a Fine Art," *Saturday Review* 53, no. 1,373 (18 February 1882): 204.

4. "A Female Fraud," *St. Louis Post-Dispatch* (6 March 1882): 7.

5. John Berwick Harwood's *Lady Flavia* (1865) involves the personation of a murdered aristocrat. And John Cordy Jeaffreson's *A Woman in Spite of Herself* (1872) follows Felicia Avalon's desperate personation of her dead brother, Felix. Inspired by Furneaux, the periodical *Tit-Bits* ran an article titled "Parallels to the Furneaux Case," which summarized nine instances, mostly from the nineteenth century, in which women assumed new identities as men.

6. "The Personation Frauds," *Birmingham Daily Post* 7,377 (24 February 1882): 4.

7. "Conspiracy to Defraud: Extraordinary Case," *Newcastle Courant* 10,806 (10 February 1882): 5; "A Woman Personating a Nobleman," *Lancaster Gazette* 5,213 (11 February 1882): 6.

8. "Miss Furneaux's Career: Frauds upon Frauds She Practiced Year After Year," *New York Times* (12 March 1882): 4.

9. "'Lord Pelham Clinton' Again," *Daily Telegraph* (8 September 1894): 3.

10. "Female," *St. Louis*, 7.

11. "Personating Noblemen," *Times* 30,427 (10 February 1882): 8.

12. "The Fearneaux Frauds," *Birmingham Daily Post* 7,637 (13 February 1882): 5; "The Fearneaux Frauds," *Times* 30,431 (15 February 1882): 10.

13. "The Fearneaux Frauds," *London Journal* 75, no. 1,937 (25 March 1882): 188.

14. "Whispers," *The Birmingham Owl* 7, no. 2 (3 March 1882): 10.

15. In 1866, John Vansittart Danvers Butler-Danvers (1839–1905) became the 6th Earl of Lanesborough. Furneaux's mother claimed to be "the daughter of the late Lieutenant John Hutchinson Butler, of the 22d Regiment, and state[d] that her grandfather was son of the Hon. John Butler, brother of the Earl of Lanesborough" ("The Frauds by an Adventuress," *Times of India* [8 March 1882]: 5).

16. "Fearneaux," *Times*, 10.

17. Edward Cox, ed., "Reg. *v.* Boulton and Others," in *Cox's Reports of Cases in Criminal Law*, vol. 12 (London: Horace Cox, 1875), 88.

18. Cox, "Reg.," 89.

19. Cox, "Reg.," 89.

20. Cox, "Reg.," 89.

21. "Law and Police," *Pall Mall Budget* 4 (24 June 1870): 34.

22. "Masquerading Extraordinary," *St. Louis Globe-Democrat* 296 (12 March 1882): 15.

23. "Personating Lord Arthur Clinton," *Nottinghamshire Guardian* 1,334 (24 November 1871): 2.

24. "Personating," *Nottinghamshire*, 2.

25. "Personating," *Nottinghamshire*, 2.
26. "Personating Lord Arthur Clinton," *Hampshire Telegraph and Sussex Chronicle* 4,098 (25 November 1871): 4.
27. "Personating Lord Arthur Clinton," *Bristol Mercury* 4,259 (25 November 1871): 3.
28. "Extraordinary Case of Female Swindling," *York Herald* 5,163 (2 December 1871): 10.
29. "The Fearneaux Frauds," *Birmingham Daily Post* 7,372 (18 February 1882): 5.
30. "The Extraordinary Career of Personation," *Liverpool Mercury* 10,636 (10 February 1882): 7; "Personating," *Times*, 8.
31. Abigail Joseph, *Exquisite Materials: Episodes in the Queer History of Victorian Style* (Newark: University of Delaware Press, 2019), 81.
32. "Extraordinary Story of Fraud," *Manchester Guardian* (9 February 1882): 8; "Law and Police," *Pall Mall Budget* 27 (10 February 1882): 27.
33. Furneaux forged letters from "the Queen, the Prince of Wales, Lord Coleridge, Mr. Justice Denman, Mr. Justice Williams, Lord Strathnairn, Lord Lytton, Lord Granville, Lord Justice Lush, Sir John Bennet, Sir Thomas Biddulph, among others" (*The History of the Year: A Narrative of the Chief Events and Topics of Interest from October 1, 1881, to September 30, 1882* [London: Cassell, Petter, Galpin & Co., 1882], 83–84).
34. "The Frauds by an Adventuress," *Times* 30,429 (13 February 1882): 6.
35. Furneaux took tracings of official seals from tombstones and had them engraved to stamp on her letters. She also "snipped out [seals] from some illustrated print copies of the Royal arms, and carefully gummed them on the outside of the envelopes" ("Extraordinary Frauds by a Woman at Birmingham," *Ipswich Journal* 8,022 [14 February 1882]: 3). After she was captured, officials found "letter heads and envelopes bearing impressions of armorial and other heraldic devices . . . in her room" ("Fearneaux," *Times*, 10).
36. "The Audacious Career of an Adventuress," *Dundee Courier & Argus* 8,914 (10 February 1882): 5.
37. "Extraordinary," *Liverpool*, 7.
38. "The Daring Frauds by an Adventuress," *Blackburn Standard* 2,417 (18 February 1882): 7.
39. "Fearneaux," *London*, 188.
40. "Fearneaux," *Birmingham*, 5.
41. "The Assizes," *Times* 30,503 (10 May 1882): 7.
42. "Audacious," *Dundee*, 5.
43. "The Extraordinary Frauds by a Woman," *Manchester Guardian* (15 February 1882): 5.
44. "Epitome of General News," *Launceston Examiner* (21 April 1882): 3.

45. Furneaux also used the alias "H. Marie J. Eugènie Butler de Fearneaux." When she was younger, she assumed the name Mary Newell to commit crimes such as robbery.

46. "The Frauds by an Adventuress," *Times* 30,430 (14 February 1882): 5.

47. "The Fearneaux Frauds," *Birmingham Daily Post* 7,368 (14 February 1882): 4.

48. "The Frauds by an Adventuress," *Illustrated London News* 80, no. 2,233 (18 February 1882): 163; "The Frauds by an Adventuress: Amazing Credulity of Her Victims," *North-Eastern Daily Gazette* 4,576 (14 February 1882): 3.

49. "The Personation Frauds," *Sheffield Daily Telegraph* 8,321 (24 February 1882): 2.

50. "The Fearneaux Frauds," *Birmingham Daily Post* 7,369 (15 February 1882): 4.

51. "The Fearneaux Frauds," *Times* 30,446 (4 March 1882): 10.

52. *History*, 84.

53. "A Singular Case of Personation," *Times* 30,427 (10 February 1882): 8.

54. "Fearneaux," *Times*, 10.

55. "Assizes," *Times*, 7.

56. "Frauds," *North-Eastern*, 3.

57. "Assizes," *Times*, 7.

58. "A Woman with a Past. Sensational Arrest in Leeds," *Yorkshire Evening Post* 1,187 (18 June 1894): 3. In *Crooks of the Waldorf* (1929), Horace Smith illustrates the life and profession of Joseph Edward Smith, the "house detective" of the Waldorf Hotel in New York City. Joseph Smith was trained by Scotland Yard and reportedly was involved in Furneaux's capture, though Horace Smith refers to her as "Frederica de Furneaux" throughout. The crimes that Smith describes are limited to London robberies, where Furneaux set up a sort of salon. Joseph Smith was a young apprentice at the time, but he joined the case, having "inclined toward the male impersonator idea" (*Crooks of the Waldorf: Being the Story of Joe Smith, Master Detective* [New York: Macaulay Company, 1929], 34).

59. "Lord," *Daily*, 3.

60. "The Fearneaux Frauds Again," *Lancaster Gazette* 6,495 (20 June 1894): 4.

61. "Woman," *Yorkshire*, 3.

62. "Lambeth," *Standard* 21,840 (3 July 1894): 6.

63. "Woman," *Yorkshire*, 3.

64. "A Remarkable Impostor," *Evening News* (7 August 1894): 3.

Chapter 5

1. Thomas Carlyle, *The French Revolution*, ed. David R. Sorensen and Brent E. Kinser (Oxford: Oxford University Press, 2019), 32.

2. Carlyle, *French*, 32.
3. Carlyle, *French*, 32.
4. Bill Brown, *A Sense of Things: The Object Matter of American Literature* (Chicago: University of Chicago Press, 2003), 4.
5. Sigmund Freud, "A Note upon the 'Mystic Writing-Pad,'" in *The Standard Edition of the Complete Psychological Works*, vol. 19, ed. James Strachey (London: Hogarth, 1973), 429.
6. Jacques Derrida, "Paper or Me, You Know . . . (New Speculations of a Luxury of the Poor)," in *Paper Machine*, trans. Rachel Bowlby (Stanford, CA: Stanford University Press, 2005), 41.
7. "The Paper Age," *American Bookseller* 18, no. 2 (15 July 1885): 59.
8. Frederick Knight Hunt, "A Visit to the Registrar-General," *Household Words* 2.36 (30 November 1850): 235.
9. John Hollingshead, "The City of Unlimited Paper," *Household Words* 17, no. 404 (19 December 1857): 1.
10. Lisa Gitelman, *Paper Knowledge: Toward a Media History of Documents* (Durham, NC: Duke University Press, 2014), 3.
11. Karl Marx, "The Power of Money in Bourgeois Society," in *Sociological Theory in the Classical Era: Text and Readings*, ed. Laura Desfor Edles and Scott Appelrouth (Los Angeles: Sage, 2015), 54.
12. Karl Marx, *Capital*, ed. David McLellan (Oxford: Oxford University Press, 2008), 83.
13. Kevin McLaughlin, *Paperwork: Fiction and Mass Mediacy in the Paper Age* (Philadelphia: University of Pennsylvania Press, 2005), 2.
14. Peter Brooks, *Enigmas of Identity* (Princeton, NJ: Princeton University Press, 2011), 4.
15. Brooks, *Enigmas*, 4.
16. James C. Scott, *Seeing Like a State: How Certain Schemes to Improve Human Condition Have Failed* (New Haven, CT: Yale University Press, 1998), 2.
17. Ian Hacking, *The Taming of Chance* (Cambridge: Cambridge University Press, 1990), 2–3. Modern social statistics developed in the 1830s via the competing work of Auguste Comte (1798–1857) and Adolphe Quetelet (1796–1874). Comte applied the term "sociology" to his positivist theories in response to Quetelet appropriating "social physics" for his own work, which sought to understand social phenomena through statistics. According to Simon A. Cole, statistics developed "to collect and store information about ordinary people," and to give them an "identity that existed outside the physical body" (*Suspect Identities: A History of Fingerprinting and Criminal Identification* [Cambridge, MA: Harvard University Press, 2001], 9, 10.).
18. Keith Breckenridge and Simon Szreter, Introduction, *Registration and Recognition: Documenting the Person in World History*, ed. Keith Breckenridge and Simon Szreter (Oxford: Oxford University Press, 2012), 1; Michel Foucault, *Power/*

Knowledge: Selected Interviews & Other Writings, 1972–1977, ed. Colin Gordon (New York: Pantheon Books, 1980), 102.

19. Edward Higgs, *Life, Death and Statistics: Civil Registration, Censuses and the Work of the General Register Office, 1836–1952* (Hatfield, Hertfordshire: Local Population Studies, 2004), 1.

20. Charles Dickens, "Received—A Blank Child," *Household Words* 7, no. 156 (3 March 1853): 49.

21. In 1850, Hunt calls attention to the "little innocent," who will "shortly be inscribed on the parchment indexes of the grand muster-roll of the British nation," and the "heartbroken widow," whose dead husband has "already passed into the black volumes of the Registrar" ("Visit," 235).

22. John Guillory, "The Memo and Modernity," *Critical Inquiry* 31, no. 1 (Autumn 2004): 113n13.

23. George Graham, *Twenty-Second Annual Report of the Registrar-General of Births, Deaths, and Marriages in England* (London: George E. Eyre and William Spottiswoode, 1861), xliii.

24. "Very Common Law," *All the Year Round* 2, no. 37 (7 January 1860): 254.

25. Edward Higgs, "The Linguistic Construction of Social and Medical Categories in the Work of the English General Register Office, 1837–1950," in *Categories and Contexts: Anthropological and Historical Studies in Critical Demography*, ed. Simon Szreter, Hania Sholkamy, and A. Dharmarlingam (Oxford: Oxford University Press, 2004), 91.

26. Henry Wyldbore Rumsey, *Essays on State Medicine* (London: John Churchill, 1856), 9.

27. Claudine Dardy, "L'identité-papier," *Les Cahiers de Médiologie* 2, no. 4 (1997): 226–27; my translation.

28. Sara Malton, *Forgery in Nineteenth-Century Literature and Culture: Fictions of Finance from Dickens to Wilde* (New York: Palgrave Macmillan, 2009), 151n9.

29. Anthony Trollope's *Orley Farm* (1861–62) features a complex plot involving a forged codicil. And in George Eliot's *Middlemarch* (1871–72), Edward Casaubon includes a codicil in his will that disinherits his wife Dorothea Brooke if she were to marry Will Ladislaw.

30. On 20 September 1792, just days after the September massacres, the French National Assembly voted to standardize the civil status of its population. This legislation was based on language from the 1791 Constitution, which vowed to "establish for all inhabitants, without distinction, the manner in which births, marriages, and deaths will be certified; and . . . [to] designate the public officials who will receive and maintain these files" (Gérard Noiriel, "The Identification of the Citizen: The Birth of Republican Status in France," in *Documenting Individual Identity: The Development of State Practices in the Modern World*, ed. Jane Caplan and John Torpey [Princeton, NJ: Princeton University Press, 2001], 28).

31. The Domesday Book (1086), commissioned by William the Conqueror, is probably the first formal attempt at registration. In the 1670s, William Petty

(1620–87) called for the registration of births, deaths, and marriages in Ireland, but his inspired inquiry was largely ignored (Michael J. Cullen, *The Statistical Movement in Early Victorian Britain: The Foundations of Empirical Social Research* [New York: Harvester Press, 1975], 3). Over a century later, Thomas Percival made an impassioned plea for the "establishment of a judicious and accurate register of the births and burials," and provided samples for how he thought these registers should be constructed ("Proposals for Establishing More Accurate and Comprehensive Bills of Mortality in Manchester," in *Essays Medical and Experimental*, vol. 2 [London: Joseph Johnson, 1773], 239).

32. The 1837 Births, Deaths, and Marriages Act was effectively two combined acts, one for registering births and deaths at the civil level rather than baptisms and burials at the parochial level, and the other for registering marriages as civil contracts rather than limiting legal marriage to Church of England services. England and Wales were the only countries covered because parish clerks in Scotland fought to have it postponed.

33. Nathan K. Hensley, *Forms of Empire: The Poetics of Victorian Sovereignty* (Oxford: Oxford University Press, 2016), 88.

34. Muriel Nissel, *People Count: A History of the General Register Office* (London: Her Majesty's Stationary Service, 1987), 24.

35. Hunt, "Visit," 236.

36. Hunt, "Visit," 239.

37. Lister asserted: "After such a preliminary arrangement as shall prevent the confusion and intermixture of papers, each leaf of the Certified Copies, and each entry thereon, is subjected to a strict examination. If any erasure, interpolation, informality, omission, or error, or defect of any kind, is thereby detected in any entry, it is immediately noted" (*First Annual Report of the Registrar-General of Births, Deaths, and Marriages in England* [London: W. Clowes and Sons, 1839], 13).

38. Lister, *First*, 71.

39. Lister, *First*, 71.

40. Hunt, "Visit," 238.

41. Hunt, "Visit," 236.

42. George Graham, *Fourth Annual Report of the Registrar-General of Births, Deaths, and Marriages, in England* (London: W. Clowes and Sons, 1842), 10.

43. As with Lister, Graham worked closely with William Farr (1807–83), the "chief statistician" of the General Register Office for over forty years, who contributed health analyses in appendices to the Annual Reports (Cullen, *Statistical*, 15).

44. Nissel, *People*, 24; Hunt, "Visit," 238.

45. Nissel, *People*, 25.

46. Pamela K. Gilbert, *The Citizen's Body: Desire, Health, and the Social in Victorian England* (Columbus: The Ohio State University Press, 2007), 3.

47. George Graham, *Thirty-Seventh Annual Report of the Registrar-General of Births, Deaths, and Marriages, in England* (London: George E. Eyre and William Spottiswoode, 1876), vi.

48. Scott, *Seeing*, 2.

49. Ronald R. Thomas, *Detective Fiction and the Rise of Forensic Science* (Cambridge: Cambridge University Press, 1999), 60.

50. In John Cordy Jeaffreson's *Not Dead Yet* (1864), Rupert Smith (né Edward Guerdon) confirms Edward Smith's aristocratic lineage by consulting a parish register, motivating him to personate his half-brother. In Hall Caine's *A Son of Hagar* (1886), Hugh Ritson travels to the General Register Office to peruse two birth registers and a marriage register to ascertain the identity of his half-brother Paul. In Wilkie Collins's *Armadale* (1854–66), Lydia Gwilt marries Ozias Midwinter (né Alan Armadale) so that she can claim the other Alan Armadale's inheritance following his death. In *The Law and the Lady* (1874–75), Eustace Macallan fraudulently signs his name as Woodville in the register following his marriage to Valeria Brinton. John Berwick Harwood's *Lady Flavia* (1866) follows the exploits of the impostor Adela Burt, who is falsely recorded to have died of heart trouble. And in Benjamin Leopold Farjeon's *The Sacred Nugget* (1885), David Bannister forges a birth certificate that permits Peggy's personation of Madge.

51. In Robert Arthur Arnold's *Hever Court* (1867), Will is taken in by Mrs. Prickett, who dreams of a better life for her adopted child. Prickett establishes a friendship with Jimmy Pitcher, a parish clerk and sexton, and wants him to "search every parish registry in England in the hope of finding evidence of [Will's] mother's marriage" (2 vols. [London: Bradbury, Evans & Co., 1867], 1.34). Thereafter, Gribble, a duplicitous lawyer, produces "the certificate of marriage of those parties" (1.135). He admits that the signatures bear "little similarity" but argues that "the parties to a secret marriage would attempt to disguise their handwriting" (1.136). As it turns out, the "register has been fraudulently tampered with," as Gribble forged "the second 'n' into a 'y,'" making "Ann Campbell" into "Amy Campbell" (2.171–72).

52. Sean Grass, *The Commodification of Identity in Victorian Narrative: Autobiography, Sensation, and the Literary Marketplace* (Cambridge: Cambridge University Press, 2019), 72.

53. Wilkie Collins, *The Woman in White* (New York: Barnes & Noble, 2005), 17–18; subsequent references to this edition provided in the text.

54. Sara Malton, *Forgery in Nineteenth-Century Literature and Culture: Fictions of Finance from Dickens to Wilde* (New York: Palgrave Macmillan, 2009), 42.

55. Helen Barrell has elucidated Hartright's reference to the "old-fashioned" register book, which contains "entries . . . made on blank pages, in manuscript" ("Parish Registers in Wilkie Collins' The Woman in White," Essex & Suffolk Surnames, http://essexandsuffolksurnames.co.uk/parish-registers-in-wilkie-collins-the-woman-in-white). Prior to the 1812 passing of Rose's Act, which established uniformity in parish registers, marriage registers took many forms. Some contained printed text with lines to differentiate dates, signatures, and witnesses, while others contained only lines, similar to notebook paper. The register that Glyde forges, however, has neither printed text nor lines. Hartright records that the entries were

separated only "by ink lines drawn across the page at the close of each entry" (491). Thus, the register book is kept insecurely and composed unreliably, allowing Glyde access and space to forge his life.

56. Gwendolyn MacDonagh and Jonathan Smith point out several blank spaces in the novel, including Laura's gravestone and Glyde's document that Laura refuses to sign. MacDonagh and Smith also argue that "the thickly-planted trees" at Blackwater Park are "the visual analogue of the forged entry in the marriage register" ("'Fill up All the Gaps': Narrative and Illegitimacy in *The Woman in White*," *The Journal of Narrative Technique* 26, no. 3 [Fall 1996]: 276).

57. John Kucich, *The Power of Lies: Transgression in Victorian Fiction* (Ithaca, NY: Cornell University Press, 1994), 91.

58. Hartright also fills Anne with Laura. Rachel Ablow observes that *The Woman in White* "explores the fantasy . . . of how a 'sympathetic' relation to one's wife could enable limitless self-recreation. Walter sees 'Anne,' names her 'Laura,' and refashions himself as the father of the Heir of Limmeridge" (*The Marriage of Minds: Reading Sympathy in the Victorian Marriage Plot* [Stanford, CA: Stanford University Press, 2007], 116). Andrew Mangham also suggests that Hartright fills Laura with himself: "Anne Catherick is a figurative *tabula rasa* onto which [Hartright] daubs the most disturbing aspects of his own character" ("'What Could I Do?': Nineteenth-Century Psychology and the Horrors of Masculinity in *The Woman in White*," in *Victorian Sensations: Essays on a Scandalous Genre*, ed. Kimberly Harrison and Richard Fontina [Columbus: The Ohio State University Press, 2006], 120).

59. Nicholas Daly, *Sensation and Modernity in the 1860s* (Cambridge: Cambridge University Press, 2009), 32.

60. Daly, *Sensation*, 34.

61. Daly, *Sensation*, 35.

62. Valerie Pedlar, "Drawing a Blank: The Construction of Identity in *The Woman in White*," in *The Nineteenth-Century Novel: Identities*, ed. Dennis Walder (London: Routledge, 2001), 80.

63. Ronald R. Thomas, *Detective Fiction and the Rise of Forensic Science* (Cambridge: Cambridge University Press, 1999), 72.

64. Rebecca Stern, "'Personation' and 'Good Marking-Ink': Sanity, Performativity, and Biology in Victorian Sensation Fiction," *Nineteenth-Century Studies* 14 (2000): 44.

65. Ann Gaylin, *Eavesdropping in the Novel from Austen to Proust* (Cambridge: Cambridge University Press, 2003), 116. Ann Cvetkovich notes Hartright's "class transition" and argues that his "incapacity to control his own body . . . permits him to rise to power without appearing to aspire to it" (*Mixed Feelings: Feminism, Mass Culture, and Victorian Sensationalism* [New Brunswick, NJ: Rutgers University Press, 1992], 77, 75).

66. Mariaconcetta Costantini, *Sensation and Professionalism in the Victorian Novel* (Bern: Peter Lang, 2014), 165.

67. "How to Prove a Will," *Chambers's Journal* 3, no. 123 (8 May 1886): 299.

68. "How," *Chambers's*, 299.

69. The 1540 Statute of Wills granted the authority to bequeath property, while the 1677 Statute of Frauds required that wills pertaining to property be produced in writing. The Wills Act legislated that a subject's gift of "personal estate" could be made "in any form" of writing: "Any scrap of paper or memorandum, in ink or in pencil, mentioning an intended disposition of the testator's property, was admitted as a will, and held to be valid" (Edward Chitty, *The Commercial and General Lawyer* [London: R. Macdonald, 1839], 722).

70. Cathrine O. Frank, *Law, Literature, and the Transmission of Culture in England, 1837–1925* (London: Routledge, 2016), 3.

71. Frank, *Law*, 4.

72. Frank, *Law*, 35.

73. Frank, *Law*, 4.

74. L. S. Lewis, "Some Peculiar Wills," *Strand Magazine* 14, no. 82 (October 1897): 441.

75. "Wills and Will-Making, Ancient and Modern," *London Quarterly Review* 108, no. 216 (1860): 223.

76. Charles Draycott, "Whimsical Will-Making," *Temple Bar* 110 (January 1897): 66.

77. "The Degeneracy of Wills," *Spectator* 86, no. 3,785 (12 January 1901): 46.

78. William Hazlitt, "On Will-Making," in *Table-Talk*, vol. 1 (Paris: A. and W. Galignani, 1825), 113.

79. Hazlitt, "On Will-Making," 113.

80. Hazlitt, "On Will-Making," 121.

81. Charles Dickens, *Bleak House*, ed. George Ford and Sylvère Monod (New York: Norton, 1977), 7–8.

82. Dickens, *Bleak*, 759, 760.

83. Charles Dickens and William Henry Wills, "The Doom of English Wills: Cathedral Number One," *Household Words* 2, no. 27 (28 September 1850): 3.

84. "Curious Will Case," *Annual Register* (London: J. & F. H. Rivington, 1861), 39.

85. "The Derbyshire Will Case," *Saturday Review* 9, no. 231 (31 March 1860): 396.

86. "Derbyshire," *Saturday*, 396.

87. "The Derbyshire Will Case," *Spectator* 37, no. 1,862 (5 March 1864): 262.

88. "Derbyshire," *Saturday*, 396.

89. "The Matlock Will Case," *Law Journal* 26 (17 October 1891): 639.

90. "Matlock," *Law*, 639; "Derbyshire," *Spectator*, 262.

91. "Matlock," *Law*, 639.

92. "Matlock," *Law*, 640.

93. "Matlock," *Law*, 640.

94. "Law Report," *Examiner* 2,927 (5 March 1864): 154.
95. "Law," *Examiner*, 154.
96. "More Matlock Codicils," *Punch* 46 (28 May 1864): 227.
97. "Derbyshire," *Saturday*, 397.
98. Eileen Cleere notes that sensation fiction and "anti-Mormon stories have much in common" ("Chaste Polygamy: Mormon Marriage and the Fantasy of Sexual Privacy in *East Lynne* and *Verner's Pride*," *Victorian Studies* 57, no. 2 [Winter 2015]: 202). While *Verner's Pride* is "[i]nstinctively repulsed by the Mormon mission," the novel "nevertheless indulges the very appealing fantasy of chaste polygamy that was on offer in a wide variety of Mormon materials in the 1860s" (202). Deborah Wynne argues that Wood was influenced by an 1861 article by Jules Rémy, titled "The Mormons and the Country They Dwell In," which "depicts Mormons as 'imposters' who set out to infiltrate and undermine British society" (*The Sensation Novel and the Victorian Family Magazine* [New York: Palgrave Macmillan, 2001], 80).
99. "Verner's Pride," *London Review* 6, no. 146 (18 April 1863): 416.
100. "Verner's," *London*, 416.
101. "Verner's," *London*, 416.
102. "Verner's Pride," *Saturday Review* 15, no. 383 (28 February 1863): 280; "Verner's Pride," *Athenaeum* 1,845 (7 March 1863): 323.
103. "Verner's Pride," *Examiner* 2,876 (14 March 1863): 165.
104. Ellen Wood, *Verner's Pride: A Novel* (Macmillan and Co., 1900), 352; subsequent references to this edition provided in the text.

Chapter 6

1. Charles Dickens, *A Tale of Two Cities*, ed. Richard Maxwell (London: Penguin, 2000), 77.
2. [Untitled], *All the Year Round* 2, no. 31 (26 November 1859): 95.
3. Daniel Stout, "Nothing Personal: The Decapitation of Character in *A Tale of Two Cities*," *NOVEL: A Forum on Fiction* 41, no. 1 (Fall 2007): 29.
4. In Rupert Greville-Williams's *Ruthven's Wrecks* (1887), Robert Ruthven personates his brother George, even though they were "widely different in appearance, manners, and feelings," merely by forging his brother's signature ([Bristol: J. W. Arrowsmith, 1887], 3). And in Ida Ashworth Taylor's *Vice Valentine* (1890), Valentine Kremleck personates her deceased cousin Valentine "Tina" Kremleck by signing her own name, thereby accessing payments from Tina's estranged husband Osmund Wynter. As in *Ruthven's Wrecks*, Valentine and Tina are dissimilar, the former having been a "little brown baby," owing to her mother being found as a "beautiful gypsy at a fair" (2 vols. [London: Ward and Downey, 1890], 1.26–27).
5. Charles Dickens, "A Paper-Mill," *Household Words* 1, no. 23 (31 August 1850): 530.

6. Michelle Allen, *Cleansing the City: Sanitary Geographies in Victorian London* (Athens: Ohio University Press, 2008), 111.

7. Dickens, "Paper," 529–30.

8. Dickens, "Paper," 530.

9. Owen Ashmore, *The Industrial Archaeology of North-West England* (Manchester: Chetham Society, 1982), 15.

10. Richard Menke, "*New Grub Street*'s Ecologies of Paper," *Victorian Studies* 61.1 (Autumn 2018): 68.

11. Michael F. Suarez and H. R. Woudhuysen, *The Book: A Global History* (Oxford: Oxford University Press, 2013), 160.

12. In 1899, C. H. Bothamley pointed to "the Evil of Wood-pulp," but admitted that "we are at present without any evidence that would justify the rejection of mounts properly made from esparto, wood-cellulose, or straw-cellulose" ("Paper and Mounts," *Photography* 9, no. 539 [9 March 1988]: 151).

13. "Paper," *All the Year Round* 12, no. 306 (10 November 1894): 442.

14. "Paper," *All*, 442.

15. "Paper," *All*, 442.

16. "Paper," *All*, 443.

17. "Paper," *All*, 443.

18. Leah Price, *How to Do Things with Books in Victorian Britain* (Princeton, NJ: Princeton University Press, 2012), 219.

19. Arjun Appadurai, "Introduction: Commodities and the Politics of Value," in *The Social Life of Things: Commodities in Cultural Perspective*, ed. Arjun Appadurai (Cambridge: Cambridge University Press, 1986), 23.

20. Natalka Freeland, "Trash Fiction: The Victorian Novel and the Rise of Disposable Culture" (PhD dissertation, Yale University, New Haven, Connecticut, 1998), 4.

21. Pamela K. Gilbert, "Medical Mapping: The Thames, the Body, and *Our Mutual Friend*," in *Filth: Dirt, Disgust, and Modern Life*, ed. William A. Cohen and Ryan Johnson (Minneapolis: University of Minnesota Press, 2005), 79.

22. Mary Douglas, *Purity and Danger* (London: Routledge, 1966), 2.

23. Douglas, *Purity*, 4–5.

24. Michael Thompson, *Rubbish Theory: The Creation and Destruction of Value* (London: Pluto Press, 2017), 10.

25. Thompson, *Rubbish*, 11.

26. Thompson, *Rubbish*, 11.

27. Alexander Charles Ewald, *The Right Hon. Benjamin Disraeli, Earl of Beaconsfield, K. G., and His Times*, vol. 2 (London: William Mackenzie, 1882), 229.

28. Ewald, *Right*, 229.

29. Ewald, *Right*, 229.

30. Edwin Chadwick, *Report on the Sanitary Condition of the Laboring Population of Great Britain* (London: W. Clowes and Sons, 1842), 5.

31. Dickens read the report in 1842 and, in collaboration with his brother-in-law Henry Austin, promoted sanitary reform throughout the 1840s. David Trotter observes that Dickens accessed a "discursive economy" that would "shape his imagining of the disposition and regulation of society," which he understood as a "system of flows and stoppages" (*Circulation: Defoe, Dickens, and the Economies of the Novel* [London: Macmillan, 1988], 104).

32. Chadwick, *Report*, 54.

33. Chadwick, *Report*, 44.

34. Lee Jackson, *Dirty Old London: The Victorian Fight Against Filth* (New Haven, CT: Yale University Press, 2014), 2–3.

35. Chadwick, *Report*, 48.

36. Allen, *Cleansing*, 2.

37. Sally Mitchell, *Daily Life in Victorian England* (London: Greenwood Press, 1996), 80.

38. Chadwick, *Report*, 370.

39. George R. Sims, *How the Poor Live* (London: Chatto & Windus, 1883), 6.

40. Henry Mayhew, *London Labour and the London Poor*, 2 vols. (London: Griffin, Bohn, and Company, 1861), 1.409.

41. Mayhew, *London*, 2.125.

42. Mayhew, *London*, 2.125–26.

43. Price, *How*, 219.

44. "Government Waste-Paper," *Chambers's Journal* 13, no. 673 (21 November 1886): 747.

45. "Government," *Chambers's*, 748.

46. "Government," *Chambers's*, 748.

47. Henry Mansel, "Sensation Novels," *Quarterly Review* 113, no. 226 (April 1863): 486.

48. "Novels," *Marlburian* 1 (20 September 1865): 2.

49. "Armadale," *Spectator* 39.1,980 (9 June 1866): 639.

50. "The Law and the Lady," *Saturday Review* 38, no. 1,011 (13 March 1875): 358.

51. Wilkie Collins, *The Law and the Lady* (London: Chatto and Windus, 1876), 296.

52. In Mary Elizabeth Braddon's *Henry Dunbar* (1864), Clement Austin receives a mysterious parcel with an envelope that he initially discards. Looking for clues to identify the sender, he returns to his dustbin, and "tosse[s] over the chaotic fragments, the soiled envelopes, the circulars of enterprising Clapham tradesmen, and all the other rubbish that had accumulated within the last two years. The dust floated up to my face and almost blinded me" (2 vols. [Leipzig: Bernhard Tauchnitz, 1864], 2.302). Eventually, he locates the envelope, marked with the name and address of a stationary company, which gives him the general location of Margaret Wilmot. In John Berwick Harwood's *Lady Flavia* (1866), Adela Burt,

personating the real Lady Flavia, whom she accidentally killed, visits a post office to send a telegram abroad. But she neglects to take her receipt. "Little oversights like this," the narrator remarks, "sometimes produce important results" ([London: Richard Bentley, 1866], 147).

53. J. Hillis Miller, *Charles Dickens: The World of His Novels* (Cambridge, MA: Harvard University Press, 1958), 281, 288. Leslie Simon similarly argues that dust "works as a central image, figuring thematically . . . as a symbol of psychological fragmentation" ("*Bleak House, Our Mutual Friend*, and the Aesthetics of Dust," *Dickens Studies Annual* 42 [2011]: 217–18).

54. Charles Dickens, *Our Mutual Friend*, ed. Stephen Gill (London: Penguin, 1985), 127; subsequent references to this edition provided in the text.

55. Sean Grass, *The Commodification of Identity in Victorian Narrative: Autobiography, Sensation, and the Literary Marketplace* (Cambridge: Cambridge University Press, 2019), 162.

56. Jessica Kuskey, "Our Mutual Engine: The Economics of Victorian Thermodynamics," *Victorian Literature and Culture* 41 (2013): 76.

57. J. Hillis Miller, *Victorian Subjects* (Durham, NC: Duke University Press, 1991), 71.

58. "Our Mutual Friend," *Eclectic Review* 9 (November 1865): 456.

59. Dickens, *Bleak House*, 491.

60. Dickens, *Bleak House*, 273.

61. "Living Novelists," *Rambler* 1.1 (January 1854): 44. Dickens's imagery resembles some aspects of John Ruskin's "The Ethics of Dust" (1866), in which the narrator tells a group of schoolgirls: "you are yourselves . . . nothing, in the eye of a mineralogist, but a lovely group of rosy sugar-candy, arranged by atomic forces" ([New York: John B. Alden, 1888], 20). A contemporaneous review of Ruskin's text, which threatens to miss its point entirely, nonetheless contains passages relevant to *Our Mutual Friend*: "Golden dust has enslaved us, but common dust breaks away our fetters. Molecules of matter have overcome us, and we hurry from city and town anywhither, we say from custom, or change, or for health; but we are in reality dust-scattered" ("Ethics of Dust," *Meliora* 9 [1866]: 99).

62. Virginia Zimmerman, *Excavating Victorians* (Albany, NY: SUNY Press, 2008), 162.

63. Simon, *Bleak*, 219.

64. Daniel Novak, *Realism, Photography and Nineteenth-Century Fiction* (Cambridge: Cambridge University Press, 2008), 76.

65. Eve Kosofsky Sedgwick, *Between Men: English Literature and Male Homosocial Desire* (New York: Columbia University Press, 2015), 171. Sabine Schülting reads the dust-mounds as "the only reliable form of wealth in the novel" (*Dirt in Victorian Literature and Culture: Writing Materiality* [New York: Routledge, 2016], 34).

66. Grass, *Commodification*, 164.

67. Grass, *Commodification*, 164.

68. R. H. Horne, "Dust; or Ugliness Redeemed," *Household Words* 1, no. 16 (13 July 1850): 380, 382. Horne introduces three eccentric characters who are employed to sift through the dust. The most unfortunate of the bunch makes a remarkable discovery—a parchment encased in a gold frame. Similar to the opening chapter of *Our Mutual Friend*, the group suddenly finds a body floating in nearby water. They manage to revive the man, who spots the framed paper. Coincidentally, the man identifies the paper as a "portion of the title-deeds he had lost; and though it did not prove sufficient to enable him to recover his fortune, it brought his opponent to a composition, which gave him an annuity for life" (384).

69. Miller, *Charles*, 281.

70. Nancy Aycock Metz observes Harmon's "crisis of identity" ("The Artistic Reclamation of Waste in *Our Mutual Friend*," *Nineteenth-Century Fiction* 34, no. 1 [June 1979]: 62); and Leon Litvack argues that Harmon is "the novel's prime example of fluidity of human personality" ("Images of the River in *Our Mutual Friend*," *Dickens Quarterly* 20, no. 1 [March 2003]: 48).

71. "Our Mutual Friend," *London Review* 11 (28 October 1865): 468.

72. Freeland, "Trash," 77.

73. "Our Mutual Friend," *Morning Post* 28,670 (1 November 1865): 2.

74. Gwen Watkins, *Dickens in Search of Himself: Recurrent Themes and Characters in the Work of Charles Dickens* (London: Macmillan Press, 1987), 135.

75. Ellen Handy, "Dust Piles and Damp Pavements: Excrement, Repression, and the Victorian City in Photography and Literature," in *Victorian Literature and the Victorian Visual Imagination*, ed. Carol T. Christ and John O. Jordan (Berkeley: University of California Press, 1995), 118.

76. *The Letters of Charles Dickens*, vol. 2, ed. Madeline House and Graham Storey (Oxford: Clarendon Press, 1969), 284.

77. Henry Morley and William Henry Wills, "Photography," *Household Words* 7.156 (19 March 1853): 54.

78. Morley and Wills, "Photography," 58, 55.

79. Morley and Wills, "Photography," 56.

80. Morley and Wills, "Photography," 55.

81. Morley and Wills, "Photography," 55.

82. In 1891, M. Lazar Popoff noted: "in a tribe in western Africa it was dangerous to make a portrait of the natives, because they were afraid that by some kind of sorcery a part of their soul would pass into their image . . . ; and the more like the portrait the greater the danger to the original; for the more life there is in the copy, the less must be left in the person" ("The Origin of Portraiture," *American Journal of Photography* 12.144 [December 1891]: 559).

83. Susan Sontag, *On Photography* (New York: Farrar, Status and Giroux, 1977), 1.

84. Sontag, *On Photography*, 2.

85. Sontag, *On Photography*, 4.

86. Sontag, *On Photography*, 12.

87. Roland Barthes, *Camera Lucida: Reflections on Photography*, trans. Richard Howard (New York: Hill and Wang, 1981), 13.

88. Barthes, *Camera*, 5.

89. Barthes, *Camera*, 9, 12.

90. Barthes, *Camera*, 14.

91. Jonathan Crary has identified a "reorganization of vision" in the nineteenth century that preceded the introduction of photography" (*Techniques of the Observer: On Vision and Modernity in the Nineteenth Century* [Cambridge, MA: MIT Press, 1992], 2). Photography becomes an "element of a new and homogeneous terrain of consumption and circulation" and helps to construct a "whole social world [that] is represented and constituted exclusively as signs" (13). Nancy Armstrong traces a similar transformation, noting that photography heralded "the substitution of the visual representation for the object represented" (*Fiction in the Age of Photography: The Legacy of British Realism* [Cambridge, MA: Harvard University Press, 1999], 33).

92. "Detection of Crime by Photography," *Monthly Law Digest and Reporter* 1, no. 8 (August 1893): 468.

93. "Photography: Its History and Applications," *British Quarterly Review* 44 (1 October 1866): 382.

94. "Photograph by Telegraph," *British Journal of Photography* 24, no. 878 (2 March 1877): 104.

95. *The Trial at Bar of Sir Roger C. D. Tichborne*, vol. 8 (London: Englishman Office, 1880), 232.

96. "The Identiscope," *Amateur Photographer* 1, no. 9 (5 December 1884): 141.

97. *The Trial*, 263.

98. Francis Wharton, *A Treatise on the Law of Evidence in Criminal Issues* (Philadelphia: Kay and Brother, 1880), 805.

99. In Wilkie Collins's final novel *Blind Love* (1889), the villainous Clarence Vimpany poisons Oxbye, who resembles Lord Harry, and then takes a photograph of Oxbye to falsify Lord Harry's death.

100. Thomas Hardy, *Desperate Remedies: A Novel* (London: Ward and Downey, 1889), 307.

101. Hardy, *Desperate*, 307.

102. Hardy, *Desperate*, 307.

103. Hardy, *Desperate*, 307–308.

104. In Hardy's *A Laodicean* (1880–81), William Dare forges a telegram and manipulates a photograph to blackmail George Somerset.

105. Sutton was a respected artist, critic, and inventor in the field of photography. He edited the journal *Photographic Notes* from 1856 to 1869 and ran the *Amateur's Photographic Album*. In 1859, he produced the first wide-angle panoramic camera, and in 1861 he patented the first reflex camera, which "narrowed the gap

between focusing and exposure" (Kaja Silverman, *The Miracle of Analogy or The History of Photography, Part 1* [Stanford, CA: Stanford University Press, 2015], 72). Jordi Cat has studied Sutton's role in developing the first color photograph (*Maxwell, Sutton, and the Birth of Color Photography: A Binocular Study* [New York: Palgrave Macmillan, 2013]).

106. "Unconventional," *Athenaeum* 2,012 (19 May 1866): 688.

107. "Unconventional," *Reader* 7, no. 173 (21 April 1866): 393.

108. Elazar Barkan, "Victorian Promiscuity: Greek Ethics and Primitive Exemplars," in *Prehistories of the Future: The Primitivist Project and the Culture of Modernism*, ed. Elazar Barkan and Ronald Bush (Stanford, CA: Stanford University Press, 1995), 70.

109. Thomas Sutton, "Photographic Society of Scotland. Ordinary Meeting," *Journal of the Photographic Society of London* 8, no. 129 (15 January 1863): 203.

110. Thomas Sutton, *Unconventional: A Novel*, 3 vols. (London: Sampson Low, Son, & Marston, 1866), 3.175; subsequent references to this edition provided in the text.

111. Sutton inserted himself into contentious debates over Oscar Gustave Rejlander's *The Two Ways of Life* (1856), which featured nude models. Although Sutton was initially supportive, he changed his view in the early 1860s, writing: "there *is* impropriety in allowing the public to see photographs of nude prostitutes, in flesh-and-blood truthfulness and minuteness of detail" ("Photographic," 203). Alfred H. Wall offered a sharp rebuke: "If . . . Mr. Sutton objects to the representation of nude models, simply because he imagines that they should be idealized, or conventionalized, before their images are fit to be presented to what he must evidently regard as a lascivious-minded British public, then I have another answer for him" ("Thomas Sutton, B.A., on Art-Photography," *Journal of the Photographic Society of London* 8, no. 131 [16 March 1863]: 244).

Afterword

1. Several writers claimed that the genre owed its genesis to the Gothic. "In the 'Castle of Otranto,'" one 1874 reviewer remarked, "we find quite a surfeit of all the elements of a sensation novel" (E. B., "The Sensation Novel," *Argosy* 18 [1 August 1874]: 140).

2. Henry James, "Miss Braddon," *Nation* 1, no. 19 (9 November 1865): 593.

3. Lewis Carroll, *Alice's Adventures in Wonderland* and *Through the Looking-Glass*, ed. Peter Hunt (Oxford: Oxford University Press, 2009), 15.

4. Robert Louis Stevenson, *The Strange Case of Dr. Jekyll and Mr. Hyde*, ed. Emma Letley (Oxford: Oxford University Press, 1998), 63; subsequent references to this edition provided in the text.

5. "Robert Louis Stevenson," *Century* 35, no. 6 (April 1888): 878.

6. Carol Margaret Davison, "A Battle of Wills: Solving *The Strange Case of Dr Jekyll and Mr Hyde*," in *Troubled Legacies: Narrative and Inheritance*, ed. Allan Hepburn (Toronto: University of Toronto Press, 2007), 147.

7. Sara Malton, *Forgery in Nineteenth-Century Literature and Culture: Fictions of Finance from Dickens to Wilde* (New York: Palgrave Macmillan, 2009), 106.

8. "Our Library Table," *Athenaeum* 3,038 (16 January 1886): 100.

9. "The Inquest on Hyde," *Saturday Review* 61, no. 1,587 (27 March 1886): 426.

10. "Inquest," *Saturday*, 427.

11. "Inquest," *Saturday*, 427.

12. "Strange Case of Dr. Jekyll and Mr. Hyde," *Dublin Review* 15, no. 2 (April 1886): 422.

13. Oscar Wilde, *The Picture of Dorian Gray*, ed. Joseph Bristow (Oxford: Oxford University Press, 2008), 79, 90; subsequent references to this edition provided in the text.

14. Kathryn Humphreys, "The Artistic Exchange: *Dorian Gray* at the *Sacred Fount*," *Texas Studies in Literature and Language* 32, no. 4 (Winter 1990): 524.

15. Wilde revered Whitman, and the authors met over wine in January 1882.

16. J. Halberstam, *Skin Shows: Gothic Horror and the Technology of Monsters* (Durham, NC: Duke University Press, 1995), 73.

17. Andrew Eastham, "Aesthetic Vampirism: Pater, Wilde, and the Concept of Irony," in *Art and Life in Aestheticism: De-Humanizing and Re-Humanizing Art, the Artist, and the Artistic Receptor*, ed. Kelly Comfort (New York: Palgrave Macmillan, 2008), 79.

18. Stephen Arata, *Fictions of Loss in the Victorian Fin de Siècle: Identity and Empire* (Cambridge: Cambridge University Press, 1996), 108.

19. Bram Stoker, *Dracula*, ed. Nina Auerbach and David J. Skal (New York: Norton, 1997), 53–54; subsequent references to this edition provided in the text.

20. Dracula's "extraordinary pallor" (24) appears only when he is wanting for blood. When he is "gorged," his youth returns, and his "white skin seemed ruby-red underneath" (53).

21. Jennifer Wicke, "Vampiric Typewriting: *Dracula* and Its Media," *English Literary History* 59, no. 2 (Summer 1992): 467.

22. Wicke, "Vampiric," 469.

Works Cited

Ablow, Rachel. *The Marriage of Minds: Reading Sympathy in the Victorian Marriage Plot.* Stanford, CA: Stanford University Press, 2007.
———. *Victorian Pain.* Princeton, NJ: Princeton University Press, 2017.
Aindow, Rosy. *Dress and Identity in British Literary Culture, 1870–1914.* Burlington, VT: Ashgate, 2010.
Allen, Michelle. *Cleansing the City: Sanitary Geographies in Victorian London.* Athens: Ohio University Press, 2008.
Anderson, Mary. *A Few Memories.* New York: Harper & Brothers, 1896.
"Alice Grey." *Leader* 6.300 (22 December 1855): 1218.
"Alice Grey." *Leeds Times* 22.1,185 (8 December 1855): 7.
"Alice Grey." *Times* 22,242 (20 December 1855): 10.
"Alice Grey, &c. &c. &c. &c. &c." *Times* 22,204 (6 November 1855): 10.
"Alice Grey, Actress." *Port Pirie Recorder and North Western Mail* 671 (7 January 1905): 1.
"Alice Grey, the Impostor." *Annual Register.* London: F. & J. Rivington, 1856. 163–65.
"Alice Grey, the Impostor." *Daily News* 2,980 (6 December 1855): 3.
"Alice Grey, The Impostor." *Lady's Newspaper* 463 (10 November 1855): 300–301.
"Alice Grey the Impostor." *Morning Advertiser* (9 November 1855): 3.
"Alice Grey, the Impostor." *Standard* 9,774 (10 December 1855): 1.
"Alice Grey in Ireland." *Morning Post* 25,549 (22 November 1855): 3.
"Alice Grey's Continental Double." *Examiner* 2,499 (22 December 1855): 1–2.
"Analytical and Critical Review." *British Foreign Medical Review* 21 (April 1846): 285–333.
Appadurai, Arjun. "Introduction: Commodities and the Politics of Value." *The Social Life of Things: Commodities in Cultural Perspective.* Ed. Arjun Appadurai. Cambridge: Cambridge University Press, 1986. 3–63.
Arata, Stephen. *Fictions of Loss in the Victorian Fin de Siècle: Identity and Empire.* Cambridge: Cambridge University Press, 1996.
"Armadale." *Spectator* 39.1,980 (9 June 1866): 638–40.

Armstrong, Edmund J. "The Remains of Edmund J. Armstrong." *Edinburgh Review* 103 (July 1878): 30–40.

Armstrong, Nancy. *Fiction in the Age of Photography: The Legacy of British Realism*. Cambridge, MA: Harvard University Press, 1999.

Arnold, Robert Arthur. *Hever Court*. 2 vols. London: Bradbury, Evans & Co., 1867.

Arnold, Thomas. "Recent Novel Writing." *Macmillan's Magazine* 13 (January 1866): 202–9.

The Art of Beauty. London: Knight and Lacey, 1825.

Ashmore, Owen. *The Industrial Archaeology of North-West England*. Manchester: Chetham Society, 1982.

"The Assizes." *Times* 30,503 (10 May 1882): 7.

"The Audacious Career of an Adventuress." *Dundee Courier & Argus* 8,914 (10 February 1882): 5.

Bain, Alexander. *Logic*. London: Longmans, Green, & Co., 1879.

———. *Mind and Body: The Theories of Their Relation*. New York: D. Appleton & Company, 1874.

Balibar, Étienne. *Identity and Difference: John Locke and the Invention of Consciousness*. Ed. Stella Sandford. London: Verso, 2013.

Barkan, Elazar. "Victorian Promiscuity: Greek Ethics and Primitive Exemplars." *Prehistories of the Future: The Primitivist Project and the Culture of Modernism*. Ed. Elazar Barkan and Ronald Bush. Stanford, CA: Stanford University Press, 1995. 56–92.

Barnard, A. M. [Louisa May Alcott]. *Behind a Mask, or A Woman's Power. Alternative Alcott*. Ed. Elaine Showalter. New Brunswick, NJ: Rutgers University Press, 1988. 95–202.

Barrell, Helen. "Parish Registers in Wilkie Collins' *The Woman in White*." *Essex & Suffolk Surnames*, http://essexandsuffolksurnames.co.uk/parish-registers-in-wilkie-collins-the-woman-in-white/. Accessed 29 August 2018.

Barrell, John. *The Infection of Thomas De Quincey: A Psychopathology of Imperialism*. New Haven, CT: Yale University Press, 1991.

Barrett, Frank. *Under A Strange Mask*. London: Cassell & Company, 1890.

Barthes, Roland. *Camera Lucida: Reflections on Photography*. Trans. Richard Howard. New York: Hill and Wang, 1981.

Barton, John Cyril, and Jennifer Phegley. Introduction. *Transatlantic Sensations*. Ed. Jennifer, Phegley, John Cyril Barton, and Kristin N. Huston. Burlington, VT: Ashgate, 2012. 1–22.

Bauman, Allen. "Epilepsy, Crime, and Masculinity in Mary Elizabeth Braddon's *Thou Art the Man*." *Nineteenth-Century Gender Studies* 4.2 (2008). www.ncgsjournal.com/issue42/ bauman.htm

Bayard, Marie. *The Art of Beauty or Lady's Companion to the Boudoir*. London: Weldon & Co., 1876.

"Beauty." *Reynolds's Newspaper* 1,023 (20 March 1870): 2.
Beer, Gillian. *Darwin's Plots: Evolutionary Narrative in Darwin, George Eliot, and Nineteenth-Century Fiction*. Cambridge: Cambridge University Press, 2000.
"The Belgian Murder Trial." *Bristol Mercury* 10,781 (2 December 1882): 5.
Beller, Anne-Marie. "Detecting the Self in the Sensation Fiction of Wilkie Collins and Mary Elizabeth Braddon." *Clues: A Journal of Detection* 26.1 (2007): 49–61.
———. Introduction. *Henry Dunbar*. By Mary Elizabeth Braddon. Brighton, UK: Victorian Secrets, 2010. iii–xvi.
———. "Sensation Fiction in the 1850s." *The Cambridge Companion to Sensation Fiction*. Ed. Andrew Mangham. Cambridge: Cambridge University Press, 2013. 7–20.
"Belles Lettres." *Westminster Review* 86 (July 1866): 125–32.
"Belles Lettres." *Westminster Review* 129.1 (January 1888): 119–26.
Bennett, John Hughes. *The Mesmeric Mania of 1851*. Edinburgh: Sutherland and Knox, 1851.
Bentham, Jeremy. *Principles of Penal Law. The Works of Jeremy Bentham*. Part II. Edinburgh: William Tait, 1838. 365–580.
Bérenguier, Nadine. *Conduct Books for Girls in Enlightenment France*. London: Routledge, 2016.
Bernstein, Susan D. "Ape Anxiety: Sensation Fiction, Evolution, and the Genre Question." *Journal of Victorian Culture* 6.2 (January 2001): 250–71.
Berrios, German E. "Memory Disorders and Epilepsy during the Nineteenth Century." *Epilepsy and Memory*. Ed. Adam Zeman, Narinder Kapur, and Marilyn Jones-Gotman. Oxford: Oxford University Press, 2012. 51–62.
Bertillon, Alphonse. *Signaletic Instructions*. Chicago: The Werner Company, 1896.
Bishop, W. J. *The Early History of Surgery*. New York: Barnes & Noble, 1995.
"Blood Transfusion." *Freeman's Journal* 107 (31 July 1874): 4.
"Blood Transfusion." *Our Young Folk's Weekly Budget* 26.748 (4 April 1885): 16.
Blundell, James. *Researches Physiological and Pathological*. London: E. Cox and Son, 1824.
Bothamley, C. H. "Paper and Mounts." *Photography* 9.539 (9 March 1988): 149–51.
Bousfield, R. M., and R. Merrett. "Report of the Trial of Daniel M'Naughton." *The Law Magazine* 29 (1843): 378–409.
Braddon, Mary Elizabeth. *Aurora Floyd*. Vol. 1. Leipzig: Bernhard Tauchnitz, 1863.
———. *The Captain of the Vulture*. London: John and Robert Maxwell, 1868.
———. "Good Lady Ducayne." *Strand Magazine* 11 (1896): 185–99.
———. *Henry Dunbar: The Story of an Outcast*. 2 vols. Leipzig: Bernhard Tauchnitz, 1864.
———. *Lady Audley's Secret*. Ed. Lyn Pykett. Oxford: Oxford University Press, 2012.
———. *Sir Jasper's Tenant*. 2 Vols. Leipzig: Bernhard Tauchnitz, 1866.
———. *Thou Art the Man*. Ed. Laurence Talairach-Vielmas. Kansas City: Valancourt, 2008.

———. *The Trail of the Serpent*. Ed. Chris Willis. New York: Modern Library, 2003.
Brantlinger, Patrick. "What is 'Sensational' about the 'Sensation Novel'?" *Nineteenth-Century Fiction* 37.1 (June 1982): 1–28.
"Bravery of a Surgeon." *Morning Post* 36,628 (7 November 1889): 3.
Breckenridge, Keith, and Simon Szreter. Introduction. *Registration and Recognition: Documenting the Person in World History*. Ed. Keith Breckenridge and Simon Szreter. Oxford: Oxford University Press, 2012. 1–36.
Briefel, Aviva. "Cosmetic Tragedies: Failed Masquerade in Wilkie Collins's *The Law and the Lady*." *Victorian Literature and Culture* 37.2 (2009): 463–81.
Brontë, Charlotte. *Jane Eyre*. Ed Stevie Davies. London: Penguin, 2006.
Brooks, Peter. *Enigmas of Identity*. Princeton, NJ: Princeton University Press, 2011.
Brown, Bill. *A Sense of Things: The Object Matter of American Literature*. Chicago: University of Chicago Press, 2003.
Browne, James Crichton. "Personal Identity, and Its Morbid Modifications." *Journal of Medical Science* 8.43–44 (October 1862–January 1863): 385–95; 535–45.
Burgess, Joshua. *The Medical and Legal Relations of Madness*. London: John Churchill, 1858.
Butler, Judith. *Gender Trouble: Feminism and the Subversion of Identity*. New York: Routledge, 1999.
Calkins, Alonzo. *Opium and the Opium-Appetite*. Philadelphia: J. Lippincott & Co., 1871.
Caplan, Jane. "This or That Particular Person: Protocols of Identity in Nineteenth-Century Europe." *Documenting Individual Identity: The Development of State Practices in the Modern World*. Ed. Jane Caplan and John Torpey. Princeton, NJ: Princeton University Press, 2001. 49–66.
Caplan, Jane, and John Torpey. "Introduction." *Documenting Individual Identity: The Development of State Practices in the Modern World*. Ed. Jane Caplan and John Torpey. Princeton, NJ: Princeton University Press, 2001. 1–12.
Carlyle, Jane. Letter to John Welsh. 13 December 1844. *Carlyle Letters Online*. DOI 10.1215/lt-18441213-JWC-JWE-01.
Carlyle, Thomas. *The French Revolution*. Ed. David R. Sorensen and Brent E. Kinser. Oxford: Oxford University Press, 2019.
———. *Sartor Resartus*. Ed. Rodger L. Tarr. Berkeley: University of California Press, 2000.
———. "Signs of the Times." *Edinburgh Review* 49.98 (July 1829): 439–59.
Carpenter, William Benjamin. *Mesmerism, Spiritualism, &c*. London: Longmans, Green, and Co., 1877.
Carroll, Lewis. *Alice's Adventures in Wonderland* and *Through the Looking-Glass*. Ed. Peter Hunt. Oxford: Oxford University Press, 2009.
"The Case of Imposition by a Female in Wolverhampton." *Morning Post* 25,531 (1 November 1855): 2.

"A Case in Point." *Law Times* 26 (10 November 1855): 90.
"Cases of Mistaken Identity." *Dublin University Magazine* 498.83 (June 1874): 733–41.
"A Casual Acquaintance." *Times* 25,462 (3 April 1866): 4.
Census of England and Wales for the Year 1861. Vol. 3. London: George Edward Eyre and William Spottiswoode, 1863.
Chadwick, Edwin. *Report on the Sanitary Condition of the Laboring Population of Great Britain*. London: W. Clowes and Sons, 1843.
Challice, Annie Emma. *The Wife's Temptation: A Tale of Belgravia*. 2 vols. London: Charles Westerton, 1859.
"Checkmate." *British Quarterly Review* 54.107 (July 1871): 248–49.
"Checkmate." *Saturday Review* 31.803 (18 March 1871): 351–52.
"Checkmate." *Spectator* 44.2,226 (25 February 1871): 224–25.
Chelius, J. M. "Organic Restoration of Lost Parts." *A System of Surgery*. Vol. 3. Philadelphia: Lea & Blanchard, 1847. 576–96.
Chitty, Edward. *The Commercial and General Lawyer*. London: R. Macdonald, 1839.
Chorley, H. F. "Armadale." *Athenaeum* 2,014 (June 1866): 732–33.
Clavering, Vere. *Barcaldine*. 3 vols. London: Hurst and Blackett, 1889.
Cleere, Eileen. "Chaste Polygamy: Mormon Marriage and the Fantasy of Sexual Privacy in *East Lynne* and *Verner's Pride*." *Victorian Studies* 57.2 (Winter 2015): 199–224.
Cohen, William A. *Embodied: Victorian Literature and the Senses*. Minneapolis: University of Minnesota Press, 2009.
Cole, Simon A. *Suspect Identities: A History of Fingerprinting and Criminal Identification*. Cambridge, MA: Harvard University Press, 2002.
Coleridge, Samuel Taylor. "Kubla Khan." *The Major Works*. Ed. H. J. Jackson. Oxford: Oxford University Press, 2000. 103–104.
The Collected Letters of Samuel Taylor Coleridge. 6 vols. Ed. Earl Leslie Griggs. Oxford: Oxford University Press, 1956–71.
Collins, Philip. "Inspector Bucket Visits the Princess Puffer." *Dickensian* 343 (1 May 1964): 88–90.
Collins, Wilkie. *Armadale*. Ed. Catherine Peters. Oxford: Oxford University Press, 2008.
———. *The Law and the Lady*. London: Chatto and Windus, 1876.
———. "Mad Monkton." *A Plot in Private Life and Other Tales*. Leipzig: Bernhard Tauchnitz, 1859. 91–188.
———. *The Moonstone*. Ed. John Sutherland. Oxford: Oxford University Press, 2008.
———. *No Name*. Ed. Mark Ford. London: Penguin, 2004.
———. *Poor Miss Finch*. New York: Harper & Brothers, 1872.
———. *The Woman in White*. New York: Barnes & Noble, 2005.
Combe, George. *A System of Phrenology*. Vol. 1. Edinburgh: Maclachlan, Steward & Co., 1848.

Conolly, John. *An Inquiry Concerning the Indications of Insanity*. London: John Taylor, 1830.

"Conspiracy to Defraud: Extraordinary Case." *Newcastle Courant* 10,806 (10 February 1882): 5.

"Conviction of Alice Grey." *John Bull* 1,841 (22 March 1856): 190.

Costantini, Mariaconcetta. "Sensation, Class and the Rising Professionals." *The Cambridge Companion to Sensation Fiction*. Ed. Andrew Mangham. Cambridge: Cambridge University Press, 2013. 99–112.

———. *Sensation and Professionalism in the Victorian Novel*. Bern: Peter Lang, 2014.

Cox, Jessica. "Representations of Illegitimacy in Wilkie Collins's Early Novels." *Philological Quarterly* 83.2 (Spring 2004): 147–69.

———. *Victorian Sensation Fiction*. London: Red Globe Press, 2019.

Cox, Edward, ed. "Reg. *v.* Boulton and Others." *Cox's Reports of Cases in Criminal Law*. Vol. 12. London: Horace Cox, 1875. 87–95.

Crary, Jonathan. *Techniques of the Observer: On Vision and Modernity in the Nineteenth Century*. Cambridge, MA: MIT Press, 1992.

Crouzet, François. *The Victorian Economy*. Trans. Anthony Forster. London: Routledge, 1982.

Cullen, Michael J. *The Statistical Movement in Early Victorian Britain: The Foundations of Empirical Social Research*. New York: Harvester Press, 1975.

"Curious Will Case." *Annual Register*. London: J. & F. H. Rivington, 1861. 37–39.

Curtis, Ella J [Shirley Smith]. *A Game of Chance: A Novel*. London: Hurst and Blackett, 1889.

Cvetkovich, Ann. *Mixed Feelings: Feminism, Mass Culture, and Victorian Sensationalism*. New Brunswick, NJ: Rutgers University Press, 1992.

The Cyclopedia of Practical Medicine. Ed. John Forbes, Alexander Tweedie, and John Conolly. Vol. 3. Philadelphia: Henry C. Lea, 1867.

Daly, Nicholas. *Literature, Technology, and Modernity, 1860–2000*. Cambridge: Cambridge University Press, 2004.

———. *Sensation and Modernity in the 1860s*. Cambridge: Cambridge University Press, 2009.

Dardy, Claudine. "L'identité-papier." *Les Cahiers de Médiologie* 2.4 (1997): 225–31.

"A Daring Female Impostor." *Albion* 13.37 (24 November 1855): 557.

"The Daring Frauds by an Adventuress." *Blackburn Standard* 2,417 (18 February 1882): 7.

Darnton, Robert. *Mesmerism and the End of the Enlightenment in France*. Cambridge, MA: Harvard University Press, 1968.

Davison, Carol Margaret. "A Battle of Wills: Solving *The Strange Case of Dr. Jekyll and Mr. Hyde*." *Troubled Legacies: Narrative and Inheritance*. Ed. Allan Hepburn. Toronto: University of Toronto Press, 2007. 137–62.

Day, Carolyn A. *Consumptive Chic: A History of Beauty, Fashion, and Disease*. London: Bloomsbury, 2017.

Derrida, Jacques. "Structure, Sign and Play in the Discourse of the Human Sciences." *Writing and Difference*. Trans. Alan Bass. Chicago: University of Chicago Press, 1978. 278–93.
De Quincey, Thomas. *Confessions of an English Opium-Eater*. Ed. Grevel Lindop. Oxford: Oxford University Press, 1998.
"The Degeneracy of Wills." *Spectator* 86.3,785 (12 January 1901): 46–47.
Depledge, Greta. "Sensation Fiction and the New Woman." *The Cambridge Companion to Sensation Fiction*. Ed. Andrew Mangham Cambridge: Cambridge University Press, 2013. 196–209.
"The Derbyshire Will Case." *Saturday Review* 9.231 (31 March 1860): 396–97.
"The Derbyshire Will Case." *Spectator* 37.1,862 (5 March 1864): 261–63.
Derrida, Jacques. "Paper or Me, You Know . . . (New Speculations of a Luxury of the Poor)." *Paper Machine*. Trans. Rachel Bowlby. Stanford, CA: Stanford University Press, 2005. 41–65.
———. *Writing and Difference*. Ed. Alan Bass. Chicago: University of Chicago Press, 1978.
"Detection of Crime by Photography." *Monthly Law Digest and Reporter* 1.8 (August 1893): 465–70.
Dickens, Charles. *Bleak House*. Ed. George Ford and Sylvère Monod. New York: Norton, 1977.
———. *The Mystery of Edwin Drood*. Ed. Margaret Cardwell. Oxford: Oxford University Press, 2009.
———. *Our Mutual Friend*. Ed. Stephen Gill. London: Penguin, 1985.
———. "A Paper-Mill." *Household Words* 1.23 (31 August 1850): 529–31.
———. *The Posthumous Papers of the Pickwick Club*. Vol. 1. London: Chapman and Hall, 1837.
———. "Received—A Blank Child." *Household Words* 7.156 (3 March 1853): 49–53.
———. *A Tale of Two Cities*. Ed. Richard Maxwell. London: Penguin, 2000.
Dickens, Charles, and William Henry Wills. "The Doom of English Wills: Cathedral Number One." *Household Words* 2.27 (28 September 1850): 1–4.
"District News." *Birmingham Gazette* 114.5,948 (19 November 1855): 2.
"The Doctor's Wife." *Saturday Review* 18.471 (5 November 1864): 571–72.
Dods, John Bovee. *The Philosophy of Mesmerism and Electrical Psychology*. London: James Burns, 1886.
Dormandy, Thomas. *Opium: Reality's Dark Dream*. New Haven, CT: Yale University Press, 2012.
Douglas, Mary. *Purity and Danger*. London: Routledge, 1966.
Draycott, Charles. "Whimsical Will-Making." *Temple Bar* 110 (January 1897): 66–71.
Du Boisgobey, Fortuné. *Where's Zenobia?* Vol. 1. London: Vizetelly & Co. 1888.
Duncan, James F. *The Personal Responsibility of the Insane*. Dublin: Fannin and Co., 1865.
The Duties of a Lady's Maid. London: James Bulcock, 1825.

E. B. "The Sensation Novel." *Argosy* 18 (1 August 1874): 137–43.
"East London Opium Smokers." *London Society* 14 (1868): 68–72.
"Eastern Counties." *Herpath's Railway and Commercial Journal* 18.869 (2 February 1856): 107–109.
Eastham, Andrew. "Aesthetic Vampirism: Pater, Wilde, and the Concept of Irony." *Art and Life in Aestheticism: De-Humanizing and Re-Humanizing Art, the Artist, and the Artistic Receptor*. Ed. Kelly Comfort. New York: Palgrave Macmillan, 2008. 79–95.
"To the Editor of the Times." *Times* 22,203 (5 November 1855): 5.
Egan, Joel Peter. *Unconscious Crime: Mental Absence and Criminal Responsibility in Victorian London*. Baltimore: Johns Hopkins University Press, 2003.
Elam, Diane. "White Narratology: Gender and Reference in Wilkie Collins's *The Woman in White*." *Virginal Sexuality and Textuality in Victorian Literature*. Ed. Lloyd Davis. Albany, NY: SUNY Press, 1993. 49–64.
Eliot, George. *The Lifted Veil* and *Brother Jacob* Ed. Sally Shuttleworth. London: Penguin, 2001.
———. *Silas Marner*. Ed. George Levine. New York: Barnes & Noble, 2005.
Eliot, T. S. "Wilkie Collins and Dickens." *The Victorian Novel*. Ed. Harold Bloom. New York: Chelsea House, 2004. 307–314.
Elliotson, John. *Human Physiology*. London: Longman, Rees, Orme, Brown, Green, & Longman, 1835.
———. "Letter from Dr. Elliotson." *Cerebral Physiology and Materialism*. By W. C. Engledue. London: J. Watson, 1842. 27–32.
———. [Untitled]. *The Zoist* 10.38 (July 1852): 151–53.
"Epitome of General News." *Launceston Examiner* (21 April 1882): 3.
"Equatorial Africa, and Its Inhabitants." *Westminster Review* 20 (1861): 137–87.
"Ethics of Dust." *Meliora* 9 (1866): 97–107.
Evans, Charlotte. *Over the Hills and Far Away: A Story of New Zealand*. London: Sampson Low, Marston, Low, & Searle, 1874.
Ewald, Alexander Charles. *The Right Hon. Benjamin Disraeli, Earl of Beaconsfield, K. G., and His Times*. Vol. 2. London: William Mackenzie, 1882.
"The Extraordinary Career of Personation." *Liverpool Mercury* 10,636 (10 February 1882): 7.
"Extraordinary Case of Female Swindling." *York Herald* 5,163 (2 December 1871): 10.
"Extraordinary Case of Imposture and Perjury." *Huddersfield Chronicle* 293 (27 October 1855): 7.
"The Extraordinary Case of Imposture at Wolverhampton." *Examiner* 2,492 (3 November 1855): 12–13.
"Extraordinary Case of Imposture at Wolverhampton." *John Bull* 35.1,821 (3 November 1855): 15.
"The Extraordinary Case of Imposture at Wolverhampton." *Leicester Chronicle* 45 (3 November 1855): 1.

"Extraordinary Case of Perjury." *Northampton Mercury* 51 (3 November 1855): 4.
"The Extraordinary Frauds by a Woman." *Manchester Guardian* (15 February 1882): 5.
"Extraordinary Frauds by a Woman at Birmingham." *Ipswich Journal* 8,022 (14 February 1882): 3.
"Extraordinary Imposture." *Sheffield & Rotherham Independent* 1,882 (3 November 1855): 12.
"Extraordinary Imposture and Systematic Perjury." *Bell's Life in London* (4 November 1855): 7.
"The Extraordinary Impostures." *Morning Post* 25,544 (16 November 1855): 4.
"The Extraordinary Impostures of 'Miss Alice Grey.'" *Lady's Newspaper* 461 (27 October 1855): 256.
"Extraordinary Story of Fraud." *Manchester Guardian* (9 February 1882): 8.
"Extraordinary Series of Frauds and Perjury." *Essex Standard* 25.1,299 (7 November 1855): 4.
"The Fatal Case of Blood Transfusion." *Liverpool Mercury* 9,159 (24 May 1877): 8
"The Fearneaux Frauds." *Birmingham Daily Post* 7,637 (13 February 1882): 5.
"The Fearneaux Frauds." *Birmingham Daily Post* 7,368 (14 February 1882): 4.
"The Fearneaux Frauds." *Birmingham Daily Post* 7,369 (15 February 1882): 4.
"The Fearneaux Frauds." *Birmingham Daily Post* 7,372 (18 February 1882): 5.
"The Fearneaux Frauds." *London Journal* 75.1,937 (25 March 1882): 188.
"The Fearneaux Frauds." *Times* 30,431 (15 February 1882): 10.
"The Fearneaux Frauds." *Times* 30,446 (4 March 1882): 10.
"The Fearneaux Frauds Again." *Lancaster Gazette* 6,495 (20 June 1894): 4.
Felix, Charles [Charles Warren Adams]. *The Notting Hill Mystery*. London: Saunders, Otley, and Co., 1865.
"The Female Form Divine." *Women's Penny Paper* 7.211 (12 November 1892): 16.
"A Female Fraud." *St. Louis Post-Dispatch* (6 March 1882): 7.
"The Female Impostor at Wolverhampton." *Cork Examiner* 15.2,104 (7 November 1855): 4.
"The Female Impostor at Wolverhampton." *Morning Chronicle* 27,722 (1 November 1855): 7.
"The Female Impostor at Wolverhampton." *Standard* 9,747 (8 November 1855): 1.
"The Female Impostor at Wolverhampton." *Times* 22,206 (8 November 1855): 10.
"Female Life in Prison." *Christian Remembrancer* 44 (1863): 365–87.
Ferrier, David. "The Organ of Mind." *Princeton Review* 55 (1879): 98–125.
"Fiction." *Speaker* 10 (28 July 1894): 109–110.
Flint, Kate. "Blood, Bodies, and *The Lifted Veil*." *Nineteenth-Century Literature* 51.4 (March 1997): 455–73.
Floyd, Courtney A. "'Take It When Tendered': M. E. Braddon's *Thou Art the Man* and the *Weekly Telegraph*'s Media Model of Disability." *Victorian Review* 45.1 (Spring 2019): 59–80.
Forster, John. *The Life of Charles Dickens*. Vol. 2. London: Chapman and Hall, 1890.

Foucault, Michel. *Power/Knowledge: Selected Interviews & Other Writings, 1972–1977*. Ed. Colin Gordon. New York: Pantheon Books, 1980.

Frank, Cathrine O. *Law, Literature, and the Transmission of Culture in England, 1837–1925*. London: Routledge, 2016.

"The Frauds by an Adventuress." *Illustrated London News* 80.2,233 (18 February 1882): 163.

"The Frauds by an Adventuress." *Times* 30,429 (13 February 1882): 6.

"The Frauds by an Adventuress." *Times* 30,430 (14 February 1882): 5.

"The Frauds by an Adventuress." *Times of India* (8 March 1882): 5.

"The Frauds by an Adventuress: Amazing Credulity of Her Victims." *North-Eastern Daily Gazette* 4,576 (14 February 1882): 3.

Freeland, Natalka. "Trash Fiction: The Victorian Novel and the Rise of Disposable Culture." PhD dissertation, Yale University, New Haven, Connecticut, 1998. 1177A.

Freeman, Mary Eleanor Wilkins. *Jane Field*. New York: Harper & Brothers, 1902.

Freud, Sigmund. "A Note upon the 'Mystic Writing-Pad.'" *The Standard Edition of the Complete Psychological Works*. Vol. 19. Ed. James Strachey. London: Hogarth, 1973. 428–34.

Gabriele, Alberto. "Transnational Currents, Intermedial Trajectories—A Global Nineteenth-Century Approach." *Sensationalism and the Genealogy of Modernity: A Global Nineteenth-Century Perspective*. Ed. Alberto Gabriele. New York: Palgrave Macmillan, 2017. 1–26.

Gairdner, W. T. *Insanity: Modern Views as to Its Nature and Treatment*. Glasgow: James MacLehose & Sons, 1885.

Galton, Francis. "Identification by Finger-Tips." *The Nineteenth Century: A Monthly Review* 30.174 (August 1891): 303–11.

Garratt, Peter. *Victorian Empiricism: Self, Knowledge, and Reality in Ruskin, Bain, Lewes, Spencer, and George Eliot*. Madison, NJ: Fairleigh Dickinson University Press, 2010.

Garrison, Laurie. *Science, Sexuality, and Sensation Novels: Pleasures of the Senses*. New York: Palgrave Macmillan, 2011.

Gates, Kelly A. "Biometrics and Post-9/11 Technologies." *Social Text* 83 (2005): 35–53.

Gaylin, Ann. *Eavesdropping in the Novel from Austen to Proust*. Cambridge: Cambridge University Press, 2003.

Gibson, Mary, and Nicole Hahn Rafter. Introduction. *Criminal Man*. Trans. Mary Gibson and Nicole Hahn Rafter. Durham, NC: Duke University Press, 2006. 1–36.

Gilbert, Pamela K. *The Citizen's Body: Desire, Health, and the Social in Victorian England*. Columbus: The Ohio State University Press, 2007.

———. *Disease, Desire, and the Body in Victorian Women's Popular Novels*. Cambridge: Cambridge University Press, 1997.

———. "Medical Mapping: The Thames, the Body, and *Our Mutual Friend*." *Filth: Dirt, Disgust, and Modern Life*. Ed. William A. Cohen and Ryan Johnson. Minneapolis: University of Minnesota Press, 2005. 78–102.

———. "Sensation Fiction and the Medical Context." *The Cambridge Companion to Sensation Fiction*. Ed. Andrew Mangham. Cambridge: Cambridge University Press, 2013. 182–95.

———. *Victorian Skin: Surface, Self, History*. Ithaca, NY: Cornell University Press, 2019.

Gilbert, William. *Our Discharged Convicts*. London: Thomas Brettell & Co., 1870.

Gilman, Sander L. *Making the Body Beautiful: A Cultural History of Aesthetic Surgery*. Princeton, NJ: Princeton University Press, 1999.

Gitelman, Lisa. *Paper Knowledge: Toward a Media History of Documents*. Durham, NC: Duke University Press, 2014.

"Government Waste-Paper." *Chambers's Journal* 13.673 (21 November 1886): 747–49.

Graham, George. *Fourth Annual Report of the Registrar-General of Births, Deaths, and Marriages, in England*. London: W. Clowes and Sons, 1842.

———. *Thirty-Seventh Annual Report of the Registrar-General of Births, Deaths, and Marriages, in England*. London: George E. Eyre and William Spottiswoode, 1876.

———. *Twenty-Second Annual Report of the Registrar-General of Births, Deaths, and Marriages in England*. London: George E. Eyre and William Spottiswoode, 1861.

Grass, Sean. *The Commodification of Identity in Victorian Narrative: Autobiography, Sensation, and the Literary Marketplace*. Cambridge: Cambridge University Press, 2019.

Gregory, William. *Animal Magnetism; or, Mesmerism and Its Phenomena*. London: The Psychological Press Association, 1884.

Greville-Williams, Rupert. *Ruthven's Wrecks*. Bristol: J. W. Arrowsmith, 1887.

Griffiths, Arthur. *Memorials of Millbank, and Chapters in Prison History*. Vol. 2. London: Henry S. King & Co., 1875.

Guillory, John. "The Memo and Modernity." *Critical Inquiry* 31.1 (Autumn 2004): 108–132.

Guthrie, Leonard. "Night Terrors, Symptomatic and Idiopathic, with Associated Disorders in Children." *Clinical Journal* 14.7 (7 June 1899): 97–109.

Guy, William Augustus. *Principles of Forensic Medicine*. London: Henry Renshaw, 1868.

Hacking, Ian. *The Taming of Chance*. Cambridge: Cambridge University Press, 1990.

Halberstam, J. *Skin Shows: Gothic Horror and the Technology of Monsters*. Durham, NC: Duke University Press, 1995.

Hamilton, Allan McLane, and Lawrence Godkin. *A System of Legal Medicine*. Vol. 1. New York: E. B. Treat, 1894.

Handy, Ellen. "Dust Piles and Damp Pavements: Excrement, Repression, and the Victorian City in Photography and Literature." *Victorian Literature and the*

Victorian Visual Imagination. Ed. Carol T. Christ and John O. Jordan. Berkeley: University of California Press, 1995. 111–33.

Hardy, Thomas. *Desperate Remedies: A Novel*. London: Ward and Downey, 1889.

Harrison, Kimberly. "'Come Buy, Come Buy': Sensation Fiction in the Context of Consumer and Commodity Culture." *A Companion to Sensation Fiction*. Ed. Pamela K. Gilbert. Malden, MA: Wiley-Blackwell, 2011. 528–39.

Harwood, John Berwick. *One False, Both Fair: Or, A Hard Knot*. New York: John W. Lovell, 1885.

———. *Lady Flavia*. London: Richard Bentley, 1866.

Haweis, Mary Eliza. *The Art of Beauty*. New York: Harper & Brothers, 1878.

Hawthorne, Julian. *The Confessions of a Convict*. Philadelphia: Rufus C. Hartranft, 1893.

Hay, William Delisle. *Blood: A Tragic Tale*. London: Swan Sonnenschein, Lowrey & Co., 1888.

Hazlitt, William. "On Will-Making." *Table-Talk*. Vol. 1. Paris: A. and W. Galignani, 1825. 113–33.

Hensley, Nathan K. *Forms of Empire: The Poetics of Victorian Sovereignty*. Oxford: Oxford University Press, 2016.

Higgs, Edward. *Identifying the English: A History of Personal Identification 1500 to the Present*. London: Continuum, 2011.

———. "The Linguistic Construction of Social and Medical Categories in the Work of the English General Register Office, 1837–1950." *Categories and Contexts: Anthropological and Historical Studies in Critical Demography*. Ed. Simon Szreter, Hania Sholkamy, and A. Dharmarlingam. Oxford: Oxford University Press, 2004. 86–106.

———. *Life, Death and Statistics: Civil Registration, Censuses and the Work of the General Register Office, 1836–1952*. Hatfield, Hertfordshire: Local Population Studies, 2004.

Hingston, Kylee-Anne. *Articulating Bodies: The Narrative Form of Disability and Illness in Victorian Fiction*. Liverpool: Liverpool University Press, 2019.

———. "'Skins to Jump into': The Slipperiness of Identity and the Body in Wilkie Collins's *No Name*." *Victorian Literature and Culture* 40 (2012): 117–35.

The History of the Year: A Narrative of the Chief Events and Topics of Interest from October 1, 1881, to September 30, 1882. London: Cassell, Petter, Galpin & Co., 1882.

Hollingshead, John. "The City of Unlimited Paper." *Household Words* 17.404 (19 December 1857): 1–4.

Holmes, Martha Stoddard. *Fictions of Affliction: Physical Disability in Victorian Culture*. Ann Arbor: University of Michigan Press, 2009.

Horne, R. H. "Dust; or Ugliness Redeemed." *Household Words* 1.16 (13 July 1850): 379–84.

Houston, Matilda. *Done in the Dark*. Vol. 1. London: Samuel Tinsley, 1877.

Houston, Natalie. Introduction. *Lady Audley's Secret*. By Mary Elizabeth Braddon. Peterborough, Ontario: Broadview Press, 2003. 9–29.
"How to Prove a Will." *Chambers's Journal* 3.123 (8 May 1886): 299–301.
Hubback, John. *A Treatise on the Evidence of Succession to Real and Personal Property and Peerages*. Philadelphia: T. & J. W. Johnson, 1845.
Hughes, Winifred. "The Sensation Novel." *A Companion to the Victorian Novel*. Ed. Patrick Brantlinger and William B. Thesing. Malden, MA: Wiley-Blackwell, 2002. 260–78.
———. *The Maniac in the Cellar: Sensation Novels of the 1860s*. Princeton, NJ: Princeton University Press, 1980.
Hume, David. *A Treatise of Human Nature*. Vol. 1. London: Longmans, Green, and Co., 1878.
Humphreys, Kathryn. "The Artistic Exchange: *Dorian Gray* at the *Sacred Fount*." *Texas Studies in Literature and Language* 32.4 (Winter 1990): 522–35.
Hunt, Frederick Knight. "A Visit to the Registrar-General." *Household Words* 2.36 (30 November 1850): 235–40.
Hurley, Kelly. *The Gothic Body: Sexuality, Materialism and Degeneration at the* Fin de Siècle. Cambridge: Cambridge University Press, 1996.
"The Identiscope." *Amateur Photographer* 1.9 (5 December 1884): 141.
Ifill, Helena. *Creating Character: Theories of Nature and Nurture in Victorian Sensation Fiction*. Manchester: Manchester University Press, 2018.
"The Impostures of 'Alice Grey.'" *Lady's Newspaper* 462 (3 November 1855): 283.
"Ingenious Impostor." *John Bull* 5.27 (4 July 1825): 215.
"The Inquest on Hyde." *Saturday Review* 61.1,587 (27 March 1886): 426–27.
J. L. "Female Impostors.—A Parallel." *Morning Post* 25,540 (12 November 1855): 3.
Jackson, John Hughlings. "A Study of Convulsions." *Transactions*. Vol. 4. London: John Churchill and Sons, 1870. 162–204.
———. *On Convulsive Seizures*. London: British Medical Association, 1890.
Jackson, Lee. *Dirty Old London: The Victorian Fight Against Filth*. New Haven, CT: Yale University Press, 2014.
Jacyna, L. S. "Somatic Theories of Mind and the Interests of Medicine in Britain, 1850–1879." *Medical History* 26 (1982): 233–58.
Jaffe, Audrey. *Scenes of Sympathy: Identity and Representation in Victorian Fiction*. Ithaca, NY: Cornell University Press, 2000.
James, Henry. "Miss Braddon." *Nation* 1.19 (9 November 1865): 593–95.
James, William. *The Principles of Psychology*. Vol. 1. London: Macmillan and Co., 1891.
Jeaffreson, John Cordy. *A Woman in Spite of Herself*. 2 Vols. Leipzig: Bernhard Tauchnitz, 1872.
"John Marchmont's Legacy." *Ladies' Companion* 25 (1864): 277–78.
Johnson, Heidi H. "Electra-fying the Female Sleuth: Detecting the Father in *Eleanor's Victory* and *Thou Art the Man*." *Beyond Sensation: Mary Elizabeth Braddon in*

Context. Ed. Marlene Tromp, Pamela K. Gilbert, and Aeron Haynie. Albany, NY: SUNY Press, 2000. 255–75.

Jones, Anna Maria. *Problem Novels: Victorian Fiction Theorizes the Sensational Self.* Columbus: The Ohio State University Press, 2007.

———. "Sheridan Le Fanu." *A Companion to Sensation Fiction*. Ed. Pamela K. Gilbert. Malden, MA: Blackwell, 2011. 269–80.

Joseph, Abigail. *Exquisite Materials: Episodes in the Queer History of Victorian Style*. Newark: University of Delaware Press, 2019.

Karpenko, Lara. "'So Extraordinary a Bond': Mesmerism and Sympathetic Identification in Charles Adams's *Notting Hill Mystery*." *Strange Science: Investigating the Limits of Knowledge in the Victorian Age*. Ed. Lara Karpenko and Shalyn Claggett. Ann Arbor: University of Michigan Press, 2017. 145–163.

Kibbie, Ann Louise. *Transfusion: Blood and Sympathy in the Nineteenth-Century Literary Imagination*. Charlottesville: University of Virginia Press, 2019.

Kingston, Charles. *A Gallery of Rogues*. London: Stanley Paul & Co., 1924.

Kling, Rebecca. "'It is only colour that you want': *Lady Audley's Secret* and Cosmetics as Discursive Fantasy." *Victorian Periodicals Review* 50.3 (Fall 2017): 560–84.

Kontou, Tatiana. "Parallel Worlds: Wilkie Collins's Sensationalism and Spiritualist Practice." *Wilkie Collins: Interdisciplinary Essays*. Ed. Andrew Mangham. Newcastle UK: Cambridge Scholars Publishing, 2007. 37–55.

Kucich, John. *The Power of Lies: Transgression in Victorian Fiction*. Ithaca, NY: Cornell University Press, 1994.

Kuskey, Jessica. "Our Mutual Engine: The Economics of Victorian Thermodynamics." *Victorian Literature and Culture* 41 (2013): 75–89.

"Lady Audley's Secret." *Athenaeum* 1,826 (25 October 1862): 525–26.

"Lady Audley's Secret." *Critic* 25.631 (December 1862): 178–79.

"'Lady' Sinett and Her Portfolio." *North-Eastern Daily Gazette* (12 August 1890): 4.

"Lambeth." *Standard* 21,840 (3 July 1894): 6.

"Latest Intelligence." *Bell's Life in London and Sporting Chronicle* (18 November 1855): 8.

Lavater, Johann Kaspar. *Physiognomy*. London: Cowie, Low, and Co., 1826.

Law, Jules. *The Social Life of Fluids: Blood, Milk, and Water in the Victorian Novel*. Ithaca, NY: Cornell University Press, 2010.

"Law and Police." *Pall Mall Budget* 4 (24 June 1870): 34.

"Law and Police." *Pall Mall Budget* 27 (10 February 1882): 26–27.

"The Law and the Lady." *Saturday Review* 38.1,011 (13 March 1875): 357–58.

"Law Report." *Examiner* 2,927 (5 March 1864): 154.

Laycock, Thomas. *Mind and Brain: Or, The Correlations of Consciousness and Organization*. Vol. 1. London: Simpkin, Marshall, and Co., 1869.

———. "Researches into the Functions of the Brain." *Journal of Psychological Medicine* 8 (1855): 512–41.

"Lazarus, Lotus-Eating." *All the Year Round* 15 (12 May 1866): 421–25.

Leask, Nigel. *British Romantic Writers and the East: Anxieties of Empire.* Cambridge: Cambridge University Press, 1992.

Le Fanu, Sheridan. *Checkmate.* Philadelphia: Evans, Stoddard & Co., 1871.

Lethbridge, Stefanie. "The Horror of Clothing and the Clothing of Horror: Material and Meaning in Gothic and Sensation Fiction." *Sensationalism and the Genealogy of Modernity.* Ed. Alberto Gabriele. London: Palgrave Macmillan, 2017. 49–68.

The Letters of Charles Dickens. Ed. Madeline House, Graham Storey, et al. 12 vols. Oxford: Clarendon Press, 1965–2002.

Levine, George. *Darwin and the Novelists: Patterns of Science in Victorian Fiction.* Chicago: University of Chicago Press, 1991.

Lewes, George Henry. *The History of Philosophy from Thales to Comte.* Vol. 2. London: Longmans, Green, and Co., 1867.

———. *The Physiology of Common Life.* Vol. 1. Edinburgh: William Blackwood and Sons, 1859.

Lewis, L. S. "Some Peculiar Wills." *Strand Magazine* 14.82 (October 1897): 441–47.

Liddle, Dallas. *The Dynamics of Genre: Journalism and the Practice of Literature in Mid-Victorian Britain.* Charlottesville: University of Virginia Press, 2009.

Liggans, John. *Opium: England's Coercive Opium Policy and Its Disastrous Results in China and India: The Spread of Opium Smoking in America.* New York: Funk & Wagnalls, 1883.

Lindop, Grevel. "Lamb, Hazlitt, and De Quincey." *The Coleridge Connection: Essays for Thomas McFarland.* Ed. Richard Gravil and Molly Lefebure. New York: St. Martin's, 1990. 111–32.

Lister, Thomas Henry. *First Annual Report of the Registrar-General of Births, Deaths, and Marriages in England.* London: W. Clowes and Sons, 1839.

"Literary Notices." *Public Opinion* 3.69 (17 January 1863): 74–75.

"Literature." *Athenaeum* 1,807 (7 June 1862): 781–83.

Litvack, Leon. "Images of the River in *Our Mutual Friend.*" *Dickens Quarterly* 20.1 (March 2003): 34–55.

"Living Novelists." *Rambler* 1.1 (January 1854): 41–51.

Locke, John. *An Essay Concerning Human Understanding.* Philadelphia: Kay & Troutman, 1849.

Loesberg, Jonathan. "The Ideology of Narrative Form in Sensation Fiction." *Representations* 13 (Winter 1986): 115–38.

Logan, Heidi. *Sensational Deviance: Disability in Nineteenth-Century Sensation Fiction.* New York: Routledge, 2019.

Lombroso, Cesare. *Criminal Man.* Trans. Mary Gibson and Nicole Hahn Rafter. Durham, NC: Duke University Press, 2006.

"London, Thursday, November 1, 1855." *Times* 22,200 (1 November 1855): 6.

"'Lord Pelham Clinton' Again." *Daily Telegraph* (8 September 1894): 3.

"M. Richet on Poisons of Intelligence." *All about Opium*. Ed. Hartmann Henry Sultzberger. London: Cannon Street, 1884. 178–80.

MacDonagh, Gwendolyn, and Jonathan Smith. "'Fill up All the Gaps': Narrative and Illegitimacy in *The Woman in White*." *The Journal of Narrative Technique* 26.3 (Fall 1996): 274–91.

MacDonald, Tara. "Sensation Fiction, Gender and Identity." *The Cambridge Companion to Sensation Fiction*. Ed. Andrew Mangham. Cambridge: Cambridge University Press, 2013. 127–40.

"Madness in Novels." *The Spectator* 39.1,962 (3 February 1866): 134–35.

Malton, Sara. *Forgery in Nineteenth-Century Literature and Culture: Fictions of Finance from Dickens to Wilde*. New York: Palgrave Macmillan, 2009.

Mangham, Andrew. *Violent Women and Sensation Fiction: Crime, Medicine and Victorian Popular Culture*. New York: Palgrave Macmillan, 2007.

———. "'What Could I Do?': Nineteenth-Century Psychology and the Horrors of Masculinity in *The Woman in White*." *Victorian Sensations: Essays on a Scandalous Genre*. Ed. Kimberly Harrison and Richard Fontina. Columbus: The Ohio State University Press, 2006. 115–25.

Mansel, Henry. "Sensation Novels." *Quarterly Review* 113.226 (April 1863): 481–514.

Mara, Miriam O'Kane. "Sucking the Empire Dry: Colonial Critique in *The Mystery of Edwin Drood*." *Dickens Studies Annual* 32 (2002): 233–46.

Martha and Mary. London: Smith, Elder, and Co., 1880.

Martin, Raymond, and John Barresi. *Naturalization of the Soul: Self and Personal Identity in the Eighteenth Century*. London: Routledge, 2000.

Martineau, Harriet. *Letters on Mesmerism*. London: Edward Moxon, 1845.

———. *Life in the Sick-Room*. London: Edward Moxon, 1844.

Marx, Karl. *Capital*. Ed. David McLellan. Oxford: Oxford University Press, 2008.

———. *A Contribution to the Critique of Political Economy*. Chicago: Charles H. Kerr & Company, 1904.

———. *The German Ideology*. Ed. C. J. Arthur. New York: International Publishers, 1970.

———. "The Power of Money in Bourgeois Society." *Sociological Theory in the Classical Era: Text and Readings*. Ed. Laura Desfor Edles and Scott Appelrouth. Los Angeles: Sage, 2015. 54–57.

———. "Theses on Feuerbach." *The German Ideology*. Ed. C. J. Arthur. New York: International Publishers, 1970. 121–23.

"Masquerading Extraordinary." *St. Louis Globe-Democrat* 296 (12 March 1882): 15.

Masters, Frederick J., "Opium and Its Votaries." *Californian* 1.6 (May 1892): 631–45.

"The Matlock Will Case." *Law Journal* 26 (17 October 1891): 639–40.

Matus, Jill L. "Disclosure as 'Cover-up': The Disclosure of Madness in *Lady Audley's Secret*." *University of Toronto Quarterly* 62.3 (Spring 1993): 334–55.

———. *Shock, Memory and the Unconscious in Victorian Fiction*. Cambridge: Cambridge University Press, 2009.

Maudsley, Henry. *The Pathology of Mind*. New York: D. Appleton and Company, 1886.
———. *The Pathology of Mind*. London: Macmillan and Co., 1895.
———. *The Physiology and Pathology of Mind*. London: Macmillan and Co., 1868.
———. *Responsibility in Mental Disease*. New York: D. Appleton and Company, 1892.
Maunder, Andrew and Grace Moore. Introduction. *Victorian Crime, Madness, and Sensation*. Aldershot, Hampshire, UK: Ashgate, 2004. 1–14.
May, Leila Silvana. *Secrecy and Disclosure in Victorian Fiction*. New York: Routledge, 2017.
Mayhew, Henry. *London Labour and the London Poor*. Vol. 1. London: Griffin, Bohn, and Company, 1861.
Mayhew, Henry, and John Binny. *The Criminal Prisons of London and Scenes of Prison Life*. London: Griffin, Bohn, and Company, 1862.
McAleavey, Maia. The *Bigamy Plot: Sensation and Convention in the Victorian Novel*. Cambridge: Cambridge University Press, 2015.
McEachin, A. B. "Personal Identity." *Southern Law Journal and Reporter* 1.6 (May 1880): 391–97.
McLaughlin, Kevin. *Paperwork: Fiction and Mass Mediacy in the Paper Age*. Philadelphia: University of Pennsylvania Press, 2005.
"An M. D." *The Pocket Magazine*. Vol. 2. London: James Robins & Co., 1829. 84–87.
Meade, L. T. *An Adventuress*. London: Chatto & Windus, 1899.
Menke, Richard. "*New Grub Street*'s Ecologies of Paper." *Victorian Studies* 61.1 (Autumn 2018): 60–82.
"Mesmerism; Its Dangers and Curiosities." *Punch* 6 (1844): 100–103.
Metz, Nancy Aycock. "The Artistic Reclamation of Waste in *Our Mutual Friend*." *Nineteenth-Century Fiction* 34.1 (June 1979): 59–72.
Milbank, Alison. *Daughters of the House: Modes of the Gothic in Victorian Fiction*. London: Palgrave Macmillan, 1992.
Miller, D. A. *The Novel and the Police*. Berkeley: University of California Press, 1988.
Miller, J. Hillis. *Charles Dickens: The World of His Novels*. Cambridge, MA: Harvard University Press, 1958.
———. *Victorian Subjects*. Durham, NC: Duke University Press, 1991.
Milligan, Barry. *Pleasures and Pains: Opium and the Orient in 19th-Century British Culture*. Charlottesville: University of Virginia Press, 1995.
Milton, John. *Paradise Lost*. Ed. Gordon Teskey. New York: Norton, 2005.
"Miss Braddon's Novels." *Reader* 1.9 (28 February 1863): 210–11.
"Miss Furneaux's Career: Frauds upon Frauds She Practiced Year After Year." *New York Times* (12 March 1882): 4.
"Mistaken Identity: A Marvellously Strange Case." *Bangor Whig* 17.66 (8 February 1849): 4.
Mitchell, Sally. *Daily Life in Victorian England*. London: Greenwood Press, 1996.
"Monthly Synopsis of Practical Medicine." *London Medical and Surgical Journal* 1.2 (1 August 1828): 157–86.

Montwieler, Katherine. "Marketing Sensation: *Lady Audley's Secret* and Consumer Culture." *Beyond Sensation: Mary Elizabeth Braddon in Context*. Ed. Marlene Tromp, Pamela K. Gilbert, and Aeron Haynie. Albany, NY: SUNY Press, 2000. 43–62.
"The Moonstone." *Spectator* 41.2,091 25 July 1868): 881–82.
"The Moonstone: A Novel." *Nation* 7.168 (17 September 1868): 235.
"More Matlock Codicils." *Punch* 46 (28 May 1864): 227.
Morgan, Benjamin. *The Outward Mind: Materialist Aesthetics in Victorian Science and Literature*. Chicago: University of Chicago Press, 2017.
Morgan, James Appleton. "Personal Identity." *Sanitarian* 5.46 (January 1877): 21–35.
Moriarty, Aubrey. *On Personation and Disputed Identity, and Their Tests*. London: Stevens and Haynes, 1873.
Morley, Henry, and William Henry Wills. "Photography." *Household Words* 7.156 (19 March 1853): 54–61.
Murphy, Sara. "'No Two Men Were Ever Alike Within': The Tichborne Trial, The Lord Chief Justice, and the Narration of Identity." *Law, Culture and the Humanities* 13.2 (2017): 244–60.
"Narrative of Law and Crime." *Household Narrative of Current Events* (November 1855): 241–48.
Nayder, Lillian. "Science and Sensation." *The Cambridge Companion to Sensation Fiction*. Ed. Andrew Mangham. Cambridge: Cambridge University Press, 2013. 145–57.
———. *Unequal Partners: Charles Dickens, Wilkie Collins, and Victorian Authorship*. Ithaca, NY: Cornell University Press, 2002.
Neaves, Charles. "How to Make a Novel. A Sensational Song." *Songs and Verses: Social and Scientific*. Edinburgh: William Blackwood and Sons, 1869. 81–84.
"New Books." *Penn Monthly* 6 (March 1875): 228–37.
"New Novels." *Examiner* 3,288 (4 February 1871): 130–31.
"New Novels." *Graphic* 112 (20 January 1872): 13.
"New Novels." *The Literary World* 37 (27 January 1888): 73–75.
Nissel, Muriel. *People Count: A History of the General Register Office*. London: Her Majesty's Stationary Service, 1987.
"No Name." *London Review* 6.132 (10 January 1863): 46–47.
"No Name." *Spectator* 36.1,802 (10 January 1863): 1501–1502.
Noiriel, Gérard. "The Identification of the Citizen: The Birth of Republican Status in France." *Documenting Individual Identity: The Development of State Practices in the Modern World*. Ed. Jane Caplan and John Torpey. Princeton, NJ: Princeton University Press, 2001. 28–38.
Norris, Margot. *Beasts of the Modern Imagination*. Baltimore: Johns Hopkins University Press, 1985.
North, Henry. "A Stolen Identity." *Belgravia* 69 (July 1889): 37–69.

"The Norwich Impostor." *Daily News* 1,990 (7 October 1852): 6.
"Notes from Our Diary." *The Lady's Newspaper & Pictorial Times* 465 (24 November 1855): 13.
"Nothing Can Be More Slightly Defined." *Times* 21,800 (22 July 1854): 8–9.
"The Notting Hill Mystery." *Athenaeum* 1,955 (15 April 1865): 520.
Novak, Daniel. *Realism, Photography and Nineteenth-Century Fiction*. Cambridge: Cambridge University Press, 2008.
"Novelettes." *London Review* 11.267 (12 August 1865): 178.
"Novels." *Marlburian* 1 (20 September 1865): 1–2.
"Novels." *Saturday Review* 67.1741 (9 March 1889): 286–87.
"Novels." *Saturday Review* 78.2,039 (24 November 1894): 566–68.
"Novels Past and Present." *Saturday Review* 21.546 (April 1866): 438–40.
"Novels of the Week." *Athenaeum* 2,307 (13 January 1872): 48–50.
"Novels of the Week." *Athenaeum* 2,578 (24 March 1877): 382–83.
Oberman, Harold A. "Organization, Functions, Regulation, and Legal Concerns of Blood Banks." *Clinical Laboratory Medicine*. Ed. Kenneth D. McClatchey. Philadelphia: Lippincott, Williams, & Wilkins, 2002. 1517–21.
"Obtaining Money Under False Pretences." *Leeds Mercury* 9,324 (2 March 1868): 3.
The Old Roman Well: A Romance of Dark Streets and Green Lanes. 3 vols. London: Saunders, Otley, and Co., 1861.
Oliphant, Margaret. "Modern Novelists—Great and Small." *Blackwood's Edinburgh Magazine* 77.475 (May 1855): 554–568.
———. "Novels." *Blackwood's Edinburgh Magazine* 94 (August 1863): 168–83.
"Our Library Table." *St. James's Magazine* (1865): 179–88.
"Our Library Table." *Athenaeum* 3,038 (16 January 1886): 100–101.
"Our Mutual Friend." *Eclectic Review* 9 (November 1865): 455–76.
"Our Mutual Friend." *London Review* 11 (28 October 1865): 467–68.
"Our Mutual Friend." *Morning Post* 28,670 (1 November 1865): 2.
"Paint, and No Paint." *All the Year Round* 7.172 (9 August 1862): 519–21.
"Paper." *All the Year Round* 12.306 (10 November 1894): 442–47.
"The Paper Age." *American Bookseller* 18.2 (15 July 1885): 59.
"The Park-Lane Murder." *Daily News* 8,103 (17 April 1872): 3.
Pearl, Sharrona. "Dazed and Abused: Gender and Mesmerism in Wilkie Collins." *Victorian Literary Mesmerism*. Ed. Martin Willis and Catherine Wynne. Amsterdam: Rodopi, 2008. 163–82.
Pedlar, Valerie. "Drawing a Blank: The Construction of Identity in *The Woman in White*." *The Nineteenth-Century Novel: Identities*. Ed. Dennis Walder. London: Routledge, 2001. 69–94.
Peña-Sy, Stephanie. "Intoxication, Provocation, and Derangement: Interrogating the Nature of Criminal Responsibility in *The Mystery of Edwin Drood*." *Dickens Studies Annual* 40 (2009): 215–30.

Percival, Thomas. "Proposals for Establishing More Accurate and Comprehensive Bills of Mortality in Manchester." *Essays Medical and Experimental*. Vol. 2. London: Joseph Johnson, 1773. 239–52.

"Personal Identity." *Lancet* 1 (1 February 1873): 180.

"The Personation Frauds." *Sheffield Daily Telegraph* 8,321 (24 February 1882): 2.

"Personating Lord Arthur Clinton." *Bristol Mercury* 4,259 (25 November 1871): 3.

"Personating Lord Arthur Clinton." *Hampshire Telegraph and Sussex Chronicle* 4,098 (25 November 1871): 4.

"Personating Lord Arthur Clinton." *Nottinghamshire Guardian* 1,334 (24 November 1871): 2.

"Personating Noblemen." *Times* 30,427 (10 February 1882): 8.

"Personation." *Spectator* 37.1875 (4 June 1864): 656–57.

"The Personation Frauds." *Birmingham Daily Post* 7,377 (24 February 1882): 4.

Petch, Simon. "Robert Audley's Profession." *Studies in the Novel* 32.1 (Spring 2000): 1–13.

Peters, Catherine. *The King of Inventers: A Life of Wilkie Collins*. Princeton, NJ: Princeton University Press, 1991.

"Photograph by Telegraph." *British Journal of Photography* 24.878 (2 March 1877): 103–104.

"Photographic Society of Scotland. Ordinary Meeting." *Journal of the Photographic Society of London* 8.129 (15 January 1863): 202–6.

"Photography: Its History and Applications." *British Quarterly Review* 44 (1 October 1866): 346–90.

"Poor Miss Finch." *Athenaeum* 2,312 (17 February 1872): 202–3.

Poovey, Mary. *Making a Social Body: British Cultural Formation, 1830–1864*. Chicago: University of Chicago Press, 1995.

Popoff, M. Lazar. "The Origin of Portraiture." *American Journal of Photography* 12.144 (December 1891): 556–65.

Poznar, Susan. "Whose Body? The 'Willing' or 'Unwilling' Mesmerized Women in Late Victorian Fiction." *Women's Writing* 15.3 (2008): 412–35.

Price, Cheryl B. "Probability and Capital Crime: The Rise and Fall of Actuarial Detection in Victorian Crime Fiction." *Clues* 34.2 (Fall 2016): 7–17.

Price, Leah. *How to Do Things with Books in Victorian Britain*. Princeton, NJ: Princeton University Press, 2012.

"The Provinces." *Spectator* 1,427 (3 November 1855): 1127–28.

Pugliese, Joseph. *Biometrics: Bodies, Technologies, Biopolitics*. New York: Routledge, 2010.

Pykett, Lyn. *The Sensation Novel: From* The Woman in White *to* The Moonstone. Plymouth: Northcote, 1994.

Radford, Andrew D. *Victorian Sensation Fiction*. New York: Palgrave Macmillan, 2009.

Rae, W. Fraser. "Sensation Novelists: Miss Braddon." *North British Review* 43.85 (September 1865): 180–204.

Reade, Charles. "Doubles." *Belgravia* 31 (January–February 1877): 319–26; 433–36.
———. *Griffith Gaunt; or, Jealousy*. Boston: Ticknor and Friends, 1866.
———. "The Prurient Prude." *Readiana: Comments on Current Events*. London: Chatto and Windus, 1883. 314–19.
"Recent Novels." *Spectator* 73.3,448 (28 July 1894): 118–120.
Reese, John J. "The Personal Identity of the Living and the Dead." *Medical Record* 15.19 (10 May 1879): 433–35.
"The Remarkable Fraud at Birmingham." *Kerang Times and Swan Hill Gazette* (14 April 1882): 2.
"Remarkable Case of Impersonation." *Manchester Times* 463 (20 October 1866): 5.
"A Remarkable Impostor." *Evening News* (7 August 1894): 3.
"The Renewing of Noses." *Birmingham Daily Post* 9,965 (2 June 1890): 8.
Reynolds, David S. Preface. *Transatlantic Sensations*. Ed. Jennifer Phegley, John Cyril Barton, and Kristin N. Huston. New York: Routledge, 2016. xiii–xxi.
Richards, Thomas. *The Commodity Culture of Victorian England: Advertising and Spectacle, 1851–1914*. Stanford, CA: Stanford University Press, 1990.
Richet, Charles. "Opium and Its Antidote." *Pharmacist* 11.6 (June 1878): 176–79.
"Robert Louis Stevenson." *Century* 35.6 (April 1888): 869–79.
Robinson, Frederick William. *Female Life in Prison*. Vol. 2. London: Hurst and Blackett, 1862.
"The Romance of Babington White." *Saturday Review* 24.622 (28 September 1867): 399–400.
"The Romance of Wicked Women." *London Review* 6.145 (11 April 1864): 375–77.
Rudy, Jason R. *Electric Meters: Victorian Physiological Poetics*. Athens: Ohio University Press, 2009.
Rumsey, Henry Wyldbore. *Essays on State Medicine*. London: John Churchill, 1856.
Ruskin, John. *The Ethics of Dust*. New York: John B. Alden, 1888.
Ryan, Vanessa. *Thinking without Thinking in the Victorian Novel*. Baltimore: Johns Hopkins University Press, 2012.
Schmitt, Cannon. "Evolution and Victorian Fiction." *Evolution and Victorian Culture*. Ed. Bernard Lightman and Bennett Zon. Cambridge: Cambridge University Press, 2014. 17–38.
Schülting, Sabine. *Dirt in Victorian Literature and Culture: Writing Materiality*. New York: Routledge, 2016.
Schwanebeck, Wieland. "'It's Never Twins?'—It's *Always* Twins: *The Notting Hill Mystery* (1865) and the Specter of Twinship in Early Detective Fiction." *Clues* 36.1 (Spring 2018): 58–68.
Scoffern, John. "Cosmetics." *Belgravia* 4 (December 1867): 208–16.
Scott, James C. *Seeing Like a State: How Certain Schemes to Improve Human Condition Have Failed*. New Haven, CT: Yale University Press, 1998.
"A Scottish Maiden." *Leader* 6.292 (27 October 1855): 1025.
Secrets in the Art of Dress. London: Jas. Gilbert, 1849.

Sedgwick, Eve Kosofsky. *Between Men: English Literature and Male Homosocial Desire.* Columbia University Press, 2015.

"Sensation Novels." *Medical Critic and Psychological Journal* 16 (July 1863): 513–19.

"Sensation Novels." *Spectator* 41.2,093 (8 August 1868): 931–32.

Showalter, Elaine. "Desperate Remedies: Sensation Novels of the 1860s." *Victorian Newsletter* 49 (Spring 1976): 1–5.

———. *The Female Malady: Women, Madness, and English Culture, 1830–1980.* New York: Pantheon Books, 1985.

Shuttleworth, Sally. " 'Preaching to the Nerves': Psychological Disorder in Sensation Fiction." *A Question of Identity: Women, Science, and Literature.* Ed. Marina Benjamin. New Brunswick, NJ: Rutgers University Press, 1993. 192–222.

"Singular Case of Imposture." *Cheshire Observer and General Advertiser* 77 (27 October 1855): 3.

"Six Stories." *Saturday Review* 64.1,678 (24 December 1887): 855–56.

Silverman, Kaja. *The Miracle of Analogy or The History of Photography, Part 1.* Stanford, CA: Stanford University Press, 2015.

Simon, Leslie. "*Bleak House, Our Mutual Friend,* and the Aesthetics of Dust." *Dickens Studies Annual* 42 (2011): 217–36.

Sims, George R. *How the Poor Live.* London: Chatto & Windus, 1883.

"A Singular Case of Personation." *Times* 30,427 (10 February 1882): 8.

"Sir Jasper's Tenant." *Saturday Review* 20.521 (21 October 1865): 520–21.

Smith, Horace. *Crooks of the Waldorf: Being the Story of Joe Smith, Master Detective.* New York: Macaulay Company, 1929.

Sontag, Susan. *On Photography.* New York: Farrar, Status and Giroux, 1977.

"St. Martin's Eve." *Saturday Review* 21.544 (31 March 1866): 387–88.

Staffe, Baroness. *My Lady's Dressing Room.* Trans. Harriet Hubbard Ayer. New York: Cassell Publishing Company, 1892.

Stallybrass, Peter, and Allon White. *The Politics and Poetics of Transgression.* Ithaca, NY: Cornell University Press, 1986.

Starr, Douglas. *Blood: An Epic History of Medicine and Commerce.* New York: Alfred A. Knopf, 1998.

Stern, Rebecca. *Home Economics: Domestic Fraud in Victorian England.* Columbus: The Ohio State University Press, 2008.

———. " 'Personation' and 'Good Marking-Ink': Sanity, Performativity, and Biology in Victorian Sensation Fiction." *Nineteenth-Century Studies* 14 (2000): 35–62.

Stevens, C. L. McCluer. *Famous Crimes and Criminals.* New York: Duffield & Company, 1924.

Stevenson, Robert Louis. *The Strange Case of Dr. Jekyll and Mr. Hyde.* Ed. Emma Letley. Oxford: Oxford University Press, 1998.

Stiles, Anne. *Popular Fiction and Brain Science in the Late Nineteenth Century.* Cambridge: Cambridge University Press, 2012.

Stoker, Bram. *Dracula.* Ed. Nina Auerbach and David J. Skal. New York: Norton, 1997.

Stout, Daniel. "Nothing Personal: The Decapitation of Character in *A Tale of Two Cities*." *NOVEL: A Forum on Fiction* 41.1 (Fall 2007): 29–52.
"Strange Case of Dr. Jekyll and Mr. Hyde." *Dublin Review* 15.2 (April 1886): 422–23.
"A Strange Case—A Family Deceived as to the Identity of a Son and Brother," *Saturday Evening Post* 28 (3 February 1849): 2.
"Striking Likenesses." *All the Year Round* 6.127 (28 September 1861): 19–24.
Suarez, Michael F., and H. R. Woudhuysen. *The Book: A Global History*. Oxford: Oxford University Press, 2013.
Sutherland, John. Introduction. *The Moonstone*. Oxford: Oxford University Press, 2008. vii–xxix.
Sutton, Thomas. *Unconventional: A Novel*. 3 vols. London: Sampson Low, Son, & Marston, 1866.
"Swindling as a Fine Art." *Saturday Review* 53.1,373 (18 February 1882): 204–5.
Symons, Arthur. Introduction. *Poems of Coleridge*. London: Methuen & Co., 1905. ix–l.
"Synopsis of Opium Inebriety." *New York Medical Journal* 55.5 (30 January 1892): 113.
T. B. M. *The Ballad of Alice Grey and the Grand Jury: A Lay of Modern Staffordshire*. Wolverhampton: Joseph York, 1856.
Talairach-Vielmas, Laurence. Introduction. *Thou Art the Man*. Kansas City: Valancourt, 2008. vii–xxiv.
———. *Moulding the Female Body in Victorian Fairy Tales and Sensation Fiction*. London: Routledge, 2007.
———. "Sensation Fiction: A Peep Behind the Veil." *The Victorian Gothic: An Edinburgh Companion*. Ed. Andrew Smith and William Hughes. Edinburgh: Edinburgh University Press, 2012. 29–42.
———. "Victorian Sensational Shoppers: Representing Transgressive Femininity in Wilkie Collins's *No Name*." *Victorian Review* 31.2 (2005): 56–78.
———. *Wilkie Collins, Medicine and the Gothic*. Cardiff: University of Wales Press, 2009.
Tambling, Jeremy. *Dickens' Novels as Poetry: Allegory and Literature of the City*. New York: Routledge, 2015.
Taylor, Alfred Swaine. "Medico-Legal Observations on Tattoo-Marks as Evidence of Personal Identity. Remarks on the Tichborne Case." *Guy's Hospital Reports*. Ed. H. G. Howse. Vol. 19. London: J. & A. Churchill, 1874. 441–65.
Taylor, Ida Ashworth. *Vice Valentine*. 2 vols. London: Ward and Downey, 1890.
Taylor, Jenny Bourne. *In the Secret Theater of Home: Wilkie Collins, Sensation Narrative, and Nineteenth-Century Psychology*. New York: Routledge, 1988.
———. Introduction. *Lady Audley's Secret*. By Mary Elizabeth Braddon. London: Penguin, 1998. vii–xli.
Taylor, Jenny Bourne, and Sally Shuttleworth. Introduction. *Embodied Selves: An Anthology of Psychological Texts 1830–1890*. Oxford: Clarendon Press, 1998. xiii–xviii.

Thomas, David Wayne. *Cultivating Victorians: Liberal Culture and the Aesthetic.* Philadelphia: University of Pennsylvania Press, 2004.

Thomas, Ronald R. *Detective Fiction and the Rise of Forensic Science.* Cambridge: Cambridge University Press, 1999.

———. *Dreams of Authority: Freud and the Fictions of the Unconscious.* Ithaca, NY: Cornell University Press, 1990.

———. "Wilkie Collins and the Sensation Novel." *The Columbia History of the English Novel.* Ed. John Richetti. New York: Columbia University Press, 1994. 479–507.

Thompson, Michael. *Rubbish Theory: The Creation and Destruction of Value.* London: Pluto Press, 2017.

Thomson, A. T. *Lectures on Medical Jurisprudence. The Lancet* 1 (26 November 1836): 313–19.

"Thoughts upon Insanity, Dreams, Hallucinations, and Self-Control." *Metropolitan* 4 (1856): 536–38.

Tillotson, Kathleen. "Introduction: The Lighter Reading of the Eighteen-Sixties." *The Woman in White.* By Wilkie Collins. Boston: Houghton, 1969. ix–xxvi.

Tolhurt, David. *Pioneers in Plastic Surgery.* London: Springer, 2015.

Torgerson, Beth. "Harriet Martineau, Victorian Sciences of Mind and the Birth of Psychology." *Harriet Martineau and the Birth of Disciplines: Nineteenth-Century Intellectual Powerhouse.* Ed. Valeria Sanders and Gaby Weiner. London: Routledge, 2017. 135–51.

Townshend, Chauncy Hare. *Facts in Mesmerism: With Reasons for a Dispassionate Inquiry into It.* New York: Harper & Brothers, 1843.

Travers, Robert. "Essay on Personal Identity, and its Proof from Physical Signs." *Dublin Quarterly Journal of Medical Science* 52 (1871): 365–83.

The Trial at Bar of Sir Roger C. D. Tichborne. Vol. 8. London: Englishman Office, 1880.

"The Trial of Mary Jane Fearneaux." *Spectator* 55.2,811 (13 May 1882): 615.

Trotter, David. *Circulation: Defoe, Dickens, and the Economies of the Novel.* London: Macmillan, 1988.

Tucker, Holly. *Blood Work: A Tale of Medicine and Murder in the Scientific Revolution.* New York: Norton, 2011.

"Unconventional." *Athenaeum* 2,012 (19 May 1866): 668.

"Unconventional." *Reader* 7.173 (21 April 1866): 393.

[Untitled]. *All the Year Round* 2.31 (26 November 1859): 95.

"Verner's Pride." *Athenaeum* 1,845 (7 March 1863): 322–23.

"Verner's Pride." *Examiner* 2,876 (14 March 1863): 165–66.

"Verner's Pride." *London Review* 6.146 (18 April 1863): 416–17.

"Verner's Pride." *Saturday Review* 15.383 (28 February 1863): 279–80.

"Very Common Law." *All the Year Round* 2.37 (7 January 1860): 253–56.

Voskuil, Lynn M. "Acts of Madness: Lady Audley and the Meanings of Victorian Femininity." *Feminist Studies* 27.3 (Autumn 2001): 611–39.
Von Krafft-Ebing, Richard. *Psychopathia Sexualis*. New York: Rebman Company, 1906.
W. D. L. "English Fiction and Scottish Law." *Scottish Law Review* 9.104 (August 1893): 175–81.
"Waiting for the Verdict." *Saturday Review* 15.389 (11 April 1863): 476–78.
Wall, Alfred H. "Thomas Sutton, B.A., on Art-Photography." *Journal of the Photographic Society of London* 8.131 (16 March 1863): 245–46.
Walker, Mrs. A. *Female Beauty, as Preserved and Improved by Regimen, Cleanliness and Dress*. New York: Scofield and Voorhies, 1840.
Ward, Charlotte. *Lending a Hand: Or, Help for the Working Classes*. London: Seeley, Jackson, and Halliday, 1866.
Watkins, Gwen. *Dickens in Search of Himself: Recurrent Themes and Characters in the Work of Charles Dickens*. London: Macmillan Press, 1987.
Welsh, Alexander. *George Eliot and Blackmail*. Cambridge, MA: Harvard University Press, 1985.
Westall, William. *Red Ryvington*. London: Cassel & Company, 1885.
Wharton, Francis. *Philosophy of Criminal Law*. Philadelphia: Kay & Brother, 1880.
———. *A Treatise on the Law of Evidence in Criminal Issues*. Philadelphia: Kay and Brother, 1880.
"What Shall They Do to Be Saved?" *Harper's New Monthly Magazine* 35.207 (August 1867): 377–87.
"Whispers." *The Birmingham Owl* 7.2 (3 March 1882): 10.
Wicke, Jennifer. "Vampiric Typewriting: *Dracula* and Its Media." *English Literary History* 59.2 (Summer 1992): 467–93.
Wilde, Oscar. *The Picture of Dorian Gray*. Ed. Joseph Bristow. Oxford: Oxford University Press, 2008.
"Wills and Will-Making, Ancient and Modern." *London Quarterly Review* 108.216 (1860): 222–45.
Willis, Martin, and Catherine Wynne. Introduction. *Victorian Literary Mesmerism*. Ed. Martin Willis and Catherine Wynne. Amsterdam: Rodopi, 2006. 1–16.
Winter, Alison. *Mesmerized: Powers of Mind in Victorian Britain*. Chicago: University of Chicago Press, 1998.
Winter, William. *Old Friends: Being Literary Recollections of Other Days*. New York: Moffat, Yard and Company, 1909.
Wolf, Peter. "Epilepsy and Catalepsy in Anglo-American Literature between Romanticism and Realism: Tennyson, Poe, Eliot, and Collins." *Journal of the History of the Neurosciences* 9.3 (2000): 286–93.
"A Woman with a Past. Sensational Arrest in Leeds." *Yorkshire Evening Post* 1,187 (18 June 1894): 3.
"A Woman Personating a Nobleman." *Lancaster Gazette* 5,213 (11 February 1882): 6.

"A Woman in Spite of Herself." *Examiner* 3,339 (27 January 1872): 103.
"A Woman in Spite of Herself." *Spectator* 45.2,277 (17 February 1872): 214–15.
"Women in Prison." *London Review* 5.115 (13 September 1862): 238–40.
Wood, Ellen. *East Lynne*. Ed. Elisabeth Jay. Oxford: Oxford University Press, 2008.
———. *St. Martin's Eve*. London: Macmillan and Co., 1901.
———. *Verner's Pride: A Novel*. Macmillan and Co., 1900.
Woodman, William Bathurst, and Charles Meymott Tidy. *A Handy-Book of Forensic Medicine and Toxicology*. London: J. & A. Churchill, 1877.
Woods, Robert. *The Demography of Victorian England and Wales*. Cambridge: Cambridge University Press, 2000.
The Works of Charles Dickens: Letters and Speeches. Vol. 2. London: Chapman and Hall, 1908.
Wynne, Deborah. *The Sensation Novel and the Victorian Family Magazine*. New York: Palgrave, 2001.
Wynter, Andrew. "First Beginnings." *Cornhill Magazine* (April 1862): 481–94.
Young, Robert M. *Mind, Brain, and Adaptation in the Nineteenth Century*. Oxford: Oxford University Press, 1990.
Zeman, Adam, Narinder Kapur, and Marilyn Jones-Gotman. Introduction. *Epilepsy and Memory*. Ed. Adam Zeman, Narinder Kapur, and Marilyn Jones-Gotman. Oxford: Oxford University Press, 2012. 1–18.
Zigarovich, Jolene. "'A Strange and Startling Creature': Transgender Possibilities in Wilkie Collins's *The Law and the Lady*." *Victorian Review* 44.1 (Spring 2018): 99–111.
Zimmerman, Virginia. *Excavating Victorians*. Albany, NY: SUNY Press, 2008.
Žižek, Slavoj. "The Undergrowth of Enjoyment: How Popular Culture Can Serve as an Introduction to Lacan." *The Žižek Reader*. Ed. Elizabeth Wright and Edmond Wright. Oxford: Blackwell, 1999. 11–36.

Index

Adams, Charles Warren, 11, 90, 92. See also *The Notting Hill Mystery*
affect. *See under* sensation genre
Alcott, Louisa May, 11, 17–18
animal magnetism. *See under* mesmerism
antiseptics, 33, 34; sterilization, 89
Arnold, Robert Arthur, 208n51
Arnold, Thomas, 75
atavism, 80, 100. *See also* degeneration, evolution
anthropometry, 3, 10, 162n18. *See also* Bertillon, Alphonse, biometrics, fingerprinting, handwriting
Aylieff, Joseph, 90

Bain, Alexander, 64, 190n50
Bakhtin, Mikhail, 168n51
Ballantine, Mary Bland, 175n38
Barrett, Frank, 177n61
Barthes, Roland, 147
Bazalgette, Joseph, 139
Beard, Frank, 87, 97
Beard, Richard, 146
Bell, Charles, 163n23
Bennett, John Hughes, 91
Bentham, Jeremy, 164–65n27. *See also* tattoos
Bertillon, Alphonse, 162n18. *See also* anthropometry

bigamy, 9, 43, 51, 74, 76, 131, 134, 172n90. *See also* forgery
Binny, John, 58
biometrics, 2, 3, 4, 6, 10, 11, 38, 39, 163n22, 165–66n31. *See also* anthropometry, fingerprinting, handwriting
birthmarks. *See under* skin
Births, Deaths, and Marriages Act (1837), 120–27, 139, 207n32, 207n37. *See also* civil registration
Bishop, W. J., 33
blank space, 27, 123, 124, 178n77, 209n56
blood, 26, 33, 39–47, 65, 79, 81, 133, 182n55; bloodline. *See under* inheritance; personal identity, 31, 33, 39–47; transfusion, 11, 31, 32, 33, 39–47; types, 39; vampire blood, 98, 158–59, 218n20; vitalism, 31, 41, 43. *See also* Blundell, James
Blood: A Tragic Tale (Hay), 11, 33, 39–47
Blundell, James, 40, 43. *See also* blood transfusion, obstetrics
Bothamley, C. H., 212n12
Braddon, Mary Elizabeth, 16, 65, 75, 161n11, 172n94, 181n33, 188n27, 191n67, 195n132, 196n137; *Aurora*

Braddon, Mary Elizabeth *(continued)*
Floyd, 68, 105, 161n11; *The Captain of the Vulture* 20, 180n7; "Good Lady Ducayne," 42; *Henry Dunbar*, 16, 18, 175n39, 213n52; *Sir Jasper's Tenant*, 20, 32, 33; *The Trail of the Serpent*, 20, 176n40, 180n7. See also *Lady Audley's Secret*, *Thou Art the Man*
brain, 64, 67, 72, 73, 163–64n23, 183n68; abnormality, 67, 76, 77, 80, 133, 189–90n50; hemispheres of, 68, 76, 77, 90, 96, 171n85; injury to. See under concussion; materiality of, 36, 89, 90, 190n57; neurology, 35, 64, 67, 77, 96, 190n57, 193n97; surgery, 35. See also localization, psychosurgery
brands. See under skin
Brontë, Charlotte, 63–65
Browne, James Crichton, 64, 70. See also double consciousness/identity
Burdett-Coutts, Angela, 146
Burney, Frances, 33

Cain, Hall, 172n94, 176n42
Calkins, Alonzo, 96
calotype. See under photography
capitalism, 7, 16, 199n49; industry, 10, 16, 128, 138; mass production, 16, 135, 159
Carlyle, Jane Welsh, 91–92
Carlyle, Thomas, 18, 19, 117; *French Revolution, The*, 117; *Sartor Resartus*, 18, 19; "Signs of the Times," 175n32
Carpenter, William Benjamin, 92
Carpue, Joseph Constantine, 34
Carroll, Lewis, 66, 153, 184n7
cartesian, 44
Castle of Otranto, The (Radcliffe), 217n1

catalepsy. See under epilepsy
Chadwick, Edwin, 139–40
Challice, Annie Emma, 198n44
Checkmate (Le Fanu), 11, 33, 36–39, 44, 181n33
Chelius, J. M., 34
chloroform, 33, 42, 107, 111
Chorley, H. F., 188n27
civil registration, 9, 119–27, 206–207n31, 208n55; General Register Office, 120, 124, 127, 207n43, 208n50; registrar fraud, 122; Registrar General, 118, 119, 120, 121; Registration Act (1837). See under Births, Deaths, and Marriages Act; Registration Act (1874), 122
clairvoyance. See under mesmerism
Clarke, Marcus, 176n42
class, 3, 5–8, 10, 16, 66, 75, 80, 82, 100, 105, 127, 139, 163n20, 168n52, 168n53, 168–69n54, 169n55, 188n26, 209n65. See also reform
Clavering, Vere, 35
clergy, 121, 127
clothes, 1, 9, 11, 15, 16, 18–23, 31, 32, 38, 58, 68, 135, 136, 150, 155, 158, 174n28, 175n35, 175n37, 175n38, 175–76n39, 176n40, 176n42. See also crossdressing, textiles
codicils. See under wills
Coleridge, Samuel Taylor, 95–96, 199n65; *Biographia Literaria*, 199n65; "Kubla Khan," 95–96; "The Pains of Sleep," 96
colonialism, 86, 98, 146, 147; imperialism, 75
Collins, Wilkie, 6, 65, 85, 87–88, 90, 97, 126, 128, 168–69n54, 172n94, 188n27, 196n137, 196n1, 196n3, 197n11; *Armadale*, 24, 141,

176n42, 198n44, 208n50; *Blind Love*, 216n99; *the Dead Secret*, 176n40; "Mad Monkton," 195n123; *The Moonstone*, 85–87, 92, 97, 98, 177n61, 196n3, 196n5, 197n11, 198n44; *The New Magdalen*, 10, 176n42; *Poor Miss Finch*, 79, 195n126; *The Law and the Lady*, 24, 141, 176n42, 177n59, 208n50. See also *No Name*, *The Woman in White*
Combe, George, 67. *See also* phrenology
commodities, 5, 7, 15, 16, 18, 118, 128, 138, 142, 143. *See also* Marx, Karl
concussions, 35, 63, 65, 79, 82
Conolly, John, 66, 67. *See also* madness
Comte, Augustus, 205n17. *See also* statistics
consciousness, 4, 10, 16, 43, 44, 46, 47, 63, 64, 67, 75, 76, 78, 79, 80, 81, 88, 90, 95, 96, 97, 99–101, 147, 155, 157, 164n25, 165n28, 189n50, 190n57, 201n98
continuity of consciousness, 4, 9, 66, 73, 85, 165n28. *See also* Locke, John
convulsions. *See under* epilepsy
cosmetics, 9, 11, 15–18, 23–30, 31, 32, 34, 71, 176n52, 177n58, 177n59, 177n61, 178n69, 178n75, 179n81
counterfeiting, 21, 23, 27, 32, 33, 112, 113, 122, 123, 130–31, 132, 149, 150, 151, 154–55. *See also* forgery
crossdressing, 21–23, 105–109, 112
Curtis, Ella J., 190n58

daguerreotype. *See under* photography

Darwin, Charles, 5, 77, 166n39; *On the Origin of Species*, 166n39, 192n82. *See also* atavism, degeneration, evolution, natural selection
De Quincey, Thomas, 95–96; *Confessions of an English Opium-Eater*, 95–96, 199n65
Degeneration, 29, 69, 74, 77, 78, 80, 83, 123. *See also* atavism; Darwin, Charles; evolution; natural selection
Denis, Jean-Baptiste, 40
Derrida, Jacques, 4–5; paper, 117; trace, 26
detective, 7, 8, 17, 28, 36, 37, 87, 147, 150, 154
detective fiction, 7
Dickens, Charles, 11, 85, 89–90, 97–98, 119, 126, 129, 135, 136, 142, 146, 164n26, 172n94, 173n98, 200n81, 213n31; *Bleak House*, 97, 129, 142, 143; *Pickwick Papers*, 162n14; *A Tale of Two Cities*, 19, 100, 135, 145, 168n52. See also *The Mystery of Edwin Drood*, *Our Mutual Friend*
Dieffenbach, Johann Friedrich, 34
disability. *See under* sensation genre
disease, 33, 41, 86, 88, 89, 91, 119, 125, 138, 140; of the brain, 64, 65, 66, 68, 76, 77, 78, 80–83, 189n37
disguise, 6, 9, 15, 17, 18, 19, 22, 25, 27, 31, 32, 33, 35, 36, 38, 145, 149, 150, 174n28, 175n38, 177n61
Disraeli, Benjamin, 139
Dods, John Bovee, 90
Domesday Book, 206n31
double consciousness/identity, 41, 44, 64, 65, 70, 72, 75, 76, 82, 90, 96. *See also* Browne, James Crichton
Dracula, 41, 43, 45, 158–59, 218n20
Draycott, Charles, 128

Du Boisgobey, Fortuné, 177n61
Duncan, James F., 67
dust, 140–45, 213n52, 214n53, 214n61, 215n68
dust-mounds. See under *Our Mutual Friend*

ego. *See under* subjectivity
Eliot, George, 41–42, 79, 132, 206n29; *Adam Bede*, 132; "The Lifted Veil," 41–42; *Middlemarch*, 206n29; *Silas Marner*, 79
Eliot, T. S., 188n27
Elliotson, John, 87, 89, 90, 93, 96; *The Zoist*, 89, 90, 93
Else, John, 130–31
epilepsy, 9, 11, 63, 64, 76–79; catalepsy, 79, 99; convulsions, 77–78, 80, 81, 193n94, 195n126; effect on personal identity, 76–83; used to describe sensation fiction, 75–76; seizures, 76–77, 79, 81, 193n97, 195n127
Esquirol, Jean-Étienne Dominque, 193n94
ether, 33
Evans, Charlotte, 180n7
evolution, 5, 77, 83, 166n39; natural selection, 5, 166n39. *See also* atavism; Darwin, Charles; degeneration

Falret, Jules, 193n94
Farjeon, 208n50
Farr, William, 207n43
Ferrier, David, 171n85
Feuerbach, Ludwig, 16
fingerprinting, 2, 3, 10, 172n95. *See also* anthropometry, biometrics, handwriting
fission theory, 44, 183n68. *See also* Hazlitt, William

forgery, 27, 39, 52, 70, 104, 109, 112, 113, 114, 119, 129, 132, 154, 170n74, 175n38, 191n75, 203n33, 203n35, 206n29; birth register, 172n90, 208n50; marriage register, 122–26, 172n90, 208n51, 208n55; uttering, 154. *See also* counterfeiting
Foucault, Michel, 119
Frankenstein, 37, 39, 43, 44, 156
Freeman, Mary Eleanor Wilkins, 191n66
French Revolution, 120, 135, 206n30
Freud, Sigmund, 4, 117. *See also* psychoanalysis
Furneaux, Mary Jane, 103–114, 202n5, 202n15, 203n33, 203n35, 204n45, 204n58

Gall, Franz Joseph, 96, 163n22
Galton, Francis, 147, 172n95
gender, 10, 22, 23, 46, 75, 100, 167n44, 169n55, 174n28, 174n29
Gilbert, W. S., 51
Gilbert, William, 187n85
gold, 52, 117, 118
Gothic, 5, 11, 31, 153–59, 166n36, 168n49, 175n37, 217n1
Graefe, Karl Ferdinand von, 34
Graham, George, 119, 121, 122
Gregory, William, 90
Greville-Williams: *Ruthven's Wrecks*, 211n4
Grey, Alice, 29, 49–59, 103, 106, 112
Griffiths, Arthur, 58
Guthrie, Leonard, 63
Guy, William Augustus, 179n5

hair, 18, 21, 24, 25–26, 29, 51, 52, 68, 70, 71, 73, 113, 159, 178n75, 179n81, 192n76. *See also* wigs
handwriting, 21, 23, 27, 52, 72, 112, 113, 123, 130, 131, 154, 155, 208n51. *See also* counterfeiting

Hardy, Thomas, 148, 175n35
Harvey, William, 39
Harwood, John Berwick, 180n7, 202n5, 208n50, 213–14n52
Hause, Luther, 1–2, 161n1
Haweis, Mary Eliza, 15, 19
Hawthorne, Julian, 186n84
Hay, William Delisle, 11, 33, 43–44. See also *Blood: A Tragic Talei*
Hazlitt, William, 44, 128–29, 183n68. See also fission theory, wills
heredity. See under inheritance
Hollingshead, John, 118
homosexuality, 105–106, 111
Horne, R. H., 144, 215n68
Houston, Matilda, 195n123
Hume, David, 165n28, 183n68
Hunt, Frederick Knight, 118, 121
Hunter, John, 33
Huxley, T. H., 192n82
hypnotism, 86, 88, 89, 159. See also mesmerism

illegitimacy, 43, 80, 128, 172n94, 178n72
imperialism. See under colonialism
impersonation. See under identity fraud
imposture. See under identity fraud
individuality. See under subjectivity
industry. See under capitalism
inheritance, 26, 27, 29, 30, 92, 93, 105, 112, 120, 131, 132, 154, 208n50; bloodline, 80–81; heredity, 43, 63, 69, 74, 77, 79, 80, 82, 127, 192n83, 195n123
insanity. See under madness
Inspector Field, 99

Jackson, John Hughlings, 76, 77, 195n126
James, Henry, 153, 188n27
James, William, 19

Jeaffreson, John Cordy, 11, 20, 22, 23, 202n5, 208n50. See also *A Woman in Spite of Herself*

Kenealy, Edward, 147
Kingston, Charles, 59
Krafft-Ebing, Richard Von, 77

Lacan, Jacques, 26; *object petit a*, 26, 178n73
Lady Audley's Secret (Braddon), 5, 7, 8, 9, 10, 11, 17, 51, 59, 65–75, 94, 169n57, 170n75, 192n76, 192n77, 192n79, 192n83, 193n87
Landsteiner, Karl, 40
laudanum. See under opium
Lavater, Johann Kaspar, 163n22
Laycock, Thomas, 66, 96, 189–90n50
Le Fanu, Sheridan, 11, 33, 36, 37, 38, 39. See also *Checkmate*
legality identity 3, 4, 7, 8, 10, 18, 30, 39, 78, 119, 128, 168n52, 168n54, 171n83, 194n116
legible identity 3, 8, 46, 119, 122
Lewes, George Henry, 41, 163n22
Lewis, L. S., 128
Lister, Joseph, 33
Lister, Thomas Henry, 120, 121, 207n37, 207n43
localization, 35, 67, 73, 76, 163n22. See also brain
Locke, John, 4, 44, 73, 79, 96, 165n28. See also continuity of consciousness
Lombroso, Cesare, 78
lunacy. See under madness
Lyle, Matilda Eliza, 175n38

Madame Rachel [Sarah Rachel Leverson], 24, 71
madness, 9, 11, 20, 23, 56, 63, 64, 65–75, 76, 80, 81, 82, 191n67,

madness *(continued)*
    192n83, 194n116, 195n123;
    insanity, 39, 40, 56, 64, 66, 67,
    68, 70, 71, 74, 78, 105, 111,
    189n37; "lunacy panic," 66; Lunacy
    Commission, 189n40
Magendie, François, 163n23
makeup. *See under* cosmetics
Mansel, Henry, 5, 69, 76, 141
Marryat, Florence, 16
Martha and Mary, 182n55
Martineau, Harriet, 90–91
Marx, Karl, 16, 118, 136, 164n25.
    See also commodities, capitalism,
    materialism
materialism, 4, 6, 9, 16, 19, 41, 89,
    90, 128, 163n19, 167n44, 190n50;
    personal identity, 2–9, 16, 19, 20,
    26, 27, 30, 36, 41, 44–46, 66–68,
    70–72, 75, 128, 136, 141, 147,
    162n14, 163n19, 164n25, 171n85,
    189–90n50, 190n57
Matthew, William, 147
Maudsley, Henry, 64, 68, 76, 77, 78,
    188n12
Mayall, John Jabez Edwin, 146
Mayhew, Henry, 58, 140
Meade, L. T., 191n66
Mesmer, Franz Anton, 88
mesmerism, 9, 11, 85–95, 96, 98,
    165n29, 192n79, 198n44, 201n90;
    animal magnetism, 85, 88, 91, 100;
    clairvoyance, 91, 197n9
Milton, John, 101
M'Naughten case, 78, 194n116
moles, 26–29, 33, 179n81. *See also*
    birthmarks, brands, scars, skin,
    tattoos
moral treatment (madness), 67–68,
    74. *See also* lunacy panic, Lunacy
    Commission, insanity, madness;
    Tuke, William

Morel, Bénédict, 77, 193n94
Morgan, James Appleton, 8
Moriarty, Aubrey, 171n83. *See also*
    legal identity
Morley, Henry, 146
Mormonism, 131, 134m 211n98
mummy, 100, 201n97
Mystery of Edwin Drood, The
    (Dickens), 11, 95–101, 201n98

natural selection. *See under* evolution
neurology. *See under* brain
Navarro, Mary de, 197n11
Neaves, Charles, 171n89
No Name (Collins), 11, 17, 23–30, 32,
    71, 87, 178n69, 178n72, 178n75,
    178n77, 179n78, 179n81, 179n82,
    198n44
Notting Hill Mystery, The (Adams), 11,
    88–95, 198–99n48, 199n49

objet petit a. *See under* Lacan, Jacques
obstetrics, 40
Old Roman Well, The, 9, 177n61
opium, 11, 85–88, 95–101, 196n3,
    197n11, 199n65, 201n97;
    laudanum, 85–88, 95, 98, 100, 111,
    200n81
Orton, Arthur (Tichborne Claimant),
    2, 104, 105, 125, 147–48, 161–
    62n11, 162n12. *See also* Tichborne,
    Sir Roger
Our Mutual Friend (Dickens), 8, 11,
    138–45, 149, 214n53, 214n61,
    215n68, 215n70
Owen, Richard, 192n82

paper, 1, 9, 26, 30, 70, 71, 72, 92,
    117–23, 126, 128, 129, 131, 135,
    136–37, 140–44, 147, 149, 150,
    154, 155, 159, 192n76, 210n69,
    215n68; esparto grass, 137, 212n12;

mechanization, 136–37, 149; "paper age," 117, 118, 120; paper trail, 72, 126, 212n12; pulp, 137, 140; recycling, 140–41
Pearl, Cora, 23–24
Percival, Thomas, 207n31
personal identity, 2, 4, 5, 8, 9, 17, 31, 68, 85, 136, 141, 153, 155, 165n28, 169n59, 171–72n90, 183n68; blood, 31, 33, 39–47; clothes, 15, 18–23; cosmetics, 15, 18, 23–30; epilepsy, 63–64, 67, 75–83; madness, 63–64, 65–75, 194n116; materialization of, 3, 4, 10, 16, 31, 32, 163n22, 164n25, 171n85; mesmerism, 86, 87, 88–95; opium, 86, 87, 88, 95–101; photographs, 146–51; refuse, 137, 138–45; registers, 119, 120–27; surgery, 31, 32, 33–39; wills, 120, 127–34
personation. *See under* identity fraud
Petty, William, 206–207n31
photography, 3, 9, 10, 11, 53, 54, 57, 107, 112, 130, 136, 137, 146–51, 212n12, 215n82, 216n91, 216n99, 216n104, 216–17n105, 217n111; calotype, 53; daguerreotype, 53, 90, 146, 147; fear of, 215n82; forensics, 147–48; fraud, 148, 216n99, 216n104. *See also* Sutton, Thomas
phrenology, 3, 21, 67, 89, 90, 96, 163n22. *See also* physiognomy
physiognomy, 3, 25, 163n22. *See also* phrenology
Picture of Dorian Gray, The (Wilde), 155–57
plastic surgery, 31–36, 38, 44, 180n12. *See also* rhinoplasty
poison, 24, 40, 42, 46, 93–94, 95, 145
Polytechnic Institution, 146

Poor Law (1834), 120, 139
Popoff, M. Lazar, 215n82
pornography, 149, 150, 151
professionalism, 169n54, 188n26, 193n87
psychoanalysis, 4, 10, 178n73. *See also* Freud, Sigmund
psychology, 10, 19, 44, 68, 90, 96, 167n44, 168n52, 171n85, 190n57, 196n1
psychosurgery, 73
Public Health Act (1875), 140

queer, 46, 109. *See also* homosexuality, trans
Quetelet, Adolphe, 205n17. *See also* statistics

Ranken, W. Bayne, 186n85
Reade, Charles, 42, 43, 79, 162n12, 195n123; *Griffith Gaunt*, 42–43, 79, 195n127; *Hard Cash*, 195n123
realism, 6, 16, 120, 157, 166n36
recommendation letter, 70, 191n75
Reese, John J., 171n88
reform, 3, 5, 6, 7, 66, 67, 138, 140, 213n31. *See also* class
refuse. *See under* waste
Registration Act. *See under* Births, Deaths, and Marriages Act
Rejlander, Oscar Gustave, 217n111
rhinoplasty, 33, 34, 180n12, 181n27
Richet, Charles, 97
Robinson, Frederick William, 58
Rumsey, Henry Wyldbore, 119
Ruskin, John, 214n61

Sala, George Augustus, 173n98
sanitation, 139–40, 213n31
scars, 1, 2, 26, 32, 35, 36, 37, 38, 54, 159, 179n5, 180n7. *See also* brands, moles, skin, tattoos

Scoffern, John, 24
Sedgwick, Eve Kosofsky, 143
seizures. *See under* epilepsy
self, the. *See under* subjectivity
sensation genre, 5–11, 35, 59, 66, 75, 94, 98, 104, 120, 122, 131, 132, 141, 148, 153; affect in 76, 94, 193n93; authorial duality, 65, 188n26; authorial hypocrisy, 10, 128, 172n94; disability in 81, 170n66, 170n75, 196n137; doubling in 168n49; evolution in 166n39; generic boundaries of 172n97; transgression in 168n51
shock, 40, 63, 187n10, 191n66. *See also* concussions
Sims, George R., 140
skin, 18, 23, 25, 28, 29, 30, 31, 32, 33, 34, 36, 37, 38, 79, 89, 100, 180n12, 218n20. *See also* brands, moles, scars, tattoos
skin grafting, 34
sleepwalking. *See under* somnambulism
Smith, Horace, 204n58
Smith, Madeleine, 24
somnambulism, 9, 86, 87, 89, 93
Sontag, Susan, 146
spiritualism, 89, 90. *See also* mesmerism
split identity, 44, 101, 153, 155, 156. *See also* double consciousness
Staffe, Baroness, 24, 34
statistics, 4, 66, 118, 119, 120, 205n17, 207n43
sterilization. *See under* antiseptics
Stevens, C. L. McCluer, 59
Stevenson, Robert Louis, 82, 153, 154, 155. See also *The Strange Case of Dr. Jekyll and Mr. Hyde*
Stoker, Bram, 41, 43, 158. See also *Dracula*

Strange Case of Dr. Jekyll and Mr. Hyde, The (Stevenson), 44, 153–55
subjectivity, 2–9, 16, 18, 19, 20, 26, 36, 41, 43, 45, 66, 67, 69, 73, 75, 79, 85, 88, 89, 90, 94, 95, 117, 118, 122, 128, 131, 136, 141, 142, 144, 153, 162n16, 163n19, 163–64n23, 165n29, 171n85, 175n37, 189–90n50
surgery, 9, 31, 33, 35, 36, 73, 89. *See also* plastic surgery
Sutton, Thomas, 11, 148, 149, 150, 151, 216–17n105, 217n111. *See also* photography, *Unconventional*
Symons, Arthur, 95

tattoos, 32, 164n27. *See also* brands, moles, scars, skin
Taylor, Alfred Swaine, 32
taxes on knowledge, 117, 136
Taylor, Ida Ashworth, 211n4
textiles, 15, 20, 28. *See also* clothes
Thomson, A. T., 15
Thou Art the Man (Braddon), 11, 79–83
Tichborne, Sir Roger, 2, 125, 147, 148, 162n12. *See also* Orton, Arthur
Townshend, Chauncy Hare, 89
trace, 26, 28, 70
trans, 46. *See also* queer
transfusion. *See under* blood
transplantation, organ, 34, 45, 183n68
trash. *See under* waste
Travers, Robert, 8. *See also* legal identity
Tremaine, Amelia Eliza, 186n72
Trollope, Anthony, 206n29
trusts. *See under* wills
Tuke, William, 67. *See also* madness, moral treatment
Twain, Mark, 19–20

unconscious, 63, 78, 101, 111, 196n1
Unconventional (Sutton), 11, 148–51

Verner's Pride (Wood), 6, 11, 131–34, 177n61, 211n98
vitalism. *See under* blood
voice, 23, 26, 27, 31, 39, 52, 106, 178n73

Warden, Florence, 176n39
waste (dirt, rubbish, trash) 136, 138–44; rubbish theory, 138–39
waxwork, 36
Westall, William, 182n55
Wharton, Francis, 8, 31, 39, 46, 101, 148. *See also* legal identity
Whitman, Walt, 157, 218n15
wigs, 25, 27, 52. *See also* hair
Wilde, Oscar, 155, 157, 218n15. See also *The Picture of Dorian Gray*
wills, 9, 11, 119, 120, 122, 127–31, 144, 210n69; codicils, 120, 130–34, 144, 206n29; Court of Probate, 127; Principal Probate Registry, 127, 129, 144; trusts, 29, 130; Wills Act (1837), 127, 210n69
Wills, William Henry, 129, 146
Winter, William, 197n11
Woman in Spite of Herself, A (Jeaffreson), 11, 20–23, 25, 202n5
Woman in White, The (Collins), 6, 7, 11, 20, 25, 26, 27, 68–69, 92, 94, 122–26, 131, 135, 158, 166n39, 189n37, 189n40, 198n44, 198–99n48, 208–209n55, 209n56, 209n58
Wood, Ellen, 6, 11, 35, 131, 132, 134, 170n75, 177n61, 191n67, 211n98; *East Lynne*, 35, 170n75; *St. Martin's Eve*, 191n67. See also *Verner's Pride*
Wynter, Andrew, 66, 68

Zeis, Eduard, 34
Žižek, Slavoj, 178n73
Zoist, The. See under Elliotson, John

www.ingramcontent.com/pod-product-compliance
Lightning Source LLC
Chambersburg PA
CBHW030535230426
43665CB00010B/897